CHILDREN'S SEXUAL ENCOUNTERS WITH ADULTS

CHILDREN'S SEXUAL ENCOUNTERS WITH ADULTS

A Scientific Study

C.K. Li
D.J. West
T.P. Woodhouse

Prometheus Books • Buffalo, New York

Published 1993 by Prometheus Books

97 96 95 94 93   5 4 3 2 1

Library of Congress Cataloging-in-Publication Data

Li, C. K.
    Children's sexual encounters with adults : a scientific study / C. K. Li, D. J. West, and T. P. Woodhouse.
        p.   cm.
    Originally published: London : G. Duckworth, 1990.
    Includes bibliographical references and index.
    ISBN 0-87975-820-1
    1. Child molesting—Great Britain. 2. Child molesters—Great Britain. 3. Sexually abused children—Great Britain. I. West, D. J. (Donald James), 1924–
II. Woodhouse, T. P. III. Title.
HQ72.G7L5   1993
362.7'6—dc20   92-43601
                                                                                                CIP

Printed on acid-free paper in the United States of America.

Contents

Preface

The two research projects reported here approached the topic of children's sexual encounters with adults from opposite directions. The first was conducted at Cambridge University Institute of Criminology, with funding from the Mental Health Foundation, by Professor Donald West and his then research associate T.P. Woodhouse. It was limited to questioning men about what happened when they were boys, because a similar inquiry addressed to women had already been completed. The results of the male and female surveys provided some striking contrasts.

The second project, also carried out at the Institute of Criminology, was a doctoral research by C.K. Li with Professor West as his supervisor. Dr Li collected accounts from men who were willing to admit to a sexual interest in children, mostly girls, and to discuss their experiences and explanations of their behaviour. He was able to compare the attitudes and theories of professional experts with those of the sexual deviants themselves.

Both reports include some commentary on the state of present knowledge, with particular reference to harm sustained by children, and both conclude that serious harm does not invariably occur. Because the reports were prepared independently, there is some overlap in the discussion of findings, but the commentaries have been left unchanged so that readers can appreciate the scope for differences in emphasis in the selection and interpretation of research findings. Li provides a more general review of both the methodological and theoretical problems of assessing evidence. West and Woodhouse are less ambitious, but call attention to differences in the reported experiences of girls and boys and to differences in findings according to the varying methods of inquiry and whether samples are taken from the community or from cases under official investigation or treatment.

Neither project claims to have achieved the impossible goal of a 'representative' sample. Self-selected paedophiles recruited by advertisement cannot be assumed to be typical. Retrospective accounts by adult men are inevitably affected by memory loss and the distorting effects of current attitudes. In mitigation it needs to be pointed out that observational studies or contemporary questioning of participants in unreported and secretive encounters are simply not feasible. One must seek information as best one can and make allowances for probable bias. These problems are dealt with in detail in the body of the reports.

D.J.W.

Part I

Sexual Encounters between Boys and Adults

D.J. West & T.P. Woodhouse

1

Background to the Project

Child sexual abuse and how to deal with it have become topics of enormous concern, a preoccupation for health professionals no less than for the media. Clinicians report numerous cases of serious disturbance in adults which is attributed to early sexual molestation. Recent evidence points to an alarming prevalence of experiences of abuse, especially by young girls who become captive victims in their own homes.

A variety of considerations prompted us to undertake this research on boys. Most previous inquiries, including one for which one of the present authors was responsible (Nash & West, 1985), have been concerned with girls, but clinicians are now reporting a substantial proportion of boys among children brought for examination in connection with sexual abuse. According to some recent statistics supplied by Paul Griffiths, lately research director to ChildLine, something like a quarter of the calls from children made to that telephone help line on the subject of sex abuse are from boys. Boys' and girls' sexual experiences with adults are thought to differ in kind. Identified perpetrators of child sex abuse are nearly always men, so it is assumed that boys' sexual encounters with adults are mostly of a homosexual nature. The use of the blanket term 'abuse', and the popular concept of 'corruption', commonly applied to all sexual contacts between children and adults, obscures the varying degrees of seriousness of the incidents in question and the varying prospects of deleterious consequences. In the case of pubertal children, boys especially, the supposed victim is often claimed to have been an active participant if not an instigator (Rossman, 1979; Wilson, 1981; Brongersma, 1987). Whereas girls' confrontations with adult sexuality are thought likely to induce anxiety and frigidity, boys' contacts with men are popularly feared to seduce them away from heterosexual interests.

The purpose of the present survey was to test the validity of some of these preconceptions by collecting recollections of early sexual experiences from a sample of men taken from the ordinary population. The questions used were designed to explore the whole range of adult child sexual encounters, not just those of a coercive, homosexual or traumatic nature. It was realised that many experiences might be remembered of a kind not usually mentioned to parents or brought to the attention of social workers or police, but it was thought that information on these matters could be helpful in providing the necessary context for evaluating incidents that are reported.

1.1 Prevalence

Population surveys have yielded remarkably different prevalence figures for adult recollections of childhood sexual abuse. Finkelhor (1979a), who questioned a sample of 530 female and 266 male college students in New England, found that 19.2 per cent of women and 8.6 per cent of men described sexual experiences with partners substantially older than themselves when they were themselves under 17. Many of their earliest experiences reportedly occurred long before they had reached puberty. In a later review of his own and others' surveys Finkelhor (1986) noted prevalence estimates that varied from 6 to 62 per cent among samples of women and from 3 to 30 per cent among males. The results clearly depended on many factors, including the method of questioning (e.g. anonymous forms or in depth interviewing), the ages that defined 'child' and 'adult', the place where the survey was carried out, whether only 'unwanted' or 'abusive' incidents were counted or whether incidents with indecent exposers, pornographic displays or sexual talk without physical contact were included. One of the largest studies was of a national sample of just over 2,000 Canadians, half of them males, who were asked about 'unwanted' sexual contacts or approaches. Over half, 53.5 per cent of females and 30.6 per cent of males claimed to have been a sex victim, and in each case about half said that their first experience of the kind had been when they were under 16 (Badgley, 1984, p. 180). In the Nash & West (1985) survey 42 per cent of 223 women registered with a general medical health service practice in Cambridge, England, reported having had some sexual experience with an adult before they were 16, but this figure was reduced to 23 per cent by the exclusion of incidents not involving physical contact – mainly confrontations with male exposers, a particularly common event for women. In MORI poll survey in England in 1984 (Baker and Duncan, 1985) a sample of over 2,000, chosen to be nationally representative, were interviewed individually in their homes in the context of a general attitude survey and asked if they had ever had a sexually abusive experience conforming to the following definition:

> A child (anyone under 16 years) is sexually abused when another person, who is sexually mature, involves the child in any activity which the other person expects to lead to their sexual arousal. This might involve intercourse, touching, exposure of the sexual organs, showing pornographic material or talking about things in an erotic way.

Of the 970 men in the sample, 8 per cent acknowledged abuse as defined, 78 per cent denied it, and 14 per cent declined to answer. Of 1,049 women the corresponding figures were 12, 76 and 12 per cent).

In a household survey in San Francisco by Russell (1983) the prevalence of women's recollections of early sexual abuse was nearly five times greater, 54 per cent. The investigator suggested that her unusually high prevalence figure might be accounted for by the use of trained and exclusively female interviewers 'sensitised' to child sex abuse and able to elicit descriptions of embarrassing incidents, especially intra-familial incidents, that might not otherwise be mentioned.

Such global statistics become meaningful only when the differing frequencies of different types of incident and the relative ages of the participants are explored. It is too readily assumed that the incidents charted in population surveys are equivalent to the instances of gross victimisation seen in clinical practice. Russell defined 'child' as 'under 18' and included non-contact experiences such as exhibitionism to obtain the figure of 54 per cent. In the MORI survey, which gave a prevalence figure of 10 per cent for males and females combined, about half of the reported incidents involved no physical contact and only 14 per cent were incidents within the family. The estimated prevalence of actual incest, i.e. sexual intercourse with a blood relative, was as low as 0.25 per cent. The average age at the time of the first recollected incident was two years later among boys (12.03 years) than among girls (10.74 years).

An American student questionnaire survey by Fritz *et al.* (1981) asked about a variety of early sexual experiences and included inquiry about encounters 'with a post-adolescent individual before the subject reached puberty' involving physical contact of an overtly sexual nature. Given this fairly strict criterion they obtained a prevalence rate of 7.7 for females, 4.8 per cent for males. As in other surveys the vast majority (90 per cent) of girls' experiences were with men. Unlike the findings of some other surveys in which it may not have been clear to respondents that boys' heterosexual experiences are also of interest, 60 per cent of the boys' encounters with older persons were with women. The sample was small (20 molested males out of 412), so the figure of 60 per cent could be unreliable. In an American national incidence survey cited by Finkelhor (1984, p. 186) 24 per cent of sexual offenders against boys were women.

Clinical samples tend to feature relatively few cases of children who have had brief encounters with outsiders. Girls predominate to a greater extent than in community surveys, possibly because their relationships are more closely monitored. Molestation by women, either of girls or of boys, rarely results in a clinical referral, but clinical samples tend to be overweighted with incidents involving an adult member of the family, often a father or step-father, these being situations particularly liable to produce detectable distress. Referrals to treatment agencies often include children with considerable emotional or social disturbance before the onset of sexual molestation (Adams-Tucker, 1981).

The proportion of boys appearing in clinical samples has tended to increase. Reinhart (1987), working in Sacramento with a typical clinical population, found that 16.4 per cent of referrals for suspected child sexual abuse were boys. In accordance with the suspicion of under-reporting by older boys, and in contrast to community survey findings, the 189 boys in

Reinhart's sample were surprisingly young, with a mean age just under 6. They were matched individually against girl victims of similar age and ethnicity. An initial disclosure by some third party was more common among the boys and the boys had much more often than the girls been involved with offenders still relatively young, such as older friends, brothers, cousins, etc. In spite of being so young, 40 per cent of the boys had been subjected to anal penetration, a finding not unusual for clinical samples, but much less common in community surveys. The report ended with a warning: 'Abnormal anogenital findings are more common in young children, and examiner experience is essential to assess the findings appropriately.'

Some physicians report an extraordinarily high prevalence of physical signs of anal sexual abuse among young children of both sexes. Over a short period of eight months' practice in Leeds, which has a child population of 146,000, Hobbs and Wynne (1986) diagnosed anal injuries from buggery in 35 children, 17 of them boys. Their ages ranged from 14 months to 8 years. In 27 of the 35 cases the abuse was confirmed through disclosure by the child or the perpetrator. Fathers were most commonly implicated, but in the case of 4 of the boys the mother was suspected.

The forensic medical examination of children is a difficult and specialised field (Enos et al., 1986). It is hard to know what to make of the Leeds findings in view of continuing controversy between experts as to the significance of some of the physical signs upon which diagnoses of sexual abuse, particularly anal abuse, may be made (Kirschner and Stein, 1985). Fissures and inflammations can have other causes. Moreover, in the majority of cases of known sexual molestation, even when the behaviour has included anal penetration, no definite physical signs are to be found by the time the child is brought for medical examination. Repeated anal penetration, however, is liable to cause bruising of the anal verge; spasm of the anal sphincter muscle on examination may occur if penetration has been forceful, painful and recent; dilatation of the orifice and diminution of the contractile power of the anal musculature may be found if penetration has been habitual. A positive response to the anal dilatation test, that is relaxation instead of the normal contraction that occurs when the buttocks are pressed apart by the examiner, is a less reliable indicator of habituation to anal penetration (Paul, 1986). An attempt to cooperate with the examiner can produce a similar effect.

Estimates of the prevalence of child-adult sexual contacts, and more particularly estimates of the likelihood of serious sexual assaults including anal penetrations on young children by family members, have more than academic importance. They have a bearing on how such allegations are viewed and must influence the likelihood of a child being placed in Care of the local authority once suspicions are aroused, decisions which can have devastating consequences for the families concerned. They have obvious implications for the allocation of resources, the encouragement of active measures of discovery and the provision of telephone help-lines for affected children.

1.2 Effects of sexual encounters with adults: the conflicting evidence

Some people are undoubtedly deeply affected by premature and unwanted sexual experiences in childhood. Media exposure of the topic has encouraged individuals of both sexes to make public declarations of hitherto unspoken, lifelong grievances about their sufferings from childhood sexual molestation. In one startling example three brothers discovered, when they were aged 37, 31 and 21 respectively, that they had all three been sexually molested by their father when they were small children. Up till then each had assumed he was the only victim. The eldest brother recalled that, as a teenager, he had told about paternal brutality but kept secret the sexual incidents in which he had been bribed with extra pocket money to masturbate his father. Over a period of seventeen years the three brothers were each in turn subjected to mutual masturbation and oral and anal sex. The case became public because the brothers decided to confront their father and demand, under threat of exposure to the police, that he seek treatment by contacting Richard Johnson (himself a victim of paternal sex abuse) who runs the Incest Crisis Line. When the father proved uncooperative and countered with his own legal threats they reported the matter to the police. The father was interrogated and they were told afterwards that he had admitted some of the acts, but the Crown Prosecution Service decided not to bring charges. Greatly angered by this, they set about collecting further evidence by contacting their father's second, divorced wife and turning over further reports to the police.

In the above instance the victims were apparently not permanently damaged. According to the newspaper report *Observer*, 5 July 1987): 'Remarkably, the brothers have recovered from their childhood experience. They all have responsible jobs; the older two are married, the youngest is engaged.' In many cases, however, self-declared victims display continuing problems in adult life which they attribute to having been sexually abused. In the Nash & West (1985) survey of females, in which half of the respondents were under the age of 12 at the time of the first remembered incident, some of the women who were interviewed subsequently became very distressed and emotional when recounting what happened. Many said that they had bottled up their thoughts and never told anyone before about what had happened, although they had brooded over it for years. Although the interviewed women said that shock or confusion had been their predominant initial response, 41 per cent of the incidents they described were said to have been pleasurable or sexually arousing at the time (Nash & West, 1985, table 7.2). Evidence that a minority of the women might indeed have been permanently affected was obtained by comparing information given at interviews by 78 women with a history of sexual abuse and 31 with no such history. A significantly larger proportion of the former (28 per cent as against 7 per cent) were without a current sexual partner.

This particular survey, in common with most other population studies, showed that the reactions to childhood sexual incidents are highly varied, some very serious, others not at all. Although the most obviously traumatic incidents, such as repeated and forceful attempts at intercourse by parents or guardians, were the ones most likely to be associated with lasting disturbance, some seemingly trivial events, such as mildly indecent fondling, could also assume great emotional significance, if not at the time, then when the girl was old enough to appreciate and absorb the social condemnation and consequent anxiety and guilt which involvement in such episodes arouses.

Surveys which have addressed the issue find that on the whole boys are less likely than girls to experience bad effects attributable to sexual incidents with adults. Finkelhor (1979a, p. 70) found that male students less often reported negative reactions than did female students – 38 per cent as against 66 per cent. In the MORI survey (Baker & Duncan, 1985, table 4) it was again remarked that girls 'find their abusive experiences more damaging than boys seem to'. As many as 57 per cent of the males who recalled some childhood experience of sexual 'abuse' thought that it had had no effect, only 4 per cent thought that it had caused permanent damage, and 6 per cent thought that it had actually 'improved life'. The corresponding figures obtained from female respondents were 34 per cent, 13 per cent and 2 per cent respectively. It was suggested that one reason for the different reactions of the two sexes might be that boys have less cause than girls to connect adverse experience with men with their later heterosexual relationships. Other reasons might stem from the different circumstances in which molestation of boys and girls tends to occur. Most surveys, including Finkelhor's and the MORI inquiry, show that boys are generally older when the incidents occur and less likely to be molested in their own homes; they are therefore in a better position to terminate unwanted situations.

In his review of evidence of the effects of child sex abuse obtained from both population studies and clinical samples, Finkelhor (1986, pp. 142ff.) makes the point that most studies refer essentially to females. Although a minority of boys are sometimes included they are usually not described separately so that it is impossible to tell to what extent the reported sequelae apply to them. Nevertheless, clinical examinations of boys referred when intra-familial sex abuse is disclosed or for disturbances following abusive experiences (Dixon et al., 1978; Rogers & Terry, 1984) suggest that those who are affected tend to react in similar ways to girls, but with greater emphasis on aggressive reactions. For instance, Lindberg & Distad (1985) describing the aggressive and self-destructive behaviour of 27 young incest victims, 3 of them boys, quote the example of one 16-year-old who had been subjected to six years of almost daily oral and rectal sex abuse by his father. He developed an explosive temper, abused alcohol and drugs, engaged in sexual misbehaviour with both boys and girls and was so manipulative and disruptive he could not be kept in the children's home in which he had been placed.

Although this is often forgotten, boys may have contacts with women as well as with men. Few complaints against female perpetrators reach official agencies, but they are not unknown. In an analysis of 1,108 cases of child sexual abuse in the files of a social agency and a prosecutor's office in Texas, Kercher & McShane (1984a) noted that of the 16.5 per cent of victims who were boys, 5 per cent had been involved with female perpetrators, compared with only 2.9 per cent of girl victims.

In another survey of 25 male victims referred to a child protection service for sexual abuse, occurring at an average age of 10.6 years, Pierce & Pierce (1985b) noted several differences between them and girl victims. The perpetrators were often fathers or stepfathers in the case of both boys and girls (48 per cent and 54 per cent respectively), but boys were more often molested by someone outside the family (20 per cent against 6 per cent), more often subjected to threats, violence or multiple sex acts and their assailants more often received severer penalties. Nevertheless, boy victims were less often placed away from home and tended to receive shorter periods of treatment.

Finkelhor distinguishes between initial reactions and long-term effects and makes the point that, though it may not be lasting, an initial disturbance in a child needs to be taken just as seriously as an adult's reactions to a personal crisis. Anxiety, phobias, depression, confusion, anger, guilt feelings, psychosomatic symptoms, worsening of school performance, truancy, enuresis and antisocial behaviour have all been reported and said to be warning signs that abuse may be happening. They are hardly specific to sexual abuse, of course, being common reactions to all kinds of stress from illness in the family to threatened parental divorce.

Long-term effects, especially on sexual life, have been described in virtually every study of sexual abuse of girls, especially abuse by father figures. De Young (1982a), who studied 120 victims of sex abuse (including 23 males) recruited from varied sources, found many lasting disturbances, including depression, marital problems and upsetting 'flashback' memories during sexual relations. Males molested by their fathers were anxious about their own sexual orientation, but 5 males who had been molested by females (2 by their mothers) were less disturbed than those who had had contact with men.

Since population studies have revealed an incidence of child sex abuse far greater than the numbers coming to official notice might suggest, the latter probably include an over-representation of the worst cases. Some evidence of this was obtained by Tsai *et al.* (1979). They compared women seeking therapy for problems associated with child sexual abuse, women who had been molested but never sought help and a control group of demographically matched non-molested women. On a measure of psychological adjustment (the MMPI), and in self-reporting of current sexual satisfaction, the therapy group were significantly maladjusted, but the other molested women were no different from the controls. It seems that clinicians tend to see individuals who have reacted badly because they were unstable before the abuse began and individuals whose disturbance may be unrelated to their sexual abuse history.

Joan Nelson (1981), who recruited by advertisement a sample of persons who had been involved in intra-familial sexual relationships, found that over half evaluated their experiences positively. Her respondents included the older as well as the younger partners in the relationships, but still a substantial proportion, 25 per cent, of the younger partners in child-adult situations rated their experiences positively. Males were much more likely than females to report positive feelings.

There is a considerable amount of evidence that some boys are quite happy in relationships with adult homosexual men so long as the affair does not come to light and cause scandal or police action. Sandfort (1987) interviewed boys of pubertal age who were in intimate friendships with men. The great majority came from apparently normal homes, but were pleased to have additional attention and patronage from a devoted adult and willingly went along with his sexual requirements, except that some began to lose interest when they began to find pleasure with girls. Ingram (1981) studied boys from problem families needing counselling who were involved in pederastic relationships. He noted that many were seeking love and attention rather than sexual play, which was less important to them than to their adult partners. In some cases affectionate relationships continued after the sexual activity had stopped, but some went on to become homosexuals and a few became homosexual prostitutes. Righton (1981), in describing his experience of counselling 39 men who had sought help in connection with their sexual desire for boys, reported that in 14 instances he had been able to compare the man's version of events with that of the boy involved. The accounts proved substantially congruent and confirmed that the men had generally shown a lasting devotion normally associated with love between adults. The boys expressed appreciation for the consideration and attention they had received, which they rarely got in their own homes, and most felt they had benefited. Constantine (1983), in a review of researches on the effects of children's sexual experiences with adults, concluded that all studies based on community rather than clinical samples found very varied outcomes and some proportion who suffered neither short-term nor long-term harm. All but one of the (then) six most recent studies revealed some who had found the experience beneficial. Brongersma (1987), in a scholarly survey of international literature, argues similarly. In the student survey by Fritz *et al.* (1981), men sometimes looked back on their early sexual encounters as a positive experience, whereas women significantly more often reported negative feelings or harmful effects. Finkelhor (1979a, p. 79) also noted that male students reported fewer negative reactions than did female students, especially when the older person had been a woman.

Steel & Alexander (1981), discussing long-term effects, note how difficult it is to separate the sequelae of sexual abuse from the effects of other noxious situations in the family background which may be either prime or contributory factors. Retreats from sexual activities and avoidance of close personal relationships, and sexual difficulties such as frigidity and impotence, are commonly attributed both to abuse and to unhappy parent-child relationships outside the sexual sphere. Consider, for example, the case of 'Marty' described by Embling (1986, p. 37). He was an aggressive, delinquent boy, nearly 13, disruptive and inattentive at school, with a conviction record for theft, vandalism, drugs and drunkenness. He had been subjected to attempted anal penetration by one of his mother's many boyfriends and at the age of 10 he had been involved in child pornography and sexual 'gang bangs'. Fatherless and subjected to cruel whippings by his alcoholic mother, this street urchin's behaviour might have been just as bad if his brutalising experiences at home and on the street had happened not to include specifically sexual incidents.

Whatever the contributions of simultaneous adversities of a non-sexual nature, most researchers and clinical observers seem agreed as to the kinds of sexual incident most likely, in themselves, to produce lasting problems. These include sexual attacks using violence or threats or causing pain or injury, and incidents in which parent-figures step out of their customary role and cause anxiety and confusion by obliging the child to participate in secret sexual misdeeds. Passive but unwilling acceptance and inability to end an increasingly unwanted relationship also seem to be associated with adverse outcomes (Constantine, 1983). In short, outcomes are variable and assertive generalisations about the consequences of abusive incidents are made too readily. Effects depend upon the nature and circumstances of the sexual behaviour and upon the victim's age, temperament, gender and stage of socio-sexual development. Retrospective opinions of adults who have been victims are informative, but subjective and liable to distortion, suppression and faulty attributions of cause and effect.

1.3 Deviances attributed to abusive experiences

Retrospective studies of specialised penal and clinical samples of neurotics, the sexually disordered, prostitutes, homosexuals, paedophiles, drug abusers and even women with anorexia nervosa have all found a remarkably high prevalence of histories of child-adult sexual contacts supposedly partly responsible for the current deviant behaviour or symptomatology.

Freud was the first to report a connection between the neurotic troubles of his female patients and their stories of sexual intimacies with their fathers when they were little. Later he developed the theory that these were wishful fantasies, but he has been sharply criticised by Masson (1984) for ignoring the reality of early sexual seduction in such cases, the evidence for which was strong and accepted by his colleague Ferenczi.

Reference to sex abuse histories in selected samples of disturbed or deviant adults are too numerous for comprehensive review; a few representative examples must suffice. Groth (1979), in a study of 348 men convicted of sexual assault (173 'rapists' and 175 'child molesters') found that 30 per cent reported some incident of sexual victimisation when they were boys compared with only 3 per cent of 67 law enforcement officers who were questioned for purposes of comparison. A majority of their assailants had been adults, in the case of those who became rapists 30 per cent were adult males and 38 per cent adult females, in the case of the child molesters 54 per cent of assailants were adult males and 18 per cent adult females. In addition to underscoring the need to consider effects of victimisation on boys as well as girls, the author noted that women perpetrators were much more prevalent than their rare appearance in crimir al statistics might suggest. This last point emerged again in a more recent report of a survey of 83 men incarcerated for rape of females over 17. Molestation by adult females, mostly neighbours and family friends, when they were boys (mean age 10.8) was reported by 49 (59 per cent) of the men (Petrovich and Templer, 1984). Of course all surveys of offenders have to contend with bias from the natural tendency of the guilty to lay claim to any extenuating circumstances suggested to them.

Prostitutes are also said to have a high incidence of histories of sexual abuse in childhood. James & Meyerding (1978) used earlier studies of 228 female prostitutes for a comparison with research on normal women. The prostitutes, compared with the control women, significantly more often had experienced incest, premature sexual advances and forced intercourse. They had received less parental sex instruction and tended to obtain information through brute experience. The investigators concluded that loss of self-esteem from sexual exploitation led women to seek a kind of status through illicit sex.

Silbert & Pines (1981) studied 200 street prostitutes, average age 22, and found that a majority reported serious and often prolonged sexual abuse, most often from father-figures. The victims suffered very unhappy emotional effects and many of them felt that their early sexual traumata had contributed significantly to their decision to turn to prostitution.

Similar claims have been made about male prostitution. Richie McMullen (1987), who worked for an organisation specialising in befriending young male street prostitutes, considered child sex abuse a frequent and important antecedent to entry into prostitution among the young men he was seeing. American authorities have made the same assertions. Justice & Justice (1980, p. 197), citing no particular authority, state that a history of intra- or extra-familial sexual abuse occurs in the backgrounds of 'many' youths who, receiving little or no nurturing at home, seek love, money and caring through street contacts with homosexual men. Coombs (1974) interviewed 41 male homosexual prostitutes and compared their backgrounds with those of normal youths of similar age, around 19. Early homosexual experience with older males was overwhelmingly more common among the prostitutes and some of their experiences were decidedly abusive. One boy had been sold to an elderly paedophile by his drunken father when he was 10. Another had been forced so often into anal intercourse that he made up his mind to relax and make it pay. Coombs concluded that early ab sive experiences taught these boys, who came from unstable homes and lacked vocational skills, that they could use sex to manipulate others and gain material rewards. Many remained, nevertheless, distinctly heterosexual in their natural preference.

Allen (1980), another American investigator, conducted a more exhaustive three-year project interviewing 98 young male prostitutes. The refusal rate was less than 10 per cent. This sample gave rather different findings. Two-thirds had had their first sexual experience with other males, usually persons older than themselves, at a median age of 13.5 years (or 12.2 years in the case of those who were full-time professional street workers or call boys). Most of the sample had been introduced to prostitution through peers with experience of the trade, but 30 per cent had started through propositioning by an older male. Unlike some previous surveys of male prostitutes (Coombs, 1974; Jersild, 1956; MacNamara, 1965; Reiss, 1961), which suggested that rather few male prostitutes are homosexually oriented, Allen found that 81 per cent of the sample rated themselves as bisexual or predominantly homosexual on the Kinsey scale, with 39 per cent exclusively or very predominantly homosexual (Kinsey rating 5 or 6). This may explain the finding that, although many of the young men came from deprived and uncaring homes, their early homosexual experiences were not necessarily referred to as abusive. A third had had their first sex experience through seduction by an older male, but 28 per cent had initiated their first homosexual contact.

Apart from the obvious question of the trustworthiness of historical accounts from social deviants, there is a problem in interpreting such claims. In the deprived and chaotic home backgrounds characteristic of many prostitutes, low social standards and general neglect expose children prematurely to adult sexuality. Alayne Yates (1978, p. 75) a psychiatrist who was far from squeamish about sex and advocated open discussion between parents and children about developing sexuality, acknowledged the undesirable nature of the sort of sexual licence found in the slums of Chicago. She had seen mothers there taking in a succession of short-lived boyfriends and children exposed to violent sexual scenes from an early age. In some overcrowded appartments children continued sleeping with their mothers after a new 'uncle' or 'fiancée' had arrived. Very early in life children were exposed to erotic stimulation and learned to stimulate themselves and others. Sexual activities in tenement hallways became a substitute for toys. Gangs of boys went around grabbing young girls for sex in alleyways. Girls who ran with the gangs to gain protection ended up despised as sluts. Anger, domination, drunkenness and physical abuse were linked with sex from the start. Under such conditions coercive or precocious sex is part and parcel of a home environment in which personal relationships are often uncaring, violent or exploitative. It may be a mistake to single out the sexual aspect of deprived and brutal upbringings as the main cause of subsequent deviations from the social rules governing intimate relationships.

Delinquency, one of the many undesirable developments said to follow sexual abuse of the young, might also be linked as a result of common background circumstances. McCormack *et al.* (1986) obtained some data relevant to this issue in a survey of adolescent runaways aged 15 to 20 entering a shelter in Toronto. No less than 73 per cent of the girls and 38 per cent of the boys complained of having had abusive sexual experiences. Compared with other female runaways the abused girls had been significantly more often arrested or in trouble with the law. A majority of the boy runaways had been arrested or had trouble with the law, but in their case the ones with a history of sexual abuse were no more likely than the others to be delinquent. From this it would appear that the addition of abusive sexual experiences makes no difference to the likelihood of a runaway boy turning delinquent, although it may do so in the case of girls.

Homosexuality is another undesirable development widely believed to be encouraged by early sexual abuse, especially of boys. Long-term follow-up studies of boys who have been involved in relationships with homosexual paedophiles are few and far between, but such as have been reported do not suggest that a homosexual orientation is a particularly likely outcome (Doshay, 1943; Tindall, 1978; Tolsma, 1957; Wilson, 1981). Retrospective inquiries among adult men and women, however, show that homosexuals recall many more experiences of homosexual contacts in their pre-adolescent years than do heterosexuals. To some extent this might be due to selective forgetting by heterosexuals of incidents repugnant to their current attitudes, but this would hardly account for the massive and consistent differences documented by Bell, Weinberg & Hammersmith (1981). These investigators compared 979 homosexual and 477 heterosexual males living in the San Francisco Bay area and found that not only did the homosexuals recall more sexual encounters with males when they were children, but the majority rated their pre-adolescent sexual behaviours as predominantly homosexual, whereas virtually none of the heterosexuals did so (op. cit., p. 100). Few of their experiences, however, had been with adult men. In contrast, Finkelhor (1984, p. 195), in his student survey, found that of 11 men who had had childhood experiences with older males, 5 were currently engaged in homosexual activity, a prevalence four times greater than among men with no such history.

In a methodologically sophisticated, large-scale re-analysis of data relating to the development of sexual orientation, taken from Kinsey's enormous sample of personal sex histories, Van Wyk & Geist (1984) confirmed the existence of a close relationship, not necessarily causal, between early homosexual contacts and homosexual arousal and later homosexual orientation. Their conclusions were broadly in keeping with those of Bell and Weinberg, who noted that homosexuals had often been aware of their same sex inclinations and sometimes actively seeking contacts at the time of their first homosexual experience. Van Wyk and Geist also found, apparently to their surprise, that looked at from a developmental standpoint, and in conformity with popular conceptions, most people could be fairly dichotomised as predominantly homosexual or predominantly heterosexual, the intermediate bisexual group being much less frequent than envisaged from Kinsey's original scaling. Demographic characteristics, such as social class, education and religion, were only weakly associated with adult sexual orientation; the most important predictor was the extent and nature of pre-adolescent sexual contacts, usually with peers, which the subject had felt arousing. Among males, once a particular outlet was found exciting, it tended to be reinforced by rehearsal in masturbation fantasies as well as by repetition.

Learning by boys from experiences with adult males was considered 'to play a small but definite role'. Interestingly, females who had had intense sexual contact with older males in childhood (genital touching, oral sex, coitus) had significantly higher Kinsey ratings, indicative of a trend towards lesbianism. It was suggested that this might be due to the different bio-social development of the two sexes, girls being less prepared than boys to indulge in full physical sex expression and possibly finding the experience of premature arousal unrewarding. Again the findings seemed to confirm a popular idea, namely that premature heterosexual experience by girls with older males may be aversive and promote lesbianism. Prepubertal boys were less likely than girls to have contact with adults of the opposite sex and when they did the age gap was generally less. The average age of female partners of prepubertal males was 20.3 years compared with an average of 33.4 years in the case of male partners of preadolescent females (op. cit., p. 520). This feature, plus the fact that boys are often the initiators, may explain why it is not suggested that seduction of boys by a female is likely to prove aversive or discourage heterosexual development.

A link between homosexual paedophilia and homosexual seduction in childhood has often been asserted, usually on the basis of a claim by offenders that they have themselves been victims in their early years. One investigator (Brunold, 1964) followed up 62 victims of child sexual abuse after some fifteen years when they were of an average age of 23. Of 12 males in the sample, 10 had married but one had become an active homosexual, 'almost certainly' as a result of sexual abuse, and had himself been punished for offences against boys. Of course it is unsafe to generalise from an isolated case and one cannot judge whether the incident may have been the cause or the effect of a homosexual orientation.

Clearer statistical evidence was obtained from a large scale American study of convicted sex offenders by Gebhard *et al.* (1965, pp. 275, 301). Only 8 per cent of a control group of unconvicted men reported sexual experiences with adult males when they were boys – a similar proportion to that found years later in Finkelhor's student survey. In contrast, roughly a third of sex offenders against boys under 16 recalled such an experience, a higher proportion than among any other group of imprisoned sex offenders. The authors wisely pointed out, however, that the statistical association they had discovered fell short of proof of a causal relationship. Moreover, the Gebhard study, like others of its kind, could not eliminate the possibility of bias caused by prisoners' self-exculpatory exaggerations. It was noteworthy, however, that paedophiles more often reported early sexual molestation than did any other category of imprisoned sex offender.

Assessment of the claim that early homosexual seduction may lead to paedophilia in males is further complicated by the tendency of some surveys to include encounters at an age when the younger partner was probably quite mature in a physiological sense and aware of his own desires and preferences. Relations between similarly teenaged girls and older males are less likely to be thought abnormal or pathogenic. Incidentally, the gender-discriminatory tendency to condemn women 'baby snatchers' more severely than their male counterparts seems to be diminishing as female pop stars can now boast of their 'toy boys'.

Research reported by Freund *et al.* (1975) was of particular relevance to the theory of a link between seduction in early years and paedophilia because they were specific about the age levels at issue and because they compared homosexuals attracted to prepubertal boys or young adolescents with homosexuals interested only in other men. There were 54 in each group, all volunteers, but the paedophiles came from a prison hospital. 'Seduction to sexual interaction' before the age of 12 was significantly more often reported by the paedophiles.

1.4 Cultural relativity

The damaging effects on children of intimate but non-penetrative contacts with adults are clearly psychological rather than physical and to a considerable extent dependent upon how such situations are viewed in the society in which the child has been brought up. Discussing this issue in relation to the women in his sample who had experienced what is now termed child abuse, Kinsey (1953, p. 121) commented: 'It is difficult to understand why a child, except for its cultural conditioning, should be disturbed at having its genitalia touched, or disturbed at seeing the genitalia of other persons, or disturbed at even more specific sexual contacts.' He suggested that it was the anxious warnings from parents against contacts with strangers, and the reactions of police and other adults when such contacts are discovered, that may disturb a child more than the behaviour itself.

Children have not always been so protected. The social historian Ariès (1962, ch. 5) finds that the convention whereby children are treated as asexual and innocent, to be shielded from the erotic talk or behaviour of adults, and on no account to be touched indecently, is a relatively recent development. In Europe, up to the seventeenth century, indecent jokes and horseplay with young children, including the handling of private parts, was commonplace. Small children regularly slept together or with adults regardless of gender. The physician attached to Louis XIII of France recorded details of the sex games with relatives and servants which the infant King enjoyed and which seemed quite natural to the adults involved. The behaviour did not include coitus or penetration, and was meant more as a joke than as a method of satisfying adult lust, but by modern standards it would count as serious molestation.

Ethnographic reports show that many non-European cultures have had few inhibitions about stimulating rather than suppressing children's sexuality. Mohammed himself had a child bride, and in Muslim societies girls can become betrothed or actually married and having intercourse at ages we should consider incredibly premature. Up to 1929, girls could be legally married at 13 in England. According to Edwardes & Masters (1970) Muslim boys often had their penis tweaked or jiggled by their mother, nurse or other attending female, such being the custom. They also cite (p. 125) descriptions of Swahili fathers in Zanzibar massaging the penis of their little boys of 4 to 6 to stimulate growth and ensure potency. Sex initiation rituals for pubertal boys were sometimes of a homosexual nature. In the Kaluli tribe of New Guinea, for example, boys of 10 or 11 would be introduced by their fathers to a man who would become for some months their training partner for penetrative anal intercourse (Herdt, 1982, p. 162). Belief in the benefit of receiving strength-giving semen as a preparation for a virile marriage justified some of these practices.

Currier (1981), in an analysis of methods of management of juvenile sexuality in different cultures, identifies a class of permissive and supportive societies in which children's sexuality is recognised and given free rein. Sexual stimulation of infants, especially of boys by their mothers, is 'a common form of parental pacification'. Children are allowed to masturbate themselves and explore each other's bodies and older juveniles to attempt copulation and adolescents to enjoy promiscuous relationships before settling down to a stable mating. The implication appears to be that such arrangements make for good adult sexual adjustment and perhaps remove the reasons for sexual exploitation or coercion of children.

Although it may seem to follow from anthropological findings that some adult-child sexual contacts may not be intrinsically harmful, since they have been found acceptable in other cultures, it does not follow that they are without harm today. It may be true that the negative views and reactions of the majority of members of contemporary society are largely responsible for the adverse effects, but, as Abel *et al.* (1984) point out, this explanation does not make the consequences any the less serious for the modern child. The topic arouses strong emotions among professional workers as well as among the public. There is a noticeable 'polarisation of opinion as to the quality and quantity of harmful effects that such activities may have on the child'.

There is no significant support for a massive move in the direction of sexual permissiveness, although some respectable authorities have advocated an adjustment of the age of consent and a legal distinction between seemingly consensual indecencies and true assault, which would avoid what many consider are over-reactions by the criminal justice system (Howard League, 1985). Against this, many others argue that young people are incapable of giving informed consent because they lack the knowledge and experience to appreciate the problematic aspects of a relationship with an older person or the force of society's condemnation, and because they are too easily swayed by an adult's authoritative persuasiveness and ability to provide rewards. The dispute is especially acute in relation to boys on account of the popular view that homosexual contacts with an adult (for which the 'age of consent' is 21) are both traumatic and corrupting and properly regarded as criminal assault. Others point to evidence that some boys seek out such contacts and find them beneficial. The organisation 'Gay Teenagers' suggests that homosexually oriented adolescents are unfairly deprived by repressive laws and social conventions from forming the relationships necessary for their emotional and sexual development (Burbridge & Waters, 1981).

1.5 A need for research

This brief excursion into the literature on children's sexual experience with adults suffices to show that knowledge on the topic is fragmented and uncertain, evidence conflicting and debate frequently more polemical than well informed. There is little agreement as to the true prevalence of the phenomenon, which is hardly surprising since definitions of 'child', 'sexual' and 'adult' differ from one survey to the next. Generalisations are put forward with little regard to the wide variety of behaviours encountered. These range from nudity and caresses in circumstances that would be considered normal by many people to horrifying brutalities perpetrated on victims too small to resist. Dubious extrapolations are made from highly deviant minorities, such as imprisoned sex offenders, which cannot give a true indication of what happens to the great majority of children who have had what is usually a rather casual, isolated encounter.

The need for yet another survey might be disputed, but it was felt that an English inquiry directed exclusively towards males, who have hitherto been somewhat neglected, and based on a non-clinical sample, might yield new information and help to counteract misguided speculation. In particular, we wanted to avoid the tendency to label as sexual abuse any and every incident in which a significant disparity in age exists between the participants, because this obscures the true complexity of the phenomenon. We aimed to encourage men who have had such experiences to describe their subsequent attitudes and feelings in their own way, without putting to them any particular expectation, leaving them as free as possible to describe the whole gamut of reactions from shock/horror to nostalgia.

2

The Student Survey

2.1 Designing the project

Inquiries about sex, especially about deviant activities, meet with much resistance. Cooperation from individual subjects, or from the authorities who control access to potential samples, is not easy to secure when the topic concerns private and sensitive experiences that many people do not like to discuss. Respondents are likely to refuse to answer questions that appear too obtrusive or seem to delve into matters that could have adverse repercussions should confidentiality be breached. Investigators may be suspected of prurient rather than scientific curiosity or of trying to give spurious legitimacy to unacceptable behaviour.

To discover all the different kinds of sexual encounters with adults that ordinary boys are likely to experience it was necessary to question a sample taken from non-clinical sources and, in view of current publicity about sex abuse, to convince respondents that the research concerned all sexual experience, 'abusive' or otherwise. Ethical and practical considerations precluded approaches to schoolchildren, so the inquiry had to be retrospective, asking adults about their recollections of events in childhood. This has unavoidable disadvantages. Memories of events long past, which may have seemed trivial at the time, inevitably fade, or they may become distorted, especially if they concern matters about which there are feelings of guilt or shame. Attitudes to the involvement of children in adult sexuality, acquired during the course of growing up and absorbing cultural mores, may make unbiassed recall of these childhood experiences peculiarly difficult. A subject may feel reluctant to reveal events which he thinks may put himself or his family in a bad light. For this reason it was felt important to allow subjects to respond to questions anonymously in the first instance if they so wished.

The inquiry was addressed to male students, predominantly those studying social sciences and psychology. Several considerations governed this decision. It was thought that students would be more likely than the average member of the public to appreciate the needs of research and to be willing and able to complete a fairly complex questionnaire. Students for whom the topic and the method of inquiry had some relevance to their studies might be better motivated to cooperate. We hoped that the heads of social science departments would be sufficiently sympathetic to the aims of the study to provide personal addresses of students so that all members of defined groups could be contacted individually by private letter. Since the project was mounted under the auspices of a responsible university department, and must therefore have passed the scrutiny of proper authorities, students could be confident of our bona fides. As students are predominantly young adults there would be no risk of the questionnaires being received by children, but at the same time many of the respondents would be removed by less than a decade from the events they were being asked to recall. Samples of polytechnic as well as university students were recruited, but even so there was inevitably an under-representation of men from working-class backgrounds. This might not bias the outcome as heavily as some would expect. When Nash & West (1985) conducted a similar kind of inquiry among women students and women townspeople the differences in regard to reported childhood sex experiences were not great, although female students did find more to relate, and certainly more to complain about, than the townspeople.

The wording of the questionnaire called for an uneasy compromise between the use of medical terminology for sexual acts, which can be misunderstood or sound prurient, and the use of less precise everyday language, readily understood but sounding vulgar. To make clear that we were interested in all kinds of sexual experience (not just what is commonly referred to as 'having sex') open-ended examples were provided (e.g. 'indecent suggestions', 'flashing', 'mutual masturbation', 'touching your private parts in a way you thought was sexual' and 'any other type of contact which you considered then or now to be sexual'). More detailed specifications (e.g. 'digital-anal-contact') were avoided.

A draft questionnaire was tested for comprehensibility and probable acceptability by giving it to acquaintances and inviting comments. A version was distributed by T.P. Woodhouse to strangers in the street, who were simply asked whether they would be willing to complete a research questionnaire. They were handed a sealed envelope for its return anonymously after completion. In all, 30 questionnaires were given out and 10 were returned. The exercise was useful in showing that people were able to complete the form and give coherent replies, but it could not be used as the source of an unselected sample or as an indication of a likely response rate. There was a natural tendency to approach men who looked amenable, and an indeterminate number would brush past or otherwise avoid the researcher standing on a corner with clipboard and papers. Once they had stopped and spoken, most potential respondents would agree to accept a questionnaire, even after asking and being told what it was about. Three men did refuse to take the questionnaire on learning what the topic was, one of them exclaiming: 'Do you think I look like a child molester?'

Following this brief pilot work a slightly altered questionnaire was prepared for use with the main samples of students. It is reproduced in

Appendix A (pp. 129-34). Separate sections of the questionnaire asked about experiences under the age of 11 with either a male or a female aged at least 16, and experiences after 11 but under 16 with men or women over 18. The division at 11 was intended to help men to remember how old they were when incidents took place. Since 11 is the age when children change school, if a respondent knew what school he was at when an event happened he could be sure whether it was before or after he had turned 11.

2.2 Obtaining access to the sample

Authorities at 17 colleges, departments or faculties in London and Cambridge were approached, in a few instances by personal contact, otherwise by letter. The nature of the research was explained, confidentiality assured and cooperation requested. Except for one graduate college in Cambridge, containing students from many disciplines, the subjects were all studying psychology or social science subjects at university or polytechnic. The request made clear that the questionnaire would need to be given to all male members of specified groups so that sampling would be unselective and the proportion of non-responders would be known. The replies could be sent back anonymously if so desired.

No answer was received from 3 institutions, either to the initial letter or to a reminder. One dean of social studies replied to the reminder explaining that four individual departments under his jurisdiction would need to be consulted. A month later he wrote that two had declined to cooperate and two others wanted an approach made via the students' union. To avoid further delay that suggestion was not pursued. The reply from one polytechnic declined to circulate a questionnaire but suggested putting up a notice asking for volunteers. As that would not have provided an unselected sample the offer was not taken up. The head of social sciences in one polytechnic responded, after a reminder, to the effect that in view of the sensitive nature of the topic the request was being passed on to the students' union. No further communication was received, but in answer to a telephone inquiry we were told that cooperation was not possible. Another reply stated simply that it was not the policy of the polytechnic to supply names or addresses to outside bodies. This was in fact the most usual reason given for declining to assist, usually together with some polite expression of regret. In London 24 colleges of further education were approached, but none were willing to help. Ultimately 9 sources agreed to cooperate, but sometimes only after months of negotiation and reference to ethical committees. A request for home addresses, to avoid consultations between respondents that might occur if questionnaires were distributed within a college, was usually refused. Only three sources supplied home addresses enabling questionnaires to be posted directly to individuals, and one of these informed us later that in doing so they had acted in error in contravention of their own rules. Otherwise, after the lists of names to be included in the sample were supplied, the questionnaires were distributed on our behalf, in most cases via student pigeon holes. We could not be sure, therefore, that every questionnaire had been collected.

No special precautions were possible to eliminate untruthful or facetious responses, but so far as could be judged those who took the trouble to reply had nearly all filled in the forms conscientiously and seriously. The last page of the questionnaire thanked the students for their help and asked if they would agree to a private interview. These subsequent interviews gave an opportunity to check that in these cases the original questionnaires had been completed fully and accurately.

One hoax reply was detected. A respondent put another student's name and telephone number on the form and filled it in with fictitious information. When contact was made by telephone it soon became clear that the person spoken to was not one of the sample, had never seen our questionnaire and would not have replied or agreed to an interview had he received one. He recognised the person who had played the trick and was considerably annoyed. He might have been angrier still if he had been told that the fabricated response alleged sexual abuse by his father. Since all those who supplied a name and address with a view to an interview were contacted, either by letter or telephone, and no other complaint was received, it seems unlikely that there were any other similar hoaxes.

Several questionnaires were returned with a variety of comments (one or two very rude) protesting at having been sent the request. One questionnaire, although completed, was returned with an erased identification number beside which was written 'Just in case I get quoted in *Private Eye*'.

2.3 Response rates and response bias

In all, 512 students were sent a copy of the questionnaire, but 8 at least were not delivered, since they were returned by the Post Office or known not to have been collected. Of the 504 probably delivered, 182 were returned completed, a response rate of 36.1 per cent.

As illustrated in Table 1, the response rates from the different sources varied widely, from 72.7 to only 12.5 per cent (Source D in the Table combines two groups from the same institution, which is why only 8 sources are shown). Four completed questionnaires were returned with the identification code eradicated, so it was not possible to say from which student group they came. If it had been possible to allocate them correctly the response rates for some of the groups would have been marginally larger than shown in the Table. The lowest response rate came from one of the London departments that distributed the envelopes in students' pigeon holes. The highest response rates came from two Cambridge sources that had links with the department from which the questionnaires were issued.

Table 1. Response rates by student sources

Student Group	Questionnaires delivered	Returned completed	Response rate	No. of positives	% positive
A	44	32	72.7	10	31.2
B	85	40	47.1	11	27.5
C	72	33	45.8	14	42.4
D	43	18	41.9	5	27.8
Sub-total	244	123	50.4	40	32.5
E	28	10	35.7	2	20.0
F	85	23	27.1	12	52.2
G	51	10	19.6	6	60.0
H	96	12	12.5	5	41.7
Sub-total	260	55	21.2	25	45.5
Unidentified returns	–	4	–	2	50.0
Total student sample	504	182		67	36.8

Notwithstanding a reminder enclosing a further copy of the questionnaire, the final response rate overall was disappointingly low; lower than had been achieved in previous research in which a rather similar questionnaire had been addressed to women students (Nash & West, 1985). In order to try to discover the reason for non-compliance a group of 17 Cambridge students who had not replied were sent, together with the reminder, a questionnaire asking them to give reasons why they might not wish to participate. Eleven possible reasons were given on the form (e.g. 'too busy', 'too personal', 'I could not see the point') which the respondent could tick, plus a space for any additional explanation. Five replied, four with completed questionnaires, four with a statement, that they had been 'too busy' to respond initially. One man explained that he was a foreign student and did not think he had anything to contribute. None of the 13 others who had failed to respond initially returned the form asking their reason for not wanting to do so.

Out of the total of 182 completed questionnaires, 67 (36.8 per cent) reported some early sexual experience with an older person. In estimating the true prevalence of such memories the low response rate might introduce bias in either direction. If some men fail to reply because they have had experiences they do not wish to disclose then the proportion of positives among those who do respond will be too low. If, however, it is more common for non-response to result from men with nothing to relate not bothering to reply the proportion of positives among those who do reply will be artificially raised. In order to discover how low response rates might be affecting the apparent incidence of early sexual encounters with adults, the sources shown in Table 1 are arranged in sub-groups, A to D having a relatively high response rate (50.4 per cent in total) and E to H having lower response rates (21.2 per cent in total). It can be seen that the groups with a low response rate are associated with a higher proportion of questionnaires claiming some sexual experience (45.5 per cent compared with 32.5 per cent). This suggests that generally non-responders have less to report than responders, and that the groups with a relatively high response rate give a better estimate of the prevalence of memories of childhood sexual encounters. Considering only the relatively high responding groups A to D, the most conservative possible estimate, on the implausible assumption that none of the men who failed to reply had anything to report, the incidence of relevant sexual memories among students would be 16.4 per cent.

Even this conservative figure represents a substantial proportion of the male population. It could be that the figure is inflated by the reporting of trivial incidents, or that the most significant, traumatic or embarrassing incidents are selectively eliminated through masculine reticence.

2.4 Findings from the students' questionnaire

The first page of the questionnaire asked for basic background information about age, composition of family of origin, occupation of parents and whether there had been any childhood separation from parents. The next section asked about any sexual approaches from or contact with a male or female older than 16 when the respondent was not yet 11. The following section asked about any similar incidents with men or women older than 18 when the respondent was aged 11 to 16. It also asked about sexual experience with girls of their own age. Finally, if any experience with an older person at any time up to age 16 had been recalled, the respondent was asked about the effects, if any, on his sexual life. So few replied to this last section that no analysis was feasible.

Students tend to be young, and most of the 182 respondents (81.9 per cent gave their age as under 30; only 9.9 per cent were 35 or more. There were only 6 born abroad, because we had avoided sending questionnaires to students with names that looked foreign. Of the 166 who were born in Britain and gave classifiable replies to the question, 30 (18.1 per cent) had spent the greater part of their life up to the age of 16 in London, 21 (12.7 per cent) in some other large British city, 72 (43.4 per cent) in some smaller town and 43 (25.9 per cent) in the country.

The proportion who reported some sexual experience with an older person when they were under 16 steadily decreased from 50 per cent of those brought up in London to 26 per cent of those brought up in the country (see Table 2, row 1). Although this contrast in percentages was substantial it was not statistically significant $\chi^2 = 2.13$, p = 0.2) Both experiences with older men and older women showed the same stepwise decline between London and country (rows 2 and 3). The most marked contrast between the London and country groups (from 23 to 7 per cent) was in regard to experiences under the age of 11 (row 4). These trends were in conformity with the expectation that the greatest likelihood of childhood sexual experiences with adults would be among those brought up in London or large cities.

Table 2. Proportion of students reporting early sexual experiences with adults by locality of upbringing

| | Brought up in | | | | | | | |
| | *London* | | *Other large city* | | *Smaller town* | | *Country* | |
	N	%	N	%	N	%	N	%
(1) Some sex experience with an older person when under 16	15	50	9	43	24	33	11	26
(2) Some sex experience with an older male when under 16	12	40	7	34	14	20	7	16
(3) Some sex experience with an older female when under 16	7	23	3	14	13	18	5	12
(4) Some sex experience with an older person of either sex when under 11	7	23	2	10	7	10	3	7
Total respondents Overall total = 166	30	–	21	–	72	–	43	–

Students who reported a break with their parents when they were under 16 (from death, desertion or divorce, etc.) reported a relevant sexual experience more often than did those who had never had a family separation. The contrast was most noticeable in regard to experiences under 11, but the differences were not statistically significant. Nevertheless, the trend is as expected on the hypothesis that a family break would be conducive to early sexual experiences with an adult (see Table 3).

From the 168 replies that gave a classifiable father's occupation it was possible to divide respondents according to occupational class of their family of origin. As might have been expected of a student sample, the majority, 133 (79.2 per cent), were in white-collar occupations – professional, managerial or clerical – the remainder were skilled or unskilled manual workers. As can be seen from Table 4, the incidence of reports of sexual experiences under sixteen was higher among

Table 3. Proportion of students reporting early sexual experiences with older persons against separations from parents

	Break with parents		No break with parents	
	N	%	N	%
(1) Some sex experience with an older person when under 16	12	50	55	35
(2) Some sex experience with an older male when under 16	10	41	35	22
(3) Some sex experience with an older female when under 16	6	25	28	18
(4) Some sex experience with an older person when under 11	7	29	15	10
Total respondents	24	–	158	–

Table 4. Proportion of respondents reporting childhood sexual contacts with adults against father's occupational class

	Father professional/ managerial/clerical		Father skilled or unskilled manual	
	N	%	N	%
Some sexual approach or contact by an older person when under 16	41	31	20	57
Some approach or contact by an older male when under 16	26	20	13	38
Some approach or contact with an older female when under 16	20	15	11	32
Some approach by or contact with an older person when under 11	12	9	7	21
Total respondents Overall total = 168	133	–	35	–

respondents from lower status families (57 per cent against 31 per cent, $\chi^2 = 3.50$, $\rho = .06$) (see Table 4).

The observations that respondents from lower-status families, from broken homes or from large cities more frequently reported early sexual experiences was unsurprising. The life of boys from higher-status homes is known to be more structured and supervised, boys who have unbroken contact with their parents are presumably likely to have less scope or inducement for associations with other adults, and boys reared in rural areas will be far away from the places where paedophiles commonly make their approaches. The fact that these trends emerged suggests that the respondents to the questionnaire were supplying serious, meaningful information.

2.5 Questionnaire accounts of sexual experiences

One section of the questionnaire asked about experiences when under the age of 11, another about experiences at 11 up to 16. In each section respondents were asked separately about sexual approaches that had not led to actual contact (such as indecent suggestions, 'flashing' etc.) and about experiences of physical contact (including masturbation, touching of private parts, etc.). They were also asked separately about approaches from or contacts with older males and older females. An additional question asked how many experiences they had had in each of these categories. Table 5 sets out the results. Several features deserve comment.

More men reported experiences when they were aged 11 up to 16 than when they were under 11 (46:22). Slightly more reported experiences with males than reported experiences with females (45:33). However, at least twice as many men reported experiences (both approaches and actual contact) involving men than involving women when they were under 11. (10:4 and 8:4). It would appear that postpubertal boys are more likely than younger boys to have experiences with older females, presumably because they have themselves become heterosexually active. Within each of the specified categories (with the exception of sexual approaches by men when boys were under 11) respondents who recalled any experience at all were likely to mention more than one occurrence. Unfortunately the question did not distinguish between repeated incidents with the same or different adults. Nevertheless, the figures show that few boys had taken action that avoided further confrontations.

In the section dealing with experiences under the age of 11, and again when the period from 11 up to 16 was under consideration, respondents reporting an incident with an older person were asked to provide a brief description of what happened. If they had had more than one encounter they were asked to describe 'the occasion which left the greatest impression'. They were asked also to circle the word that best fitted how they found the experience. The possibilities listed were: 'very disturbing', 'disturbing', 'indifferent', 'pleasant', 'enjoyable'. Some respondents failed to answer all the relevant questions, but enough did so to reveal some obvious trends. Of the 61 incidents cited, 19 happened under the age of 11. In 56 instances the age of the older person was stated; 16 (28.6 per cent) were 20 or younger (including 5 who were under 18); 17 (30.4 per

Table 5

		Number of respondents answering 'Yes' N	%	Number recalling more than one experience	Number who did not reply to question whether was repeated
Sexual approach from older female when 11-15 incl.	aged 11-15	25	13.7	13	3
Sexual approach by older male when 11-15	aged 11-15	28	15.4	17	0
Sexual contact with older female when 11-15	aged 11-15	16	8.8	9	1
Sexual contact with older male when 11-15	aged 11-15	11	6.0	7	1
Sexual approach by older female when under 11	aged <11	4	2.2	3	0
Sexual approach by older male when under 11	aged <11	10	5.5	2	2
Sexual contact with older female when under 11	aged <11	4	2.2	3	
Sexual contact with older male when under 11	aged <11	8	4.4	4	1
Any approach or contact when under 11 with older person		22	12.1	–	–
Any approach or contact 11 to 15 with older person		46	25.3	–	–
Any approach or contact up to 16 with older male		45	24.7	-	–
Any approach or contact up to 16 with older female		33	18.1	–	–
Total responding positively		67	36.8	–	–

cent) were 35 or more. Of the 57 who answered the question, a majority of 32 said they had not mentioned the incident to anyone at the time, only 5 had reported to parents, 20 had told other persons, mostly friends of similar age. Of the 60 cases where information was given, roughly equal numbers of encounters with females (31) and with males (29) were cited, although only 6 of the encounters with females were at ages under 11. In incidents with males, the older person was significantly more often said to have been 'not previously known' than was the case with female encounters (18 of 30 against 9 of 28, $\chi^2 = 4.52$, p = 0.02). Where ratings were given, the great majority of encounters with older females, even those that occurred when the respondent was under 11, were endorsed 'pleasant' or 'enjoyable', whereas the reverse was true of encounters with males (24 out of 29, 82 per cent against 2 out of 29, 7 per cent, $\chi^2 = 13.80$, p < 0.01). Indifference was the most commonly endorsed reaction to the male encounters (15 of 29); but those occurring at 11 or later were more often endorsed 'disturbing' or 'very disturbing' than those at an earlier age (10 of 17 against 2 of 12). This may reflect the fact that very young boys did not always realise the social significance of the incident at the time.

Encounters with older persons (i.e. over 30) were less often rated positively than encounters with younger people (5 of 19 against 21 of 36, $\chi^2 = 5.11$, p = 0.05).

The questionnaire asked about sexual experiences with girls around the same age when respondents were under 11 or 11 up to 16. A majority of the respondents, 113 out of 182, did report some heterosexual experiences with peers at 11 up to 16, and these included a relatively higher proportion who had had some approach from or contact with an older person (45 per cent against 23 per cent). A smaller number, 58, acknowledged sexual experiences with girls around the same age when they were under 11. These also included a relatively higher proportion who had at some stage had approaches from or contact with an older person (53 per cent against 29 per cent). Although these trends were not statistically significant, they were suggestive of a connection between sexual precocity and sexual involvement with adults.

Descriptions of early sexual experiences are examined in more detail later when the sub-sample of students who were interviewed is discussed. The brief statements included on the questionnaires provided some preliminary impressions which served to confirm trends suggested by the numerical analysis. For example, 19 respondents gave short descriptions of approaches from or, in 16 cases, contacts with females much older than themselves when they were aged 11 to 16. These were usually noted with expressions of pleasure rather than concern, as in the following examples, all rated 'enjoyable' and all happening at age 15:

(283) 'During a party I went into another room with a girl (aged over 18) and became involved in "petting".'

(999) 'I was at a party and the older woman (aged 30) and I talked politely. We both had quite a bit to drink. Both of us were obliging. There was no intercourse, just mutual masturbation.' 'It made me more confident about sex in general'.

(106) 'This person [aged 27] was a friend of my brother's who used to pay my brother regular visits. From the start I liked her – I was about 14 – and started showing it to her. It took a whole year. I guess she waited for

me to grow up a bit! We eventually made love in her car after we had had a cold ice cream.' Commenting on the effects of such incidents this man described them as 'beneficial' – 'so long as the child is old enough, I would say above 13 years old ... because it relaxes you, gives you a secure feeling ... [but only] if the persons involved have some sort of a mutual feeling of likeness or sympathy.'

Only a few respondents said they had been disturbed by heterosexual contacts. Here are two examples:

(411) When aged 8 'I had been playing board games with a school friend in his parents' flat when my friend's mother insisted that it was "bathtime". We were both undressed by his mother and then all I really remember after this is feeling cold inside. I stood with my friend in two inches of water whilst his mother kept lathering my lower half with soap. The worst aspect of this was my inability to laugh along with my friend. I was confused because this game was more serious and in ways I could not understand.' The incident was rated 'disturbing'. The woman involved was 25 to 30. This same student, commenting upon petting games he had had with a woman of 19 when he was 13, wrote: 'This was all clean fun and rather like a dream come true for a 13-year-old boy whose estimation among his friends reaches a new level ...'

(213) An experience with a woman of 25 when he was a schoolboy (age not stated) was rated 'disturbing (slightly)': 'I drank to excess at a party with people from a supermarket where I had a weekend job, and as a result I slept with one of the girl employees. Full intercourse did not take place. The morning afterwards I felt awful thinking about what had occurred. I left my job soon afwards, without the relationship developing further.'

Feelings about incidents of a homosexual kind were generally endorsed 'indifferent', as in the following examples:

(315) When aged about 7 'I was offered money in a public toilet, refused.'

(359) When aged 15 'I was on a train coming back from a soccer match and a man [aged 45 to 56] got in the carriage – just the two of us. He started asking me harmless questions to strike up a conversation. He then told me about how he was a boarding teacher in the Midlands and related many indecent stories about the sexual activities he got up to with the boys there. Suddenly we arrived at my station.'

(402) At 12 'I was told by a soldier [aged 18] to masturbate him in the locker room. At the time it did not affect me since I had no idea what was going on.'

(476) At 14 'at a public bathing place I was approached by a man who asked me to take a drive with him. His attitude seemed a little odd to me. [He was aged 25 to 30.] I became a little frightened and departed.'

(005) An experience at 15 with a man of 30. 'The person was someone I used to chat to about all my normal adolescent frustrations. He once asked if I wanted to be shown how to masturbate. It sounded a bit dubious to me so I said "No". It wasn't particularly disturbing and didn't stop me talking to the person. There was no element of threat involved ... I would rather not be interviewed, mainly because at the time I promised not to talk about the experience, and as I still occasionally meet the person involved, I'd rather keep the promise.'

(144) At 11 'When leaving the school library one of the "known" gay people in the school [aged 17] decided to "flash" himself, and tried to persuade me to stay with him for a while. I disagreed, and escaped.'

Some of the homosexual incidents which were rated 'disturbing' seemed not much worse than the ones recorded as 'indifferent'. Here are some examples:

(102) At the age of 12 'A man [of 25] in a public lavatory commented on the size of my penis.'

(019) When aged 15 'I was in a strange town in the park. I asked an oldish man [56 years] the time and then went to a public lavatory. The toilet cubicle had a hole drilled in the door and I saw an eye looking at me. I was frightened. A finger then appeared through the hole and wiggled in a suggestive way – I kicked it. I got up, opened the door to leave and the old man just stood there grinning. I fled, but he did not follow me. It was frightening, but after describing it to friends [some time later, about nine months] it seemed funny.'

(228) At 12: 'Forced into mutual masturbation by the friendly, authoritative air of the person involved' [a man of 46]. After answering 'No' to whether the experience had had effects on his sexual life this student commented: 'In the presence of older homosexuals, the atmosphere can be unnerving.'

It was noteworthy that none of the accounts mentioned physical violence. In fact in almost all of the heterosexual incidents the boys were willing if not enthusiastic participants. Most of the unwanted homosexual incidents took place in situations that were rather easily terminated. Unlike the incidents recalled by women the great majority of the encounters remembered by men had occurred outside the home, very often with total strangers. A few incidents involved relatives or family friends visiting the home. No examples of sexual approaches by their own parents were reported by these respondents.

3

Interviews with Students

3.1 Casual incidents

All the students who agreed to be interviewed were contacted by letter or telephone. Because it had not been decided initially that they should be included there was a longer interval before attempts were made to contact those who had reported no relevant sexual experiences on their questionnaires. Due to this delay and to the fact that men with nothing to report were less likely to volunteer for interview, only 13 of these were seen compared with 24 of the students who had mentioned some positive experience. In effect, one of these 24 was properly counted as 'negative' since it emerged that the incident he described had happened after he had turned 16.

The extracts which follow are quoted as far as possible verbatim from the tape recordings of the interviews. Judged by the length and detail of the descriptions, incidents with older males had made the most impression and were generally recalled as having been unwanted and vaguely unpleasant or anxiety-provoking – possibly because of the homosexual implications. In general, homosexual incidents happening in early adolescence to respondents who regarded themselves as hetero-sexual were mostly casual, isolated encounters that were quickly terminated by the boy without much difficulty and without thought of reporting the matter to parents or other adults. Here are a few examples of the kind. The interviewer's questions and comments appear in italics.

Case 002

A 36-year-old married, heterosexual student recalled an encounter with a man when he was aged 15. He found the experience 'disturbing', although at the time or shortly after he had a sexual affair with a woman five years his senior, which he found 'rewarding'.

Well I was a bit confused about that questionnaire, because I think it was the only incident where I've ever been approached by a man, and I think I probably explained it there. When I was about 15 to 16 there was – I sort of had quite a long-term relationship with a girl who was much older than me. She was sort of 20. And I wasn't sure whether that was [wanted] – I didn't know what you were driving at actually.

Right. That's OK. Could you just go through the male one and then we'll go through the female one.

Yes, sure. Again the details are probably a bit hazy. I tried to get as clear a picture as I could. Essentially, I used to work at a butcher's and deliver meat and there was some works going on. Now I think they were outside the shop. If they weren't they were outside a place where I used to regularly deliver to. That sort of thing. And they were quite obviously long-term workings because the people were there on several occasions, or the one guy was there on several occasions. And he used to chat to me sort of – about what are you doing delivering meat and all that sort of thing. And he used to chat about things and offer me a fag, smoking, and talk to me about 'Do you go to pubs?' and that sort of thing. I thought he just seemed a reasonable sort of guy so I just chatted to him. On this occasion I can remember – it's quite difficult to put it down in words – but when I was sitting on a bicycle and I've got one foot on a pedal like that and he's got a fag in his hand and says, 'Have you got a light?' And as he leant over for a light he sort of put his hand on my knee and started to move it up towards my genitals and at the same time he started rubbing himself on the knee that was there. So I felt, 'Hello!' So I gave him the light and so I said, 'I've got to go', and I cycled off. I don't like this at all.

What age was he?

I reckon about 30s. Again it's all pretty hazy.

You just cycled off?

Oh sure, yes.

You didn't say anything?

No, I didn't say anything to him. I chose to sort of ignore the incident.

Did you see him again after that?

Funnily enough no.

He just disappeared?

That's an interesting sort of aside. Because when I spoke to my mate about it that night – Terry and I were good buddies at that time – and Terry was all for getting the boys together and going round and sorting this queer out. Which I suppose I was sort of along those lines as well I suppose when I stopped to think about it. At the time I thought, 'Oh I don't want this.' I thought to retreat out of the way was the best thing to do. So I think – I mean I never saw him again, but I can't really remember whether I tried to avoid that area or tried to sort of think 'I don't want to go along there again in case I see him.'

Did you find it embarrassing?

Did I? Yes, I think so. And yet I can remember talking to Terry about it and sort of I suppose I sort of played it, you know. I don't really remember how I played it. A sort of macho – what this bastard did – you know.

That's right, yes.

So I got it out in that sense. That's probably how I overcame the embarrassment. Sort of, you use the sort of classic stereotype. Maybe that's what I'm doing.

Besides embarrassment, were there other sorts of feelings? Disgust, revulsion? – I don't know – fear, nervousness, anything like that?

I was certainly nervous in as much as I was a bit worried, you know. Christ, am I going to have to have a punch up with this guy or something. That sort of approach.

Actually slightly frightened, maybe?

Yes, possibly so. Yes, because it was unnerving for sure. And I didn't really handle it at all. I didn't know what to do except to ride off. And of course it was easy to get out of the way. All I did was just ride away and that was it.

You seem to sort of – you were clear about what went on. You knew about these men who approached, or you seemed to know.

Yes. I suppose it's the old, old joke. You read about it in the papers. You can hear about it till you are blue in the face but until it actually occurs to you you're not sure. And it's easy to make non-involved comment and judgment. But when you are actually there confronted with the situation and it happens to you it's very, very different.

Did you tell your parents?

No.

You didn't tell any adults?

No.

Do you know why that was? Can you remember why that was?

Well, I could guess and say that I'd be embarrassed to tell them that sort of thing. I don't suspect that my parents would have reacted in a sort of bad way. They wouldn't have wanted to sort of get the police and get this man arrested and what have you. I think they would have been more concerned about what actually happened and whether I was actually assaulted in any way. [*Yes.*] But I didn't tell them, no. And I suspect, well it was almost pure embarrassment. I mean at 35 years old it's a lot easier to talk about it. At 15 you sort of struggle a bit.

Do you think it had any other effect on your life? Did it make you more wary about being on the street or more wary about particular places or particular men or anything like that?

I don't think so. I really can't remember feeling that way. So, I mean at the time, so maybe for a week or so I did, but I certainly can't remember it. Life just went on as it did before. Just forgot about it.

What about the relationship with the woman; you said she was about 20.

Yes. When I say it was long-term it was months rather than years, but we sort of once – it wasn't my very first, but she was one of my very early steady girlfriends and I can't even remember how we got together to be honest. I remember at the time we met certainly when I was helping to run the cub pack as a sort of one of the more senior scouts, and she was the sister of the cub pack leader and she used to come down and help out now and again. And eventually we just got talking to each other and started going out. I mean it was sexual in as much as we were both well aware that we were both potentially – that there was a sexual relationship to be had there. It never actually resulted in intercourse or anything, but there was plenty of sort of sexual fondling and things like that. It was sexual in that sense. Lots of people when you say you have a sexual relationship immediately infer that it was an intercourse relationshihp, which it was not.

So what does sexual fondling mean?

Oh groping, yes basically. What we as teenagers would call groping. Playing with each other's private parts I suppose is another way of putting it. Heavy petting was it? [*Heavy petting can mean fellatio*] Yes, well it wasn't that. [*So there was no ... orgasm?*] Yes, certainly, on my part. [*She used to masturbate you?*] Yes.

Why did it end?

Why did it end? Can't remember, I really can't. I don't know whether she left the area or it just petered out. I really can't remember. I think relationships are very on off at that age anyway. [*Yes*] I think my son who is 15 now, he's just finished with his first girlfriend and he's already on the 'phone to someone else …

Did you enjoy the relationship?

Oh sure, yes. Absolutely great. Had a really good time, yes.

What about your parents, did they know about it?

I think they that I was sort of seeing this girl, but I don't think they knew to what extent we were sort of sexually engaged. They obviously have to – they have to just guess I suppose. We never talked about it, let's put it that way. I never made it explicit to them. I don't think they really wanted me to either.

What about your friends then, was it discussed?

Yes, I think it was. Maybe not in full, lurid details.

Did anyone make any comment about the age difference?

No, I don't think so.

On his questionnaire, in response to the request to comment on sexual involvement of adults with children, this man had written:

It is difficult to assess the divide between adults and children – for exmple I had a long-term sexual relationship at the age of 15/16 with a woman of 20. Was I a child? Was she an adult? I appreciate this may not be what you mean when you refer to much older in Section D.

Case 179

A mature, married research student aged 36 recalled one incident which he interpreted as homosexual that happened the first time he visited London and found that there was no room at the house of a friend who had invited him to stay.

When I was about 15, I remember disappearing off to stay with somebody in London, and this was about Easter, Easter 1965. I went with a boy from school, and it became very apparent when we got down there that we were not expected to stay where we were supposed to be. This was probably on a Friday and we didn't particularly feel like going home, so the pair of us stayed in London. We probably stayed for about three nights. Kings Cross Station on a Friday, Paddington on the Saturday and back to Kings Cross Station on the Sunday I certainly remember.

You actually slept in the station?

Well, in the waiting room, but I am sure we didn't get much sleep. If you pop down to Kings Cross, I don't know what it's like now, but a lot of people sleep in the waiting rooms over there in various places, it is particularly warm. The waiting room gets emptied about 2 o'clock by the police and people creep back in there on the pretext of having a train to catch for Edinburgh or somewhere at 6.30 in the morning. No, I certainly remember, it was not the first night, probably the second night, being approached by somebody. It was 2 o'clock in the morning. It was a very strange feeling. I remember thinking afterwards, you know, that I was a bit slow there. I didn't realise what was happening – I mean I was with a friend as well.

Were you asleep?

No, we were just sort of walking around.

And then somebody came up to you?
Yes.
Was it a male?
Yes. It was a fella.
What sort of age was he?
I suppose somewhere between 40 and 50.
And what did he say?
Well after, you know, preliminary chatting about what we were doing and what we were up to and the rest of it, he suggested giving us a cup of tea somewhere. We had no intention of going. We probably just sensed something not quite right. While it's nice other people being quite friendly, you don't anticipate it 60 miles from home at 2 o'clock in the morning, so I would say that, you know, we began to get a bit nervous. You'd think, afterwards, looking back, why didn't we just say time to disappear and run. But somehow you don't. Well the outcome was um-er, sort of thing. It's a very funny story. A younger lad came along. I can only guess he'd be about 25 or 30, and started trying to make similar intimations, at the same time as trying to suggest to the other fella, the older man, that he'd disappear. Now whether the taller, younger man had been drinking or not I don't know, but they ended up arguing, you know, about who was here first and all the rest of it. [laughs] It really was this funny. I know the great temptation to elaborate after 15 to 20 years, but it really was this funny. And whilst they were arguing with each other we did just – well literally – run for our lives.
Can you remember any of the sort of things that they said?
Really no. They were just trying to encourage us back to where they lived, you know, to stay for the night and have breakfast. There was certainly towards the end a certain amount of fear, because as a 15-year-old I wasn't a particularly sort of big fella, I was really quite small. Obviously it stayed vividly in my mind ever since.
With your friend afterwards, when you talked about it, what did you say?
It's a funny thing, but we didn't actually talk about it very much. I think it was just taken for granted that we both knew what we had almost become involved in, without actually saying anything.
Why do you think it was that you didn't speak about it?
[long pause] I don't know, I don't know why we didn't speak about it at all. I think probably because we both understood, you know, what was happening. We certainly understood that the approach made to us was not a normal approach. And when the two started fighting –. Maybe we were more naive than I thought. Maybe that was particularly worrying and maybe it made us think a bit harder about what was happening. And certainly the younger lad was a big lad, you know he could just have picked you up and put you on his shoulder and disappeared into another part of the station.
Did you think that?
Maybe fear set in at that stage.
Do you think embarrassment played a part?
I wasn't, not consciously, aware of embarrassment. Maybe with hindsight, whenever you are almost taken for a ride, you feel a bit embarrassed. It doesn't matter whether it's somebody shortchanging you at a market or whatever ...
Did your parents know that you were sleeping on a railway station?
No.
You didn't tell them?

No. As far as my parents were concerned, we went to stay with somebody in London for three days.

Was this the first time they allowed you to go off on your own?

To London certainly. In fact I had been to stay with other people, but probably not with the same degree of freedom that I enjoyed on that particular occasion.

Did you speak to your parents about what had happened? I suppose you couldn't really.

No.

Did you ever mention it to anyone else?

I'm quite sure I have, yes. Maybe with the years it becomes – well it's never difficult talking about it. I just didn't talk about it [then], but now it does raise the odd laugh in appropriate conversations, you know.

Would you say that [incident] was particularly significant?

Well, I remember it very well. Obviously, it must have had an impact of some sort, but I wouldn't have said it was a huge impact. It's just an experience that you've got to use.

When you said you ran out of the station, did you literally run?

Yes, we did. I think this is the sort of thing: you both look at each other and you'd both walk away backwards for about six or seven paces and yes, you do run, literally run.

Did you think of reporting to the police?

It didn't occur to me. In fact with the police emptying the waiting rooms out every three hours you were supposed to clear off. If you saw a policeman you looked the other way. I'm sure we were aware as well that probably at the age of 15 staying rough in London wasn't an accepted way of behaviour. I'm quite sure that any policeman catching us would want to know what we were up to and dispatch us off on the 6.30 train.

When asked about his earliest sexual interests he mentioned 'falling in love' and 'certainly inexplicable feelings, not physical feelings', from age 8 or 9, all directed towards girls. At the time of interview he had been married fifteen years and had three children. He was still having marital intercourse several times a month. He had warned his children casually about not accepting lifts and that some adults were not as nice as they might seem. Unlike the previous respondent, he expressed no strong feelings about paedophilia. His comments were somewhat tentative:

I don't have any sexual desires towards children and I can't see any personal gain from it myself. I must assume that people who do have that particular bent, who I assume are different, have different appetites, requirements, whatever, from mine. We all like to think that we're normal and we all know that we're probably not. [laughs] So I suppose you just have to you know – it's not so much punishment as much as, well you have to protect children from it. Punishment, I'd say probably not. It's not like a theft or anything. But treatment, I don't know. I don't know how treatments work, how effective they are, or anything. I just don't know enough to comment at all.

Case 489

An unmarried, heterosexually oriented, 27-year-old postgraduate student had one incident to report when he was 14. Coming home late one evening from air cadets, he was standing at a bus stop when a car driver in his mid-30s stopped and asked directions.

He then asked 'Are you going that way too?' I said yes. I got in and, when we got to about where I was supposed to get off, I said you can let me off here. And he said 'No, no, I will drop you off to your door'. I resisted, but then he insisted and he brought the car close to my home and we got near to my house. He then stopped and parked and – this is very vague, my memory, but the thing about it that stands out was that I used to be very very skinny. He claimed over the journey to be a physiotherapist working for a rugby club or something, or a football club, and that interested me. I was already interested in how to develop my body and become bigger and so on, and he then said, 'Well let me have a look at you and see what you are like.' You know, how muscley you are. And I think he wanted to touch me. I don't know what muscle this is above your knee, but that's the one he wanted to look at and in order to do so he had to put his hand down my trousers. [At the time he was wearing long trousers which the man had to unbuckle to reach down his leg.] Now it was done on a very professional basis, or at least the way he argued his case was a very professional one, but at the time I was very, very wary of what was happening. I was a very cynical little boy at the time, not so bright as I am now, but cynical and sarcastic, and my wariness brought this sarcasm out, and it certainly came across to him. He picked it up and he tried to put me at ease and I ended up letting him touch the muscle to see how big or how hard it was or whether I would be growing into a big boy or whatever. And – um – that was it, nothing else happened. After he did it he then replied, 'See, nothing happened.' That was it and I left the car feeling rather – I don't know – a certain weakness in myself for letting it happen and wondering how my parents would respond to that episode if they were to know about it. And that was it.

You said he claimed to be a physiotherapist. Didn't you believe him at the time?

Then, no. Looking back on it I would assume if the guy was simply a straight guy it wouldn't have happened, the event wouldn't have happened the way it did happen. He wouldn't have insisted to go off the main street, the back street close to my home. He wouldn't have pushed to examine me, to overcome my resistance, if he was simply straight. It wouldn't have been important to him, but the fact was that what came across to me was it did seem to be important to him, when faced with my rather tenuous resistance, and that's why I doubted his story.

After the event I thought it interesting. It showed me someone that I'd never met before, a personality as opposed to a person, a personality which I had never met before and this is – you know – sort of like, being who I am, um, on that part it was interesting. Not only him, it was interesting for me as well, interesting in the way I handled it and so on. The events themselves take a minor role, funnily enough.

Were you frightened?

I was frightened, I was frightened if I resisted too much I may get hurt. So

I remember thinking – I'm probably fabricating here slightly – I remember thinking, um, if I were to resist would I be able to handle it, handle him. You know, I was very little and he was a man and so I think that did come into it.
You didn't tell your parents?
No, I never told my parents, no.
Why was that, do you think?
Yeh, I remember walking away from the car thinking to myself, laughing in fact, or giggling, not giggling, smirking, that if I were to tell my parents – My God! What would they think? You know – how silly I was. Whereas I was trying to sort out the situation by thinking, well, wasn't it an informative experience. That sort of thing. I was rather intellectual about it, whereas of course my parents would be much more paternal about it.
[In fact he did not discuss the incident with anyone at the time.] The friends I had at that time, we didn't discuss that sort of thing because of its explicit sexual nature. We weren't a very discursive clique, we were very physical, you know, playing games and things like that.

He recalled one other ambiguous homosexual situation. Since the age of 11 he formed a platonic friendship with a male teacher, then in his late 30s. He enjoyed chatting with this man who, unlike his parents, encouraged his intellectual interests, but

... the kids at school ... would have a go at him because he was feminine, so according to them he was gay, or whatever, but according to me I liked him ... even though he would be effeminate towards me and even more affectionate than was socially acceptable, or whatever. I'd never jumped to the conclusion that he was gay.
[Later, when he was 16,] my relationship with my English teacher developed. I used to go and see him and chat quite a lot. It's where I began to develop myself intellectually, became myself, an academic proper. One of the supports of the relationship for him was he had an attraction towards me and he wanted to encourage an attraction of myself to him. Um, and in doing so his homosexuality came out, he confronted me with it and so on ... He put it to me that the reason why I came to see him was because I was attracted to him. This of course meant that if I was to continue going to see him, because I enjoyed seeing him, he would continue interpreting it otherwise. So the relationship stopped ... The only [thing] you could do was stop going to see him, which is what happened.

This student described no early homosexual attractions or homosexual experiences with peers. His first remembered sexual interests, when aged about 9, were towards girls he felt he wanted to touch. At 12 he had fantasies about a woman teacher who wore sexy mini skirts: 'I wanted to go to bed with her. I didn't know what I would do in bed, but I knew I wanted to go to bed with her.' At 18 he fell in love and had full intercourse for the first time. Various sexual affairs followed, but he has always felt some conflict between his 'passion' for studies and on the one hand the demands of girlfriends and on the other the 'distraction' of sex 'playing on your mind a bit' if the opportunity for it is not immediately available.

At the interview this student seemed to be trying to portray himself as sophisticated and self-assured. It could be that at the time of his experience with the car driver he was less sure about what was happening than he cared to admit.

Case 381

A heterosexual student, aged 26, described some homosexual gestures from a teacher at his single-sex boarding school and one encounter with an importunate man in a cinema.

The one thing that comes to mind immediately … was this teacher.
What did he do?
He was just generally inclined that way. I didn't understand the motivation behind it.
This was at prep. school?
Yes.
So you would be what age?
Well 11 I suppose, by the time it happened 11 to 12. He used to come round and put his arm round you in the classroom, or tell the good-looking boys to stand up, he was incredibly open about it … I think today's kids would latch onto it very quickly.
The other kids at school, what did they think about him?
Well by the time we were 13 and ready to leave it was a known fact and we were not exactly overjoyed about it … One time I was in the dining room and I had a blazer button undone and this lunatic told me to take all my clothes off since I liked going around stripped. I thought that's very odd and I went to the headmaster and said I have to phone my father, I have had enough of this school. He asked me what had happened and I told him. You can imagine the little panic stations that ran then …
Do you know what happened to the teacher? Did he continue to be at the school?
Yes he did, and carried on with what he was up to. In fact he was very vindictive because he used to try – He would say everybody but [me] can do this or that … [My] parents will only come down and complain …
He doesn't sound like he was very frightened by it all.
Well, he could not admit to it. I think he meant well … One half of him was warm and considerate and the other side was slightly crooked.
But did he ever do anything other than making comments such as the one you mentioned, and his hands sort of touching?
Well, all I remember is he had boys to his house – each teacher had a house – and what happened then I have no idea. I mean there were rumours abounding, but that could happen to anyone …
Was that the only incident that you remember?
I had an incident once in a cinema, but this was just basic. I was watching the film *Carrie* and this fellow just put his hand on my knee …
What age were you at this time?
That must have been about 15 or 16 …
You were at the cinema on your own?
No I was with a friend of mine and I was just watching the film. And then

the fellow just did that, so I moved two seats along and he did it again you know actually.

You mean he actually followed you?

Oh yes. Moved up two seats.

And the second time?

What, that he did it?

Yes, what did you do?

I left the cinema.

Had the film finished?

No it had not finished ...

What did you notice about the man, what sort of age was he?

I can't remember a thing about him. I suppose, deep down, the first time it happened it was more of a – what on earth does he think he's doing? get back! I wanted to get back to the film. The second time I think I was very frightened. I just wanted to get out of the cinema.

Why do you think you were frightened?

Um, because I knew what it was about and yet had never thought about it ... a sort of, um, ignorance of the situation.

What about your friend? Did you explain to your friend that you were leaving?

Oh yes. I told him, definitely.

And what did he say?

I cannot remember at the time what he said. I suppose it was just like, 'Right, we will leave the cinema.' It was in that situation.

You said you were frightened, did that last?

I have obviously never forgotten it ... [it was like] an approach from a yobbo threatening to beat me up, it was that type of fear, sort of being out in the open and vulnerable like that. I have often thought if it happened today I would react a lot differently.

How do you think you would react?

I hate to say it, but a little violently as I am bigger and stronger now. I didn't like the way I was very young and vulnerable then, and I rather resent that.

In the space on the questionnaire asking for comments about sexual involvements of adults with children this man had written:

Positively damaging to the child. Although this is a value judgment – I believe that children are totally unequipped and unprepared to suffer the intimate or lust (whatever) involvement of an adult. Furthermore, unless the child is extremely advanced mentally and physically, which is another matter (although still unnatural) the 'adult' undoubtedly has a personality disorder not to control his/her actions with the child.

At interview he amplified these views, saying that he would rule out sex with any adult, male or female, familiar or stranger, and classify it as abuse, regardless of whether the child, out of curiosity or ignorance, thinks he wants it. Children are just not developed sufficiently to cope with the emotions that sex contacts with adults may arouse.

When interviewed, this young man said that he had had a regular sexual relationship for about three years with a particular girlfriend with whom he had intercourse 'roughly three times a week'. He had attended a mixed secondary school and had no difficulty recalling that from the outset his sexual interests had been towards girls:

> *Do you remember the first time you were interested sexually in someone else?*
> Yes, I do. I was probably about 7. I can remember very very early.
> *Who was that?*
> Oh, that was a teacher, a woman teacher at school, a maths teacher. I was just trying to think, I used to have a mad childhood crush on Diana Rigg in *The Avengers*, so that must have been very early on ...
> *Was it fairly uncomplicated having a girlfriend and discovering about sex?*
> At public school? Well, first of all they had 'hops' as they were called. That was where you met your girlfriend. Or you were in class with them, as it was mixed, and naturally your dormitory mates would talk about it, all what they did. So it was again very easy because you were together, it was a natural progression. I got teased I remember when I found a girl I liked, yet that was natural.

Coming from an affluent, well educated background, with a father who was a gynaecologist, this young man appears to have been relatively sophisticated about sexual matters from an early age, and, unlike some others who were interviewed, well able to interpret and react to homosexual situations in the manner he saw fit.

Case 484

This 35-year-old, who rated himself exclusively heterosexual, recalled several episodes involving males which had made no great impression because he was already strongly oriented towards girls and could not appreciate male homoeroticism.

> There were these two incidents I vaguely recall. One was to do with an older boy when I was, I guess, about 11 and he was about 16 or 17. This was while I was actually on a train-spotting trip. We came back on a train, about five or six of us and he was – I sort of looked across at the other seat and there was one of my friends who was actually touching him, you know, touching his genitals. He had quite a large – this was under his trousers – quite a large erection. I couldn't imagine, I didn't know what it was that was going on. I was curious about this and I did say, 'What are you doing?' I don't know what was said but the guy was just touching him and he was lying back displaying this thing and he said, 'Go on, do you want to touch it, have a go.' And I did actually touch it – because I was quite surprised at the size of it, the extent of this thing, and it felt odd. It certainly was arousing, not necessarily in a positive sense, but there was something that made me touch it. Then I just kind of stopped. I knew it was wrong, somehow.
> *You said it was arousing. What did you mean?*

Just that I felt vaguely – maybe it was the naughtiness of it I think which was what aroused me. There may obviously have been some sort of sexual component as well, but I was not aware of it at the time, although I was aware obviously that it was something about it. I was drawn to it. I cannot imagine why I would have wanted to touch it, but perhaps wanting to is putting it a bit strong. But just thinking that – I don't know – I think that was the first time that I was ever aware that there was such a thing as sort of male sexual contact. In actual fact I couldn't imagine why he wanted this boy to touch him like that. As far as I knew it was far better touching girls. That was what you were supposed to do as well. That was naughty enough. Why! This must be really bad, or conversely it was totally normal. I didn't know. I forgot it very quickly, obviously. I say obviously, but it's an odd thing to remember now.

Asked about his earliest sexual interests he said that from early childhood, since 3 or 4, he had played a lot with girls. In junior school

I had always somebody that I would call a girlfriend there at a given time, and we used to spend quite a lot of our time when I was train spotting or whatever just going out and hanging around on the estate with girls, getting up to various things, nothing sexual, but just pairing off, that sort of thing.
The first time I actually felt any sexual arousal I was about 8 or 9 I should think and there was this girl, a girl who lived down the bottom of our street, and she was about 12 or 13, and she took me into the shed and blacked out the windows and took all her clothes off. And she undressed me from the waist down as well, and we were in there for ages. I do not know why I was enjoying it, but I was really enjoying it I remember. After a while, it must have been a couple of hours I guess – just sort of looking around and playing around – I felt it was desperately naughty, but I felt that I enjoyed it and we must do this again sometime.

After going to secondary school at 11, for several years he had little to do with girls and was into boys' gangs. At this point he felt rather shocked by the revelation of adolescent forms of sexuality and talk of masturbation and orgasm and was rather naive. Since the age of 16, however, he has had a continuously active sexual life with one girl or another, most of the time cohabiting, and now contemplating marriage.
His later experience of homosexual approaches came when

I guess I was 15 to 16. I became aware then that there were queers in the town and there were places where the queers went, but I did not know actually what these queers looked like or anything like that, but there was a pub which was a queer's pub. And I started to understand what all these writing on the walls of the toilets were, that it was not actually heterosexual it was homosexual. I had wondered, you know, how these women got in to write these things on the wall, it was a naive thought that crossed my mind ...
As a quite early teenager, often I used to, most night I was out, I would walk up from my girlfriend's house. And on several occasions there was one

particular car that would cruise. The guy used to live fairly close by and he would stop on my side of the road, usually around about one particular toilet that I used to step into on the way home, just because, I don't know, I was very fascinated by all these graffiti. I must say I was intrigued by it and this seemingly must have been a well known 'cottage'. I remember this guy would stop in the car and I would cross over and he would drive on and stop on my side of the road. This happened on two or three occasions. I knew who he was. He was a significant person in the town, well known. In fact that's an odd thing about it in a way, because it wasn't a big town. He was a very well known person and he was a well known homosexual.

Did he follow you in his car? Is that all that would happen?

Usually, because I would avoid it, yes. I would cross. I would get quite close and [laughs] I would cross over to avoid it. I don't know how close I would get before I crossed over. I don't know if I was just in some way leading it on. I don't know.

Do you think, suspect you might have done?

I do think so, yes possibly, but I don't think that I – I certainly would have run a mile rather than get in the car or anything.

When you went into the lavatory, in the evening you said, was it being used as a – [meeting place]?

I don't think so.

Did you ever see any people other than that one man?

I think probably on maybe one or two occasions, I think that people would come in and take an unusual amount of time.

Did you understand what was going on?

No, I didn't at all. I really didn't. It was only really that during the time that I started to find out about homosexuality, because certain friends of mine were actually working for this guy. Apparently he used to try to pick everybody up all the time. He was constantly cruising most guys, and he used to employ quite a lot you know – teenage boys in his business – in the summer, it's a very seasonal place, and he used to be always approaching them, making lewd comments, suggestive comments, telling them stories about these things. He was looking for a response. So I think it was probably because of this guy being around that I started to find out about homosexuality, and then, at this time, also on two or three occasions, he tried to pick me up. Nothing restricted to me. It was just that he was out looking.

What did you think about this?

I couldn't understand it. I couldn't imagine why, why he could possibly –

Did you feel nervous about it?

About?

About a man approaching you?

Yes, in a way, but I was confident I could get away.

Why were you so confident?

I used to run for my school, apart from anything else, and he was an ugly fat man. But I wasn't at all frightened. Even if I had got in the car he couldn't have. I was not at all worried that there was any real threat from him …

Did you tell your parents?

No.

Did you tell anyone else?

Yes, my friends – schoolfriends, the ones that worked for him. It was by way of a joke that he tried to pick me up last night.

Had they had similar experiences?

I think one had, actually, with the car business, but a couple of others that worked for him and had these sort of joking approaches, sort of touching them, coming up behind them while they're serving and saying, 'Are you wearing underpants, I can't feel any?' – that kind of thing. It was a sort of common bond in that area, this joking about it, which made it seem not too threatening or too terrifying – it was not.

Asked about his views on sexual contacts between adults and the young he commented:

I don't think it is a good idea, I don't think that the younger person necessarily is emotionally equipped to deal with it ... I can't see any way in which it is going to be good for a young person, you know, a very young person, to be sexually involved with somebody who is significantly older.
Do you think it makes a difference if the older person is male or female?
Um [laughter] There, my instinct is to say that it might be less damaging for a younger man with an older woman, but I do not know why I should say that. I don't know whether it is possibly because I felt I might find it exciting and I could deal with it, but I don't know ...

Case 166

A 29-year-old heterosexual student reported an episode at age 11 or 12 with a man of about 35. This man had started up a campanology group and our respondent had been a keen participant, travelling around the country with the bell-ringers. The same man, together with a friend, another adult male, also took boys caving.

I thought this was great fun and I think we went several times. On a couple of times, I'm not sure how it happened, but it basically involved – I mean, this was usually at the end of a cave system and he spun this story about doing scientific research on the development of young boys. I think to begin with I very naively believed this was genuine and the only way he could get his data. Anyway it wasn't, I don't think it was, a particularly serious thing, but he tried to masturbate me, completely unsuccessfully, and I did the same for him.
I didn't like it at all, but I think it involved – going along with it involved – being used to him and getting a lot out of him in other ways. Probably also being a very timid child and not liking to make [trouble]. I think I knew that if I brought it up or if I made a stand that would destroy the whole caving and everything. Also I remember, at one time anyway, that he made a big point of saying we were at the end of the cave and I didn't know my way back, which was quite true.
Did you feel that as a threat?
Yes, yes I was frightened, frightened physically of being in the cave and not able to get back and going against someone of authority. And the large repercussions of being in trouble with my parents.
Was it a threat when he said that about being at the end of the cave?
Well I don't know about – I suppose if I talk rationally about it I realise he

could not have left me down there, but yes, I think it did make me feel more dependent.

Did he talk to you about whether you should speak about these events?

Yes he did, he said you mus'n't, you definitely mus'n't tell anyone.

You make it sound as if you felt slightly that you cooperated in the situation for your own ends.

I don't think I thought a bit like that. Thinking back on it, I was mainly wanting to avoid – for instance why I didn't tell my parents was wanting to avoid all the very – I mean a lot of upset. It was mainly going to be directed against me, and just be an unpleasant thing I am sure. Also I mean, I realised at the time, this group of bell-ringers that I was happy with would be destroyed ...

You seem to suggest that you were aware at the time that in some way what was going on was wrong. Is that right?

Yes. I think, you know, implausible as it sounds, I believed that scientific story to begin with because I think I sort of asked him [about it] later, perhaps the next week, and he had probably forgotten about it or didn't want to talk about it. And then I suspected.

What about the other boys who went in the cave?

Well, I'm not sure. One of them stopped going [but] I don't think he liked caving. The other one was about [pause]

Did it happen to him?

No, I don't know, I didn't talk to him about it ... Looking back on it, it was highly suspect. These two men always went around together. I've never told my parents about this, but talking about that time later my mum said he was a strange fellow. She never felt quite safe or happy with them, or my going off with them caving. I have forgotten why I stopped going, whether he just stopped, I mean we only went two or three times caving.

Did you continue to see the man on other occasions?

Only for a short while. I really can't remember why ... The whole bell-ringing thing folded up for some reason ...

Sorry, I didn't really ask, how many times did this happen?

I think twice.

Was it always exactly the same thing on both occasions?

Yes. It was pretty much the same. I think probably, on the second occasion, I got less of a story about research and, er, I think perhaps he expected me to be enjoying it. I don't know.

But you didn't?

No, no.

This man said he was in an active sexual relationship with a girlfriend over the past seven months, that all his sexual relationships since 16 had been with women and that 'as a small boy I was always falling in love with girls'. Nevertheless, at adolescence he had had some worries about homosexuality. He did not mention any link between this and his experiences in the cave:

Did you worry about sex when you were an adolescent?

Yes I think, I am sure, I did.

What sort of worries?

I think probably things along the line of was I normal, whether I was developing normally, that kind of thing. I was certainly developing very slowly, and, you know, whether I'd turn out to be heterosexual or homosexual.

Was there any particular reason why you might be worried about your sexual orientation?

No, I don't. There was no particular incident, it was just, I think for an adolescent at school it's a very big joke. Homosexuality is a big joke. And I remember reading just a little of a book that said one in nine of people were homosexual and suddenly realising here am I and it was not at all impossible that I would be one of these terrible people. You know, we thought it was so funny.

As to his views about adults approaching children for sexual contact he said:

It just seems sort of selfish. I would question that children could get anything out of it that would do them any good, and I think it could also do them a great deal of harm, but at the least it could give them a lot of worries.

Case 429

This 21-year-old man had reported on the questionnaire that he had been approached by a middle-aged man when he was 9. He also reported that he had had sexual contact with a woman over 18 and had often been approached by women over 18 before he was himself 16. He was interviewed, but no tape recording is available, so the account is taken from notes made at the time.

The incident with the man occurred when he was on holiday with his mother and younger brother. At the time his mother was divorced and did not remarry until later, when he was 13. At interview he said he thought he was 10 on the occasion when the three of them were together shopping in a souvenir shop when a man, who was in his late 40s or early 50s stood close to him and brushed against him three times. His mother was in another part of the shop. He went over to her and told her what had happened. She was shocked, but did not report the incident to the shopkeeper or to the police. The only other details he recalled were that he had felt 'perhaps surprised' and that the man looked 'seedy and dirty'.

When asked about the experiences with older females he mentioned two episodes. When he was 13 or 14 he was 'seeing' a woman of 18 and at 12 he was 'seeing' a 16-year-old girl. There was no sexual intercourse with either of them, just 'heavy petting'.

At interview he rated himself as exclusively heterosexual and all of the sexual contacts he mentioned were with women or girls, all of them older than he was. His most recent sexual relationship, which had ended a week before the interview, was with a divorced woman with children. He described her as 'much older' than himself.

On the questionnaire, in answer to the request for an opinion about adult sexual involvements with children, he had written:

> I would think the greater the age difference then the chance for it disturbing the young person would increase, but for it to be OK for two 16-year-olds and not for a 14 to 15-year-old and a 16-year-old seems a rather arbitrary marking off of when sexual relations are acceptable and unacceptable.

*

None of these seven heterosexual students, all of whom remembered approaches from older males during their early adolescence, reported any adverse effects or attributed any great importance to what had been odd, isolated and essentially casual experiences. Though they may have experienced some anxiety at the time, they had coped with the situations without much trouble and generally avoided unwanted involvement. Those students who also recalled adolescent contacts with older females regarded these as pleasant episodes, reserving their negative comments for the experiences with men.

3.2 Repeated incidents

The next two cases concerned boys who had had repeated contacts with older males. Neither had become permanently homosexual. The first man felt he had been led into homosexual activities when he was too young and innocent to understand the implications. The second man, who reported complete indifference to homosexual approaches as a young boy, in later adolescence went through a phase of 'flamboyant' and active homosexuality that included an 'affair' with a male teacher.

Case 239

This 35-year-old mature, married student rated himself on the Kinsey Scale as 'predominantly heterosexual, only insignificantly homosexual. His story was different from those of other heterosexuals in that he had been a voluntary participant in continuing sexual encounters with an adult man when he was 13. He recalled also one guilty incident of having sex with another young man when he was 17. He described undemonstrative parents with whom he had had great difficulty in communicating, especially on sexual topics. He had no sisters, attended sex-segregated day schools, and claimed to have had little chance to mix with girls. Of all the students interviewed he was the only one who seemed anxious to ventilate continuing concern about sexual incidents long past.

> There was this thing about sex. It was something that the grown-ups would not tell you about, that there was sort of – things that you didn't understand

that you dealt with. You dealt with it in collusion with your peers. I don't think that it was until much later that we really sort of analysed things and said this was sexually attractive and this was not ... I suppose that I was sexually attracted to the boys, to the peers that I was with, really because there was no other.

Yes. Right. You mentioned one incident. Can you describe what happened?

Well in what perspective? I mean I can tell you without the social interaction and the way it came about, what I felt about it. I can tell you the actual physical details, but I don't think you are going to gain a great deal from the physical details. I mean, I don't know –

Well, I wanted to know how you met and where you went and who else was there and what –

As I said, when I went to the secondary school there was one particular friend I had known at my previous junior school ... He was just someone that I knew, that I could relate to. And it was about that time that we were sort of interested in the new feelings that we were discovering and the sexuality that was emerging. It was nice to play with yourself and it was something that none of the grown-ups talked about. And it was a big thing, you know, to compare notes and to even sort of play with yourself mutually you know. And he was the one who actually introduced me to the chap called Jim who I described in the questionnaire.

How did he introduce you?

I think he must have been part of a group of several lads who knew this chap and he just introduced me to the group of them, and said, 'Every so often Jim takes us swimming and you can come along' – sort of thing.

So you went swimming.

Yes. There was nothing about that occasion that was really not normal, but – er – there was a sort of connotation about this chap and –

Were there suspicions about this chap Jim before you got to meet him?

Well, I don't know, I have – yes, I think I had some realisation that there was going to be things that were, I don't know, not normal about it.

Did that put you off or were you curious?

I think, I think I was curious, I think that was the overall feeling about it. I think that if I had developed a bit more socially, and I was not relying on any information from this particular friend that I had, I would have seen more into it than I did; but I was, thinking back, I was very naive about the whole thing.

So you mentioned that nothing happened on that occasion, what about subsequent occasions?

On subsequent occasions there was a group of boys who knew him and his acquaintances and it was in that group that things happened.

What sort of things happened in what sort of situations?

Er – well I think it all really focused around his taking this sort of group of boys out for trips, you know, in an old ambulance that he had.

This was at weekends?

Yes.

Did your parents know?

No, they only knew that I was meeting this schoolfriend.

Why didn't you tell them?

Er – [long pause] – I think at the time there just wasn't the communication between us. There was a certain amount of conflict because they were very much into achieving things, academic things. Really their perception of what was happening socially to me seemed to be very limited at the time and almost unimportant.

So you went away for a weekend –
It was only days, just sort of days out.

I see. How many of you would there be?
About five or six I think.

That is four or five boys?
Four or five boys. Yes.

What sort of things happened?
I cannot remember very much of the detail, but I know that one or two of the boys were very much more involved than I was. I was pretty much a latecomer.

What sort of places did you go to?
I can't remember actually the details of where we went to.

It doesn't matter.
I think, if you're interested in the way the whole scene happened, this chap Jim had a room in with a family that one of the boys belonged to. He had obviously got quite heavily involved with that particular boy. I'm not sure whether it was just a case of, sort of between these two, of you toss me off and I'll toss you off, sort of thing, or whether it actually went further than that. My guess is that they probably went further. And that sort of thing was talked about amongst the group, but it was very much, as I said, the whole atmosphere of the thing was rather secretive and sort of, you know, very much a competition between the group of boys. What have you done with him and what I've done with him, sort of thing. So I mean, I think that there were several in the group who were more involved than I was.

What sort of things did you do with him?
Well the thing about these trips that we went on was that – er – we had sort of four of us in the back of this ambulance and we were encouraged to do certain things like strip poker and that sort of thing, and there was this treat. The thing was that you were, you would take a turn of sitting in the front with Jim and you'd play with him and he'd play with you, sort of thing.

Was this while he was driving along?
Sometimes it was, sometimes it wasn't.

That was really about the sum total of it?
On my part anyway.

So he would just toss you off and you would do the same for him.
Yes.

How long did this go on for?
It went on for about two or three months.

How was it that it ended?
It was quite a complicated situation because – it is a bit difficult to remember the exact details because it is quite a few years ago. I'm not quite sure whether it came out from one of the other members of the group, either to their parents or at school, but it came out into the open. And I remember that everybody in the group was obviously asked who the other members were and I think at one stage the police were involved. And I can remember having to, I didn't have to discuss the details of what happened, at least I cannot remember discussing the details of what happened with the police, but I know it got to a stage where I had to explain to my parents what had happened.

What was their reaction?

Their reaction was what I would have expected in a way, in that it was non-emotional and very matter-of-fact and something that was to be talked about and got under the table sort of thing, to be pushed away. I think there was a great deal of tension and a great deal of feeling – I think in some ways it might have been better if the whole thing had, sort of, you know, if we had had a big blow up about it. It certainly had quite a marked effect. I am not quite sure how to describe it really. I felt, once it had been brought into the open, I felt very, very guilty about it, very guilty about having to discuss it. But it was very difficult because – when that sort of experience, the experience in a group of boys and the experience with Jim, was the only thing that you really knew about sexuality you had no guide to say, I mean I could not convince myself that it was wrong. I had no way of making any judgments for myself that I felt were valid about it. It was never such a thing to be put out of the way. It was never really fully discussed and I felt that was perhaps the worst thing about it. And there was nobody, I mean I didn't feel relaxed about talking about it with the parents and there was nobody else that I could – that I would be able to discuss it with. I mean I think that it was almost, when you think about it, about morality. And certainly from what I have done since, this thing about feeling that something is wrong if you get found out was very much what I felt. There was not any sense of the particular things that I had been involved in. I didn't have a self-image of this being wrong, only of what other people saw.

In answer to questions about his early sexual development he explained that his heterosexual interests started late, about 15 or 16. Early lack of sexual knowledge and lack of contact with girls

... forced me into a very one-sided view of the world and it really took about ten years before I – even then I didn't feel happy about relations and sexual contacts with girls, and I feel that was very regrettable. I mean there are still some things that still hang over me from that now.

[He recalled] One particular incident when I was about 17. I was quite keen on going to Country and Western clubs, folk clubs, and there were two particular singers who were a duo who I quite liked. I used to go and see their shows and in fact one of the duo was homosexual. I actually had another sexual experience with this chap, and that really did leave an impression because he had homosexual intercourse with me. It was not until, well, not very long after that happened that I actually realised the full implications of that, and that made me feel quite sick, and I imagine that really choked me off. It was not until probably three or four years after that, that I started to feel happy with relationships with girls and [with] the beginning of sexual relationships, that you may have expected to have begun when I was about 15.

In the light of the history given at interview this man's comments on the questionnaire about adult-child sexual contacts become more understandable. He wrote:

As teenagers we lacked the responsibility and moral judgment of most adults and found sexual experiences compelling, pleasant, unknown. I now feel that before the age of consent children and teenagers *must* be allowed to discover their own sexuality. Adult involvement is immoral, irresponsible, and screws kids up, whereas openness and education and non-sex-segregated schools help.

At the time of interview he had been married twelve years. He described their sex life as

really good for the first four or five years. Since then it has had its ups and downs ... I think that in some respects it leaves something to be desired, but on the other hand I feel that we have a good personal relationship.

Case 050

This 25-year-old student rated himself exclusively heterosexual in behaviour with only 'insignificant' homosexual feelings. In earlier years, however, he had had extensive sexual contacts with peers of both sexes and as a boy he had been involved with adults of both sexes. He was unusually forthcoming in his account and was the only one of the interviewed students to admit to having had what amounted to a protracted relationship with an adult male.

Although he had attended a mixed school his earliest recollections of sexual interest were towards boys when he was about 10. 'I seem to remember that I wanted to have a torrid affair with the person I sat next to at school. It was a case of "I'll show you mine if you show me yours". It was interesting and pleasant, but not in any adult sense.'

His earliest experience with a man was around the same time.

He was the father of a sort of playmate of mine. It just used to be the thing that he would drive us somewhere, or whatever, or come round to our house and all the rest of it.
Was he a friend of your parents as well?
No, he was just an acquaintance of theirs. They met at a local social club. It was a social club where you could take your kids as well sort of thing. I mean, so they knew each other just to chat briefly, that's all.
And he used to take you swimming?
With his son, yes. And things happened, like he would send his son off to get some sweets or whatever and, as I put in the questionnaire, just touch my penis.
Anything else?
No, not really. I say he touched me and there was only one time when he had me stay round at their house overnight. It was a weird situation and God knows what his wife thought. She was in the house you know, made breakfast in the morning and his son was in the room on a bed or something.
Were you sharing a room with the son?
Yes, well I seem to recall sharing a double bed with his father and he was, the son was, in another part of the room on another bed. And after the lights

were out he furtively groped around the penis and backside, that's all.

Did he have an erection, do you know?

I don't. I don't seem to recall. I presume he did, but I was never made aware of that. He didn't make me touch it or I don't recall him using it against me. He didn't try anything like. He didn't try anal sex or anything like that.

What did you think about it?

I was almost wholly indifferent, it was bloody embarrassing, but I was almost completely indifferent to the whole thing. I don't seem to recall having – I mean it was a nuisance that I was being kept awake. Other than that it was slightly embarrassing I seem to remember.

Did you have any understanding of what was going on?

No, I wouldn't have said so.

Did he ever talk to you about it. I mean did he say anything?

No, not really. I mean he just had a curious euphemistic way of speaking. 'Do you mind being tickled?' It seemed a curious euphemism for it. No, he didn't really talk about it, he just sort of said 'Do you mind, are you happy?' I just sort of nodded yes. I was almost completely indifferent.

Did he ever warn you not to tell anyone?

No, I don't seem to recall that he did. I think he did, yes. I think he said something, you know, but I don't recall him making a big deal of that.

Did you tell anyone?

No, not at all.

You didn't tell your parents?

No, not anyone.

Did you ever tell anyone subsequently?

Not until very much later, and certainly not anyone like my parents who would have been in a position to do anything about it or make a fuss about it. I told my girlfriend Caroline, and things like that, but no I didn't really tell anyone.

Do you think it had any effects, was there any change, did you feel nervous about that man?

No, no. Because at no point was he threatening or unpleasant or violent. He was always a very nice, pleasant person that took us swimming and had a strange habit of shoving his hands up the bottom of my shorts. Other than that he just seemed a slightly quirky version of the parents of any child.

Did you think it was unusual?

Yes, I mean yes, I thought it was unusual and I was also slightly aware that it was wrong or bad or naughty or something, but not in the sense of being 'Oh God, isn't it awful!' Because it wasn't. It was, as I say, boring really. I remember thinking 'It's wrong, it's naughty, this does not happen every day'.

Although he did not warn me against telling anybody the fact that it was done furtively and was done when nobody was around made it fairly obvious that there was something not right about it. But other than that I didn't feel, I don't seem to recall it being particularly bad.

How long did it continue? It began when you were around 10, how long did it go on for?

It's difficult to tell, I cannot really remember. I think my memory is playing around with the time-scale somewhere, but it seems to have gone on for a couple of months, only it happened half-a-dozen times or whatever, or eight to ten times, over an indeterminate period. I cannot really remember.

Do you know why it stopped?

No, I don't know why it stopped. I had a fairly good idea it was because he was found out or something. I think either his wife or somebody must have told my parents, because they questioned me about it you know – 'Did he touch you?' and 'What did he do?' and all the rest of it. To which I replied, 'Nothing, he didn't touch me at all.' I think that is why it stopped. It sounds as though someone let the cat out of the bag and I seem to recall he had a heart attack as well. I remember hearing about it, but whether he died I don't know because I just sort of stopped seeing him and someone told me he had a heart attack and maybe died. Maybe it was all too much for the poor sod. I don't know.

When your parents questioned you about it, did they accept what you said?

Yes. I think they did. I think they suspected maybe I wasn't telling them, because they questioned me a couple of times, sort of thing, and I stuck to my story that nothing happened and it was all right. I don't know why, I think it was the thought that they would think I had done it or I would get into trouble. It might be a bit of that. I also think that maybe I didn't want to upset them as well. It was obviously something that they were finding disturbing, so I thought well maybe it's best not to tell them. I mean I'm not sure I thought anything as sophisticated as that at the time. I don't recall having that sort of [precise] idea, but maybe it was that as well.

Did you feel partly responsible for the situation, guilty?

Yes. I mean I suppose in so far as I thought I'd get into trouble for it I think I felt partly responsible for it.

Asked about other experiences with men he went on to explain:

I think it was just a case of slightly curious old men that would come up and start talking to you, that you were aware was vaguely odd. I think it happened a couple of times.

What, men in the street, that sort of thing?

Yes, just odd sort of characters. I remember being at a football match once and this curious gnome-like character came up and started talking to me about school medicals and did I have a school medical and what happened. I was vaguely aware of what he was getting at and I sort of moved away quietly.

What sort of age were you then?

13 or 14. I just seem to recall it happened a couple of times, just slightly odd old men come up and start talking weird about things I thought were strange, and being aware that it was odd and just moving away.

Was that your only reaction, just to move away?

Yes. Just sort of go.

Did you find it unpleasant?

Slightly unnerving. I mean it was just a case of laughing about it like with kids at school you know. Some dirty old man came up to me, and that was it.

You mentioned sexual contact ten to twenty times with a man, was that the same man?

Later, when I was about 15. I just had an affair with my drama teacher, at school. That was a fairly reasonable, nice, adult homosexual relationship.

Why did it begin, how did it happen?

Just started. I was being supposedly measured for a costume – I think that was a ruse on his part – it was for a small production. I was finding myself turned on by that and it was fairly obvious.

What, you had an erection?

Yes, I'm being rather coy here. Yes, standing there with a flaming great hard on and so it led to sex on the floor of the drama room of all places.

What kind of sex was it?

Mutual masturbation, oral sex. Initially it was just to get him going down on me, but later, as I say, it was a fully developed, reasonable, adult gay relationship. No anal sex involved. I just don't think it was his personal taste, like; I don't think it was mine either at the time. As I say, it was oral sex and mutual masturbation. I went and stayed at his flat a couple of times.

Was it mostly in the school?

No, it happened only once or twice at school in a stockroom. I went over to his flat.

Did you used to stay with him?

Yes, I used to stay with him the night quite a few times.

Did your parents know?

No, I just said I was going to stay with a friend. By this time my dad had died, you see, and my mum let me have a fairly long rein, I think. It was not very difficult, I mean I was staying out, it was not unusual for me to stay out all night, more or less to say I'm going to stay with my drama teacher because there is a play over at the Greenwich Theatre and it is going to be too late to get back. All those sort of things.

Did you go out together socially?

Yes. I mean not a lot. To the theatre sometimes, but that was with other kids as well doing drama at school.

Did anyone know about what was going on?

I think a few people might have guessed. A few of his friends maybe ...

Why did it finish?

Um. I don't know. He moved jobs for one thing. I don't know whether things were starting to be said, because at that time, at the same time, I started thinking 'Well this is good', and I started actually regarding myself as gay. I'd flamboyantly turn up with a badge that cryptically said 'Avenge Oscar Wilde', and I actually started to make a bit of an issue of it and started to pressurise the school librarian to take *Gay News* in the school library and things like this – you know, along with the *West Indian World* or whatever. So I suppose the fact that I started to make it a bit open and embraced it as a political issue as well – I don't know, maybe things were starting to be whispered and he thought he had better change his job. Maybe he went away and it ended like that.

Was there an explanation? Did he explain?

No, not really. He just sort of obviously wanted it to peter out, and it did, which was sad ...

During this time, when he was 15 to 16, he also engaged in sexual activities with other boys of similar age but, he explained, 'throughout all of that, when I regarded myself as gay, I was always bisexual and would try to get into bed with a woman as well'. Up to the age of 16, his heterosexual activities fell short of full intercourse, being limited to mutual masturbation and 'heavy petting', but then he met and had intercourse on four or five occasions with a woman of 23. They met while both were looking after children at a summer camp. On the first occasion, 'I ejaculated prematurely, but generally the experience was lovely.' He told his mother and brother. They were 'pleased, if anything, that the youngest lad had lost his virginity at last'.

At the time of the interview he was leading an active heterosexual life with a girl with whom he had been cohabiting for eight months. He was expecting to marry her 'sometime next year'. Up to the age of 17 his sex activity had been mainly with men, but then he acquired a steady girlfriend for the next three years during which time he would 'have sex with a few blokes as well'. That first heterosexual affair led to others until his sexual outlets became exclusively with women, except for 'just one night, with a bloke, a couple of times, about a year ago'. He commented: 'My bisexual phase, whilst enjoyable at the time, has been a little embarrassing at times.' He seemed to want to put it behind him.

Commenting on the questionnaire about adult sex involvements with children he had written:

> I can see that some relationships can cause trauma. I cannot feel that this is necessarily so. It is not my experience that I was caused any harm. The most traumatic thing I remember was being questioned by my parents. The 'Where did he touch you?' type questions made me feel quite guilty. The experience itself aroused little emotion.

At interview he added:

> The assumption is often made that it is always traumatic. That is based on some sort of assumption that children are pure, innocent, sexless, blank slates. From my experience children have sexual experience as well. I think there are definite questions about whether they fully comprehend. I mean I don't think I did when I was eleven or eight or whatever. What I'm saying is that I don't think it's always horrible. It's always pictured as being brutal and violent. In fact I can't help but feel that most sexual occurrences between adults and children are probably pretty gentle really, because an adult that is going to find a child attractive is usually going to be quite attached to them and isn't generally going to attack them or hurt them, because it's not what they want usually.

3.3 Experiences under the age of 11

Descriptions of sexual incidents that happened when boys were not more than 10 years old suggest that most of them did not understand at the time the significance of the male adult's behaviour. The reactions of parents or others when matters came to light, or a personal realisation in later years of the homosexual implications, were what gave the episodes importance and fixed them in memory. This was particularly evident in the case of young boys faced with odd behaviour by teachers whose instructions were ordinarily accepted unquestioningly.

Case 036

A student of 20 gave this story in a relaxed, matter-of-fact way. The tape recorder was not operating at this interview, so the notes are not verbatim. He recalled an incident at his boarding school when he was only 8. At the time he slept in a dormitory with about six other boys. He described what happened as 'pretty simple and painless'. At bedtime a master would come round to turn off the lights. One of the masters, a man of about 27, before saying good night, sat on the end of his bed and put a hand down inside his pyjama trousers saying things like, 'What an interesting pelvis you've got.' He used to think 'What a funny man! Why is he doing this?' He was completely innocent as to the real purpose of the master's actions, honestly believing the interest to be 'purely biological'. He thought this routine must have happened several times, he could not remember definitely. In addition, he used to be invited to this master's room and given cokes to drink and allowed to watch television. On these occasions the master would begin 'fun fights' with him.

The incidents didn't seem anything important at the time and he never told anybody then and he never told his parents either then or since. In his later years at preparatory school he heard people referring to the master in question, saying, 'Don't you think he's funny?' It was not until his later teens, however, that he learned about homosexuality from television and jokes. When he was 14 he went back to the school to visit his younger brother, who was still a pupil there, and he saw the master once more. He intended going up to speak to him, but the man was obviously embarrassed and he wondered why. The reason for the behaviour dawned upon him then. It was not until his late teens that he would mention the episode sometimes to friends over drinks, citing it as a vaguely funny prep school story. He recalled no other incidents with older people when he was a boy.

Asked about his earliest sexual interests he remembered having masturbation fantasies when he was 12 featuring women who were matrons at his school; then at 14 he had a crush on a girl of similar age, but he thought that those sexual fantasies might have been 'exploded' if real physical contact had taken place. 'Real' heterosexual sex did not begin until he was 18. He admitted to one romantic crush on another boy when he was 15. This lasted for two years, but there was no overt sexual behaviour between them, although he would have liked that to happen. Since then he has had no further homosexual inclinations.

Case 487

A 27-year-old man remembered embarrassing behaviour by the headmaster of his junior school when he was 8 or 9.

It was as a result of my being in the 'B' stream. From the second year of the 'B' stream up until the fourth year, so that's for two years, he used to, at least once a week, I used to be sent to his office to have a little chat. He used to tell me that if I worked hard and was a good boy I might get into the 'A' stream. What I remember of him is he used to sit me on his knee in the office and ask me to go through my books to show him the work I had done. It was the sitting on the knee that I found funny – well being sent to his office was a bit strange. It was always made clear to me, though perhaps not explicitly, that it was a personal thing between him and me, and he'd intimate that if I worked hard and was a good boy for him, sort of thing, that he would put me in the 'A' stream.

Did anything else happen as you were sitting on his knee?

Not that I remember, it's quite possible I couldn't remember it.

Yes.

It used to disturb me. I mean I remember that I used to feel that I ought to be flattered that he had the interest in me and I ought to be pleased about that, but at the same time I was apprehensive. It's funny I was thinking that on the bus on the way here and I was remembering that the teacher of the class, particularly the second-year teacher, used to be clearly worried at me going, and he used to ask me in detail what he'd said when I came back. And I believe, it's funny, that this headmaster had a very high profile in the local community as a wonderful human being; but after he died there were a lot of rumours about this. Apparently I wasn't the only person that this had happened to, and there were rumours that he came to us after having been sacked from another school for sexually molesting children. I honestly don't know whether that's true or not, but a lot of people have similar stories to tell. So I'm not aware of anything else happening [with me] but it could have.

Do you think you might have repressed that memory?

I'm a psychologist, I can't help considering the possibility. It seems funny that it worried me so much if it was only sitting on his knee. I can't remember.

Did your parents know that you had this special relationship with the headmaster?

They knew, I assume they knew I was being sent to his office. I'm sure they did, yes ...

So why did it stop do you think?

I don't remember exactly. I think it became less frequent as I went up through school. I seem to remember it particularly in the second year of the junior school. I think it was still happening in the third year. I don't know about the fourth year. In fact he lost interest in me. And also I became more confident in my ability. I was perhaps less vulnerable then because other teachers began to accept that I was bright and was perfectly capable of managing on my own.

You said you found it disturbing. What did you mean?

Well I remember having – it's just that I had very mixed feelings about it. I mean if it had been entirely innocent I should have viewed it positively, but I didn't view it positively you know. I remember walking down the corridor apprehensive ...

You said in the questionnaire that reading the questionnaire made you view it differently.

Because I mean I had talked about it to other people, but I hadn't really viewed it as sexual, not assault, but as a sexual contact – just a strange experience from a slightly strange man. But thinking about it for your questionnaire it became obvious to me that it was, for him anyway, a sexual experience.

Who had you spoken to about it?

Parents to some extent, not very seriously.

Is that recently?

Yes, recently, in the last few years. And to schoolfriends, but none of my immediate schoolfriends had any contact with him. I gather other people have ...

If something sexual had happened would you have known that it was sexual?

No, I suspect I wouldn't.

At that time you weren't particularly a sexually knowledgeable child?

Certainly in the second and third year I was totally ignorant of anything sexual.

Asked about his earliest sexual interests he recalled, at the age of 12 or 13, seeing pictures of women Go Go dancers and realising why everyone else was finding them interesting. From then on he viewed women 'in a different way'. He described his current behaviour, since 16, as exclusively heterosexual, but rated his *feelings* as no more than 'predominantly heterosexual, but significantly homosexual'. He also mentioned, however, that he was having very frequent sexual intercourse with a girlfriend of two years' standing.

Asked for comments about adults having sexual contacts with children he replied:

I understand the argument of people like the Paedophile Information Exchange, or whatever they are called, that it can be a good relationship, but don't believe in reality it is ... I suppose basically I want to be liberal about it, but I don't believe that children can ever benefit from it. I think they almost always suffer ... [With older, sexually knowledgeable children] they know what's going on, they have some idea of what's being done. A child of the age and knowledge I was at, it's a very different sort of situation, it's just something that someone chooses to do to you, and you don't know why they are being interested. At least you are in a position, I suppose, to inform someone if you are unhappy.

Do you think it makes any difference if the adult is male or female?

No, I don't.

Case 310

This 43-year-old man, studying at a polytechnic, who rated himself exclusively heterosexual, had been brought up in poor circumstances. His mother died when he was 6 and he spent a lot of time on the streets with companions described as 'drop-outs'. He was sent as a 'charity boy' to a middle-class preparatory school as a boarder where he felt lonely and ostracised. It was there he had an odd experience with a physical education instructor which he did not understand at the time.

At the time I didn't think anything of it, other than being uncomfortable. What he used to do was to take us out, that is a group of us, a whole class, into the field over the road and he used to have this game where we all ran round in circles trying to pull each other's shorts off. Now I don't think any of us particularly liked this, it's only on reflection that I think that since he did it so often, organised it so often, that my feeling is there was something in it for him.

What sort of age was he?
I would reckon about 40.
Did anyone succeed in pulling the shorts off?
That's the whole thing, he more or less kept the game going until everybody had got their shorts off.
Were you embarrassed by that?
I don't know whether it was embarrassment, I think it was just uncomfortable.
What did the other kids say about it?
I think we all tended to be a bit uncomfortable or embarrassed about it ... It was very much 'Oh God! Here we go again!' sort of thing.
When was it that you began to think that it may have had a sexual bearing, that it was for his pleasure?
Not until my early 20s. I was talking to somebody about boarding school and things like that and I found, as I told the story, I thought, 'Yes, it was really weird.' I hadn't thought about it for years.
So was it simply that conversation that triggered it off?
Yes.
At the time did you think that though it made you uncomfortable that it was fairly ordinary? What was it you thought about it?
I think at the time – you have to remember we're in the fifties, we're in a private boarding school. There authority is everything. I think you just bend to authority and that is it, because if you don't bend you find yourself in trouble.
So what age were you?
I think that probably it was about 9, 10, 11, I can't exactly remember. I know the guy came to the school, he wasn't there when I first went, but I can't remember at what point.
Did you ever speak to any other adults about this?
No.
Do you think any of the other kids did?
I don't know because, as I said, that was probably one of the only experiences at boarding school at which in fact I did have communication with a lot of my group. Obviously people didn't like it, but I don't think anybody did speak to their parents or anybody else. I assume not for it seems to have gone on from when he came to the school till when I left.
What about otherwise, what was he like?
No, the thing was that a lot of people liked him. He had a dog, a beautiful dog, you know we were all longing to take it out for walks. An absolutely stunning, beautiful dog which he looked after very well. You know there was that, and also he was not authoritarian, not as I remember it.

What, was he more friendly?
Yes, I remember him as being friendly, approachable.
Did you ever spend time alone with him?
No.

This man recalled another incident when he was 12, this time with a grown-up woman. At the time a friendly woman who was living in another part of the house used to let him read the *News of the World*, a paper banned by his father.

Anyway, quite often I'd be up there when this Irish girl came. She would say things like something about my reading. I'd be reading a rape thing or something like that. She would sort of say 'How would you like to be raped?' and be jocular, suggesting I might somehow like to. I don't know, it was all very jocular.
So there was only, sort of, verbal suggestions?
Yes.
She never attempted to touch you, or anything like that?
No.
What age was she?
I would imagine, probably in her middle 20s. It's very difficult to remember ...
Did it make you apprehensive at all?
No.
How did you treat it?
As a joke.

Asked why he remembered this incident he explained that he had a lot of affection for the rooming house where it had happened and for the people there who had 'in fact gone a long way to making me the person that I am today and the way I think'.

Asked about early sexual interests he recalled attraction to the opposite sex from the age of 6 or 7, but 'at first oriented – and I'm going to sound horribly Freudian – to older women, I mean they would be anywhere between 20 and 40'. Nevertheless, his early knowledge of sex was scanty, picked up from talk and activities 'behind the bicycle shed'. He was shy of girls and until around 15, when he started playing the guitar successfully and became more confident.

He was still unmarried and although he had had several regular sexual partners none had lasted except one – 'a very on and off thing. It went on and on for three years ... I think I have a problem with women generally. I think it is that I still do not know where to place my affection. I have difficulty in sustaining relationships.'

Asked for comments about sexual relationships between adults and children he remarked:

Well it seems to me that sexual abuse of children is in principle no different from any other form of sexual abuse, so it doesn't seem to me terribly out of whack with the rest of criminality as far as I am concerned. [He went on to explain that he had worked in prison and disapproved of the morality that singled out sex offenders for special condemnation and allowed other criminals to dole out punishments.] As regards sex offenders, I find I'm not revolted by them at all. I don't understand it. It's a very strange way of getting sexual gratification as far as I can see, but certain people do get their gratification that way. I don't like the way we treat them.

Interestingly, in view of his own experience with an older woman, when asked about relationships between boys and older women he found them as abusive as relationships involving men: 'No, I think it's no more correct than the reverse situation, in the sense that one person is taking advantage of another person who is inexperienced.'

3.4 Police involvement

When incidents involve boys well below puberty who are genuinely bewildered by sexual approaches they are probably more likely to be mentioned to parents and thus to come to the attention of the police. Police involvement can have varying effects upon the boys concerned, as in the next three examples.

Case 170

A heterosexual man, aged 30, remembered an incident that happened when he was aged 10 and travelling by bus one cold winter morning to meet his uncle who was finishing work at lunchtime on a Saturday:

So I was going on the bus and I had sat down in front. I was wearing shorts of course, and there was this oldish fella, or so he seemed to me, and he started to talk to me and he said, 'Oh, come and sit over here'; so I did. In the course of his conversation, [just] small talk, he did say something like, 'I bet your legs are cold this weather.' And he did rub them with his hands, rub my thighs with his hands. Anyway I don't remember this as being – that his hands were any higher – that he did anything else. I think I would certainly, I think I would have been alarmed if he had done anything more than that. Because at that age I had already had a situation with one of my friends, the same age as me ...

[On that occasion he had been in a friend's bedroom] and he wanted us to dress up or something, and I had taken my clothes off to sort of dress up and he tried to fondle me. Actually, he tried to get hold of my prick you know, but I sort of fought him off and got dressed. It was not something I wanted to be done [but] it didn't affect our friendship.

Anyway, the bus got into town and as I got off the bus he stayed where he was and somebody who'd been sitting behind moved at that point. I don't know whether he went to this other guy first, but certainly when I got off the bus he started asking me for my name and address. He didn't explain why, and I thought, well I don't know, what are you asking me for. And he was being insistent about this, urgent about it, and I was asking why and the guy wouldn't say, so I began to think I had done something wrong.

Anyway I started crying, and then my uncle showed up at the bus stop and the guy said to my uncle what had happened, that the guy had been rubbing my legs. I mean obviously my uncle would have known the significance of this I suppose. Then we went off to the police station and reported the incident and all the rest of it. Never at any point was it explained to me. Well, firstly, initially, my reaction was that I had done something wrong, because of the way I was questioned. Anyway my uncle managed to assure me that I hadn't, but then of course I asked him a question about this bloke, what he had done wrong. I mean, because to me he was being a friendly old man really. The physical side of what he had done didn't strike me as being particularly unusual, because my family were an affectionate family. I mean we would get sort of cuddled by mother, father and even, I suppose, my uncle, when we were young. And even at that age with my mother and father there was still affection to us and so physical contact between me and an adult just didn't strike me as being anything odd, certainly not the kind that he had done.

At the police station he was questioned in the presence of his uncle. He had only a vague recollection of what was asked. He remained confused about the incident and his parents did not enlighten him:

They might have said, 'You shouldn't talk to strangers,' or something like that, but certainly nothing was mentioned in the way of an explanation as to what this guy had done wrong.
When was it that you realised what it was all about?
Well probably only when I actually really understood what homosexuality was about, and I suppose that was probably not before I was what – 14 – that it actually dawned on me what the fuss had been about.
Did you tell people at school about what had happened?
I don't remember. I probably wouldn't have done because it was something with which I was left feeling vaguely as if it had been more of a misdemeanour on my part.

He recalled acquiring his sexual knowledge from playgroup gossip and being unconfident about sex as an adolescent. He was having fantasies about girls at 15 or earlier and on a couple of occasions, when he was only about 10, when together with a slightly older girl, a friend of his sister, they had both stripped naked and touched each other, but she had been the keen one. He rated himself exclusively heterosexual, had had a short period of heterosexual cohabitation and was presently in an active sexual relationship with a girlfriend of three years' standing.

Asked for comments about sexual relations between adults and children under 16 he remarked:

I would have to say, and also from reflection on my own lack of maturity at that age, that it should be something that should be discouraged ... An impressionistic person of that age doesn't really understand their sexuality or what they want and can be very easily exploited and taken advantage of.

He went on to mention the possibility of a homosexual approach altering the development of a boy's sexuality or making him confused about whether or not he is homosexual. As for sexual contacts between boys and adult women, he laughed, 'That's the standard adolescent fantasy. I'm far too old for it now.'

Case 303

A student, aged 30, self-rated exclusively heterosexual, recalled two incidents with men when he was a young boy.

I was molested twice as a child, when I was fishing, when I was about 8 ...
Can you tell me what happened on the first occasion?
I mean he just sort of fondled me, basically. I remember the second one quite vividly after the experience of the first one.
Hold on. Could I ask you where this all happened? Could we just go through it, as much as you can remember?
The actual place? The town park, the first time.
Were you in the park on your own?
On my own, yes.
Were you just walking, or – ?
I was fishing.
Then someone came along, right?
Yeah. This is as much as I can remember.
What can you remember of what happened?
Not offhand, no. Not how it came to be, you know, but I can remember it afterwards. I was just lying on the river bank in a town park, up a slope, a big slope – that's about all I can remember. And I remember the interview with the police.
You came home and told your parents, is that right? What was their reaction?
It was that you'd better go and see the police, and I said there was no point. Anyway, I didn't really see the point. Anyway the police came round. I remember this burly copper saying 'I'll castrate the bastard, if ever we get hold of him' – that kind of thing. But it did have an effect on me. I know, because the second – you see it's sort of interlinked with the second time which wasn't long afterwards. It was that I let this guy do it. I immediately knew what he was doing was wrong, but I thought so long as I let him do it he's not going to hurt me, and then I'd go and report it again.
So you said your mother telephoned the police – [the first time]
No. She went down to the police station. It was about two days' afterwards, it wasn't that day. It was during the school holidays, it must have been.
So he said he'd castrate them?
Yes, something like, you know what I mean, if he could get hold of them or something. Give them a good hiding or something – it's twenty years ago.
So then, after that, this second occurrence?
This was at the River Lea.
So it wasn't the same person.
No. no.

So you were fishing there, were you alone?
I was fishing with some mates at the time, I think, but I think they went or something like that. I know there was a group of us at first. This guy had been around for a couple of days, sort of chatting to everyone. I mean, at the time, he seemed a friendly guy.
He'd been going to this particular place?
Down to the Lea, yes.
So you'd noticed him before.
Yes.
So you were on your own, and then what happened?
I think he took me to the – yes, he did, I remember, he went over the back of some long grass. He just took some photographs.
Did he make you take your clothes off?
Just my trousers.
And he took photographs?
Yes, and he paid me for them.
How much did he pay you?
I think it was a shilling those days.
What else did he do?
He just sort of fondled me generally, nothing else.
Did he play with himself, or anything like that?
No, I can't remember.
You said earlier that you knew it was wrong.
But I thought that as long as I went along with it I wouldn't come to harm.
Is that one of the things that you felt, that you might come to harm, to some physical harm?
Yes, because of the experience of the first time. When you're eight you're sort of naive. It was the experience of the first time and the police saying this is wrong, this is wrong. Obviously I knew it was wrong to have the police come round, so obviously it wasn't right. So I kept that in my mind and I thought if I go along with this I'm not going to get harmed and then I could sort of run for home afterwards. In fact I went straight to the police station myself.
You went to the police station, and then what happened?
I cannot remember, really. I don't think anything happened. I think they would just patrol the Lea for a while. That's about what I can remember. It sounded like it was quite a common occurrence near the school.
Did they question you?
Yes. They questioned me.
And were you able to tell them as much as you remembered?
Yes.
How did that affect your subsequent life? Did you avoid going out on your own, fishing and things like that?
No, no, never. Even at 8 I thought I could look after myself, that sort of attitude really.
It had not shaken or affected you in any way?
No, no. I mean perhaps I was lucky, I don't know. I didn't feel it affected me in any way.
What about your mother, your parents, were they more protective, did they try to stop you going out?
They didn't want me to go too far or anything like that. They didn't ever really try to stop me, 'cause what can you do in the school holidays, you can't keep a child cooped up at home.

This man recalled no particular problems in sexual development. He attended a mixed school and remembered an incident when he was 10 when he felt a young girl's growing breasts. Although still unmarried he was leading an active sex life and having frequent intercourse with two different girls.

Asked his opinions on adult sexual involvement with children, he commented:

> I still think children should be protected. I had this argument with a gay friend of mine the other day, and he was saying that I was denying a child their natural sexual thing, you know, that a child is a sexual thing. But I think children should be protected until at least 15, I am not saying 16, but at least till they are 15.
> *Why do you think that?*
> I think it can have a damaging effect on children.
> *What sort of damaging effect?*
> I think it could probably scare them off sex when they get older. I think that probably it could make them very biassed towards certain people. I think it can have a mental effect. I may be wrong, but I just think probably it could happen.
> *But you don't think any of these things happened to you?*
> No, I don't think so. I mean I don't – I mean obviously Freud might say something different ...

Asked about early contacts with women he went on to explain that he thought that might not be so bad, but still not a good idea under the age of 15.

Case 199

A 25-year-old heterosexual recalled an incident when he was about 10. He was out walking with two other boys, one of them an elder brother of his, when they were led into a wood by a stranger and ordered to submit to sexual manipulation. This was different from nearly all the other incidents described in that it involved overt coercion by means of implied threat.

> *What time of the day was this?*
> It was certainly daylight, bright daylight. I would imagine it was after school, because I was more likely to see my friend then than at the week end. So I would say four o'clock, but I really can't remember well. It was definitely bright daylight and it was very quiet, which is unusual for that part of Edinburgh.
> *So what sort of place was it that you were walking?*
> Not a main road, but a very well made road which stretched from where I lived down to the promenade by the sea. On one side there were service buildings and a caravan site and stables and so on. On the other side there were playing fields and woods and a couple of hotels, that was the area.
> *So what happened?*

Well, we were all very interested in wildlife, so I think we were probably looking for birds in the woods at the time.

So you were not on the road, you went into the woods looking for birds?

Yes.

And then?

Well, we were approached by this man [in his mid-to-late 30s]. We didn't try to get away.

When you say approached, did he speak to you? What happened?

Well, he came through the wood, not directly towards us, but in our general direction. I think he probably did speak to us – he must have spoken to us in a non-threatening way because I am sure we would have run off. I don't think he actually grabbed any of us, but I'm sure he must have laid his hand on one of us and held his grip so that person could not get away, which meant that the other two of us wouldn't run away. I don't remember any actual snatching. I think it must have occurred that way.

So what happened then?

Well he told the other two to follow.

You mean he got hold of you and told them to follow?

No, he took hold of one of the others – I was trying to think of his name ... I'm pretty sure it wasn't me, probably the youngest person.

Yes. And he told you two to follow?

Yes, he took us into the woods. They were very thick, but there were parts of them where there were rhododendron bushes and so on, so it shielded the ground from sunlight. It was just covered in dead leaves. So he took us to an area like that and asked us to lie face down on the ground. He told us to loosen the button on the top of our trousers and then he lay between us, presumably in pairs. We were lying down parallel to each other. He must have lain down between one set of two and then moved over to the next set of two. I don't remember that so well.

Then what happened?

He put his hand into our trousers and fondled us for about a couple of minutes I should think.

Fondled your genitals?

Yes.

And what did you feel about that?

He kept saying that as long as we didn't make a sound we'd be OK. So I never felt that I was going to come to physical harm. So I don't think I was particularly worried.

How did it develop? What happened then?

Well after this, or during this perhaps, he asked who was the youngest of us three. Yes, that was during the sex play.

Yes.

So I obviously knew that I was younger than my elder brother, but the other boy and I had a certain conversation to work out who was the younger, and he told the two of us to wait behind while he went away with the youngest one. And he said that if you keep quiet the younger one will be OK. And to stay where we were ...

So what happened then?

They returned a few minutes later, and I think he told us to remain there until he had gone, until he was out of sight.

And so what happened then?

We went back to my house.

Did you stay there for a while as he told you?

Yes, well thirty seconds or so I should imagine. The woods were thick enough for him to get out of sight pretty fast.

And then you went home. What were you feeling about it at that point?

I think it was just the novelty of a new situation; this was, er – that we'd been in danger, it was exciting in so far as that.

Were you upset?

No, I shouldn't say so.

Were the others upset?

I think possibly they were.

Did you tell anyone?

Yes, we told my parents as soon as we got home.

What did they do?

They phoned the police. The police came round and we were interviewed by them.

One at a time?

Yes.

Do you remember what sort of questions they asked?

I can remember a lot of questions about the physical appearance of the guy.

What did you feel about being questioned by the police?

I didn't mind it. It was exciting again, I suppose – all this attention.

You said in the questionnaire that you didn't realise it was sexual. What did you think?

I didn't know what it was about. Confused. Puzzled about it.

Do you think it affected you in any way?

No.

When did you come to realise it was a homosexual thing?

I don't think I ever did logically, I never suddenly said, 'Hah, ha, it was a homosexual.' ...

Did the youngest boy ever say anything about it?

He was very shy to begin with but he did tell us what happened when he was taken away on his own – which surprised me. Well, the man took down his trousers and asked him to fondle his genitals, to fondle the man's genitals.

And he did that?

Yes.

This student denied any sexual problems, past or present, recalled a strong sexual interest in a particular girl of his own age when he was about 12 and said he was currently having intercourse with two different girls.

3.5 Experiences with females

One man who had reported a boyhood incident with an older female on the questionnaire, and been counted accordingly in the numerical analysis, when recounting the event during the interview described a smaller age differential between himself and the girl in question, thus placing the experience outside our strict definition of a boy under 11 with someone turned 16. Nevertheless the description is worth noting in view of the subject's untypical reaction of mild panic.

Case 483

This 21-year-old heterosexual student said he was 11 to 12 when, through a friend, he met a girl who was between 15 and 16.

> We ended up at this bloke's house, and they were all 14 and 15 years and they were all sort of having sex and not caring about it. I mean they knew what they were doing, and there was me there, 11 years old. She kind of took me into this bedroom and I just sort of lay there on the bed, not quite knowing what to do. And we kissed for a while and then – um – how did it happen – she just started undressing herself or something. And [she] just like got hold of my hand and sort of – that was it basically – showed me what to do. I was quite intrigued. I was a bit scared, I was very scared.
> *Why were you scared?*
> Simply because the only information I had got on sex and everything, the only attitude I had been able to glean from adults, or people I thought knew about it, was [from] my parents, who seemed to make out that it was something really bad and really sort of dangerous and you should not mess about with it until you are very much older ... I was very scared in case I was getting drawn into something that I was going to have to explain to my parents later on ... I got a big love bite on my neck as well that took ages to go away. I was quite embarrassed about that, well not embarrassed, more scared. I was convinced that I had got VD, that that [love bite] was VD ...
> *Did you enjoy it at the time though?*
> ... As much as you enjoy going on a roller coaster for the first time. I mean like you are scared shitless, I suppose, but you just enjoy it because you know you have got to go on and do that to develop ... I was intrigued to know what it was all about, everybody else seemed to be doing it ...

He told some friends about it. Their reaction, impressed but a bit scared, did not help. Despite his ambivalence about this early introduction to heterosexuality he seems to have had no problem forming heterosexual relationships in later adolesence and leading an active sexual life.

*

Few of the men whose experience was limited to some pleasurable incident with an older female during their adolescence volunteered for interview. The following Case 337, however, illustrates well the classic stereotype of an idyllic introduction to the delights of heterosexuality at the hands of an experienced older woman. The next case (139) illustrates a more ambivalent reaction by a boy exposed to adult female sexuality at a much earlier age. The last example (279) is of an unusually inhibited adolescent who found a woman's approach somewhat shocking.

Case 337

A heterosexual man of 32 recalled a sexual episode when he was 14 involving a married woman in her early 30s, listed as 'enjoyable' on the questionnaire and described as follows:

> The family of a close friend at school moved to a new home on the south coast and invited me to spend part of the summer holiday with them. My friend had made new friends, however, and I was not accepted by their group. I began spending more time with his mother with whom I had always been close. I believe she welcomed the company in a new location as her husband worked away from home for long periods. We quickly became very close with increasing flirtation and physical contact until intercourse took place one afternoon, after a particularly physical rough-and-tumble, at her suggestion and with my full consent and cooperation. The affair continued throughout the holiday, but was never resumed on any subsequent occasion.

At interview he supplied further particulars:

> [My friend] was not younger in years, but he was younger in his attitude perhaps, and the kind of things that he was doing, you know, playing football, going fishing, didn't so much appeal to me. As I say he was very much in with this new crowd of friends ...
>
> [His Mum] was very kind of young in her attitude and was very easy to get on with. She was also quite small, about 5 ft or just over, 5 ft 1 or 2 ... in a lot of ways I didn't relate to her as a kind of, like a Mum or an adult, she was just someone I liked and I started spending more and more time with her and talking with her and going out with her. I used to go shopping with her ...
>
> [Once] when we got back it was a really warm day and we went into the garden and sort of sat about chatting and we just sort of started messing about, which got quite physical, and I think, I think she was certainly as keen as I was for some kind of sexual thing. I had become very attracted to her physically and in the process of just sort of messing about and tickling each other it just got very intimate and we ended up making love in the garden. It was quite a secluded garden, a place right out in the middle of nowhere ...

He found the experience most exciting and was able to remember well his feelings at the time. Although sexually inexperienced

> I knew the sort of mechanical workings, I had a sort of rough idea, but she was I mean quite obviously experienced and, you know, I just sort of sensed that, rather than thought of it, and just kind of let her make most of the running ... I think most people when they first have a sexual involvement with someone of the same age, when they're very young, it can often be disastrous. There are so many expectations and different things in sexuality – if you get over excited and ejaculate too quickly, or she decides she doesn't want it at the last minute – it can have a lasting effect. That [encounter] did

help me with that. As I say I did get quite experienced in the next couple of weeks, probably because again I was young, it was a lot easier. I guess it did help me in a way. I feel I have never had any kind of problem about the physical side of sex.

Case 139

This 30-year-old student, who had been in an active heterosexual relationship with the same partner for the past 13 years, declined to have the interview tape-recorded. He described an unhappy early life, due to conflicts between his parents finally ending in divorce. He had often stayed with his grandparents and spent a lot of time out of the house in the company of street gangs. As a young teenager he had been fat and felt left out of sexual pleasures. He had heard of 'dirty old men' and as a child he had been very worried about meeting one, but he never did.

When he was 8 to 10 years of age the family used to have parties and an aunt, aged about 35, used to come. She would dance with him in a very sexual sort of way. At other times she would touch him on the buttocks and the genitals and tell him she wanted to take him to bed. She would be more open about it after she had been drinking. Other people must have noticed. He found it pleasant, but sometimes a bit embarrassing. It stopped because there were no more parties.

He reported no sex problems, except that he liked to be passive in his sexual relations, letting his girlfriend take the initiative. He indicated that he had some slight homosexual interest, but no overt behaviour. In the apparent expectation that the investigators were anticipating condemnatory remarks about sexual behaviour between boys and women he had written on the questionnaire:

The taboos that exist when the idea of women approaching men in a sexual way is contemplated are very destructive. Much the same is true of a relationship between a younger man and an older woman, it is seen as in some way immoral or indecent. It's about time a mature society was able to rid itself of such stupid ideas. Boys over 14 are not in a great deal of moral danger from women, so why all the fuss if both parties are consenting. It's a mad world when kids of 13 can get hold of a cigarette, glue, alcohol, drugs and yet we are worried about such inane matters as sex between young males and older women.

Case 279

This heterosexual student, aged 20, had a history of psychological disorder and problems in relationships with girls. He recalled one incident at the age of 14 with a woman in her 30s which he had found disturbing. At the time he had been in the midst of what he referred to as 'an infatuation with a girl', but she was pursuing the relationship so intensely that he became 'a mental wreck'. This was at the time he was taking his 'O' level examinations, and as a result he had to resit them.

[The woman was] the next door neighbour's sister, and it was at a New Year's Eve party and we had both had a drink. This is pretty mild, what happened, but it shocked me a bit, being a good Methodist and the like. My parents were there as well. We were dancing and she started to kiss me, rather passionately you might say, rather smuttily I would say. Like I say, I gave in I think, but I do not remember. I was pretty drunk, but the main part of it was she started to squeeze my genitalia and she suggested we went upstairs. I just laughed it off and went back home. That was it really.

Your parents were at this party?

Yes, they were, and this woman's boyfriend. She had a bit of a reputation, I found out later. She was married at the time and also had a boyfriend. She was on a kind of friendly separation trial, during which time she was on the rampage ...

Did you mention this happening to anyone?

No, you are the first person I have told.

Why do you think you didn't?

Well, I didn't want to get the woman into trouble. She was drunk and it could have been – someone could have been bolshie, I don't know. And besides, I didn't want to create a rift between us and our neighbours ...

You said you found it disturbing.

I was just shocked by it, you know. I felt a bit cold. Whether or not it affected me, my sexual development, I don't know ... Soon after this incident I was to split up with my girlfriend, which also had an effect on me, so I can't say ... I just sort of laughed it off. I sat down for about an hour and then went home.

Asked about his earliest sexual interests he gave an unusual reply:

It has never really interested me until now. I think adolescents or people in general are very much pressurised by social pressures into sexual activity when perhaps they should take stock of things and say, 'Well now I don't really want sex, I just want companionship.' ... I just felt the need for companionship. It has become sexual now, but not totally sexual, that only forms a small part of my desire.

He explained that he had no active sexual relationship currently, but he resumed seeing the girlfriend of his schooldays. He had had psychiatric treatment following the trouble with his girlfriend. 'I think the ability to talk about one's psychological problems can do a lot to allay them ... I bottled up my feelings for my girlfriend when I shouldn't have, and that's what caused my breakdown.'

Commenting on the questionnaire about adult sexual involvement with children he had written:

I believe that there are occasions on which children below the age of consent (but not too far below, say 14 years at the extreme) *can* make decisions about deep physical-emotional relationships with older people and that genuine love can actually exist between an older person and a young pubescent adult. The laws should be amended as such.

3.6 Homosexual and bisexual students

A minority of the students who came for interview declared themselves to be wholly or partly homosexual. There were more of them than might have been expected from a random sample of the young male population, possibly because persons with unorthodox sexual inclinations have an interest in discussing their experience. As might have been predicted, some of the homosexually inclined men admitted that they had been willing participants in, if not actual initiators of, early sexual involvements with adult males. The example which follows illustrates how a boy, long before he reaches 16, may develop strong sexual preferences as to age and sex.

Case 249

This 22-year-old student, who rated himself 'predominantly homosexual, only insignificantly heterosexual', when asked about his earliest sexual interests replied that from the age of 8 or 9 he had been interested in boys rather than girls, but this might have been because the group that he mixed with as a schoolboy were nearly all boys.

I think we had a lot of sexual goings on and carryings on and things like this, you know, together.
Was that at school?
No, not at school, this was with people who lived in my area.
What in each other's houses?
No, not in houses. Things like would go on in the hay fields and just sort of take our clothes off and sort of, you know, lie on top of each other and all these sorts of things and generally fooling around. This is maybe up to the age of 12 with this crowd.
All of you were boys?
Well, there was one girl who featured, I remember, sometimes. She didn't live in our area, she lived in Edinburgh and she used to come – she was a bit of a tomboy – and she used sometimes to become involved. But that was only rare, only sometimes, it was mainly with just friends.
What about when you were a bit older?
Well, with that group of friends, it just stopped when we went to the secondary school and then it only ever happened once again, a few years later, at about 14 I think. It happened once, that was all. These things always seemed to happen, it was never planned, let's go and do this or anything, it just seemed to happen and it was never actually discussed after the event.

He went on to explain that by the age of 15 he looked physically very mature and willingly indulged in sex with older males. He used to tell them he was 18 because he knew they wouldn't do anything with him otherwise.

On the questionnaire he had mentioned several boyhood experiences with older males, the earliest being an incident when he was 13.

Myself and another friend, we lived in a countryside area, and went out on our bikes one day and we went to this tributary of a river which had a pool, and we went in there swimming. And this man came by and he walked by with his clothes on, and then he went away behind the bush and came back with his clothes off and came into the water with us.
Was he completely naked?
Yes. He was not, I mean – We were what, about 13 or 14 and he was about, I mean he was not a dirty old man, he was only about 30, maybe 20s, between 25 and 30, I'd say.
Then what happened?
Well, initially he just started talking and then he started masturbating himself, you know, but to make sure we'd see, and then he tried to masturbate us.
You said he tried?
Well he did, I mean he did ... I can't remember exactly, but I know he did it to both of us ... [Both had erections and ejaculated]
What did he say to you?
Not very much. He just said really stupid things like 'Is the water deep here? He was very nervous and so were we. He was asking things like how deep is the water or what time is it, and we were standing there with nothing on and he was asking us what time it was. He was a strange person.
Did you and your friend talk back?
No. Well, the thing was I was quite into it, but the other person was not really. I think he was probably taken aback by the whole thing. You know, he was not quite into it. It was never spoken about again.
You never told anyone else about it?
No, not then.
Do you think he ever spoke about it?
No, I don't think so.
You said you enjoyed it?
Yes I did. I don't think he did.
The older person, did he just get out, what happened afterwards?
Well, his clothes were at a different part from ours and our bikes. We – I don't know – we just sort of dispersed ... I never saw him again.
Did you go back to the same place?
Of course I did, in the hope he would be there. I went back a few times but I never saw him again. He was a very nice person, very nice looking. But when I say I went back my friend never came with me, not that I think I would tell him I was going out there.

In describing the next incident, in which the older man concerned was unattractive to him, he expressed very different feelings:

This really old man on a bus, he was sitting beside me and he started touching me up and things like that. Well, I mean, it was really disgusting, you know, I mean he just kept on pressing. It was a really crowded bus as well and I could feel his thigh against my thigh and then I could feel his fingers in between my thigh and his thigh and his fingers were moving and you know it was horrible. I mean he must have been 70-odd easily.

What age were you then?

I should say about 14.

And what did you do?

What did I do? Well, I could not really do anything at the time, because it was like – not near my destination. So I had to sort of grin and bear it and the bus was really crowded and I just sat it out. But I didn't participate in any way. I meant to move, but he was moving up, you know what I mean, so I could not get away from him. The thing is he didn't realise that I knew who he was, because I knew his wife. He was married, he is dead now, he died two years ago, but it was horrible. He didn't know me, I'm sure he didn't know who I was.

Did you think to complain?

No, because even when I was that age I knew some old men did that sort of thing. I just didn't. I mean it would be too embarrassing, and what's your evidence? I mean to complain about something like that.

What did you think would be embarrassing?

Well, I mean, just imagine the position of a 14-year-old. For a start, who would you tell? The bus driver who was driving the bus? That an old man tried to touch you up? He's hardly going to do anything. A policeman? I mean it would just be too much, it would be too embarrassing. They would ask you 'What did he do?' And then they would say it was a crowded bus, it was just innocent physical contact, even though it wasn't. He was definitely sort of at it. I mean that's what his thrill was, just a wee bit of touching I mean, but he wasn't a nice person.

The next incident, which happened when he was 15, was while he was travelling by train in an empty self-contained compartment with two facing seats and a sliding door.

[A man got in and] he sat across from me and he started rubbing his leg against mine and sort of, he sort of picked me up as it were on this train. We got off the train and went away up to this –

Was he just rubbing your leg?

No, that was the start of it. Then he put his hand down his trousers and started to run himself and all this sort of thing. And he initially started off just by touching my leg and then he was really rubbing it. Initially I didn't realise, I thought the train was moving his leg beside mine. I didn't know and I moved my leg and then his leg got harder and I wondered what he was doing. So I moved mine away and he followed me with his leg and I realised, 'Oh Gosh, he's after me,' you know. So then he was really rubbing his leg and he was putting his hand in his trousers and that sort of thing, you know. We got off the train and we went up to this place. It is called the Caledonian Canal and it is quite quiet and we went up there and we sort of had sex.

What do you mean 'sort of had sex'

Well just sort of masturbating, and oral sex I'd say at the time.

Was that in the open?

Yes it was, actually. It was a very stupid thing to do, looking back. He'd have got done for it if we'd got caught.

Were there other people around?

Well I remember I had to, a couple of times, sit up and try to look innocent. There were other people around, yes, it was a public place. The train got into the city centre, so obviously we couldn't go anywhere there, so we had to go up to this place, which is not far from the city centre. At the bank of the canal the grass goes down, but people walk along the tow path, so we had to watch what was going on.

Did you speak with him at all?

Yes. He said he had never done this sort of thing before. So I said, 'I don't do this often.' You know, pick people up on the train. He said he was a riveter in the shipyards.

What sort of age was he?

He was about – I don't know – about 28 or 30. He said he had never done it before. But I mean, I was very well aware of the fact that I had my school uniform on. I kept thinking that he must realise that I'm only – quite young sort of thing. When he came into the carriage I just didn't think. It was just somebody on the train, it could have been anybody, but it was really bizarre. That's why I kept on thinking, 'It can't be. This is just innocent, his leg is just touching mine innocently.' It definitely wasn't. I kept thinking to myself, 'I am in school uniform and this man cannot be after me, he wouldn't.' But he did. He said he had a girlfriend, a fiancée, and that sort of thing, and I arranged to meet him again, actually one week later. He turned up and we went to the same place and did the same thing again. Then he said he didn't like it, didn't like doing it, and thought it would be a good idea just to forget what had happened.

Did you ever mention the age difference?

No I didn't, actually, because the second time I met him I was really quite paranoid about it. I went in sort of civilian clothes because I did look old for my age and tall and things, so I didn't wear the same clothes the second time. And then after the second time he said he wanted to forget it. I thought that if I had worn a uniform maybe he would have wanted to meet me again, because maybe that's what he was attracted to, you know, sort of schoolboy type in uniform.

When you said you were quite paranoid about it, what did you mean?

Well I mean the fact that someone could pick someone up on a British Rail train having a school uniform on, I mean it is a bit sort of strange set-up. I didn't know what to think. Some sort of pervert, you know ... He may have been wanting to do something kinky, which I wouldn't have been interested in ... I didn't want him to do anything to me that might hurt me.

He mentioned that some few years later he met up with the man again in a gay bar, but he seemed very nervous and confused, giving the impression that he was leading a double life and had just sneaked out for a few hours.

As regards his views on adult-child sexual involvements, he had written on the original questionnaire:

I think that all forms of child abuse should be outlawed ... No way do I think that my early sexual experiences could be called abuse.

When, at interview, he was asked to elaborate, he commented:

I just don't see how an adult can have any satisfaction from having sex with a child. I mean really – the child is not physiologically or physically or mentally developed enough to participate ... I mean sex should be a two-way thing, I mean especially when you talk about people who have sex with children under 10. OK, there might be some children who are physically developed by the time of 12, but I mean it is just too much, I cannot agree with it, well I personally can't, I think it is wrong and they are just taking advantage of the child. I see people who do that in terms of them having some sort of psychiatric problem ...

I think in a way that with slightly older children you must try and suss out with the child if the child was willing. When I was 15 I used to tell people I was 18 and things like that ... then I should be the one to be blamed, not them.

*

In the next case, an early experience of homosexual contact with a young man was plainly an opportunistic expression of the subject's own pre-existing desires.

Case 031

This 19-year-old student said he had been a practising homosexual for some time, but his experiences with older men did not begin until he was 17. Asked about his earliest sexual interests he said:

I seem always to have been sexually interested in other people. I don't know if I've invented it, but I am pretty sure I can remember as far back as infant school. The school playground was above a pit showers. I can remember watching – I suppose it was curiosity.
Was your interest in males, females?
Males. I don't think it could really be defined as sexual. I found them interesting, but I don't think I found them interesting in sexual terms only.

He recalled one episode when he was 9 which seemed more an expression of his own developing sexuality than a response to another's initiative:

[The other person] was only 16 at the time, but he seemed older because he was my uncle. He was babysitting for my sister and me. He couldn't get home by the time my parents got back. He was telling them he didn't have a car, so they thought it was all right if he slept in my bed.
Then what happened?
It was me more than anything. It was my curiosity. I suppose I was just interested in his private parts and then it just ended up with a quick fumble. We played with each other most of the night and then went to sleep together. It just didn't happen once, it happened three or four times, because he came to babysit that often.
What does fumbling mean?
We'd hold each other.

Was there any masturbation?
No.
Did he have an erection?
Yes.
Did you?
Can't remember.
Why did it stop?
He just stopped wanting to babysit. I don't know why. I think my Dad explained it by him wanting to go out himself Saturday nights.
Did you tell anyone?
No.
Ever?
Not until a few months ago. I'd actually forgotten about it.
Do you think it made any difference to you?
No, I don't think so. I think I became more curious.
What form did that take?
I had a cousin about a year younger than me and after my uncle stopped babysitting I started having sex with my cousin. I used to spend Saturday nights at my grandparents and my cousin was there as well.
So you were fumbling with your cousin?
Yes.
Was that the general pattern until you were 16, having sexual encounters with kids your own age?
Usually about my own age, yes. The same age and a bit younger, definitely no one older. Occasionally with girls as well.
Oh, with girls too?
Once or twice.
Were these encounters sexual in the sense of erections and orgasms?
Erections, yes, not orgasm.

On the questionnaire this student's comments about the effect of the episode with his uncle were as follows:

The relationship was short – approximately three weeks – but it could be said it was the beginning of sexual activity with people my own age. Personally, I don't think this experience had any effect on my sexual attitudes.

In response to questions about his current situation he explained that he was leading an active sex life but that since 16 his contacts had been exclusively with men.

*

In the next example a student described very mixed feelings about the homosexual experiences he had had with men during his adolescence. He had been warned strongly against homosexuality by his parents.

Nevertheless, he deliberately sought out men who wanted sexual contacts.

Case 261

This student, aged 27, rated himself 'predominantly homosexual but significantly heterosexual'. He recalled various boyhood incidents with adult men, both welcome and unwelcome; the first was when he was 14:

I was in this shop and I noticed through the shelves – you could see right through the shelves – that this guy kept looking at me. I didn't take any notice at first, and I walked along looking around and he kept following me. Then I noticed that he had this overcoat on, but he was masturbating beneath the overcoat. Well, I couldn't actually see anything, but I could see his hand moving up and down. So I walked out of the shop. He was still following me and there were a couple of policemen standing together on the side of the road, so I just stayed near to the policemen, I didn't actually plan to say anything to them, and the guy walked off.

Did you mention this to anyone?

Yes, I told my mother about that.

How did she react?

She went mad. She phoned the police and I had to give a description of the man. She was very agitated. Then I got all the warnings about being more careful of people and then my mother's attitude to gay men surfaced, which was along the lines that they can't help it, they are sick, more to be pitied than anything else.

Did you actually go to see the police?

No. It was on the telephone.

Do you know if they did anything about it?

I have no idea.

What did you feel when your mother reacted – ?

It certainly made me more aware.

Did it make you nervous?

No, I wouldn't say nervous. If people looked at me, particularly men, that I would be more aware of and think it was probably for some purpose. Plus I began to – at this stage – to know more about homosexuality.

What do you mean?

Well, at school, with the other boys in the class. It was at that time when we were all discovering ourselves ...

Were you approached on other occasions?

Yes, this is before 16, isn't it? Yes, there were a couple of times I realised that people, men, were looking at me and following me around, not getting too close, but I mean I had the distinct impression of being watched, which worried me a bit. But so long as they didn't come too close, you know, I was OK. I'd just go off home – get on the bus and go off home.

Did you do anything to avoid these situations?

Yes, I used to make sure I was with plenty of other people and go into a crowded shop or whatever so I wouldn't feel so vulnerable as just walking down the street. And I certainly felt safer if I was with other people.

You mentioned that you had actual sexual contacts as opposed to approaches.

Yes, the first time was with – I'd had a few sexual experiences with boys at school. That was more just sort of wanking together and things like that, it was nothing heavy, and a lot of the boys were doing it. But this was on the way home, and it was in the summer, and this car pulled up by the side. And it was a sports car and this guy called out. I walked over to the side of the road. He thought that I was somebody he knew, and he said, 'I'm sorry, I've made a mistake.' And he started to ask me questions about myself – where I was going and what my name was, and he said would I like to go for a ride. So I did and we went off to this park. I was very, very nervous, but I didn't go away. I mean I could have gone away, but I didn't. We went off to this park and he took down his trousers, took down mine, and I just masturbated him.

What age were you at this time?

About 15.

Do you know why you went with him? You mentioned other occasions when you were approached you had avoided it.

I have no idea, no idea.

When you had sex in the park, what happened then?

Well then he suggested that we arrange to meet again and I just agreed, but I had no intention of doing so. I felt terrible about the whole thing and I just went off home.

He didn't give you a lift?

Well he offered to, but I wouldn't, I just wanted to get away.

Did you tell anyone?

No. No.

What did you feel about it?

I felt very guilty about the whole thing.

Do you know why?

Well I think a lot of it was because my upbringing was very strict Catholic, coupled with my mother's attitude towards these people that I had done this dreadful deed with meant that there was no one I could turn to, not in my family anyway.

Did you see yourself as being like these people your mother didn't like?

No. I didn't see myself being like them because I didn't see myself as sick, which was the impression she had given me of these people. I just saw myself as being bad.

Did you ever see the man again?

No.

What about other occasions?

Well after that, once I had calmed down from that, I went through a series of meeting men and having similar experiences.

Where did you go to meet them?

I didn't go anywhere in particular, it was just probably the same sort of men that I was seeing before who I'd steered away from. It was the same sort of people, but actually meeting them, going off to the same sort of places – parks, there was a load of parks – and actually when going back from school, because I used to have to walk across the Downs.

Did these men wait deliberately, do you think?

I think only one did that.

Do you think they were just waiting around on the off chance?

I think so, yes.

Did you get to talk to them?
No, I tried to keep conversation to a minimum.
Did you enjoy the sex?
I did and I didn't. I know that sounds a bit iffy, but I, er, I mean it was exciting in one way but repelling in another.
But it wasn't so repelling that you didn't go back.
I think it was more a case that I began to enjoy the notice that these people were taking of me. These adults were interested in me – a mere boy sort of thing.
Did they ever give you things?
No, there was nothing like that.
Did they ever warn you not to tell anyone?
Oh yes, yes.
Was that usual?
Yes.
What sort of things did they say?
Well they were very concerned – I think they were very nervous too – very concerned about being caught.
Did you wear a school uniform?
Yes.
So it was obvious you were under age. Were they all different men or did you have a regular?
No, I never had a regular. I had a fairly, well, fairly regular relationship with one of my teachers.
What age were you then?
Coming up to 16.
How did that go?
Well, he used to see quite a few boys actually. We used to go round to his flat, he used to live nearby, and I went with friends round to his place. He was thought a very liberal teacher that we could go and call on him after school. This was laid back and easy going, and he used to show us these blue movies, heterosexual home movies. And then I found out that he had been having sex with a couple of boys and then he approached me, and I wasn't particularly – I wasn't very keen to do anything at first, but I did.
Was it spoken about among the boys at school?
No.
How did you find out that he was having sex with some of the boys?
It was he that told me.
When he showed the blue movies, was that all that happened?
We would sort of mess around you know, have bundles and things like that, but apart from that there wasn't anything. I mean obviously it aroused us all, but –
When you started having sex with him how long did that last?
About six months.
What sort of sex?
Just oral sex.
What did you think of the relationship, did you see it as a relationship?
No. I just saw it as relief I suppose, when I was really sexually aroused.
It was purely sexual?
Yes.
Did anyone else know about it?
Not so far as I know.

What about your parents?

My parents were beginning to get worried about me going out and not being willing to tell them where I was going ... So I was beginning to get a few hassles from home ... [He explained that his mother tried to vet his friends and stop him going out.] She did get really concerned.

Do you think she ever had any inkling of the kind of things you were getting up to sexually?

No, I don't think so.

What about your father, did he get involved?

He just – I used to get these cryptic comments – 'Be careful who you go around with son, be careful of men', but that's all he would say, he wouldn't elaborate. I thought he was just being obnoxious, as usual.

What about sexual relations with peers at that time, were most of your sexual contacts at that time with older people?

As far as the men went, yes, it was older men, but I was also having relationships with girls about the same age or a bit younger, say a year younger.

This man also recalled one experience with an older woman when he was about 14 or 15, travelling on a bus.

This woman was sitting at the back of the bus. She kept smiling at me and she seemed a lot older. And I was sitting near the back of the bus and there wasn't many people around. I kept looking at her because she kept smiling at me and I thought she was not all there. I used to live near a mental home, so I thought perhaps she was from the mental home. And she kept touching her breasts and between her legs and smiling at the same time.

And did you respond in any way?

No, I felt quite disgusted actually.

Why do you think you felt disgusted?

Because, I presume, she was from the mental hospital. I think I was quite intrigued by her breasts.

So how did the situation end?

I just got off the bus at my stop and that was it.

What sort of age was she?

I think she was probably around 19 to 20.

Did you mention that to anyone?

No.

Asked about his thought on adults having sex with under-age boys he commented:

I can only relate it to my own experience. I think it can be quite frightening for a boy.

Do you think it was frightening because you were sexually naive?

I think so, yes ...

But you got involved – Why?

I don't know. I think for me it was a bit of an identification thing with these men who would take a lot of interest in me, you know, sort of like the father who I perceived did not have much interest in me.

What do you think about these men now? Would you do the same?
No, I would not get involved in that at all. If I was going to have sexual relations with somebody I would like them to know exactly what it was all about, and you know go into it with their eyes open.

As to his current sexual habits, he explained that he had lived with a woman up till the age of 21 for two years. Since then his contacts had been half and half with men and women, but his present sexual partner, of two years' standing, was a man. He mentioned he had had some psychoanalysis which had helped with the guilt feelings he had used to have about sex. He used to have the idea of an all-seeing God looking at the bad things he did: 'A remnant from my Catholic upbringing.'

*

The next two cases, 297 and 008, came from backgrounds that seem to have been more loose as regards sexual morality than were those of most of the students in the sample. This may account for their having had a multiplicity of early experiences involving adults of both sexes. In the first example (297), the respondent described a clear preference for males and a deliberate seeking out of contacts in public lavatories when he was a boy of 14 or 15. The final example (008) was a man who claimed to have enjoyed sexual contacts with persons of all ages and both sexes ever since he was a boy.

Case 297

A 23-year-old homosexual student, who said he had not had sex with a female since he was 16, reported a multiplicity of sexual experiences with older people before that age. He had had an unusual upbringing. His parents were said to be middle-class, but 'week-end hippie' types who 'used to take quite a lot of drugs'. Both worked full time and he saw rather little of them. His father died when he was 10. He spent a lot of time staying at the homes of schoolfriends whose parents felt sorry for him because he seemed neglected. His closest attachments were to a peer group of young rebels and delinquents. His sexual history fitted the well-known stereotype of the deprived child seeking gratification from adult strangers.

In spite of some youthful sexual experiences with females he had always been more attracted to males. His first vague sexual feelings at age 9 or 10 were directed towards a male friend of similar age. 'I remember at the age of 12 and 11 looking at porno books and moaning about the fact that they had no men in them.'

Can you tell me about those sexual approaches from adults when you were younger?
Well, the first one, I mean the first one from a woman that I remember – I

don't know what age it was – but the woman lived about three doors away from me. Her son I knew reasonably well and me and my elder brother went round there one day. And she was just kind of saying, 'You're very attractive, both of you are going to be very good looking when you grow up. And you're going to be nice big boys when you grow up' – this kind of thing. And, you know, having her arms round both of us and stroking us, but nothing beyond that, but I mean it was definitely sexual.

You don't remember what age you were?

... I suppose 12 or 13 maybe. Could have been later.

And what sort of age was she?

At the time she must have been about 38, 39.

Did it happen on any other occasion or only once?

Not with her. It happened with, I mean that I actually had sex, with a lesbian friend of my mum's, when I was 15 or 16, who happened to be staying there at the time. But that was actually, I mean that was very intimidating. I really felt quite intimidated by that. Because I was fascinated by the fact that she was a lesbian, and she used to come around and stay with her girlfriend, and I think at one time there might have been something going on between her and my mother. I don't know, my younger brother was ill at the time, she was looking after him, and there was nobody else really in the house. It was a very intimidating situation you know. She just suggested that we should have sex, and it was very basic and I felt kind of intimidated. It was not very, not particularly, much fun.

Why do you say that?

Why – I suppose I really didn't. I was not attracted to her at all. I was attracted about the idea of having sex with a woman, you know, that was quite interesting. But I had known her for about three years and it was just kind of, just something I felt very odd about, as though I was kind of betraying something, somebody. I had already before that decided I was gay and that I wasn't really interested in having sex with women. And I did have sex with another woman at about that time, but that was a schoolfriend of mine, and that was quite a funny situation, that was much more fun and I quite enjoyed it.

She was the same age as you?

Yes, we were all about that age and my mother was away and there was nobody else in the house and there was the four of us, me and a gay friend of mine and two women. You know, like, we were all quite rebellious. We just thought it would be nice to take pictures of each other with no clothes on ...

This lesbian friend of your mother's, what age was she?

About 28 or 29.

Did you talk to other people [about that]?

No, not at all. I didn't even mention it to my friends, because at that time it just didn't seem the right idea to mention it. If that had happened with a man I'd have gone and told them all straight away. But as it had happened with a woman I felt – perhaps it was something to do with feeling inadequate at the time. One of her friends was somebody [I knew], one of her man friends. As I say mother had known her for quite a long time because they used to wo together. And I had actually tried to pick up, when I was about 13, her man friend when he was staying the night after a party. I mean he was gay, I found that out afterwards, but it was kind of very embarrassing. He was spending the night in my bedroom and there were two beds, one faced that way and there was another one against the wall, and just at three o'clock in the

morning, this was when I was 13 I remember because it was 1976, it was very hot and so I thought I would get up and have a look at, you know, what he was like with no clothes on. So I pulled back the sheets and it was really embarrassing, because he woke up and it was a kind of difficult situation, but I thought nothing's going to happen so I went back to bed and that was that. But I felt, I think, slightly embarrassed that he had told her about that. It was, you know, a few years later.
Did she know you were gay?
Well if he had told her I suppose she would have had some suspicions ...

Asked about experiences with older men he started talking about encounters in lavatories.

I was always aware that you could kind of could meet men in public toilets. So I mean, I used to, this was really quite interesting to me.
Any idea how you found out?
No, I think it was just like going to use the toilets and seeing the writing on the walls and wishing to – kind of thinking you know, this is really interesting. I can remember being about the age of 11 and going in with friends of mine and seeing what the latest writing on the wall was. We never really thought it was disgusting, just quite interesting. So I suppose there were a couple of occasions when I have had sex with people in toilets around about where I lived, but it was not what I would tell my friends about. If I came up to London for the weekend and slept with a man, then I would tell them about that. But I wouldn't [otherwise], I think they would have disapproved – I don't know.
What did you do when you went to the toilets?
Where I used to go there was just one cubicle, and there was a urinal [close] along there, so you kind of poked your way out and it was really quite notorious. I mean you just had to go into the cubicle and then if people came in and they sort of pushed the door and there was somebody in there they obviously knew there was someone there. There was a hole so you could see out, so they just got their cocks out and started wanking, and, you know, that was that, just like that. But I never really talked to them. If I did talk to them I always told them I was older than I was.
What age were you?
I suppose I was doing that from about 14. But I can remember, say at the age of 12, being in a swimming pool and having men make advances to me.
Did you respond?
No, because I was never in a situation where I was able to respond. I was always with people ...
I suppose after the age of 13 it began to dawn on me that not everybody did this. Perhaps not everyone wanted to know that you were getting advances or you were having sex with people. But I mean it was all, as I said earlier, I was learning that you could use sex as a kind of power. When I used to meet people in the toilets, I mean as far as I was concerned it was quite fun, but it was also meant, you know, they would buy me things. I could get money out of them. I suppose this is just, you know, a justification for doing it at that age, but that was always as much on my mind as anything else, that I could actually ...
Did you ask them for money or did they offer it?

No. They always offered it, but 1 always expected them to offer it. It wasn't always money. Sometimes they gave me like porno books and things like that. I think I was learning at the time that if you were a 14-year-old or a 15-year-old you have a lot of power over some people like that, you know I was learning to use it ...

During this period, before you were 16, were you mostly attracted to adult men, did you mostly go with them or with people your own age?

No, I mostly went with adults, but it was not for the want of trying. I told all my friends I was gay at 15 anyway, and their reaction, they thought it was quite amusing. They didn't think anything else of it, I was kind of notorious, and I had sex with one 13-year-old.

Was that when you were – ?

When I was at school. I mean he was a friend, a brother of somebody in my class, I don't know how it came about exactly.

Was he younger than you?

He was 13. I was 10 at the time. But apart from that they were all adults.

On the questionnaire this student had written the following comments:

Just to point out that in my own (and others to whom I have talked) experience, it was usually me that instigated the sexual contact. At no point was I ever engaged in activity that I didn't enjoy or consent to ... All I can say is that having had many sexual encounters below the age of 16 I have now a greater appreciation of its value within a one-to-one relationship. What would really have 'fucked' me up would have been if I had been caught and my partner sent to prison for what I had in most cases instigated.

At the interview he was slightly less sanguine about adult-child sexual contacts. Although he knew no one who had been harmed in that way he thought it all depended on the age of the child and the distance in age between the child and the older person.

Case 008

This 50-year-old bisexual man acknowledged that, although he had never married he had sexual relations during his adult life with partners of either sex, on occasion with boys and girls he supposed might be under 16. He was still friendly with a man now in his 20s with whom he had had a brief sexual relationship when that person was a boy.

Unlike most other student respondents, this man was from a rough, under-privileged background. He was born illegitimate and reared for the first seven years by a lone, working mother, after which he was exposed to a bullying stepfather whom he hated. In boyhood his closest ties were to the delinquent peers with whom he engaged in street-life escapades. He entered the army as a boy recruit.

He had early sexual feelings for and experiences with both males and females and seemed to have difficulty recalling all the incidents that might be relevant. When he was 10 a boy a year or two older, 'exposed himself in my bedroom. I was curious about his erection and he showed me how to masturbate.' Later, possibly around 14,

I think I do remember, there was this guy, his name was Billy, or he was called Billy, and he used to play football for [the town]. He was a great hulking brute. I mean there was very little doubt, I knew what he meant, he exposed himself you know, near some bushes. And I remember he had quite a big plonker and I thought, 'My God, I'm not getting anywhere near that' ...
Was that your only reaction? To think what a big –
I think so, yes. Somewhat amused. I remember telling my friends about it. Used to say, 'Billy has got a beauty, hasn't he?'
Did he have a reputation for exposing himself?
He had a reputation for going further – for actually having sex with boys.
Was this common knowledge?
Well, it was common knowledge amongst the adults and common knowledge amongst us ... He must have been about late twenties, something like that. A lousy football player. And we'd [tease] people – 'Ah! You've been with Billy! Did you enjoy it?' Some did go with him.
Did any of them admit to that?
Oh yes.
Was that acceptable?
It was acceptable, I think, providing you didn't go too often. I think, looking back, what was not acceptable actually was any emotional involvement with the person. Going behind the bushes for wanking was quite acceptable
Did you ever consider going with him?
Yes, I considered it. He just didn't turn me on.

He recalled two occasions of approaches from adult women when he was under 16. As to the first,

I am still not certain whether it was a sexual approach. I think that that was just a case of, you know, being provocative. The idea actually of an older woman approaching a boy, although it happened, you know it did happen. I don't think we really quite cottoned on. I think she was just a bit too provocative and flaunted herself and I got aroused by it. I don't think I really was too keen.
Who was she?
Just a neighbour.
What sort of age?
Early 20s.

The second episode, when he was 15, was with a chaplain's wife.

She was a randy cow, this was at the army school. She invited me for tea on my own. Somebody older in the year above us said, you know, 'Nudge nudge, wink, wink, you're all right.' I mean I knew about sex, but I was still a bit naive you know. I sat down and had a nice tea and that and I said, 'Where's the chaplain?' She said, 'Oh, he's away at a conference' and something like we won't be disturbed for some time, and I began to think, 'Funny!' and then

I became aware of what she wanted and I thought, well, you know, this is OK.
Was there conversation, did she touch you?
I mean by the time she touched me I knew very well what she wanted and I was saying yes in my mind.
Did she make the first move?
Oh yes, I let her.
You had sexual intercourse?
Yes.
That was on three occasions?
Yes.
Did you enjoy it?
Yes, yes.
Did you tell anyone?
No, I didn't. Even at that age I just felt that you didn't tell other people about things like this. It wasn't right. There were quite a lot of questions asked and I just said we had a nice tea. I think they cottoned on.
This happened on three occasions. Why did it stop?
I think she probably found somebody in the year beneath me.
You think she liked young men?
I think there is very little doubt about it.

3.7 Vulnerability to sexual 'abuse'

In addition to the 23 interviewed students who had some experience to report, a further 14 who volunteered to be interviewed were also seen, none of whom recalled early sexual contact with an older person. The interviews were semi-structured, with a framework of topics and questions to be covered in each case, mainly about family background and upbringing. The numbers were far too small for statistical treatment, but from the wealth of qualitative information supplied it was hoped some clues might emerge as to why some boys had been exposed to sexual experiences and others not.

Dividing the interviewees into the 23 'positives', who reported some sexual experience, and the 14 'negatives' who did not, it was apparent that several unfavourable background features, which had been elicited in response to direct questions, were more prevalent among the 'positives'. Thus 15 of the 23 'positives' (65 per cent) were coded as having working-class parentage compared with only 2 of the 14 'negatives' (14 per cent). Again, 8 'positives' (35 per cent) compared with 3 'negatives' (21 per cent) had been at some stage the child of a one-parent family. Asked whether they remembered their childhood as happy or unhappy 9 (35 per cent) of the 'positives', but only 2 (14 per cent) of the 'negatives' categorised it as unhappy. Regular absences from the boyhood home (at least several times a week) during which they were unsupervised by adults were reported 13 (57 per cent) of 'positives', but only 1 (7 per cent) of the 'negatives'. The interviewer made a judgment (based on information about the type of discipline experienced, whether as a teenager the student had been involved in vandalism or other antisocial activity outside the home, and whether he was often left unsupervised) as to whether each interviewee's upbringing had been relatively lax or strict. Of the 'positives', 12 (52 per cent) were assessed as having had relatively lax upbringings compared with 4 (29 per cent) of the 'negatives'.

Naturally, the attributes of lax discipline, absence of supervision, working-class origin, unhappy childhood and single-parent family were not independent, but viewed collectively they seemed to support the stereotype of the vulnerable boy as coming from a not very happy or attentive and possibly broken home and spending a lot of time out of doors unsupervised. This suggests that there is some basis for the notion that sexual abuse is associated with disorganised families and alienated children seeking attention elsewhere. More important than this, however, is the wide variety of backgrounds and circumstances within which the reported sexual incidents occurred. Many did not fit the stereotype. As the accounts already quoted have shown, there were differences according to whether the contacts were unwanted or welcomed, heterosexual or homosexual. An over-simple categorisation of all sexual contacts between boys and adults as the 'abuse' of 'vulnerable' children hampers rather than aids understanding of the variety and complexity of these events.

Looking back at the cases already described, one can identify some which fit the stereotype of a rough, unloving background, lax supervision and exposure to a good deal of open sexuality. This was certainly true of the bisexual man (Case 008) who had been physically abused by both his mother and stepfather. Of the latter, he said: 'The time I most felt at ease with him was when I dropped his ashes overboard from a rowing boat.' As to the atmosphere at home, he said: 'I couldn't get out of the house quick enough to play with my friends.' Case 239, who was drawn into a group of boys who were sexually involved with a middle-aged paedophile, was also in some ways emotionally deprived. Both his parents were teachers and he was left to the care of his grandmother most of the time. The incidents happened at the age of 13 when 'there wasn't the communication. There was a certain amount of conflict because they [my parents] were very much into academic things and really their conception of what was happening to me socially seemed very limited.' He blamed his sex-segregated school and lack of sex information for the naivety that allowed him to get caught in secret deviance without realising the full significance of the behaviour.

In complete contrast, Case 337, who had had a relationship with the mother of a schoolfriend, came from a secure, supportive background. He commented: 'I was quite an obedient child, especially as far as my parents were concerned. They were very good in that ... they weren't sort of severe, but they insisted on a certain level of behaviour.' It seems that, having arrived at an age when he could respond, he just took advantage of an unusual opportunity to gain heterosexual experience in a pleasant, unthreatening situation.

In the cases of two of the homosexual men there were no obvious environmental precipitants. Case 249, who had been aware of his homosexual feelings from an early age, simply took advantage of whatever opportunity arose to have sexual contact with young adult males. Case 031, from the early age of 9, when he initiated contact with a youthful uncle, continued actively to seek experiences with other boys. On the other hand, in the case of the other two homosexual men interviewed there were uneasy relationships with parents which may have encouraged them to seek attention elsewhere. Case 261 described himself as very much a loner as a boy. He felt somewhat estranged from his highly religious parents. He said of his father: 'We just didn't see eye to eye on anything and I felt when I was younger that he was not particularly interested in what I was doing or what I was interested in ... I was always under the impression that he would never listen to me at all ...' About his adolescent experiences with older men he remarked, tellingly: 'I think for me it was some sort of identification thing with these men who would take a lot of interest in me you know, sort of like the father ...' The other homosexual, Case 297, had plainly felt neglected: 'Especially after my father died [mother] was working so much that I maybe saw her three hours a day. She didn't really enjoy coming home ...', 'I never really had a close relationship with anybody in my family'; 'From when I was very young most of my friends have been outside the home'. Totally unsupervised, he was left free to stay out at nights and sleep with homosexual partners as he felt inclined.

Of the 14 heterosexual students who described unwanted sexual approaches by older persons, all but one of the incidents involved older males, most of them strangers. In several of these cases the boy had grown up in the inner city in an environment where it was acceptable for quite young children to play in the streets in the evening or after dark. Some of the incidents happened when the boys were not yet in their teens and when unusually lax parental supervision may have been a factor. For example, Case 303, who recalled being approached when he was 8 and again at 10. On both occasions he had gone fishing alone in a large park in London. Although the first incident was reported to the police he was allowed to continue visiting the same park on his own. He was an illegitimate child and his mother worked part time, but there was already a stepfather in the household when the incidents took place. In another case (489) a boy of 14 accepted a lift in a car from a man who fondled him. It appeared he was a boy who led a fairly independent social life outside the home. Even when at primary school he and his friends of similar age would travel long distances unaccompanied. He mentioned going to London airport, over 10 miles away. He also stated that as a boy and a young adolescent he went out almost every evening.

Once again, it is easy to find a contrasting case (170), in which a boy of 16 was fondled by a man in a bus. In that case there was no suggestion of any lack of parental watchfulness. He had been warned about strangers and although he was alone on the bus he was being met by an uncle.

These examples of unwanted contacts with strangers highlight the diversity of backgrounds and circumstances in which such incidents occur. Although possible contributory factors are discernible in some of the accounts, on the whole they suggest that it is not possible to specify a consistent stereotype of 'at risk' boys that would have any great predictive validity.

As mentioned earlier, questionnaire responses about the effects of early sexual experiences were too few and too scanty for meaningful analysis. Among the students interviewed only one (239) described a significant effect 'that forced me into a very one-sided view of the world and it took really about ten years before I ... even then I didn't feel happy about the sort of relations and sexual contacts with girls and now I feel that was very regrettable. I mean there are still some sort of things that hang over from that even now.'

Since this man also attributed his problems to school and parents keeping him ignorant of sex, it is unclear whether he was blaming the early homosexual experiences themselves or the lack of sophistication which led to them.

4

Electoral Register Studies

The disappointingly low response rate from students left doubt as to the true prevalence of boys' sexual contacts with adults. We decided to try other methods of obtaining an estimate, approaching samples better representative of the population at large, but restricting inquiry to a basic minimum of questions in order to secure maximum cooperation. One method considered was the telephone survey. Names were taken at random from the London directories, some with male Christian names shown, others with initials only. Calls were made until 50 men had been contacted.

The caller (either D.J. West or T.P. Woodhouse) began with a prepared introductory explanation: 'I'm sorry to trouble you. You don't know me. I'm a university research worker doing a survey over the telephone and I would be grateful if you could help. Is it convenient to talk for a moment?' If permitted to continue the caller went on to explain: 'The topic is sexual contacts between adults and children. There's been a lot about this in the news lately and we are trying to find out how common it actually is. It's an important thing to know and we hope you will help. Just three questions. We keep the answers absolutely confidential and anonymous.' Again, if allowed to do so, the caller went on to ask: 'First question. How old are you? Ever married? Now the main question: Can you remember, when you were under 16 years old, did you ever have any experience of a sexual kind with a man or woman who was over eighteen?' If the answer was 'No' the caller prompted the man, explaining that anything sexual was meant, including propositioning, exposing, touching – 'anything like that'.

In all 34 (68 per cent) of the men were prepared to listen and reply to the questions. However, after this brief trial the telephone method was discontinued because it was found to have serious disadvantages. An unexpected telephone call from a stranger was scarcely conducive to a leisurely and carefully considered response to a complex personal question. Although a substantial proportion of the men gave what seemed to be straightforward, matter-of-fact replies in a quite friendly way, the investigators got the impression that other responses such as 'No, nothing like that', delivered in a swift, dismissive tone, may have been given simply as an easy way to terminate an unwanted call. It was evident from voices in the background, and from the fact that the man had sometimes to be called to the phone by a third party, that some of the respondents were not alone when replying and might have been embarrassed to make anything but a negative reply. One respondent, while admitting to some contact with a man when he was 14, declined to give any particulars. Another, who gave a negative reply in a somewhat doubtful manner, actually remarked that the telephone lacks privacy.

The proportion of outright refusers, 32 per cent, was comparatively small and included some cases in which wives answered the telephone, asked the purpose of the call, and then declined to bring the husband or else refused on his behalf. A few of the refusers expressed disapproval or suspicion, sometimes demanding precise information about the identity and authority of the callers. One said: 'Do you know you are speaking to a policeman?' He went on to refuse with the comment: 'I get enough of this at work.' Only one was rudely abusive and he answered the questions finally.

Of the 34 men who answered, 5 (15 per cent) reported some positive experience, one had had sexual intercourse with an older female when he was 15, three described an approach from or contact with an older male when they were 14 or 15 (one in a public lavatory, one in a cinema and one unspecified) and one had been confronted at the age of 8 or 9 by a 'flasher' in some woods near his school.

*

A larger and more effective survey was carried out by postal questionnaire addressed to men whose names appeared on electoral registers. They would be, by definition, aged not less than 18. It was hoped the exercise might achieve a better response rate than had been obtained from student groups and a better estimate of prevalence through being addressed to a sample of all classes and ages, closer to the general population.

Since the main concern was to obtain a supplementary estimate of prevalence rates, the questionnaires used for the electoral register samples were shorter and simpler than those sent to students (see the example reproduced in Appendix B on p. 135). Apart from preliminary questions about age, marital status, class of family background etc., the inquiry was limited to a few direct questions about possible experiences with an adult man or an adult woman which respondents could tick either 'Yes' or 'No'.

In order to tap a wide range of social backgrounds, names were taken from the registers of three contrasting areas, Ealing and Islington in London, and Cambridge. Names were chosen on a random basis. In the first Cambridge sample 3 names were taken from each of 33 wards, choosing the first and last clearly masculine and English sounding name in each of the 33 relevant booklets together with the first listed male English name on the right-hand page when the booklet was opened in the middle. One name was left out to produce an even total of 98 which could be divided into two equal groups. In Islington, 25 names were taken from each of 4 polling districts, selected by dividing the total number of names listed by 25, to yield a number n, and choosing every nth name on the list – or the nearest subsequent male name if the initial choice was not clearly male. A similar system was used for the Ealing and second Cambridge samples.

The Cambridge questionnaires, the first set to be sent out, were addressed to each individual by name and accompanied by an introductory letter and a pre-paid and addressed envelope for returning the completed form. The inquiry was entirely anonymous, recipients being instructed: 'Do not write your name or address on the questionnaire unless you wish to be contacted.' In order to encourage responses a promise to contribute £1 to the NSPCC for each completed questionnaire was included in half of the accompanying letters. Two weeks after the first posting a reminder was sent to all 98 addresses. Ultimately, 50 completed questionnaires were received, 26 from those who had received letters mentioning a contribution to the NSPCC. The inducement had made no appreciable difference to the response rate.

In Ealing, 100 questionnaires were posted to addresses in three polling districts, 50 of them containing in the accompanying letter an offer to pay £5 to the respondent, or to a named charity, in return for a completed form. Ten days later a reminder letter was sent, and in a further ten days a second reminder with a further copy of the questionnaire and a stamped envelope. The last page of each Ealing questionnaire bore a code number which identified the forms that were returned and enabled the reminders to be sent only to those who had not responded. A total of 35 completed questionnaires were received, 17 from men who had been offered money, 15 of whom requested the payment as promised. It would appear that this monetary inducement had made no difference to the likelihood of a response.

Because of complaints from Ealing (described later) a small modification of the procedure was introduced for the Islington inquiry. The 100 questionnaires were sent out with a letter that stated that if the addressee did not wish to participate he could return the questionnaire uncompleted with his name on it and he would receive no more correspondence. Two weeks later a reminder letter was sent, with a repeat questionnaire and a stamped envelope, to those who had not replied. Those who had replied were identified by a code number concealed underneath the return address label. Only 25 completed forms were received, 9 of them following the reminder.

The response to the postal questionnaires was smaller in Ealing and Islington than in either of the Cambridge samples. Except for 50 cases out of the second Cambridge sample respondents were not asked, as they had been in Ealing and Islington, whether they were willing to be interviewed. Since the response rate in the subgroup invited to be interviewed (48 per cent) was not significantly different from that of the rest of the Cambridge samples, the inclusion of this request could not be held to account for the lower response rates in Ealing and Islington. It seems more likely that the project's links with Cambridge University encouraged a better response in that city.

The response rates from the postal inquiries are shown in Table 8. The estimates are inexact since it was impossible to know how many questionnaires failed to reach the target individual. The registers are not up to date and people may have moved. When a new register is prepared about 1 in 5 have a different address. Calls at specified addresses are apt to find some 4 per cent unoccupied or derelict. Of the forms sent out, 5 per cent were returned undelivered by third parties or by the post office. Others may have been thrown away by the current occupants of out-of-date addresses. The response rate from all four postal inquiries combined was 44.5 per cent, not a low figure in view of the nature of the topic and impersonality of the approach, but still too low for a confident estimate of incidence of relevant experiences.

Table 8. Responses from electoral register samples

	Ealing	First Cambridge Sample	Islington	Second Cambridge Sample	Doorstep inquiries		Total
					London	Cambridge	
Total of questionnaires dispatched	100	98	100	192	80	45	615
Returned undelivered	7	5	4	8	–	–	24
Questionnaires completed	35	50	25	102	52	34	298
Response rates	38%	54%	26%	55.4%	65%	75.6%	50%
Total reporting a sexual experience	7	12	6	17	11	7	60
Proportion of questionnaires reporting a sexual experience	20%	24%	24%	17%	21%	21%	20%

*

In a determined effort to achieve a better response rate than was possible by means of a postal inquiry T.P. Woodhouse tried calling in person at addresses of men whose names were on the electoral register. From the Ealing register 50 names that sounded English and masculine were selected from addresses in streets in the immediate vicinity of a particular station. The area proved to be a wealthy suburban neighbourhood with a preponderance of imposing detached houses. Since this might be producing bias only 30 of the intended 50 addresses were approached. The procedure was to ring the doorbell and ask for the respondent by name. If the door was answered by someone saying the respondent was not available the investigator explained that he was a researcher from Cambridge, that the name had been obtained from the electoral register, and asked if the gentleman might be in on one of the next few evenings so that he could call again. Regardless of whether any answer was obtained no more than three calls were made at any one address. In one case (counted as a refusal) a wife told the caller not to come again as her husband would not be willing.

When a potential respondent was met it was explained that the researcher was working for Cambridge University and would be grateful if he could complete a short questionnaire. It dealt with personal matters, but there was no need to put a name on the form. An envelope was provided which could be sealed. The researcher waited while the respondent went off to fill in the form. When it was returned he placed the sealed envelope directly in his briefcase without discussion.

If a man hesitated or asked for more information before agreeing to complete the form it was explained that the topic of the research was child sexual contacts with adults. If child sexual abuse was mentioned it was explained that we were interested in the whole range of sexual contacts, with men and women, consensual and non-consensual. The 14 contacts achieved from these 30 addresses yielded 10 completed questionnaires. A further survey was begun in some nearby but less exclusive streets, but was abandoned after 4 contacts had been made and two completed questionnaires obtained. This curtailment followed complaints about the research from the local Member of Parliament, but doorstep approaches were continued elsewhere, in Islington and Hackney, where 62 contacts yielded a further 40 completed questionnaires giving a total of 52 completed questionnaires from 80 contacts in London, equivalent to a response rate of 65 per cent – considerably better than with the postal method. Since postal inquiries had yielded a better response in Cambridge than elsewhere it was decided to attempt a further round of doorstep contacts there, sufficient to bring the total up to 125 contacts. The 45 contacts in Cambridge produced 34 completed questionnaires, a response rate of 75.6 per cent.

Of 215 targeted addresses (excluding the curtailed Ealing sample where all the targeted addresses were not visited) only 121 yielded the individual sought. No reply after repeated calls accounted for most of these failures, but in 34 cases, 16 per cent, either the place appeared unoccupied or the occupant claimed that the person sought was no longer there. This confirms the suspicion that the response rate from the postal inquiries may have been significantly lowered by failure to reach the person intended, since not all stray questionnaires would have been returned via the post office.

Out of the total of 298 completed questionnaires 20 per cent reported some early sexual experience. As shown in Table 8, the proportion with positive experiences to report varied in the six sub-samples from 17 to 24 per cent but was seemingly not much affected by high or low response rates or whether contact was made by post or personal call.

4.1 Risks of causing offence by unsolicited questions on sex

Approaching members of the general public, via electoral registers or by any other means, carries certain risks. Students were generally made aware that the male members of their entire class were being approached with the consent of their instructors or college authorities, so no individual had reason to suspect he was being specially selected. One man from a group of students not so informed wrote: 'I would require you to furnish me with details of the source supplying my name, status and recent address before participating in your project. I am most surprised that such an auspicious institution has recourse to unsolicited response to a questionnaire of such a personal nature.'

Men whose names had been taken at random from the electoral register were told in the accompanying letter that this had been done, but they had no means of checking the statement except by making written inquiry. In the case of the student samples failure to respond was apparently mostly due to apathy, expressions of annoyance being exceptional. An Ealing resident who received one of the questionnaires was offended at having had it posted to him unsolicited and drew it to the attention of a Member of Parliament. The MP supported the complaint and without, apparently, making any approach to the researchers or the Institute of Criminology to find out the purpose of the project, he informed the Press Association that he intended to put a question to the Home Secretary. According to a report in the *Daily Telegraph* (20 May 1986) he intended to ask for a suspension of all public funding to the Institute immediately 'until an investigation has been carried out into what many people may regard as prurience masquerading as scientific research'. He added: 'I fail to see how this can be legitimate research, and why taxpayers should fund what I think people will regard as a sordid and squalid survey.' In the event, the Home Secretary responded to the effect that Home Office funds were not being used and that recipients of questionnaires were free to ignore them. The following week the MP was reportedly protesting that some sex education books used in schools were too explicit. We were fortunate that notwithstanding this unfavourable publicity, which might have had repercussions on other more 'innocent' research projects, our sponsoring authorities were prepared to continue their support.

It may be only a small minority who take offence at being asked about sexual matters, but their resentment can be as strong as it can appear to others irrational. One questionnaire was returned by a wife on behalf of her elderly, ailing husband. She wrote: 'Your letter upset him. He has no time for this rubbish and neither have I. We are sick and tired of the local council and their ideas ...' Her last remark was thought to be a reference to recent publicity about the council in question reportedly giving money towards a 'lesbian centre'. Another respondent wrote criticising the 'poverty' of the questions and wrote 'I am appalled that your University should fritter away its hard come by grants on, in my view and that of many to whom I have spoken, such a useless project – useless in the sense that your conclusions will have no meaning, for I am convinced that any completing the questionnaires will give you untruthful answers, and in any case what good do you consider your conclusions will do.' He added 'Until there is a return to a belief in God, the moral standards of this or any other country will not improve and therefore nor will the crime rate drop. I am sorry that you are wasting your time and the country's money ...' A third man wrote: 'I dislike having been, as you see fit to put it "selected randomly" ... I regard this type of quasi-scientific inquiry as both valueless and impertinent.'

No adverse comments were sent in from people contacted in the doorstep inquiries. This suggests that a face-to-face request, by an interviewer who looks and is plainly serious about what he is doing and anxious not to offend and willing to answer questions, is less likely to be viewed as an unjustifiable intrusion.

4.2 Findings from the electoral register samples

The questionnaires addressed to the general public (see Appendix B) were shorter and simpler than those addressed to students. The first page asked solely for background information, such as age, marital status and social class. The second page asked whether the respondent had had any of eight specified sexual experiences with someone over 18 when he was under 16. Boxes were provided for ticking 'Yes' or 'No' to whether an adult man or woman had 'made sexual suggestions', 'touched my sex parts (bottom, breasts or genitals) in a sexual way', 'exposed to me in a sexual way' or 'had sex with me'. Respondents answering yes to any of these items were asked to state their age when it first happened. Space was provided for comments and a description of experiences. Finally, the questionnaire invited opinions as to whether sexual contacts between men and boys or between women and boys were 'not harmful', 'harmful', 'very harmful' or 'no opinion'.

Electoral register respondents differed significantly from the student samples. Most were married. Only 23.2 per cent said they were under 30, compared with 81.9 per cent of students, but 54.4 per cent were 40 or more compared with only 3.3 per cent of students. Of the 289 electoral register respondents who gave the information, 66.8 per cent said that they had been brought up in 'working-class' families. The proportion nationally reporting working-class parentage was 78.6 per cent in a British Attitude Survey, 1984 (Social and Community Planning Research). This figure could not be compared directly with the student respondents, who had been classed according to paternal occupation, but it pointed to a much higher proportion of working-class origin than was suggested by the 20.8 per cent of student respondents whose fathers were skilled and unskilled manual workers.

The results from the questions about sex experiences are set out in Table 9. Only 20.1 per cent had some relevant experience to report,

Table 9. Electoral register samples

Questions	Replies		
	No	Yes	% Yes
A woman made suggestions	283	15	5.0
A man made suggestions	261	37	12.3
A woman touched	288	10	3.3
A man touched	273	25	8.4
A woman exposed	290	8	2.7
A man exposed	284	14	4.7
A woman 'had sex'	286	12	4.0
A man 'had sex'	291	7	2.3
Positive endorsement of any of the above	238	60	20.1
Endorsement of any involvement with a male	249	49	16.4
Endorsement of any involvement with a female	281	17	5.7

compared with 36.8 per cent of the students. The difference was most striking in regard to incidents with older females, reported by only 5.7 per cent of the electoral register respondents compared with 18.1 per cent of the students. Incidents with an older male were reported by 16.4 per cent compared with 24.7 per cent of the students.

The numbers were too small to provide much help in identifying the reasons for the differences between the responses from the general public and the students. Students, besides being mostly from a generation exposed in youth to a greater abundance of sexual information, are perhaps more reflective than the average and hence more likely to recall and identify a sexual meaning in incidents that others might not find significant. The students had been encouraged to be as comprehensive as possible by the wording of their questionnaire which asked them to include 'any other type of contact which you considered then or consider now as sexual'. The briefer instructions in the electoral register questionnaires may have been insufficient to dispel the common idea that researchers would be interested only in sexual incidents of an unwanted or 'abusive' sort.

Because the electoral register respondents were on average much older than the students one might have expected the forgetting of events in the distant past to be one of the reasons why fewer of them reported relevant experiences. In actuality rather more of the electoral register respondents who were over 30 reported an experience than did those who were not yet 30 (21.0 per cent of 229 against 17.4 per cent of 69). However, only 6 of the 55 electoral register respondents who stated an age when their first sexual encounter occurred said that they had been under 11 at the time, whereas 22 of the 67 students who reported an experience mentioned an incident before they were 11. The fact that the students' questionnaires asked about experiences before and after 11 in separate sections may have helped prompt their memories.

Unlike the student sample, in which those from working-class homes were more likely to report some experience, there was no such difference in the proportion reporting experiences, either with older males or with older females, in the electoral register samples. The discrepancy could be due to the latter having been classified by their own rating of class background whereas the students were classified according to their parents' occupations. Marital status, or being parents themselves, were likewise not significantly related to positive responses in the electoral register samples. Among those who answered 'Yes' to the question whether they had been warned not to talk to strangers, rather more reported having actually had an experience than among those who had not been 'warned' (23 per cent of 157 against 16 per cent of 126).

A short description of sexual incidents they had experienced was given on their questionnaires by 25 of the electoral register respondents. Only one concerned an incident within the family, 3 were with women. The homosexual encounters were mostly casual incidents outside the home and the comments showed that some boys were quite knowing about deviant sexuality and readily refused approaches they did not like.

Age category of respondent	Age at incident	Description
50-60	9 & 14	Mutual masturbation with a man about 30 when I was 9 or 10 – at the swimming pool in the changing cubicles. When I was nearly 14 doing a paper round a woman gave me oral sex while I played with her.
over 60	10	A scout master, well known to us informed youngsters, made the most delicate of moves and was soon seen off.
30-40	10	Local church. Organist – single man living with his mother, teaching me, then a chorister, to play the organ. Began fondling me – embarrassed, moved away, went home. Kept this to myself – felt ashamed – kept my distance. The man was sick – not aggressive, pitiful.
over 60	11	An Indian (I think) locked the door of a bathroom and fiddled with my genitals. I was frightened. This happened on a P & O boat.
40-50	11	Uncle touched private parts.
over 60	12	Overcrowding at home. Slept with my uncle. I woke to find my uncle pushing his penis to my bottom. I had my first climax.
50-60	12	Asked GI for gum. He said 'follow me'. He went into a gents'. When I went in he shut door and dropped his trousers and I had to suck him off.

Age category of respondent	Age at incident	Description
40-50	12	Was 'befriended' by a scoutmaster.
30-40	12	Asked me to touch his private parts.
30-40	12	A homosexual teacher consistently moved conversation towards sex and sexuality and asked to be massaged whilst nude under his sun lamp.
50-60	12	Headmaster of junior school touched my genitals when he summoned me to be caned for some minor breach of school rules ... The incident was disconcerting but not serious. I was too embarrassed to tell anyone about it until a year or two later when the man's behaviour with boys came dramatically to light ... Boys from the senior school smashed up the office of the man one night. He instantly resigned (or was dismissed) and was never seen in the school again. No hint of why he had left was given in the school magazine or the local press ... It was rumoured that one of the senior boys involved in smashing the room had a brother who was abused. The matter was resolved without any publicity damaging to the school. The school authorities succeeded in keeping the whole thing quiet in spite of the fact that a junior headmaster was involved. All this happened 40 years ago. I have scarcely thought about it since.
50-60	13	When I was train spotting with a friend at a station near Sheffield the porter said he would report us for trespassing. He took us to the porters' room, he fondled my genitals and had oral sex with me. I never told my parents.
20-30	13	An old age pensioner approached me whilst I was on my own by a river bank and proceeded to tell me about his first masturbating experiences when he was down a mine when he was 11 years old.
40-50	14	Incident very casual. In crowded rush hour train.
40-50	14	Bus conductor in Yorkshire (my home at that time) asked the size of my penis – no further conversation took place after my riposte!
20-30	14	Simple exposure of sexual organs (penis) on the public highway – not very important but remembered by me.
under 20	14	I was sleeping round my mate's girlfriend's house when her mother got into my bed and started to climb all over me. It was then I knew what she wanted. She started to touch my penis and rub my body. Then I put my hand between her legs and pushed my finger up her cunt. Then we had sex.

Age category of respondent	Age at incident	Description
50-60	15	I was in a tube train and a man, about 50, got in and asked me if I saw my friends in the shower, then if I had ever let someone look at me having an erection and if they offered to pay me for it. He then got off the train.
50-50	15	Made love to a friend of my sister when I was about 15. She was married.
30-40	15	Accosted by a young man in a train. Taken to a quiet place and indecently assaulted.
30-40	approx 15	Cannot recall age exactly but whilst in the public toilets in one of the local cinemas a man aged somewhere around mid-50s glanced over my shoulder as he was leaving making some comment to the effect 'You have a nice one there.' Then left the toilet. No other people were in the toilets at the time. I left feeling somewhat unnerved.
30-40	15	My boss (office manager) – now recognised and known to be homosexual, suggested we meet with some idea in mind – which I rejected.
30-40	15	I used to do a paper round and collect the money on a Saturday morning. The woman invited me in to collect the money as she usually did and she seduced me while her husband exposed himself.
20-30	15	One evening while walking over the common an elderly man made advances to me. I was too afraid to do anything. I later realised I was gay.
20-30	15	Approached by older (50+) man on tube station who offered money for sex. After ignoring him for 5 minutes he went away.

Except in the first Cambridge sample all the questionnaires used in the electoral register surveys included an invitation to endorse an opinion about the harmfulness or otherwise of sexual contacts between boys under 16 and women over 18 or men over 18. The specified alternatives were filled in as shown in the table on p. 103.

A majority of 58 per cent considered contacts with men 'very harmful', but only 16.4 per cent endorsed that opinion about contacts with women. Highly condemnatory attitudes were less prevalent among those reporting actual sexual experiences. Only 3 (6.8 per cent) of 44 respondents reporting some experience endorsed the views that both contacts with males and contacts with females were 'very harmful', whereas 29 (14.7 per cent) of 197 reporting no experience endorsed these

	boys with women		boys with men	
No opinion	39	16%	21	9%
Not harmful	63	26%	19	8%
Harmful	102	40%	62	26%
Very harmful	40	16%	139	58%
(Not answered)	4		7	

totally condemnatory views. Those who classed themselves as 'working class' were more likely than others to endorse these very condemnatory opinions (16 per cent of 124 against 10 per cent of 110).

5

Early Seduction and Later Homosexuality

5.1 Contrasting outcomes

Given the restricted sample size and the dependence upon student volunteers the present survey may well have failed to reveal incidents of a relatively unusual kind or experiences that are particularly embarrassing to acknowledge. One popular explanation of the development of homosexual orientation in the male supposes that it is the direct result of a boy being sexually awakened by an adult man. None of the students' accounts suggested such a sequence. From the electoral register samples only 5 of the 37 who completed forms reporting some sexual experience expressed willingness to be interviewed and 2 of these failed to keep their appointments when an interviewer called by arrangement. The 3 actually seen were therefore such a highly selected group that it was not to be expected that their experiences would be representative. One of them was of particular interest because it was the only example we came across of a homosexual orientation said to have been the result of an early seduction experience. The man in question was a troubled homosexual aged 48, living alone and rather sad, who probably felt a need to talk. Although he blamed his situation on a childhood encounter with a man in a cinema, it became clear that other factors were involved, including homosexual relationships when he was in the forces. The transcript of this interview is reproduced in full:

Case 801

You are how old?
48.
And you are employed, of course, what is your job?
I'm an undertaker.
And what sort of area did you live in when you were young, under 16?
In a country town.
And what sort of school did you go to, day school?
Day school.
Do you have brothers and sisters?
Yes I do, two brothers and one sister.
And where do you come in the family?
I am the baby.

Are they very much older?

There's a five, ten and twelve-year gap.

And who is next, your sister?

My sister is.

And were you brought up by both parents?

Yes, I was, but my mother died when I was 11.

O.K. Now you tell us that you'd had one experience with an older person when you were young.

That's right.

Could you tell me about that?

Yes.

How old would you have been?

I would have been I should say 11 or 12. It was in the local cinema, and that was with an older man.

An older man, about how old do you think he would be?

It was very difficult to judge at that age, but I should say 45 to 50.

What sort of time of day was it?

An afternoon.

What happened?

I was accosted by the man while I was watching the film.

What did he do?

He put his hand on my knee and continued to do so for about half an hour. I realise now that I should have moved away, but I didn't.

Why?

Because, I suppose, it was some sort of affection.

You supposed it was some sort of affection?

Yes. [pause]

What happened?

I left the cinema with him and went to a caravan site where he had a caravan.

Yes?

Nothing dreadful happened.

What happened?

Well it was just – he touched me.

This was inside the cravan?

Inside the caravan, yes.

Did you get undressed?

No, not fully undressed.

Did he?

He did, yes.

Fully undressed?

Yes.

And what did he do?

Well, not very much, not very much at all.

He touched you?

Yes.

Did he masturbate you?

Yes.

And at that age were you able to ejaculate?

Oh yes.

And did you?

I did, yes.

And did he get you to do anything to him?
No.
He didn't want you to?
He would have liked to, but I was very frightened.
He would have liked you to masturbate him?
I think he would, yes.
But you were frightened?
Yes.
So what happened then?
Well it was getting late and I wanted to leave. [Long pause]
Yes?
He was trying to persuade me to stay, but when I made up my mind he
didn't force me in any way to stay longer.
And so you left?
So I left, yes.
Did you arrange to meet him again?
No, well actually yes, but I didn't go.
Why not?
Because this whole business made me feel ashamed and I realised it was
wrong.
I see. Did you tell anybody about it?
No. That is the trouble, I never had anybody I could talk to, nobody I could
tell in confidence, you know.
So did it affect you in any way?
I think it did affect me a great deal, actually.
In what way?
Well because it was confusing and in later life my thoughts were towards
men instead of women.
*Do you mean that you think this may have caused you to have thoughts
towards men?*
I think it did, in fact.
So at present would you count yourself as homosexual or heterosexual?
I count myself as bisexual ... [interview interrupted by telephone] ... It had
something to do with sex drive towards women.
You mean you had not much sex drive?
That's right.
So how old were you when you got married?
22.
How long did it last?
Eight years.
Children?
No children.
So it was the sex aspect of marriage that was the problem?
Yes.
Were you able to have intercourse?
Oh yes, often.
Then what was the trouble?
Um. Lack of interest. I tended to have sexual relations with my wife to
please her not to please me.
And while you were married did you have relationships with other men?
No, not at all.
And since?

Er – no, well I have, yes. Not a great deal.

So how would you rate your feelings now. Would they be equally towards men and women or rather more towards men than women?

More towards men.

Did you have any other experiences when you were –?

Not as a youngster. I feel that that episode in the cinema was to influence me greatly during the next four or five years and also up to the present time.

What happened during the following five years?

It was – it was a very confusing time, because I didn't know whether it was right or whether it was wrong.

You said you had nobody to talk to. You had a father though.

I had a father who was not the sort of man you could talk to, he was a very Victorian man and my brothers were of course so much older than myself that I was just a child to them, so therefore I couldn't talk to them.

Had you friends at school?

Well yes, at school everybody was talking about this sort of thing, but nobody seemed to know the answer. Was it right or was it wrong?

Did you have any sex experiences with boys your own age?

Not at that time, years later.

How old were you then?

Probably 16.

And did you have sex experiences with girls as well?

Oh yes. Most definitely.

How old the first time that you had any sex contact with girls?

15.

How old was she?

14, I should think.

And what happened between you?

Just straightforward intercourse.

And what did you feel about that?

I enjoyed it very much.

So you didn't have any trouble then?

No trouble at all.

When did the trouble begin?

The trouble began when I joined the Royal Air Force.

How old were you then?

18.

What happened?

I met an officer, one of the officers at the camp where I was stationed, and he invited me for drinks, which I accepted. Afterwards I was taken back to his quarters. During the time I was staying in this particular camp I met him on a regular basis.

And so you had sex. What sort of sex did you have with him?

I played the dominant partner.

So you had anal intercourse and you were the one on top, so to speak?

Yes.

Yes, and did you find that enjoyable at the time?

Yes, I enjoyed it very much.

So again, when did trouble begin?

Well, this particular man was posted and I met a girl, a local girl, and after six months got engaged. That fizzled out after another six months.

Why?

Well one thing was I lived in London and she lived miles away, it was commuting backwards and forwards.

And were you able to have sex with her all right?

A perfectly normal sexual relationship.

Yes.

And then I got married, I met somebody else and I got married.

When did trouble begin then?

After the end of the first year of marriage. I think the novelty wore off.

Yes.

But she came from a very good family.

Was she your own age?

Yes.

When you say the novelty wore off, did you start getting other kinds of sexual thoughts then?

No, not really, just boredom really.

I see, but you remained faithful to her.

Oh yes.

And what happened?

Well I – I decided that I'd had both types of life and I was determined to keep the marriage together.

When you say you had had both types of life you told me that you had had both types of sex, but had you mixed in what's called gay circles?

No, not at all.

Went to gay bars?

Not in those days, no.

So it was mostly an idea in your mind, a feeling more than anything actually happening?

Yes it was. Also in those days it was not like it is now, where you can do exactly as you please and no one would question you. In those days it was the expected thing for you to be married and stay married.

Did anyone know about this homosexual feeling of yours?

No. But one or two close friends.

Did your wife know?

She did when we were divorced, but not during our marriage.

How did she come to know when you were divorced?

I told her. I felt that she deserved to know.

Has she remarried?

She has remarried, yes.

And so you really think that this incident in your childhood had an important effect?

I know it did, basically because losing my mother at 11 years old and not having anybody to take her place.

How did she die?

She died from a tumour of the brain.

What had that [her death] to do with it?

Well, had my mother been there and I'd had the love and attention I know for a fact that I would never have wanted the attention of anybody else.

So that was why you went off with him?

That's right.

And you felt you did wrong, you said you felt guilty or something.

At the beginning I felt guilty, but a couple of years later of course I didn't feel guilty at all.

What made the change?

Because at the time I thought I was the only one; as I got older I realised that I was not a freak, there were other people similar to myself.

I see. So really you are saying that you could have avoided this man, but because you were looking for affection you didn't.

Well, that's what I think ... It was at a very early age.

Yes. Now going back to this question of whether you are homosexual or heterosexual, these are Kinsey scales. [Page with Kinsey seven point scales displayed] First of all you think about your behaviour and then your feelings. But first your behaviour, would you say you have more homosexual behaviour than heterosexual?

Now, yes, yes.

So you would put yourself about here would you, 'predominantly' homosexual?

Yes, predominantly homosexual.

And if you were thinking about your feelings, would that be the same or different?

That would be the same.

So this has been the main worry about sex, homosexual feelings?

No, actually, it's not just that. I had a bad illness as well, a very serious illness.

Oh. What was that?

Renal failure.

How old were you when this happened?

I had total renal failure in 1974 [aged 36], but of course the illness was ten years before that. It went on a long time until it totally failed.

I see, and did this affect your sexuality?

Yes, because I was on dialysis. My marriage had just finished.

So you weren't in a position to look for sexual relationships?

No. I think my whole life would otherwise have been a lot different from what it is now.

In what way?

Well I would probably either have been married again or gone completely the other way.

I see. Now what's your view about whether it's harmful for older men to have contact with boys. Do you think this is harmful?

I think it is very very harmful, there couldn't be anything more serious.

And what about boys' contacts with older women?

No, that's quite all right as far as I am concerned, I think they should be given every encouragement.

Did you ever have any such experience?

No. I only wish I did.

Is there anything else do you think that is relevant to all this?

Not really. All I would like to say is that if I had a choice, of being able to choose, I would definitely choose heterosexual.

Why is that?

Because you lead an orderly, respectable life.

Yes. Have you ever had trouble with the law?

No, no.

This example illustrates the difficulty of deducing cause and effect from a personal history. The man was convinced that it was because he was starved of affection that he allowed himself to be seduced by an older man and that that was why he eventually became predominantly homosexual, an outcome he felt was regrettable and unhappy. That is not necessarily the most plausible explanation. He may well have had a predisposition in that direction, for, notwithstanding his strong guilt feelings about it, he was already erotically very responsive when the 'seduction' occurred and he continued to be homosexually responsive at adolescence and again as a young man in the RAF, in spite of coexisting heterosexual opportunities and experiences.

5.2 Lasting homosexual relationships

The present survey was limited to information supplied by men who had once been the younger participant in adult-child sexual contact. The published accounts of self-admitted adult homosexual paedophiles frequently refer to long-standing sexual friendships with boys which are said to have been educational and socially beneficial without interfering with normal heterosexual development (Wilson, 1981; Sandfort, 1987). We found no evidence of this, since none of the heterosexual respondents reported continuing sexual contact with an adult male when they were young. This might be because such events are rare in the histories of heterosexuals, or because heterosexuals are reluctant to confess such experiences to survey investigators.

Dr Edward Brongersma (1987), a Dutch authority on the subject, who has amassed a large collection of paedophile case histories, would doubtless argue that if such events do not emerge in the reminiscences of heterosexual men it is probably because they are being less than frank. He was good enough to put us in touch with an articulate and successful English businessman who was willing to be interviewed and to provide a written account of a type of experience that our samples had not revealed. Here are extracts from these notes:

I am a 63-year-old married man ... I live contentedly with my wife to whom I have been married for 31 years. We have raised three sons and one daughter who was killed in a car crash at the age of 21. Our three sons have all left home, are aged from 19 to 28, and are all well balanced and achieving people.

I have enjoyed orthodox sexual intercourse hundreds, indeed thousands of times during my adult life. Before marriage I had some experimental affairs with girls and in particular remember a night spent with a quite lovely girl of 17 in my bed when I was about 25 ...

From the age of about 12 I had had grand passions for young girls – this running concurrently but alternating with having crushes on other boys. My first love was a frizzy-haired girl of about 11 named Margaret. I can't remember the names of others but there were a few. The relationships were entirely chaste but powerful all the same. I don't remember girls featuring strongly during my three years in the RAF. It was somewhat a society of 'lads' – flying aeroplanes and swilling beer.

After the RAF I ... had romantic attachments with one or two girl students and one very intense affair with a brunette ...

Later I complied with all the requirements of good citizenship. I married and played my part in making that marriage a lasting success. I shared in the birth and raising of four normal and achieving children ... I have helped to provide a stable background for our children, I worked hard, paid my way and my taxes and set not a bad example of ordinary good behaviour. Sorry if that sounds smug.

The account describes a conventional, upper-middle-class upbringing by caring and well-intentioned but strict and emotionally aloof parents.

Most of the time [my brother and I] were required to be quiet, to be well behaved, to be clean, to be punctual at meals – and so on ...

I think I first learned to masturbate at the age of 9. My mother caught me doing it one morning while I was still in bed and withdrew in shock to insist that my father do something about it. I believe I was 10 at the time. He stood beside my bed and told me what a damaging thing it was to do. He finished by saying that if I didn't stop, 'it' might have to be cut off. I continued as before but took care not to be caught again.

By the age of 10 he was having 'dry orgasms' and masturbation fantasies centred around male sex games. He and two other boys enjoyed the privacy of a playroom where 'I used to play elaborate games which had a Biggles-like story line and often ended with somebody's penis being taken out.' From the age of 12 he attended an all-male public school where homosexual horseplay was commonplace.

I became aware that there was a sexual subculture in action. Enormous and varied activity was going on although not all boys were involved in it. It was a common sight to see a small boy running and weaving through the crowded playground chased by a bigger one with the inevitable ending – the small boy being marched or carried to the lavatory block and there made to submit to sex ... Another time I came across a group of some five boys standing in a semi-circle with their penises out. They were all mature enough to be able to ejaculate and the contest was to see who could fire his semen the furthest. The main reaction to all these events was laughter. I don't remember these experiments in sex ever being heavy or oppressive.

At school I learned that some of the masters were having sexual affairs with boys ... [One master] used to wrestle me to the ground and make noises into my ear which went with a good deal of slobbering over me. He used to take me out in his car blackberrying ... Once he came into my bedroom to look at some of my homework and, having jammed the lid of a tin under the door, pulled me down face upwards to lie on top of him on my bed. I would have been about 14 at this time and was astonished (but not alarmed) at the large size of his penis. He had just pulled my trousers down and was starting the usual routine of moving his penis between my thighs when my brother attempted to open the door to see what was going on. The tin lid held long enough for us both to leave the bed and tidy our clothes up. I could see that [the master] had had a considerable fright.

To this point all the sex acts I had experienced had been 'quickies' with no real relationship developing. However a boy with whom I had been friendly since I was about 7 told me repeatedly of a man he knew who wanted to meet me. Due to shyness I was not very cooperative about this but eventually ran into the man by chance ... A smartly dressed smiling man of about 40 ... I was 14, but a young 14 and rather immature I think and was rather overawed by the meeting.

'R' asked me if I would like to see an underground railway being built, going right up to the tunnel face. I said 'Yes' and he said 'Let's talk to your parents about it' ... They had quite a long and cordial chat and my friendship with the grown-up R was formalised.

The visit to the underground site followed very quickly. He drove me in the Alvis, which was a thrill in itself for me because I was fascinated by cars ... Almost as soon as the drive began R began to ask me about what sex practices we indulged in at school. The more I told him the more he obviously approved. I found that very interesting and reassuring ...

He took me to his office ... He pottered about the office for a while beside me, and then very suddenly put his arms around me and began a lengthy hugging and kissing session whispering passionate endearments into my ears. I was amazed at this and wondered for a while if he had gone of his head. It is interesting to reflect that at school, although it was commonplace for boys to have 'crushes' on each other and very common for sex acts to take place, nobody ever said 'I love you' or went in for passionate kissing – indeed any kissing to my knowledge.

Inevitably my trousers came down ... He inspected me, played about with me but I don't think brought me to orgasm ...

He lived as a bachelor about two miles from my family ... and took tu dropping in quite often for a cup of tea with my mother and, of course, me.

Early in the relationship he took me out one evening in the Alvis after dark. We parked in a lane by a common and he masturbated me ... [He] asked me if I was ready 'to come'. When I said I was he crouched down and fellated me. It was the first time I had heard of such a thing but I remember enjoying the experience.

I spent much of the weekends with him, often staying overnight. Other boys often came to the house and later I realised he was almost certainly taking them into a bedroom or somewhere out of my sight to have quick sex with them. Also I became very useful to R as a procurer of boys – although I didn't know that was the role I was playing. I would bring young friends to his house and then find myself allotted a task to take me out of the way ... I for the most part didn't even suspect. Very naive of me, I confess.

From time to time R asked me to do things I didn't want to do. He tried to penetrate me once from behind but I disliked the preliminaries and he didn't persist. Also I declined to fellate him – and again he accepted that ...

On the other hand he used to wonder whether he was doing bad things in the eyes of God ... This was the cue for me to assure him that he wasn't doing harm, a view which I did hold. It is a view I still hold.

There is a point to make about the liberating nature of my friendship. My parents were strict, they were also narrow-minded although, of course, well intentioned. I had always felt a disappointment to my father whose disapproval and authoritarianism were never far away. To make this worse I was a very sexual human being from the age of 10 or younger. My grown-up friend fulfilled several emotional needs. He admired me to a point which was almost absurd and, presumably, off-set my father's aloofness; then he banished all my stored away guilt feelings about sexual pleasure; he provided me with a great deal of knowledge about sex but also about other aspects of life like music, and broadened my horizons enormously – almost every weekend there would be a programme of things to do.

The sex aspect of my relationship with R had died out when I was about 17 and still, I think, looking young for my age.

It all came to an end when a boy – a 9 or 10-year-old – went home from R's house and complained to his mother ... He was sentenced to three years in prison and it emerged that he had relations with over 2,000 boys. By this time I was 19 and in the RAF ...

The man who befriended me had many youthful partners in sex and I saw some of them later in life when the signs were all of sexual orthodoxy. I believe I mentioned previously one boy, slightly older than me, who tried to introduce me to the paedophile man, an effort that was overtaken by [our meeting independently]. I met that boy again when we were both about 40. He was with his wife, to whom he was clearly devoted and they had their two children with them. The days of paedophile procuring were long since past.

I would like to end by making two obvious but neglected points ... One is that a sexually eager child brought up in a narrow-minded family can be profoundly relieved to find a friendly adult to whom sex is not sinful or harmful. Second, sexually active children may much enjoy sex with an admired and caring grown-up, and to describe such enjoyment as abusive is to stand logic on its head.

[As to] the question whether some paedophile or homosexual inclinations have remained with me: of homosexual inclinations the answer is no, none have remained. Of paedophile inclinations the answer is yes. However, I have concluded that paedophile feelings, fondness for children, liking to be with them and to cuddle and fondle them – is not abnormal unless it is obsessive, and can be seen in most imaginative and sensitive adults.

In contrast to such benign outcomes one must also consider cases in which serious damage is said to have been produced. In clinical experience men troubled by recollections of incidents of sexual molestation in childhood are not uncommon. For example, a man of 27 was referred to the writer on account of depression, suicidal attempts and fears that he might attack women. Recently he had become obsessively preoccupied with memories of an incident when he was aged 7. He had been urinating in a public lavatory when a man pulled him into a cubicle, undressed him, fellated him and then made him do the same in return, forcing him to swallow semen in the process. He says that he did not understand what it was all about at the time, but was terrified. The man wanted to meet him again the following week, but he kept away. Ne never told his parents or anyone else what had happened to him. He felt guilty about it and thought that he would be blamed.

These painful memories had come flooding back suddenly some two months previously when a girlfriend of 22, with whom he had hoped to have sexual intercourse, had unbuttoned his clothing and fellated him, thereby reminding him of what had happened to him before. Ever since he had been unable to get these thoughts out of his mind. He felt wretched and had taken an overdose of his prescribed sedative in an attempt either to kill himself or to get some help.

As is almost always the case, this patient had many other unrelated problems to explain why the sexual incident assumed such great significance. He was mentally impaired, unable to read properly, had enormous difficulty in communicating, was envious of his more successful siblings and very frustrated because he had never managed to achieve heterosexual intercourse owing to his shyness and unattractiveness. His troubles had been rendered worse by teasing and bullying when he was a schoolboy and by having parents with whom he felt he could not talk freely and who did not seem to appreciate his efforts to improve. He felt guilty about his interest in heterosexual pornography, about his desire to touch women and his frequent erections in response to sexual thoughts.

The incident at the age of 7 was linked in his mind with another at the age of 19 when he had been persuaded by a young man to engage in mutual masturbation. He feared the two incidents might mean he was 'queer'. He explained that on two occasions he had been tempted to pounce on women and sexually assault them because, as he put it, he had never been able to see a naked woman.

This man's confused, guilt-ridden attitudes, his feelings of masculine insecurity and ineptitude, and the gloomy thoughts reflecting his state of depression, could not all be blamed on early sexual molestation. Nevertheless, the episode provided a focus for his worries and to that extent made a significant contribution to his distress.

5.3 A homosexual sample

In an effort to follow up impressions obtained from interviews with those few students who said they were homosexual, it was decided to give the questionnaire to some known homosexual men. In all, 22 completed questionnaires were collected. Because of the methods of distribution it is impossible to specify a response rate, but in any event this would not be particularly informative since the self-selected nature of the population created its own bias. Questionnaires were distributed to 40 patrons emerging from a gay bar, of which 7 were returned, but an indeterminate number of men were able to avoid being handed a questionnaire and 3 refused to accept one. The 'Gay Teenagers' Group in London were given 20 questionnaires, of which 11 were returned completed. At a talk at a gay club 5 members of the audience volunteered to accept a questionnaire and 3 returned one. Finally, one questionnaire was completed by an acquaintance of the investigators.

The 22 respondents ranged in age from 16 to 44, 9 being 36 or more and another 9 being under 21. They were mostly from middle-class backgrounds with fathers in professional or managerial occupations. The apparent scarcity of working-class men among volunteers from gay men's organisations was noted in a previous survey (Thompson *et al.*, 1985).

As many as 14 (63.6 per cent) of the 22 homosexual respondents reported some relevant experience, 9 with males, 1 with a female and 4 with both male and female. These figures are in conformity with the expectation that homosexual men would have an unusually high incidence of early sexual experiences with older males, but they cannot provide confirmation of this because of the self-selected nature of the sample. Nevertheless, descriptions of the circumstances of the occurrences and of reactions at the time might give some indication of differences in early sexual confrontations according to future sexual orientation.

Of the 11 respondents who gave written descriptions of one or more boyhood incidents with an older male, at least 5 were clear that they had undergone an unsolicited and unwanted experience.

One man described what amounted to a true assault when he was 13: 'I was sexually and physically assaulted by somebody I knew [aged 18]. He made suggestions, both physical and verbal, and when I refused he became violent and forceful. I did not give any sexual advances towards him beforehand or then that I was aware of. Eventually I managed to escape after being bruised and hurt mentally. I never told anybody because I thought they wouldn't believe me and I didn't want to go through it again – i.e. police pressing charges.' He rated the incident 'very disturbing'.

Another man described a 'very disturbing' incident when he was 10. 'We went to stay with my mother's aunt and uncle. During the night my uncle came into my room and took down my pyjamas and touched my private parts.' The same respondent reported some 15 to 30 occasions of sexual contact in later years with older males, describing one such incident at age 15 as 'enjoyable'. 'I went to a gay club in London and I was picked up. The man [aged 25] and I went to his flat. We then had sex.'

A 21-year-old respondent recalled an incident with a man of 46 or more when he was 12 which he found 'disturbing'. 'A neighbour who I got Sunday papers for came to the door naked on one occasion. He kissed me. He also asked if he could take photos of me naked. When he kissed me I was shocked. At a later date I told him not to do it again.'

A 20-year-old respondent recalled an incident at the age of 16 with a man of 35 which he found 'very disturbing' and a later incident at the age of 15 with a man of 21 which was 'enjoyable'. In the earlier incident, 'The male was my theatrical agent and he asked my parents if I would pose for some modelling shots. When we got to his house he asked me to undress and put on a pair of shorts, which I did. Suddenly he pushed me down onto the bed and sat on my chest and began to play with me. He then lowered his mouth onto my penis and began to suck. I told him I wanted to go to the toilet and he let me get dressed.' In the later incident, 'I was going to the toilet in a public lavatory when a man leaned over and put his hand on my penis. He asked me if I would like to come back to his flat. I did and after horseplay he screwed me. He then dropped me off home.'

A fifth respondent described an incident at the age of 13. 'I came in [Woolworths] buying something. This man was hovering around looking at me. Every time I moved to another counter I found he was looking at me. I got outside the store, went to the library and he followed me there. Well I got worried then ... as I stood at the bus stop he stood behind me and opened his coat and pushed against me.' Frightened, he spoke to a woman in the bus queue saying he thought he was being followed. 'She put her arm round my shoulder and he bolted.'

This respondent recalled one other incident when he was 16 and out cycling on his own looking for blackberries. A man stopped in his car, ostensibly to ask the way. He found the man sexually attractive and had thoughts that it would be nice to cuddle him. Nothing happened then, but he kept thinking about this man and hoping he would see him again. He did see him again and the man proposed going into a field, but he got frightened and declined, remembering stories of children being murdered in such situations.

A respondent aged 33 recalled two incidents; both happened when he was 15, one with a man and one with a woman, both of which he rated as 'pleasant' on his questionnaire. 'I was walking home one night about 6 o'clock (it was still light) and an Indian man [about 35] asked me to show him the way somewhere. I did, and then he asked me to have a cup of tea in his house. We went to the bedroom and he started touching me and masturbating and ejaculated over my slacks. I remember wondering if my mother would notice when she washed them. Though I didn't find the man attractive I was glad the incident had taken place because I had always been attracted to men and to other boys at school.'

In response to questions during a subsequent interview he explained that the man, whose English accent wasn't good, had asked to be shown where a particular road was and obviously wanted to be taken there. He obliged, but on arrival the man said it wasn't the right house, but that his own place was nearby and would he like to come in for tea. He accepted, the man made tea and then said, 'We can drink it in the bedroom.' Immediately the boy 'knew perfectly well what was going to happen', but until then he hadn't thought the situation unusual, although he now realised the need for directions to a place close by was certainly a ploy. He was not much sexually aroused by the encounter, but 'quite excited' and probably 'a bit scared' and 'a bit tense' because it was something that had never happened before. It was his first experience of sex, apart from with people his own age: 'There's a difference.' He left after the man ejaculated. He felt the incident had been 'very unromantic'. He saw the man again once or twice walking in the town. They said hello but did not arrange another meeting.

The incident with a woman happened later, but probably when he was still under 16. 'I worked in a nightclub on a couple of nights a week collecting glasses. I became friendly with the [male] manager and the [56-year-old woman] cashier and they took me out for a drink one night. I told them I thought I was gay and the woman said I should have some 'sex lessons' from her. The next week, after the club had closed and the staff had had their free drinks we went back to her house and she and I got into bed and the manager watched. I did manage to get an erection, but only by thinking about men.'

He explained at subsequent interview that his job at the club was at weekends and his parents did not know about it. He used to tell them he was out with friends. When the staff were drinking together after the club closed the woman cashier would sometimes take off her clothes and serve drinks in her tights. When he went home with her and her friend all three got into the bed. They knew he was gay and he was not nervous, but he thought it 'bizarre'. He found it 'enjoyable', but 'didn't get much out of it' and didn't want a repetition. The man who had mostly just watched was also gay and drove him home afterwards and then kept telephoning suggesting a meeting and failing to turn up. He was disappointed by that because he found the man attractive. Asked if the experience had confirmed he didn't want sex with a woman he replied, 'No, I had a girlfriend at the time.'

Other respondents with experiences to report also made clear that at the time they had known quite well what they wanted or did not want by way of sexual contact with an older person. For example, one man of 34 recalled that at the age of 14, 'A stranger approached me and took me to a basement of a derelict building and jerked me off. He wanted to give me money. I refused. It was all a bit sordid and he wasn't very attractive and I suppose it was a bit dangerous.' He rated the experience as 'slightly' disturbing.

A 36-year-old respondent recalled experiences at the age of 14 to 15 with a 50-year-old man. He rated his feelings as 'indifferent'. 'It was a classic case of the local vicar touching up members of the scout group. The members of the group all knew about it and regarded it as a big joke.'

One 44-year-old man recalled as 'enjoyable' an experience when he was only 9 with a man of 30. 'The older man involved was extremely lonely and isolated. He sought the affection of young boys, and several of my friends became involved with him. He basically liked to fondle while relieving his own tensions.' This same respondent described a later experience with a man of 35 when he was 15 as 'disturbing'. 'Having commenced working in London at the age of 15 I was picked up by an American tourist who subjected me to sexual practices with which I was not familiar. I found this distressing.'

Finally, a respondent aged 25 ranked as 'indifferent' an encounter at 15 with a man of 28. 'I was in a public toilet where I knew such activities occurred and I was confronted by what I considered to be a very attractive (both physically and sexually) man. I knew at the time I was gay but because of no experiences with older men panicked and left quickly but regretted it afterwards. I do remember being *strongly* sexually attracted to men when I was 11 to 16 years old. My only experiences at that time were with other boys the same age.' This man, who also reported having once been sexually approached by an older woman, commented, 'Women do not offend/threaten in any way but do *nothing* for me sexually.'

*

The impression gained from these homosexual respondents was that they had been unusually open to homosexual approaches, especially as teenagers, while at the same time being well aware of the partners and practices that interested them and of the confrontations that were unwanted or frightening. So far as they go their comments tend to support the view that many boys exercise considerable self-determination in their sexual interchanges with adults. As with the experiences described by heterosexual respondents, the incidents were overwhelmingly attempts at seduction rather than assaults.

6

Conclusion and Implications

6.1 Findings

Methodological difficulties set limits to what can be discovered through retrospective surveys on sexual topics. Obtaining access to suitable samples was difficult. Students' rights to privacy were jealously guarded by authorities. Members of the public sometimes took offence at unsolicited postal enquiries. The response rate from different groups was varied. Usually a lower response rate went with a higher prevalence of positive reports, suggesting that individuals with nothing to report were less likely to reply. Personal contacts achieved the highest level of cooperation.

It would seem that the kind of incidents reported were sufficiently impressive to be retained in memory indefinitely. In the community samples the older respondents were just as likely as the younger ones to recall approaches from adults when they were boys. Analysis of the questionnaires returned by students, by virtue of their internal consistency and conformity to a general pattern, suggested that they had been completed conscientiously. Only one attempted hoax was discovered. Students who were prepared to be interviewed provided the most information on the detailed circumstances of boys' sexual confrontations with adults. Reinterpretations of the past in the light of present preconceptions and illusory memories could not be eliminated, but most of the accounts obtained appeared frank and factual.

A high prevalence of recollections of boyhood sexual incidents with adults was obtained. In the student inquiry, among the more cooperative groups in which a half of the subjects returned a completed questionnaire, 32.5 per cent of respondents claimed to remember at least one sexual experience with an adult or much older person when they were boys under 16. On the very conservative assumption that no more than 10 per cent of the students who failed to reply had anything positive to report, that would still mean a prevalence of at least 1 in 5 men able to recall a relevant incident. If experiences with older females were discounted, that might reduce the prevalence of boyhood experiences involving men to 1 in 7 or 8.

The electoral register samples were probably unreliable on contacts

119

with women, but 1 in 6 respondents recalled some boyhood experience
with a man, and that proportion was seemingly unrelated to the response
rate. Even so, to allow for possible non-response bias, once again a figure
of 1 in 8 would be a conservative estimate of the prevalence of
recollections of early sex experiences with men.

Prevalence rates of more than 10 per cent imply enormous numbers of
individuals. Precise estimates are not of great practical importance. It is
more important to know what kinds of sexual involvement are in question
and what is the likelihood of adverse effects. The findings from the
detailed enquiry among students could be regarded as reassuring. Unlike
impressions gained from clinical studies or from cases dealt with by police
or from retrospective surveys of samples of women, nearly all the
incidents with boys concerned encounters with adults outside the
immediate family. No instances of parental sexual molestation were
reported (except by the one would-be hoaxer). The use of force, brutality
or even threats was very rare. No significant physical injuries were
reported by anyone and none of the 67 students who reported incidents
had been subjected to significant violence.

Of the adults involved with boys only a minority were middle-aged or
elderly. Most of the encounters with women were when boys were
pubertal and were recollected as enjoyable, although that was not the
case with the exceptional instances where boys under 11 were concerned.
Most of the incidents with men consisted of approaches, touching or
propositioning in public places or at school by male teachers. Most of
these attempted contacts were rejected and feelings at the time were
described as indifference, mild anxiety or annoyance. Few such incidents
were mentioned to parents or were said to have had any lasting effect. In
this last respect the men differed markedly from women similarly
questioned, many of whom expressed more serious and sometimes
continuing negative feelings.

A few students had had repeated contacts with the same man, but on
the whole extended sex-based friendships were reported only by those
interviewed students who classed themselves as homosexual or bisexual
or who had experienced a protracted homosexual phase (as in Cases 239
and 050). Our findings suggest that, apart from this minority, boys in
general are uninterested or resistant in the face of sexual advances from
adult men. Most incidents were described as off-putting rather than
seductive, and approaches from the elderly elicited particularly negative
reactions. Paedophiles who find boys more welcoming (O'Carroll, 1980,
p. 47) are probably being highly selective in whom they approach or
particularly adept at communicating with youngsters. Their claims in
this regard may be exaggerated, but so also may be the accounts of some
adult heterosexuals who report that as boys they instantly repulsed
homosexual propositioning.

In the case of one or two respondents, who were currently confused
about their sexuality, early experiences with homosexuals may have
exacerbated their uncertainties. Some of those who remembered

incidents when they were very young had reacted less negatively than older boys to approaches from men, possibly because at the time they did not appreciate the significance of the behaviour or the great social stigma attached to it. It is possible that intra-familial incidents and forcible sexual assaults were under-reported in this study because they were too painful to recall. It would need a remarkable degree of under-reporting, however, to invalidate the finding that most of the incidents that collectively produce alarming prevalence statistics are relatively innocuous.

There was some suggestion from the present findings that urban living, working-class origin, uncohesive families and relative lack of supervision exposed boys to increased likelihood of sexual encounters with adults. Parental warnings were recalled more often by those who reported having had encounters, but it could be that their own habits, attitudes or circumstances had prompted such warnings. Interestingly, those who had had some relevant experience less often endorsed extreme views as to the harmfulness of sexual encounters with adults than did those who had had none.

The small supplementary enquiry among homosexual groups confirmed the impression that homosexual men tended to recall more boyhood contacts with adult males than did heterosexuals. Unlike the recollections of similar incidents described by heterosexuals, homosexual respondents often reported that their early experiences with men had been welcomed or even sought after, although some of them also recalled being subjected to approaches they definitely did not like.

Except for the very young, who might be bemused by approaches from older persons, it appeared that boys were generally aware of what they wanted or did not want, were not easily persuaded into unappealing sexual acts and had not much difficulty extricating themselves from unwelcome situations. Some respondents had been quite knowing about the homosexual predelictions of certain teachers. The great majority of the sexual incidents reported in the survey had never been mentioned to parents, sometimes because boys felt that they might incur blame for getting themselves into such a situation, more often because they were not in the habit of discussing their sex lives or thoughts with their parents.

Because the result runs counter to a popular stereotype, it is of interest that half (33) of the (67) students with some experience to report mentioned incidents with older females. The great majority occurred in their pubescent years and usually the boys had been willing if not eager participants.

There were some striking contrasts between the present findings and those from the previous surveys of women which had been conducted on similar lines (Nash & West, 1985). As might have been expected, the proportion of men who had some positive experience to report was smaller (37 per cent against 54 per cent in the student samples), and of course a majority of the men's reports, but virtually none of the women's reports, concerned involvements with older persons of the same sex. Very few of the incidents recalled by men, but a substantial minority of those recalled by women, involved family members. At the time of their earliest remembered experience, a half of the women had been under 12 years of age. Boys' encounters were more frequent in later years when they spent more time and had more contacts outside home.

Suggestions that children from unhappy, broken or poorly supervised home backgrounds were more vulnerable to sexual encounters with adults emerged from both the male and female surveys, and in both surveys only a tiny minority of the incidents recalled had been reported to police and not many had been mentioned to parents, especially not by boys. A particularly striking contrast between the sexes, however, was in their reactions to sexual confrontations. The reactions at the time remembered by women were predominantly of fear, unpleasant confusion and embarrassment, even though a substantial minority also recalled some positive feelings, such as enjoyment, amusement or curiosity. Men's remembered reactions were mostly either of indifference, tinged perhaps with slight anxiety, or of positive pleasure, the latter being particularly evident in contacts with the opposite sex. Of the interviewed women who had reported early experiences a substantial minority (22 per cent) described what they considered were consequential emotional or sexual effects that continued adversely into adult life. A few of the women were obviously distressed when recounting what had been for them highly traumatic incidents. In contrast, hardly any of the men reported any lasting effects, the only exceptions being one or two who were concerned about sexual orientation development and thought that homosexual experiences might have contributed some confusion.

6.2 Discussion

Caution is needed before drawing conclusions from one small-scale survey, but one implication of the present findings is that sexual encounters between boys and adults are surprisingly common, but that most such events appear to be relatively minor episodes with no particular consequences. Gross and continuing pressures, or entrapment in family situations from which they see no way of escape, seem to be rare, and certainly rarer than among girls. Serious cases of sexual abuse of young boys such as come before police and social workers, which may include venereal infection or ano-genital trauma in addition to great mental distress, are altogether different from any of the incidents revealed in this survey. The apparently alarming statistics produced from victim studies such as this cannot be taken to imply that really serious sexual abuse is common. Most incidents recalled by men were either relatively trivial approaches that were soon rejected or else minor indecencies which boys looked upon as unimportant. Undoubtedly, some incidents are welcomed and enjoyed by the younger participant.

These observations suggest a need for discretion in evaluating incidents that come to light through the suspicions or disapproval of a third party without any complaint from the child or young person. When a teacher or member of staff of a residential institution is found to have behaved indecently with boys in his charge it often emerges that he has had contact with many children over a long period, but that most of the boys involved have not taken the behaviour at all seriously or felt the need to make an official complaint. In such situations it may be unwise to over-dramatise what has happened or to do anything to suggest that the children are themselves abnormal or blameworthy.

Media publicity has led to greater awareness and to many more boys as well as girls being referred for suspected sex abuse. Abusive physical treatment of children has to reach a certain level before drastic action is taken, but mere suspicion of sexual irregularities is often held to warrant removal from home. These interventions can have consequences worse than the sexual indecencies involved. Social services have been alerted to this by the Cleveland controversy in the summer of 1987 when unusually large numbers of children were taken into care on the basis of disputed medical evidence of sex abuse. Whether justified or not, interventions sometimes let loose uncontrolled passions. One of the Cleveland fathers killed himself and another couple were said to have been unable to press for their children's return because fire raisers had destroyed the family home (*The Times*, 29 August 1987).

When the fate of an entire family rests on the outcome of inquiries into sexual incidents, the responsible authorities have good reason to proceed cautiously. Imprisonment of a parent, followed by divorce and all the social, economic and emotional problems associated with child-rearing by a single working adult, are consequences that often conflict with the child victim's wishes and perhaps his or her best interests. Indeed, anticipation of these eventualities, which is sometimes exploited by an offender to deter a child from speaking out, accounts for many failures to disclose. In England social workers are instructed to report disclosures to the police. The primary duty of police is to collect evidence for prosecution once allegations have been made, and the declared policy of prosecuting authorities is only in exceptional cases not to proceed against a suspect if the evidence seems likely to secure a conviction. In the Netherlands the confidential doctor system permits sexual situations to be reported in confidence and dealt with by a variety of medical and social services without reference to the criminal justice process, so long as all concerned cooperate and the misconduct is effectively brought to an end (Christopherson, 1981). In this way reactions can be adjusted to meet the different needs of particular cases. Of course the system does not meet with universal approval, a common objection being that if offenders go without being publicly disgraced and punished others will not be deterred from similar misbehaviour.

As this survey has confirmed, boys' sexual contacts are mostly with adults other than their parents, such as teachers, visitors to the house or strangers casually encountered. Disclosure in these cases does not usually pose a threat to the integrity of the family home, unless standards are so low or control so inadequate that the boy is considered to be exposed to 'moral danger' and therefore a candidate for a care order. Usually boys can distance themselves successfully from the events and let the adult bear all the responsibility for whatever improprieties may have occurred. Nevertheless, police may be called in and interrogations, to say nothing of physical examinations, can sometimes be traumatic, especially if the boy has been a participant, willingly or otherwise, in sexual activity on one or more occasions with a man. Suspicions about his own sexuality are aroused and he may suffer blame from elders and ridicule from peers.

None of the three interviewed students in the present survey, who remembered being questioned by police when they were boys, said they had been unduly upset by it, although the experience seemed to have impressed upon them the seriousness with which adults viewed the situation. One was confused and puzzled, not quite understanding what the fuss was about, another was struck by the policeman's violent comment, 'I'll castrate the bastard', the third found all the attention exciting. It may be that children are less worried by questioning than professionals believe. Tedesco & Schnell (1987) prepared a child victim questionnaire asking for impressions of the effects of investigation, rating helpfulness and harmfulness separately on seven point scales. 'Helpful' was scored much more often than 'harmful', especially by boys, but this may have been influenced by the fact that 'the vast majority' of these children were in some sort of therapy at the time. Having to give evidence in court was associated with more frequent ratings for harmfulness.

Treatment rather than punishment for the offender would sometimes be in the child victim's best interest, and in the interest of potential victims of the future, but demands for castration receive more publicity than demands for better treatment facilities, the scarcity of which limits what reforms in child abuse management can accomplish. Proposals to use video recordings to relieve the stress on child witnesses in court are being pursued, but in many criminal proceedings the sex victim remains simply a witness without a legal representative to protect his or her interests.

Admission to local authority Care following reported sexual abuse disrupts schooling and friendship networks, often breaks up the parental home and is highly stigmatising for the child. Ironically, it may even fail to provide protection from sexual molestation if the child is placed in an institution among youngsters with multiple behaviour problems and under the supervision of a variety of adult strangers, some of whom could have a sexual interest in children. Poppy Smith (1987) quotes one 20-year-old man who related how, when he was 13 and in a children's home, he hated the man who used to exploit him sexually under the noses of other members of staff who failed to notice or do anything to stop it. Children abused by foster parents or child-care workers may disclose the fact only years afterwards for the reason that at the time they calculate, possibly correctly, that their word would count for little against that of a professional.

Sensational media reports quoting high prevalence figures from population surveys of child sex abuse, juxtaposed with lurid examples of exceptional cruelty, promote an atmosphere of moral panic that can have unfortunate repercussions. Well-meaning instruction to children about the possible evil intentions of any adult they might meet, coupled with advice on how to make curt and rude replies if spoken to, or how to protect themselves by hitting out at vulnerable spots on a potential assailant's body, could encourage similar responses to peers or to relatives in situations where they would be inappropriate. Nicholas Tucker (1985) pointed out the danger of setting children against adults implicit in advice given in such books as the American *Sometimes I Need to Say No!* and the British *It's OK to Say No.*

The fear that some young people may exploit the moral climate in malicious allegations against innocent adults they dislike is not altogether unfounded (Jones, 1987). Meldrum & West (1983) give one example of a group of boys, annoyed by their headmaster's disciplinary methods, and inspired by a homosexual scandal that had attracted much press publicity, concocting a story of sexual molestation that narrowly missed bringing about the man's imprisonment. Exposure of the conspiracy occurred at a late stage when one of the witnesses broke down under cross-examination at the trial.

Panic about child sexual abuse, first in America and later in Europe, has given some unscrupulous parents an opportunity to embroil their children in their battles with an estranged spouse. Children can be persuaded or coerced into making spurious allegations in the interest of the adult's wish for revenge or demands for exclusive custody. Cantwell (1981), reviewing a small sample of unfounded allegations of child sexual abuse, notes that false testimony engineered by adults appears sadly more prevalent than stories invented by children spontaneously. Schuman (1986) and Bentovim *et al.* (1988) note how children caught up in the emotional turmoil of divorce may be manipulated into accepting sinister interpretations of paternal behaviour. On the other hand, children from cohesive homes have no particular motive and much to lose by making sexual allegations against a parent.

Young children, it is thought, very rarely invent stories of sexual molestation. In one exceptional example investigated by a psychologist (Trankell, 1972), a boy of 5 told his mother that some sweets he had brought home came from a window cleaning man whose penis he had been made to suck. Fortunately for the man concerned he was cleared by evidence that he had not encountered the boy as alleged. It emerged that the story, which the boy was suspiciously reluctant to repeat to outsiders, was motivated by his wish to escape blame for having left his trouser buttons undone and for having been out with a companion disapproved of by his mother. He had probably picked up information about the sexual act, or at least the words to describe it, from other boys. According to

Faller (1984) infantile fantasies about sex are usually recognisable by their vagueness and unreality. A genuine incident may receive confirmation from the infant's inappropriately crude sexual gestures towards adults, suggesting that experience has led to belief that this is an acceptable expression of affection: 'Thus a little girl may rub a male worker's penis, or wiggle her bottom on his lap. A boy who has been a victim of a female perpetrator may attempt to squeeze a nurse's breasts.'

Precocious sexuality, some indications of which featured in the histories given by one or two of our interviewed students, has been said to be one of the most common sequelae of sexual abuse. Data congruent with this hypothesis was noted in the Nash & West (1985) survey in relation to age at first sexual intercourse. Whether premature sexual developments sometimes precede and perhaps facilitate adult-child contacts is unclear, but their presence is not in itself proof of abuse by an adult. Children's interest in and exposure to explicit adult sexuality can come about in any number of ways. Nowadays information can be acquired and interest stimulated by viewing pornographic videos, not necessarily with the parents' knowledge and consent.

The present study reinforces the notion of great contrasts between the sexes. Men are more prone than women to attempt sexual approaches to children. Boys are less often targets of sexual molestation in their homes, and outside home they seem better able to protect themselves from predators. Premature heterosexual encounters are felt by boys as less shocking and far less likely to have bad effects, but confrontations with men may provoke anxiety in boys about their own susceptibility to homosexuality. In both boys and girls reactions can be idiosyncratic, extreme to what seem minor incidents or minimal to what seems major abuse. Individual and gender differences in response to these situations would be fruitful topics for research. It might be found that the differences in cultural expectations and sexual socialisation training for boys and girls make a large contribution to the phenomenon of sexual abuse.

Surveys such as this provide a corrective to some alarming misconceptions of the incidence and seriousness of diverse sexual incidents involving children. Events mistakenly thought rare, highly abnormal and likely to produce disastrous consequences tend to evoke unnecessarily extreme reactions. In the days before Kinsey's surveys demonstrated otherwise, homosexuals were depicted in mental health literature as a tiny and seriously pathological minority. The slightest involvement in homosexual behaviour was thought to portend lifelong social and sexual deviance. This research and others like it have shown that boys' sexual encounters with older males and females are far from rare and for the most part fairly innocuous. They also show what calm reflection might predict, namely that violence in these encounters is exceptional. Men who approach boys are generally looking for what amounts to a love relationship and they employ gradual and gentle persuasion. The average pederast is no more seeking a rape-style confrontation than is the average heterosexual when looking for a congenial adult partner. Severely punitive and counter-therapeutic attitudes towards those guilty of relatively minor indecencies with boys not only fail to promote more acceptable behaviour by the offenders subsequently, but can have bad repercussions on the boys involved, some of whom may feel they share the blame.

When properly interpreted, surveys suggest that the more serious kinds of adult-child sexual interaction are unusual. A needlessly worrying impression that incest is common might be derived from some inaccurate media coverage. Health professionals, a majority of whom, when asked to assess the prevalence of incest as defined by English law, put the figure at 1 in 500 or less, were probably being more realistic (Eisenberg & Glynn-Owens, 1987). In spite of recent clinical interest in these situations, sexual molestation of boys by adult relatives in the home appears also to be relatively rare. Although it was found that boys' sexual experiences with older females were more prevalent than might have been expected, these were rarely traumatic. The results echoed the conclusions of Fritz *et al.* (1981) that whereas the early sexual experiences of girls tend to be regarded as violation, those of boys are considered initiation.

These anodyne conclusions in no way contradict the occurrence or dispute the seriousness of sexual crimes against children of either sex, some of which are extraordinarily brutal and gruesome. We do not suggest that offences perpetrated by threat or force or moral blackmail are anything but decidedly harmful, nor do we argue that indecent behaviour by parents towards their children is other than confusing and worrying, especially when the child becomes old enough to appreciate the strength of the taboo. It is just that adult-child sexual interactions include a wide range of behaviours and situations, many of which are much less horrendous than the cases that turn up among police and clinic referrals or in sensational media accounts.

Appendix A

Questionnaire used with the student samples

UNIVERSITY RESEARCH SURVEY

This research is funded by the Mental Health Foundation, a charitable body, and is based at the University of Cambridge. We are collecting information on the sexual histories of males up to the age of sixteen. We are particularly interested in adult/boy sexual contats and their effects, about which little is known, although they occur more commonly than is generally realised. We hope this research will contribute to a general understanding of adult/child sexual contacts and towards alleviating problems of abuse when they occur.

We would be very grateful if you would fill in this questionnaire. Absolute confidentiality is guaranteed. All names and addresses supplied will be kept separately from completed questionnaires.

Although our particular interest is in adult/boy sexual relations it is also very important to have information from those who have not had any such experiences. So please remember that all completed questionnaires are of help.

Please return questionnaire in envelope provided

1. SECTION A

(1) What is your age?   ...Years ...Months

(2) In which area, town or city did you
live for the longest period until you were
sixteen?   ....

(3) How many adults lived in the
household where you were brought up?   Mother ... Father ...Others ...
                                                                              (please specify)

(4) How many brothers and sisters lived
with you?   Sisters ... Brothers ...

(5) Were there other children in the
household who were not brothers or
sisters, if so how many?   ....

(6) Did you live with both your natural
parents up to the age of sixteen?   Yes ... No ...

(7) If you answered no to the last
question, please state age and circum-
stances when a break occurred   ....
(e.g. at age five parents separated).   ....

(8) What were the occupations of your   Mother ....
parents or guardians?   Father ....

The next section asks about your sexual history. If there are any of these
questions which you prefer not to answer leave them blank, but please return the
form all the same, if possible stating in the space below the reason why you do not
wish to answer. If you do not wish to complete a questionnaire, but are willing to
be interviewed, please complete the last page.

2. SECTION B

Please note. This section is concerned *only* with the period before you were eleven
years old.

(1a) Before you were eleven did you
have any form of sexual experience with
a girl of your own age? (Please include
exposure of private parts as well as other
forms of sexual contact.)   Yes ... No ...

(1b) If you answered yes, what age were
you when this first happened?   ... Years

(2a) During this period were you ever
approached by a woman who you think
was older than sixteen in a way you
thought was sexual but which *did not*
lead to any sexual contact? (e.g. indecent
suggestions, 'flashing' etc.)   Yes ... No ...

(2b) If yes, approximately how many
times did this happen?   ....

(3a) During this period were you ever
approached by a man who you think was
older than sixteen in a way you thought
was sexual but which *did not* lead to any
sexual contact? (e.g indecent sug-
gestions, 'flashing' etc.)   Yes... No...

(3b) If yes, approximately how many
times did this happen?   ....

(4a) Did you have any form of sexual
contact with a woman who you think
was older than sixteen? (Include mutual
masturbation, the person touching your
private parts in a way you thought was
sexual as well as any other type of
contact which you considered then or
consider now as sexual.)   Yes ... No ...

(4b) If yes, approximately how many
times did this happen?   ....

(5a) Did you have any form of sexual
contact with a man who you think was
older than sixteen? (Include mutual
masturbation, the person touching your
private parts in a way you thought was
sexual as well as any other type of
contact which you considered then or
now as sexual.)   Yes ... No ...

(5b) If yes, approximately how many
times did this happen?   ....

(6) What age were you when you first
ejaculated, this may have happened
spontaneously (e.g. a wet dream) or
through experimenting with masturbation? Even if you were older than
eleven please give an approximate age.   ...... Years

(7) If you had any form of sexual experience during this period with either a male or female who you think was older than sixteen (i.e. if you answered 'yes' to questions 2, 3, 4 or 5), try to answer the following questions. If you had more than one experience choose the one which left the greatest impression and answer the questions with reference to that occasion.

What age were you?   ...... Years

Was the other person male or female?   Male ... Female ...

About what age was he or she?   ...... Years

Did you know him or her beforehand?   Yes ... No ...

How did you find the experience? (ring   Very disturbing, Disturbing
the word which fits best)   Indifferent, Pleasant, Enjoyable

After it happened did you tell anyone?   Yes ... No ...

Who did you tell?   ....

If you did tell anyone, did their reaction   Felt better ...
affect your feelings about the   Felt worse ...
experience? (please tick the phrase   No change ...
which fits best)

Try to say in a few words what happened on this occasion. Please use the space below:

3. SECTION 3

Please note. This section is concerned *only* with the period from when you were eleven to sixteen years old.

(1a) Did you have sexual experiences
with girls of around the same age as
yourself during this period?   Yes ... No ...

(1b) If yes, did these experiences include
sexual intercourse?   Yes ... No ...

(2a) During this period were you ever
approached by a woman who you think
was older than eighteen in a way you
thought was sexual but *did not* lead to
any sexual contact? (e.g. indecent sug-
gestions, 'flashing' etc.)   Yes ... No ...

(2b) If yes, approximately how many
times did this happen?   ....

(3a) During this period were you ever approached by a man who you think was older than eighteen in a way you thought was sexual but *did not* lead to any sexual contact? (e.g. indecent suggestions, 'flashing' etc.)   Yes ... No ...

(3b) If yes, approximately how many times did this happen?   ....

(4a) Did you have any form of sexual contact with a woman who you think was older than eighteen? (Include mutual masturbation, the person touching your private parts in a way you thought was sexual as well as any other type of contact which you considered then or consider now as sexual.)   Yes ... No ...

(4b) If yes, approximately how many times did this happen?   ....

(5a) Did you have any form of sexual contact with a man who you think was older than eighteen? (Please include exposure of private parts, mutual masturbation, the person touching your private parts in a way that you thought was sexual as well as any other type of contact which you considered then or consider now as sexual.)   Yes ... No ...

(5b) If yes, approximately how many times did this happen?   ....

(6) If you had any form of sexual experience from when you were eleven to when you were sixteen with either a man or a woman who you think was older than eighteen (i.e. if you answered 'yes' to questions 2, 3, 4 or 5), try to answer the following questions. If you had more than one experience choose the one which left the greatest impression and answer the questions with reference to that occasion.

What age were you?   ...... Years

Was the other person a man or a woman?   Man ... Woman ...

About what age was he or she?   ... Years

Did you know him or her beforehand?   Yes ... No ...

How did you find the experience? (ring the word which fits best)	Very disturbing, Disturbing Indifferent, Pleasant, Enjoyable
After it happened did you tell any one?	Yes ... No ...
Who did you tell?	....
If you did tell anyone, did their reaction affect your feelings about the experience?	Felt better ... Felt worse ... No change ...

Try to say in a few words what happened on this occasion. Please use the space below:

4. SECTION D

(1) If you did have any sexual experiences with anyone who was much older than you *at any age before you were sixteen*, please try to answer the following questions:

Do you feel that it has made your sexual
life more difficult for you?   Yes ... No ...

Do you feel that it has made your sexual
life less difficult for you?   Yes ... No ...

Do you feel that it has had no effect on
your sexual life?   Yes ... No ...

Are there are areas of your life were you
feel that these sexual experiences have   ....
made a difference, please specify?   ....

(2) Please use the space below if there are any comments you would like to make about sexual involvement of adults with children:

Thank you for filling in this questionnaire. We would like to interview people who have filled in this questionnaire. We hope you are willing and, if so, please fill in your name and address where you can be contacted. Interviews will be conducted by one of the two researchers and can be arranged at your home or in a private room in the London or Cambridge area, again we must stress that all information will be treated in the strictest confidence. Tear off the address and sent it in an envelope separate from the returned questionnaire if you wish for stricter security.

Name: ....

Address: ....

....

Telephone number: ....

If you can be contacted by telephone please indicate the best time to ring:

Appendix B
Questionnaire used with the electoral register samples

First some information about yourself. (You cannot be identified from this information)

Put a tick in the appropriate box

Where did you live *mainly* as a child?	England/Scotland/ Wales/N. Ireland	☐
	Eire	☐
	Elsewhere	☐
Are you male or female?	Male	☐
	Female	☐
What is your age?	Under 20	☐
	20–30	☐
	30–40	☐
	40–50	☐
	50–60	☐
	Over 60	☐
Are you married or living as married?	Married/Living as Married	☐
	Single	☐
Do you have any children of your own?	One child	☐
	Two children	☐
	More than two	☐
	No children	☐
Most people see themselves as belonging to a social class. Which would you say you belonged to?	Upper middle	☐
	Middle	☐
	Upper working	☐
	Working	☐
	Poor	☐
	Don't know	☐
Which class would you say your family belonged to when you were a child?	Upper middle	☐
	Middle	☐
	Upper working	☐
	Working	☐
	Poor	☐
	Don't know	☐

These are some things which happen to children and young people. If any of these happened to you put a tick in the 'yes box' otherwise put a tick in the 'no box'.

You may find some of these questions embarrassing but remember this questionnaire is completely confidential.

	Yes	No
My mother told me the facts of life	☐	☐
My father told me the facts of life	☐	☐
My childhood was less happy than most children's	☐	☐
My childhood was similar to most children's	☐	☐
My childhood was more happy than most children's	☐	☐
My parents warned me not to talk to strangers	☐	☐
An adult woman (someone over 18) made sexual suggestions to me when I was younger than 16	☐	☐
An adult man (someone over 18) made sexual suggestions to me when I was younger than 16	☐	☐
An adult woman touched my sex parts in a sexual way when I was younger than 16	☐	☐
An adult man touched my sex parts in a sexual way when I was younger than 16	☐	☐
When I was younger than 16 a woman older than 18 exposed herself to me in a sexual way	☐	☐
When I was younger than 16 a man older than 18 exposed himself to me in a sexual way	☐	☐
Before I was 16 I had sex with a woman over 18	☐	☐
Before I was 16 I had sex with a man over 18	☐	☐

If you replied yes to any of these questions about sexual incidents with adults, how old were you when this first happened?   Aged......Years

Please say in a few words what happened. Use the space below:

Please give your opinions on the items listed below:

I think that sexual contacts between
women over 18 and boys under 16 are usually: Not harmful   ☐
                                                    Harmful   ☐
                                                    Very harmful   ☐
                                                    No opinion   ☐

I think that sexual contacts between men over 18
and boys under 16 are usually: Not harmful   ☐
                                      Harmful   ☐
                                      Very harmful   ☐
                                      No opinion   ☐

I think the law should deal in a similar way with
men and women over 18 who have sexual
contacts with boys under 16:   Agree   ☐
                                    Disagree   ☐
                                    No opinion   ☐

Use the space below for any further comments:

Thank you for filling in this questionnaire. *Whatever you have answered* it would help our research if you were willing to be interviewed. What you say will be strictly confidential and the interview can be arranged in your own home or elsewhere – wherever is most convenient for you.

If you *are* willing to be interviewed please complete the following:

My name is ....

Either   Please contact me on telephone no.............
                to arrange a convenient time and place.

Or   I do not have a telephone. Please contact me at
             Address: ....

             ....

             ....

             A convenient day and time would be ....

Now please return the questionnaire in the envelope provided

For office use only.

```
Research AB
Allocation AC
Batch AF

Comments
```

Part II

Adult Sexual Experiences with Children

C.K. Li

The research on which this work was based was carried out during the period from summer 1983 to the end of 1986 while I was at the University of Cambridge. The project was generously supported by a Commonwealth Scholarship from the Association of Commonwealth Universities, a research grant from Trinity College, Cambridge, and a Research Fellowship from St Edmund's College, Cambridge.

I wish to acknowledge the guidance provided by Professor D.J. West throughout the research, and would also like to thank Dr Martin Richards and Dr Kenneth Plummer for their helpful comments.

7

Adult-Child Sexual Contact
as a Social Problem

7.1 A highly sensitive issue

Sex between adults and children is a very sensitive issue, because it conjures up in one's mind an image of a child being sexually assaulted in a brutal manner by a callous stranger, and then left to die of fatal wounds and traumatic shock in a hidden ditch. In the 20 December 1985 issue of the *Guardian*, there was a report about a pensioner who, at the age of seventy-nine, got a life sentence for doing just that to a 7-year-old girl. The report says:

> He lured her to his old people's bungalow, ... sexually assaulted her, and then inflicted more than 70 wounds on her with a kitchen fork and breadknife.

The age of the perpetrator, far from being a mitigating factor, has added a terrifying dimension to the whole incident – a seemingly benign old man has turned out to be a child murderer.

An equally frightening observation is that organised child prostitution and pornography are becoming a serious social problem.[1] Perhaps the most unnerving, especially to parents of nursery-age children, is the recent case in California.[2] The McMartin Pre-School, hitherto a popular nursery school in Manhattan Beach, is alleged to be a place where young pupils have frequently been sexually abused:

> Up until last March, Virginia McMartin, 76, ran a prestigious preschool in Manhattan Beach, Calif. Then the police arrested McMartin, along with other staff members: her daughter, a grandson and granddaughter and three female employees. The authorities charged that for at least a decade, more than 100 children at the private school were fondled, sodomized and

---

[1] Examples of studies on this problem can be found in Burgess, Groth & McCausland (1981), Burgess (1984), Densen-Gerber & Hutchinson (1979), R. Lloyd (1979), Pierce (1984), Rush (1980), Sereny (1984), and Tyler & Stone (1985).

[2] This case is referred to in the Special Report on Sexual Abuse in the 14 May 1984 issue of *Newsweek*, and also the 18 November 1985 issue of the *Guardian* (p. 10).

raped, and there are suspicions that some of the tots may have been hired out for photography and prostitution. With growing numbers of working mothers and single parents, American society is increasingly dependent on day-care facilities, and the Manhattan Beach case still seems unbelievable to many people. How could such a thing go on for so long? Why didn't the children tell? (*Newsweek*, 14 May 1984, p. 37)

Why didn't the children tell? The *Newsweek* report said that the alleged perpetrators threatened the children by slaughtering in front of them pets like rabbits and birds, warning them that if they ever told anybody they would be similarly treated. Such gruesome detail made the story sound very frightening indeed.

Many parents are extremely worried that this case may turn out to be not only true, but indeed just one case among many. Reports of similar cases are nowadays not a rarity.[3] The average reader would certainly feel outrage towards such abominable acts. It would be difficult, if not actually impossible, to convince the public that there are many more complex issues to be discussed with respect to the phenomenon of adult-child sexual contact than, say, a simple demand for the reinstatement of the death penalty.

Given the sensational nature of these cases, which usually get the biggest possible media coverage, it is not surprising to find that many parents are now ready to organise into pressure groups to demand from the government more drastic action against adults who have molested children. One such British group, which calls itself CHILD, was formed after the murder of 3-year-old Leonie Keating of Suffolk. The first task of this group is to 'bring about a national referendum to consider the reinstatement of the death penalty for child murder, and a life sentence – 'which means life' – for child rape or for child killings with a sexual element' (Caudrey, 1985, p. 450). The following quotations, from some of the organisers of this pressure group, convey the intensity of the hatred directed against child molesters:

> They should be trussed up in the local market place. You should be able to throw things at them and they should have no protection. Then they should be hung, drawn and quartered. That may be barbaric – but that's what they are ... Why should they have any protection? The children they kill don't have any.... What do you do with a rabid dog? You have him put down. (Caudrey, 1985, p. 450)

In addition to the printed word, there have been, in recent years, a

---

[3] Jones & Krugman (1986) have discussed in detail another sensational American case in which a 3-year-old girl was abducted, sexually assaulted and then dropped down a 10-foot sewage pit by her attacker. Luckily the girl survived and was able to provide crucial evidence which led to the identification and conviction of the ruthless perpetrator. It is rare nowadays to practise in the social work field without coming into contact with child sexual abuse cases. In a recent American survey of over 1000 social workers, about three-quarters have indicated experiences of handling such cases (Johnson, 1981).

number of television and radio programmes on child sexual abuse,[4] often with phone-in 'audience participation'. The message is clear: child sexual abuse must be publicly discussed because no child is ever immune from this danger, since not even the home is always a safe place. For example, a recent BBC radio programme began with a 16-year-old girl reading out a poem that she had written:

> I hate the letter I, it stands for incest, it stands for me;
> I hate the letter N, it stands for nasty, and that's how he is to me;
> I hate the letter C, it makes me think of the lies, the crap he tells my Mum;
> I hate the letter E, just because it's in that word, reminds me of what he's done;
> I hate the letter S, because it stands for sex; they say I'll feel different one day, but
> I love the letter T, it's the last letter, the end.
> It's the one that stands for telling, the one that stands for truth.[5]

The impact of this poem is immediate – how can anyone respond to the girl's experience except by sharing her feelings of sadness and rage?

The home is not necessarily a safe place, because a molester is not necessarily an unusual person. Rather, he (and it is nearly always a 'he') may well be a perfectly ordinary chap, or even a member of the family. This is the message put across by a feminist publication:

> The first thing we can do as adult women is realise that any man, no matter how much you trust him, is capable of sexually assaulting a girl. (London Rape Crisis Centre, 1984, p. 94)

The message is clear: any man *can* become a child molester. The intensity of this 'moral panic' is so great that, according to a recent American survey, 'child molestation' ranks top as the most serious sexual deviance in the mind of the general public, even more so than bestiality, necrophilia or rape.[6] Given this growing concern about sexual abuse of children, it is not surprising to find new organisations being set up to teach children how to defend themselves physically.[7] Call for more cautious and less hysterical reactions is rarely heard.[8]

Whether adult-child sexual contact is acceptable is so sensitive an issue that often polemics take the place of rational discussion. In the United

[4] There are also video programmes specially produced to teach children how to discern and react to possible sexual abuse, e.g. 'Kids Can Say No!', produced by Rolf Harris Video, London.

[5] The programme was broadcast in the evening of 31 October 1985 on BBC Radio 4. An article based on the programme written by Jenni Mills can be found in the *Listener* published on the same day.

[6] See French & Wailes (1982).

[7] For example, an organisation in New York, which calls itself Safety and Fitness Exchange (SAFE), teaches children (even toddlers) fighting skills in their children self-defence programmes (Burns 1984).

[8] One such call, from a British developmental psychologist, is Tucker (1985).

States, researchers or professionals who have shown some liberal
tendencies regarding this question are often castigated by the popular
media. For example, in two *Time* articles, people like John Money, Larry
Constantine, Frits Bernard and Floyd Martinson[9] are characterised as
'intellectually disheveled', 'self-styled sexual radical'; and their views are
called 'reprehensible', 'propaganda campaign', 'simple-minded', or 'a
satire on how to raise children'. Moreover, such authors are attacked as
propounding their libertarian view (against the cross-generational sex
taboo) for ulterior and irresponsible motives:

> In the world of sexology, prestige usually comes from attacking taboos and
> repression, not from assessing the psychological damage of the ideas
> unleashed. And few sexologists are trained to assess such damage. (*Time*, 7
> September, 1981)

The position of mainstream orthodox opinion is tersely summarised by
the following assertion:

> The literature [of sexology] shows absolutely no attention to psychological
> realities: that often an adolescent and surely a small child can hardly
> produce anything like informed consent to an adult it depends for life and
> guidance; or that the lifting of the incest barrier would invite the routine
> exploitation of children by disturbed parents. (*Time*, 14 April 1980)

While there is a strong movement, comprising lay volunteer groups like
CHILD, and organisations such as Childline and BASPCAN,[10] which is
opposed to any form of adult-child sexual contact, there is nevertheless a
steady current of counter-opinions spearheaded by the 'pro-incest' lobby
and paedophile organisations in many western countries.

The pro-incest lobby argues that not all incest, even that between a
father and a daughter, is necessarily a negative experience – there is the
possibility of what is called 'positive incest'. Intergenerational sex within
the family is seen as a legitimate form of expression of affection and love.
Allied to the pro-incest lobby is the paedophile 'liberation' campaign,
which is trying to put across the argument that paedophilic relationships
between adults and children are a legitimate form of sexual love, that
such relationships are often consensual, and that the only harm that can
arise is that which results from society's condemnatory reactions towards
paedophilic love.[11] These libertarian views have aroused fierce opposition
from many people.[12]

[9] Works of these authors can be found in the Bibliography.

[10] Childline is an organisation, set up on 30 October 1986, offering a free phone-in service
to children in distress, particularly children who have been sexually abused.

BASPCAN = British Association for the Study and Prevention of Child Abuse and
Neglect. See, for example, their Guidelines for Social Services Departments, *Child Sexual
Abuse*. London: BASPCAN, 1981.

[11] For example, see O'Carroll (1980), Moody (1980), PIE (1978), Tsang (1981).

[12] For example, see De Mott (1980), Finkelhor (1979b).

While the anti-incest, anti-paedophile movement finds its chief protagonists in the child-protection institutions, there is another stream in this movement – the feminist camp. Some pro-paedophile activists have put up the argument that the decriminalisation of paedophilia and the abolition of the age of consent are part and parcel of a progressive politics of liberation for oppressed sexual minorities, and as such should be integrated with the feminist and homosexual/lesbian rights movements, but many feminists are openly hostile to the pro-paedophile campaign, accusing it of misogyny and hypocrisy – paedophiles are attacked as men who simply want to exploit younger females for their own gratification.[13] Thus not all anti-paedophile opinions are conservative with respect to sexual morality – feminists are against sexual abuse of children by men, but at the same time they strongly advocate the sexual liberation of all females, including underage girls.[14]

In Britain, there was a 'coming out' of paedophiles towards the late 1970s, which proved to be a fiasco.[15] Unlike the homosexual rights lobby, the pro-paedophile campaign is unlikely to gain much public support. Indeed, this 'coming out' aroused a witch-hunt, spearheaded by the tabloids (mainly the *News of the World*), which eventually led to the imprisonment of paedophile leaders like Tom O'Carroll.

The clamp-down on paedophiles in Britain, supported by celebrities such as Mary Whitehouse[16] and Geoffrey Dickens, MP[17] continues right through to the present time. Its most significant manifestation was the Private Member's Bill introduced to Parliament in June 1984 to ban all paedophile organisations.[18] Under great pressure from the criminal justice system, paedophile organisations in Britain have virtually ceased to exist.[19]

---

[13] See Isherwood (1981).

[14] For example, in the recent Gillick saga, which culminated in the House of Lords ruling in October 1985 that guaranteed GPs' right to prescribe contraceptive pills to underage girls, feminists have argued for the sexual rights of underage girls and rejected Mrs Gillick's campaign (for example, see Ceresa, 1981; McFadyean, 1985).

[15] See O'Carroll (1980), Plummer (1980, 1981b).

[16] Mary Whitehouse, perhaps the best known moral crusader in Britain, is vehemently opposed to any reform that would relax the current social and legal sanction against adult-child sexual contact. See Whitehouse (1978), ch. 4, Whitehouse (1982), ch. 13 and Whitehouse (1985), ch. 8.

[17] The recent furore, in March 1986, about a Humberside vicar who was alleged to be sexually involved with a boy of 11, ended in the vicar resigning under severe pressure engineered by Geoffrey Dickens, Conservative MP for Littleborough and Saddleworth, who was trying to invoke parliamentary privilege to name the vicar openly in the House of Commons. Although the Speaker of the House blocked Dickens's attempt to reveal the name of the vicar, Dickens had never given up his campaign.

[18] Paedophilia (Protection of Children) Bill, *Hansard*, 27 June 1984. This Bill was introduced by Geoffrey Dickens, and it aimed at banning all organisations that could be even remotely associated with anything to do with adult-child sexual contact. Being a member of such an organisation would make one liable to prosecution. The Bill failed to get a second reading then due to the lack of parliamentary time.

[19] In the July 1984 issue of *Paedophile Information Exchange (PIE) Bulletin*, the PIE executive announced that they were closing down their organisation 'because of various

Not only is it unlikely that paedophiles will receive any public support for their decriminalisation campaign, it is also highly improbable that they could rally professional opinions to their side. In 1973, the American Psychiatric Association deleted 'homosexuality' as an illness category in the second edition of their Diagnostic and Statistical Manual of Mental Disorders (DSM-II) and inserted a new category of 'sexual orientation disorder' in the section on 'psychosexual disorders'. This category was finally modified to 'ego-dystonic homosexuality' in the third edition of the manual (DSM-III) published in 1980.[20] This new category, formulated with special reference to homosexuality (with no comparable category for heterosexuality), subsumes cases of individuals who experience distress or adjustment difficulties as a consequence of their homosexual orientation. While it is true that 'homosexuality' *per se* is no longer considered a mental disorder, the very fact that a specific category is created to include 'distressed' homosexuals within an illness classification reflects the fact that mainstream psychiatry still considers homosexuality as a rather special 'condition'. If the acceptance of homosexuality is so qualified, it is not to be expected that paedophilia, which is often seen as more 'deviant' than homosexuality, will ever be deleted from the illness classification of any psychiatric manual. Indeed, it is still categorised under 'sexual deviations and disorders' in both DSM-III and the International Classification of Diseases. Thus, although the Wolfenden Report (1957) has formulated a more liberal view of adult homosexuality – a view which has definitely influenced a substantial part of British public opinion – paedophilia as such is never considered a viable candidate for decriminalisation.[21]

7.2 The ever-growing literature

While it is true to say that in the past the subject of sexual contact between children and adults was a taboo topic, and that there was a dearth of information about the phenomenon, it is no longer the case now. In the last ten years or so, a sizeable body of literature has come into existence, covering topics from paedophilia and incest to child

---

difficulties'.

[20] There had been some very acrimonious debates among American psychiatrists regarding the deletion of 'homosexuality' from the illness categorisation. The new diagnosis of 'sexual orientation disorder' underwent several revisions, from 'homodysphilia' to 'dyshomophilia', then to 'homosexual conflict disorder' before finally changed to 'ego-dystonic homosexuality'. The heated debates surrounding this issue are documented in Bayer & Spitzer (1982). It is interesting to note that in another classification manual, the International Classification of Diseases, ICD-9 (World Health Organisation, 1977), homosexuality is still listed under 'sexual deviations and disorders' within the mental disorders categorisation, although according to West (1983b, p. 224), the Parliamentary Assembly of the Council of Europe had passed a resolution recommending that the WHO delete this category from the ICD.

[21] For instance, a Working Party of the Anglican General Synod has produced a report (General Synod, 1979) fairly favourably disposed towards homosexuality within certain limits, but paedophilia is ruled out from the start as categorically unacceptable.

prostitution, and from theoretical treatises to treatment and evaluation reports.[22] Not only can the growing body of the literature on adult-child sexual contact be seen in books and journal articles, there is indeed a great deal of unpublished material on the topic, among which theses and dissertations are the most important since they reflect the kind of research activities going on in institutions of higher education and learning.

A search of the USA *Dissertation Abstracts International* from 1979 to 1984 has yielded no less than 60 entries of PhD dissertations directly related to adult-child sexual contact.[23] The number would increase enormously if Master level theses were included. Child sexual abuse was 'rediscovered' in USA as the 'final frontier of child abuse' during the 1970s – psychiatrists, psychologists, paediatricians, counsellors, social workers and other 'human services providers' began to pay greater attention to this problem in both practice and research. Despite this growing body of publications, however, there are still authors who routinely begin their book or article on the subject by referring to a lack of data in the area. For instance, Mannarino and Cohen (1986) have this to say at the beginning of their paper:

> Despite the frequency of its occurrence, and its potentially harmful effect, until recently the area of child sexual abuse has received little attention from researchers or mental health practitioners. As a result, very little is actually known about the children who are abused, their families, the abusers, or the psychological impact of child sexual abuse. (p. 17)

Statements such as this help to create and maintain the impression that there are not enough data on adult-child sexual contact, and hence more resources should be devoted to research and professional intervention into the life and families with this 'problem'. However, as Tucker (1985) has cautioned, there is already more than enough attention paid to this subject, and the upsurge of popular publication has reinforced the

---

[22] Detailed bibliography can be found in the Bibliography at the end of this book, and also in the annotated bibliographies of G.P. Jones (1982), W. Parker (1985), Rubin & Byerly (1983), Ryan (1986), Schlesinger (1982), Schultz (1979) and Weinberg & Bell (1972). A list of the more popular-type publications is given here: first-person narrative or journalistic account: C.V. Allen (1980), Armstrong (1978), Newman (1982, 1983), *Newsweek* (1984); non-technical publication for lay consumption: BASPCAN (1981), Delin (1978), Geiser (1979), Justice & Justice (1980), Kempe & Kempe (1978, 1984), S. Nelson (1982), Walters (1975). According to reviews by Rossman (1973) as well as B. Taylor (1976), themes of sexual relationship between adults and children are common in many literary works, including biographies, autobiographical writings, novels, poetry, etc. *Lolita* (Nabokov) and *Death in Venice* (Mann) are perhaps the most widely known novels with a paedophilic theme.

[23] While these 60 dissertations span quite a wide spectrum in terms of their research topics, a majority of them have their focus on the construction of profiles for either the adult perpetrator or the child victim (using personality inventories and other written tests), or on the effects of such sexual contact and the kind of treatment programmes available. A search of the British *Index to Thesis* from 1953 to 1983 has found not a single entry relevant to the topic of sexual contact between adults and children. This might be a consequence of the lack of efficiency in the compilation of the *Index*, or the lack of adequate funding for such research in Britain, or both.

Table 1. Estimated rates of child sexual abuse

Study	Estimated rate (%)		
	Male	*Female*	*Overall*
Clinical/child protection samples			
Mrazek, Lynch &			
Bentovim (1981, 1983) (UK)			0.3
NSPCC (1986) (UK)			0.025
De Francis (1969) (USA)*			0.15
Retrospective surveys			
student samples			
Nash & West (1985) (UK)		25.0	
Finkelhor (1979a) (USA)*	8.6	19.2	
Fritz, Stoll & Wagner			
(1981) (USA)	4.8	7.7	
Fromuth (1986) (USA)*		22.0	
Landis (1956) (USA)*	30.0	35.0	33.0
Schultz & Jones (1983) (USA)*			43.8
Waterman & Foss-Goodman (1984)			
(USA)	3.3	16.7	
population samples			
Hall (1985) (UK)		21.0	
MORI (1984) (UK)*	8.0	12.0	10.0
Nash & West (1985) (UK)		22.0	
Newman (1983) (UK)*		36.0	
Finkelhor (1984) (USA)*	6.0	15.0	12.0
Kercher & McShane (1984a) (USA)*	3.0	11.0	7.4
Kinsey *et al.* (1953) (USA)*		24.0	
Russell (1983) (USA)			
age <18		38.0	
age <14		28.0	
Wyatt (1985) (USA) age <18		45.0	
Canadian Committee (1984)			
National Population Survey			
assaulted	4.9	10.6	
touched	5.0	11.1	
population sample of teenagers			
Hall & Flannery (1984) (USA)			
age 14-17	2.0	12.0	

*These studies used a broad definition of child sexual abuse which includes non-bodily contact such as indecent exposure.

N.B. The NSPCC and the De Francis studies provide incidence rates, all others provide prevalence rates.

atmosphere of near-hysterical panic. This situation might in the end prove counter-productive to the achievement of an appropriate social response.

As the literature on adult-child sexual contact is vast, the present review will have to be highly selective. In this chapter, the questions of statistics and profiles, as well as the debate on effects, will be discussed. In the next chapter, a survey of theoretical models on adult-child sexual contact will be presented.

7.3 Research data on prevalence of child sexual abuse

Many studies contain information on estimated incidence or prevalence rate of child sexual abuse. Table 1 summarises the various rates derived from these studies.

The prevalence rate of child sexual abuse in Britain estimated by Mrazek and her colleagues (0.3 per cent) is one of the lowest among the studies listed in Table 1; yet in absolute terms, it means that over 40,000 children were sexually abused.[24] In studies where the estimated rates are much higher, the number of children involved will be extremely large. For example, Baker & Duncan (1985), drawing on the data of the MORI (1984) survey, have made the following estimates: over 4.5 million adults in Britain *have been* sexually abused during their childhood, and over 1.1 million children *will* be sexually abused before they reach 15 years of age. Among these 1 million children, about 150,000 will be abused within their own family. These figures are breath-taking indeed.

In the United States, an estimate made in the 1960s put the yearly national incidence of child sexual abuse at 360,000 cases (Chaneles, 1967). More recently, Finkelhor, an American authority on child sexual abuse research, has made an estimate of 150,000 to 200,000 cases per year (Finkelhor & Hotaling, 1984), which, while somewhat smaller than the Chaneles figure, is still very large. Perhaps the incidence rate estimated by Kercher (1980) for the State of Texas alone is more startling – 64,000 cases per year. If there were over 60,000 child sexual abuse cases per year in just one State within the USA, the national incidence must exceed the million mark.

However, even a cursory inspection of Table 1 above will immediately raise many questions. The rates estimated by different studies vary so greatly that it is doubtful whether a 'true' rate can be obtained. The problems involved in the estimation exercise conducted by these studies are many:

(1) The sampling procedures involved varied from study to study: some used clinical samples, some students, while others used particular population samples, such as samples drawn from GP

---

[24] As the mid-year estimates of the UK population under age 16 in 1977 (the year in which the data of Mrazek *et al.*, 1981 were collected) is 13,466,400, a rate of 0.3 per cent is equal to 40,399 children.

practices (Nash & West, 1985) or driving licence records (Kercher & McShane, 1984a). On the whole, clinical and child protection studies tend to give much smaller estimates, which are not comparable to figures derived from retrospective surveys because clinical studies do not cover *unreported* cases. However, as will be argued later,[25] retrospective surveys tend to exaggerate the extent of child sexual abuse, and so their estimates cannot be taken at face value either.

(2) The definition of sexual abuse also varied from study to study: some used a narrow definition, while others adopted a broad one[26] which would inflate the statistics. A more serious problem is that in some studies even *consensual* contact is included as abuse (e.g. Schultz & Jones, 1983).

(3) In some studies, 'victims' older than 16 were included (e.g. Russell, 1983; Wyatt, 1985), while in others the age of 13, 14 or 16 was used as the ceiling for a 'child' victim. Likewise, the age criterion for offenders varied from study to study: some included teenage 'perpetrators' (e.g. Newman, 1983; Schultz & Jones, 1983; Wyatt, 1985) while others did not. Obviously if the victim age criterion is raised and the perpetrator age criterion lowered, the magnitude of the estimates will be increased.

(4) In some studies, the non-respondent rate is high (e.g. 44 per cent in Nash & West, 1985, and 45 per cent in Wyatt, 1985). It is not sure what proportion of these 'non-respondents' would have reported incidents of child sexual abuse. This further contributes to the uncertainty of the rates obtained.

Despite these difficulties, one conclusion seems certain: the once-cherished view of 'one in a million'[27] is far from an accurate estimation of the extent of sexual contact between adults and children. The figures discussed above are enormously higher than this early estimate. Indeed, most authors usually start their discussion of the seriousness of child sexual abuse by providing some staggering statistics. It is rare to read the opening sentence of a chapter on sexual abuse which says, for example, 'The number of reported sexual offences is not increasing.'[28] The affirmation that child sexual abuse incidence is extremely high underlies the call for more professional intervention as well as the attempt by moral crusaders to impose a more stringent sexual morality on society. Yet one major issue is often ignored – the proportion of child sexual 'abuse' cases involving *consensual* activities. Walmsley & White (1979) have estimated that of all the convicted cases of serious sexual offences in 1973, 43 per cent involved consensual activities (80 per cent in the case of homosexual contact and 34 per cent of heterosexual contact). According to

[25] See §7.6 below.

[26] Broad definitions usually cover very disparate events, from obscene telephone calls or verbal advances, to indecent exposure, to sexual intercourse.

[27] This view was derived from Weinberg (1955), one of the earliest studies on incest.

[28] West (1984a), p. 1.

the description of their methodology, this is a *conservative* estimate because all cases involving children under 10 were automatically classified as 'non-consensual', and a very stringent criterion of consensuality was applied to the rest of the sample.[29] It is, therefore, reasonable to suggest that the figure of 43 per cent is most unlikely to be an over-estimate. Although it is not known how far this particular statistic can be generalised, it is plausible that contact is consensual in a substantial proportion of adult-child cases. Before the call for more legal and professional intervention into sexual activities involving children is heeded, it is essential to examine whether some of these activities are consensual and hence could be tolerated.

7.4 Profile statistics

7.4.1 *The sex of the child victim*

Related to the statistical description of the gender of children involved in sexual contact with adults is the question whether girls or boys are more 'at risk'. While there are authors who treat 'paedophilia' as a homosexual aberration or a form of homosexuality,[30] there is an argument that since most men are heterosexual, they would be more likely to seek girls rather than boys if they want sexual intimacy with children.[31] Perhaps authors who suggest that paedophilia is a homosexual variant are actually *defining* paedophilia in terms of *pederasty* (sexual love of boys). Thus, Masters (1966) used the term 'nymphophilia' to describe sexual relationship with, or desire for, young girls, and confined the term 'paedophilia' to sexual relationships with boys. Table 2 summarises the relevant information, from various studies, on victim gender in child sexual abuse cases.

The discrepancy between studies listed in Table 2 may to a large extent be due to differences in sample size. For example, the smallest study is based on a sample of 28 children (Adams-Tucker, 1981), while some of the larger-scale studies have a sample size of several thousand (e.g. the US National Reporting Data discussed in Finkelhor, 1983). Nevertheless, apart from Mulcock (1954), these studies support the claim that the majority of children involved in sexual contact with adults are girls.

It is possible, however, to argue that the observed difference is a consequence of sex-differentiated reporting:

(1) There is a much greater public tolerance of sexual activities

---

[29] 'Sexual behaviour with a person under the age of consent was only assessed as consensual where the *documentary* sources gave clear evidence to that effect; where a young person submitted through fear or merely out of obedience the behaviour was assessed as non-consensual' (Walmsley & White 1979, p. 6, italics added)

[30] See, for example, Power (1976, 1977), Roche (1950).

[31] See, for example, West (1981, 1982).

Table 2. Ratio of girl to boy victims

Study	Ratio of girls : boys
Criminal statistics	
Gibbens & Prince (1963) (UK)	7:3
Mulcock (1954) (UK)	1:3
Frisbie (1959) (USA)	7:3
Jaffe, Dynneson & ten Bensel (1975) (USA)	7:1
Canadian Committee (1984) National Police Survey	7.2
Wolters *et al.* (1985) (Holland)	4:1
Reifen (1975) (Israel)	5:2
Clinical studies	
Mrazek, Lynch & Bentovim (1981) (UK)*	6:1
Adams-Tucker (1981) (USA)	4:1
Hunter, Kilstrom & Loda (1985) (USA)	8:1
Mannarino & Cohen (1986) (USA)	7:1
Canadian Committee (1984) National Hospital Survey	6:1
Mian *et al.* (1986) (Canada) (victims' age below 7)	10:3
Child protection services data	
NSPCC (1984b) (UK)	4:1
De Francis (1969) (USA)	7:1
De Jong, Hervada & Emmett (1983) (USA)	9:2
Finkelhor (1983) (USA)	7.1
Kercher & McShane (1984b)	5:1
Pierce & Pierce (1985a, 1985b) (USA)	7:1
Canadian Committee (1984) National Child Protection Survey	6:1
Retrospective surveys	
MORI (1984) (UK)	3:2
Finkelhor (1979a) (USA)	5:1
Fritz, Stoll & Wagner (1981) (USA)	2:1
Kercher & McShane (1984a) (USA)	5:1
Landis (1956) (USA)	5:2
Canadian Committee (1984) National Population Survey	7:3

* In this particular study, the gender of the victim was not known in 51 per cent of cases. The ratio given here is derived from the other 49 per cent of cases.

involving boys than those involving girls, not least because of the lack of any risk of pregnancy. Admittedly it can be argued that since *homosexuality* still arouses much hostility from society, man-boy sexual contact is likely to be less tolerated. Yet it can also be argued the other way round – that precisely because homosexual activities are still stigmatised, man-boy contact is more furtive and hence less likely to be discovered.

(2) When parents or other caretakers find that their children have had sexual contact with adults, they would be much more anxious to have the girls undergo medical examination (for fear of pregnancy) or other forms of protective remedy. Thus girls tend to be sent to hospital or other public agencies more often than boys, hence biasing the statistics.

(3) In retrospective survey, more male respondents might be holding back from revealing their childhood sexual experiences with adults because

(i) they were more likely to be consensual partners, and hence might either feel a certain degree of guilt, or tend not to construe the contact as abuse;

(ii) their childhood sexual experiences with adults would often be of a homosexual nature, and given the social taboo against homosexuality, they might feel unable to admit to such experiences.

Given these considerations, the question whether man-boy contact is less reported or actually happens less cannot perhaps be ascertained. Although compared with girls there are fewer boy 'victims' represented in the statistics, the prevalence of sexual abuse of boys is said still to be very high: Finkelhor (1984) has estimated that it ranges from 2.5 to 8.7 per cent of the general population, and has concluded that many more boys are being sexually abused than is commonly thought. Thus Pierce & Pierce (1985b) have argued strongly that the study and treatment of boy victims must not be neglected.

7.4.2 The age of the child victim

As pointed out earlier, the age criterion for the definition of a 'child' varies from one study to another, and this creates problems for comparison. Certain trends can nevertheless be seen (see Table 3).

Finkelhor (1979a) has reviewed a number of studies and presented a detailed comparison of the age distribution of victims found by these various studies. Table 4 is adapted from his analysis.

Table 3. Age trends of child victims

Study	Mean age	Peak age range	
Offender samples			
Cambridge University			
Criminal Science			
Department (1957) (UK)		8-13(c)	
Gibbens & Prince (1963) (UK)	8-9(b)		6-16(g)
Mulcock (1954) (UK)		10-12(c)	

Table 3. Age trends of child victims (continued)

Study	Mean age		Peak age range	
Walmsley & White (1979) (UK)			5-15(b)	13-15(g)
Frisbie (1959) (USA)*	12.3(b)	8.8(g)		
Jaffe et al. (1975) (USA)	10.7(c)			
McCaghy (1967) (USA)	9.0(c)			
Canadian Committee (1984) National Police Survey			7-11(b)	14-15(g)
Mohr, Turner & Jerry (1964) (Canada)	12.2(b)	9.4(g)		
McGeorge (1964) (Australia)	11.4(b)	10.2(g)	10-15(c)	
Law (1979) (Hong Kong)	12.8(b)	8.6(g)		
Child protective services samples				
NSPCC (1984b) (UK)	11.3(c)		10-14(c)	
De Francis (1969) (USA)	11.6(c)			
Finkelhor (1983) (USA)			13-16(c)	
Kercher & McShane (1984b) (USA)	10.9(b)	10.8(g)	7-16(c)	
Pierce & Pierce (1985a, 1985b) (USA)	8.6(b)	10.6(g)	14(c)	
Weiss et al. (1955) (USA)		9.2(g)		
Canadian Committee (1984) National Child Protection Survey			<7(b)	7-11(g)
Clinical studies				
Ingram (1981) (UK)	9.2(b)			
Mrazek, Lynch & Bentovim (1981) (UK)			11-15(c)	
De Jong, Hervada & Emmett (1983) (USA)	8.6(b)	10.4(g)	7(b)	6,15(g)
Hunter et al. (1985) (USA)	9.2(c)			
Canadian Committee (1984) National Hospital Survey			7-11(c)	
Retrospective surveys				
Baker & Duncan (1985) (UK)	12.0(b)	10.7(g)		
Nash & West (1985) (UK)		11.6(g)		
Finkelhor (1979a) (USA)	11.2(b)	10.2(g)	8,10,12(c)	
Kinsey et al. (1953) (USA)				10-12(g)
Landis (1956) (USA)	15.4(b)	10.4(g)		
Canadian Committee (1984) National Population Survey			14-15(c)	

b = boys, g = girls, c = both boys and girls.
* The figures for this study are median age rather than mean age.

Table 4. Victim age in different studies

Types of studies	Mean age	
	Boys	Girls
I. Retrospective population surveys	15.0	10.2
II. Studies based on victims' reports to public agencies	8.5	9.1
III. Studies based on incarcerated offenders	12.6	10.1

From Finkelhor 1979a, p. 154.

While the figures in Table 3 do not follow exactly the pattern as observed in Finkelhor's analysis, they do tend in a similar direction. Comparing I and II in Table 4, it seems that retrospective studies of the general population have yielded a higher mean age for victims than data from public agencies. This might be due to greater public anxiety over the protection of younger children against sexual abuse, such that public agency intervention into cases of adult-child sexual contact tends to focus on the younger age groups, lowering the mean age of samples based on agency data. In population studies, on the other hand, more consensual, and hence unreported, sexual contact between adults and relatively older children is involved, thus raising the mean age of the 'victims' surveyed. *Retrospective* surveys may also be predisposed towards producing a higher mean age of victimisation due to more recent incidents being remembered.

Studies with offenders (especially those currently involved with the criminal justice system) naturally tend not to produce results indicating younger child victims since such admission might have serious legal implications. This is also true of data from paedophile organisations. For instance, the British PIE survey showed that its members preferred boys in the age range of 11-15 and girls of 8-11, rarely younger (PIE, 1976; O'Carroll, 1980). Bernard (1985) also found that the active members of a Dutch paedophile group showed a preference for children around the age of puberty.

Although these different age ranges obtained in different types of studies are not strictly consistent with each other, they nevertheless suggest that the majority of children involved in sexual activities with adults are in a developmental stage just before and around puberty. It is usually suggested that girl victims tend to be younger than boy victims because girls reach puberty sooner. Although this is not always borne out by research, there does seem to be such a trend among studies listed in Table 3.

While it is fair to say that the majority of adult-child sexual contact cases involve peri-pubertal children, there are nevertheless studies which show that some very young children have also been victimised. For instance, Gebhard & Gagnon (1964) identified a group of 60 offenders who had persistently molested children aged 5 or younger. Similarly, Cantwell (1981) found that 15 per cent of his sample of child sexual abuse cases involved victims below the age of 6, and Adams-Tucker (1981) also found 25 per cent of her clinic sample below 6. More recently, Mian *et al.* (1986) found that one-third of their hospital sample of nearly 400 child sexual abuse cases were below the age of 7, and Mannarino & Cohen (1986) found that about 50 per cent of their clinical sample of 455 sexually abused children were below the age of 5. Even though this constitutes a minority among all cases, their existence still causes a great deal of concern.

The data on age distribution of both offenders and victims presented in Walmsley & White (1980) show that there is a tendency for older offenders (over 50) to be associated with younger victims (under 10) in both USI (unlawful sexual intercourse) and indecent assault cases. This is particularly so if the victim is female.[32] This is perhaps understandable: older men might not dare to approach adolescents (who are more difficult to handle) and so tend to turn to younger children. While this seems to confirm the 'dirty old man' image of the 'child molester', it must be emphasised, as the next section will substantiate, that sexual involvement with children is far from being confined to elderly men. Indeed, the group of 60 offenders in Gebhard & Gagnon's (1964) study had a median age of 27, with 18 per cent in their late teens, 35 per cent in their 20s, 23 per cent in their 30s and only 7 per cent in each of the three subsequent age groups, (40s, 50s, 60s).

7.4.3 The age of the perpetrator

Research data on the average age and peak age of child sexual abuse perpetrators are summarised in Table 5. Despite the fact that most of the studies listed in Table 5 included adolescent perpetrators in their samples, it is nevertheless clear that the young and middle adult groups constitute the majority of the perpetrators of adult-child sexual contact. Perhaps if all teenage perpetrators were excluded, the mean age would move up somewhat – but most probably still within the 30 to 40 range. One interesting feature in the study by Mohr and his colleagues is that the offender age distribution falls into three ranges. Mohr (1981) has interpreted this distribution in terms of the different types of paedophilic tendencies involved: the adolescent type as a result of heterosexual courtship difficulties, the middle-age type as a result of marital problems, and the old-age type as a consequence of bereavement, loss and loneliness.

7.4.4 Relationship between perpetrator and victim

Not only is the paedophilic offender rarely a 'dirty old man', he is actually

[32] Walmsley & White (1980) explicitly pointed out that for unlawful sexual intercourse with an underage girl and indecent assault on a female the inverse relationship between the age of the offender and the age of the victim is marked (pp. 23, 35).

Table 5. Age of perpetrators in various studies

Study	Mean age	Peak age
Offender samples		
Fitch (1962) (UK)	35-36	31-40
Mulcock (1954) (UK)		39-44
Frisbie (1959) (USA)		20-39
Gebhard *et al*. (1965) (USA)	36-39	
Jaffe, Dynneson & ten Bensel (1975) (USA)	28	
Kercher & McShane (1984b) (USA)	34	
McCaghy (1967) (USA)	37.3	
Mohr, Turner & Jerry (1964) (Canada)*	35.3	15-19
		30-40
		55-59
Nedoma, Mellan & Pondelickova (1971)		
(Czechoslovakia)	37	
McGeorge (1964) (Australia)		20-40
Law (1979) (Hong Kong)		15-29
Victim studies		
De Francis (1969) (USA)*	31.3	<20, 30-34
De Jong, Hervada & Emmett (1983) (USA)		<20
Pierce & Pierce (1985a) (USA)	34.1	
Retrospective surveys		
Nash & West (1985) (UK)	35	16-20
Finkelhor (1979a) (USA)*	27.9	

* Figures in these studies are median rather than mean.
N.B. All studies except Nedoma *et al*. (1971) explicitly stated that teenage perpetrators were included in their samples.

often someone known to the child. Table 6 summarises the relevant research statistics on the relationship between the adult perpetrator and child victim.

The statistics presented in Table 6 vary considerably from study to study because of the variation in samples and research focus. For instance, if indecent exposure is included in the definition of child sexual abuse, the proportion of stranger perpetrators will be raised (e.g. Baker & Duncan, 1985; De Jong *et al*., 1983; Kinsey *et al*. 1953; Landis, 1956; Nash & West, 1985); whereas in studies which have drawn on data from family services agencies or social services departments, more intra-familial or incest cases are represented (e.g. Canadian Committee National Child Protection Survey, 1984; Pierce & Pierce, 1985a). Despite this variation, the overall picture is that a majority of the perpetrators in adult-child sexual contact cases are known to the victims or are actually members of the same family. Complete strangers constitute only a minority, particularly if encounters with indecent exposure are discounted.

7.4.5 Other perpetrator characteristics

In the past, child sexual abuse or incest was taken to be a specifically lower-class phenomenon. This is highlighted by studies like Fitch (1962), Gebhard *et al.* (1965), McGeorge (1964), or Mulcock (1954). Perpetrators involved in child sexual abuse tended to come from the lower strata of society: they were working class, with relatively less formal education and more often came from 'problem' families. However, the over-representation of lower-class families or individuals in the statistics might be a result of their vulnerability to becoming the subject of state intervention. Indeed, all four studies mentioned above are based on prison or offender samples, which comprised individuals under state surveillance and control. Moreover, since the size of the wealthy classes in a society is very small, even if there is a uniform distribution of child sexual abuse across different social strata, lower-class offenders would still be much more 'visible' because of the relatively much larger *number* involved. So while some studies have found lower socio-economic status a risk factor for child sexual abuse (e.g. Finkelhor, 1980b), other studies have found that class differences do not play a significant role (e.g. Baker & Duncan, 1985).

In this connection, it is worth noting that members of paedophile organisations tend to come from the more educated sectors of society. For instance, Bernard (1975, 1985) found that in his Dutch sample of homosexual paedophiles, the proportion of university graduates (20 per cent) is higher than the national average. This is also the case with PIE in Britain – in the study of Wilson & Cox (1983), 38 per cent of their sample of PIE members had a professional career. Although this observation cannot be generalised to all types of adult-child sexual contact (since pressure groups tend to comprise more educated people as members), it nevertheless should caution us against accepting uncritically the stereotype of the 'lower-class' nature of the phenomenon.

As far as the sex of the perpetrator is concerned, while on the whole research studies and official statistics show that nearly all perpetrators of child sexual abuse are male, there are nevertheless a minority of cases in which a female perpetrator is involved. For instance, in a recent review of child sexual abuse in Texas, 35 female offenders have been found among 1,000 cases (3.2 per cent) (Kercher & McShane, 1984b). A similar percentage (5 per cent) of female perpetrators has also been found in a retrospective victim study with female students (Fromuth, 1986). Thus Finkelhor & Russell (1984) have concluded that since women constitute only a very small minority of all perpetrators, child sexual abuse must be seen as a gender-related issue.

The marital status of the 'paedophile' offender shows some correlation with the kind of 'paedophilic' involvement he has. For incestuous

Table 6. Perpetrator-victim relationship

Study	Perpetrator known to victim (%)		Perpetrator stranger (%)
Offender samples			
Wamsley & White (1980)			
Buggery with boys <16	83.5(a)		16.5
1A* on boy <16	56.0(a)		44.0
1A* on girl <16	69.5(a)		30.5
Frisbie (1959)	26.0(b)		
Canadian Committee (1984) National Police			
Survey	20.8(c)	38.0(d)	35.9
Mohr *et al.* (1964)	15.0(c)	50.0(d)	10.0
Child protection data			
Gibbens & Prince (1963)	21.0(b)	29.0(d)	32.0
Cantwell (1981)	>50.0(b)		16.5
De Francis (1969)	38.0(c)	38.0(c)	25.0
Pierce & Pierce (1985a)	62.0(b)		
Canadian Committee (1984) National Child			
Protection Survey	86.4(c)	9.8(d)	1.0
Clinical studies			
Mrazek *et al.* (1981)	42.5(c)		26.0
Adams-Tucker (1981)	50.0(b)	14.0(c)	
De Jong *et al.* (1983)	53.5(a)		46.5
Mannarino & Cohen (1986)	38.0(b)		
Canadian Committee (1984) National			
Hospital Survey	46.9(c)	29.5(d)	17.8
Retrospective surveys			
Baker & Duncan (1985)	49.0(a)		51.0
Nash & West (1985)	17.4(c)	27.3(d)	55.4
Finkelhor (1979a)			
Boy victims	70.0(a)		30.0
Girl victims	76.0(a)		24.0
Fromuth (1986)	88.0(a)		
Kinsey *et al.* (1953)†	55.0(a)		52.0
Landis (1956)			
Boy victims	30.5(a)		68.0
Girl victims	33.8(a)		65.2
Russell (1983, 1984a)	29.0(c)	60.0(d)	11.0
Canadian Committee (1984) National			
Population Survey	23.8(c)	57.4(d)	17.8

* IA = indecent assault

† In Kinsey *et al.* (1953), % of reported *experiences* rather than of victims was used, thus the figures add up to more than 100.

a = known victim, including relatives and friends.

b = fathers and father-figures.   c = family members and relatives.

d = friends, neighbours and acquaintances.

N.B. Percentages in some studies do not add up to 100 because of incomplete information.

offenders, it is obvious that they tend to have marriage experience – indeed their offences have occurred in the context of a matrimonial home. On the other hand, for male paedophiles who are attracted to boys, marriage is rather infrequent. The British PIE members survey (1976) found that only 21.3 per cent of their members were or had been married, and of these a large proportion were heterosexual paedophiles. This is in agreement with Bernard (1975, 1985), who found in his Dutch sample (which was predominantly homosexual) 90 per cent of the paedophiles unmarried.

Research studies on prevalence statistics and typical profiles are often used to highlight the ubiquity of child sexual abuse. The next step is to draw attention to the damaging effects of molestation on children. This focussing on statistics and the negative outcome of adult-child sexual contact serves to establish the conclusion that this phenomenon is unmistakably a very serious social problem. In the next section I shall discuss the question to what extent sex between adults and children is harmful.

7.5 Adult-child sexual contact: effects on children

7.5.1 The question of the 'willing child'

While the greater part of the burgeoning literature on adult-child sexual contact stresses the harm done to the children involved, there are nevertheless studies which suggest that children might willingly engage in sexual activities with adults.[33] These authors talked about 'participant victims', 'victim-precipitation', 'the seductive child', 'the willing child', 'collaborative contact', etc. Not only is it possible for the child to be a willing participant in the sexual relationship, some of these authors observed that some children actually initiated the contact themselves. Even Mohr (1962), who saw paedophilia as 'pathological', concluded that 'many children are psychologically or socially predisposed to such acts and some are openly seductive' (p. 206).[34]

This is without doubt far from the dominant view in academic and professional circles. Many researchers and practitioners see much evil in such notions as 'victim-precipitation' or 'child seductiveness'.[35] They argue that children would never intentionally solicit sexual attention from adults – what children want is affection and love, not sex. If children did appear to participate in the sexual activity, they were only being bribed, seduced or coerced into doing so. Therefore, children involved in

---

[33] See Bender & Blau (1937), Bernard (1981), Brant & Tisza (1977), Burton (1968), Gagnon (1965a), Gibbens & Prince (1963), Ingram (1981), McGeorge (1964), Mohr, Turner & Jerry (1964), Sandfort (1982, 1984), Schultz & Jones (1983), Virkkunen (1981), Walmsley & White (1979), Weiss *et al.* (1955), P. Wilson (1981).

[34] The page number here refers to Mohr's article reprinted in Schlesinger (1977).

[35] See de Young (1982b), Finkelhor (1979a, 1980b), Gruber (1981), Johnston (1979).

sexual contact with adults should never be blamed.[36]

In relation to the question of the validity of a child's report of sexual abuse, Summit (1983) has proposed the notion of 'accommodation syndrome' to interpret the sometimes apparently capricious behaviour of a child after disclosure of sexual involvement with an adult. Summit argued that even if the child's accounts of what had happened were inconsistent over time, or if she wanted to retract her initial allegations, professionals involved in handling the case should understand such seemingly suspicious behaviour in terms of the pressures that the child was experiencing from various sectors of the adult world. The child is not strong enough to persevere under the threat of family disintegration, the pressure of criminal justice proceedings or the intense guilt feelings engendered by the prospects of 'causing' somebody to be sent to jail, particularly if that 'somebody' is a parent or some other significant person in the child's life. The child has to 'accommodate', to yield, to get out of the situation as quickly as possible – to retract from the original allegations may be her only option.

In this connection, the argument that the child who tells of an incident of sexual abuse must always be believed and never blamed[37] is the orthodox attitude that professional practitioners tend to take while handling children showing the sexual abuse 'accommodation syndrome'. The motto is: 'The child is always telling the truth.' The evidence is that a child can never make up stories which contain accurate detail about the sexual aspects of such an encounter with an adult. While it is found that both false allegations of child sexual abuse as well as false retractions are possible,[38] the dominant view is that to talk about 'participant' or 'seductive' victim is not professionally responsible.

7.5.2 Review of outcome research

Harmful effects of sexual abuse on children have been widely documented, although not all researchers believe that *every* form of sexual contact between adults and children is damaging to the child. The studies discussed below serve as *recent* examples of this documentation of harm.

Mannarino & Cohen (1986), in their study of a clinical sample of sexually abused children, found that 69 per cent showed some psychological symptoms immediately after the occurrence of the abuse. Such symptoms included nightmares, anxiety reactions, clinging

[36] However, in a survey of a sample of college students, Waterman & Foss-Goodman (1984) found that over one-third (N=360) of the respondents attribute some fault to child victims of hypothetical child sexual abuse cases, particularly with respect to older children. The major reason given for this fault attribution was that the child 'should have resisted'. In contrast, virtually all respondents held the perpetrator guilty of abusing the child, and the 'fault' attributed to the perpetrator was always rated as extremely serious.

[37] See Berliner (1977), Faller (1984), Rosenfeld, Nadelson & Krieger (1979).

[38] See Goodwin, Sahd & Rada (1982).

behaviour, enuresis and inappropriate sexual acting out.

In a recent English retrospective study on sexual abuse of girls, Nash & West (1985) found that among the respondents to their questionnaire survey, only 14 per cent of the GP sample and 22 per cent of the student sample said they have sustained some long-term harm because of childhood sexual abuse experiences. With respect to immediate reactions, however, a majority of the respondents indicated the experience of fear, shock, confusion, and similar negative feelings at the time of the occurrence of the abusive incident. But on the other hand, Nash and West have pointed out that a substantial proportion of their respondents (31 per cent of the GP sample, 50 per cent of the student sample) had experienced positive reactions such as enjoyment, excitement, or amusement during or after the sexual experience (1985, p. 63). Similarly, in the smaller sample of their follow-up *interview* study, 41 per cent of the informants indicated some experience of pleasure or excitement during their childhood sexual involvement with adults, although negative reactions were still more prominent.

One important point observed by Nash and West, and also by other researchers, is that child victims of sexual abuse often experience fear *and* excitement at the same time – that is why they feel confused, guilt-ridden, and have a sense of being trapped by something unknown to themselves. Such a psychologically unstable state may constitute one source of the 'accommodation syndrome' described by Summit (1983).

In three large-scale surveys conducted by the Canadian Committee on Sexual Offences against Children and Youths (1984), both current clinical samples as well as retrospective survey samples have been used, and findings of the harmful effect of childhood sexual abuse were reported. Table 7 is adapted from the Report of the Committee (p. 212).

Table 7. Effects of sexual abuse

	Physical injury %		*Immediate emotional harm (%)*		*Long-term emotional harm (%)*	
National Population Survey	3.9(b)	19.9(g)	6.8(b)	24.0(g)		
National Police Survey	6.1(b)	13.8(g)				
National Hospital Survey	10.8(b)	24.8(g)	54.0(b)	48.8(g)	18.9(b)	17.6(g)

b = boy victims
g = girl victims
From Canadian Committee, 1984

From these results, the Committee concluded that child victims of sexual abuse, both boys and girls, tend to suffer from emotional rather than physical harm.[39] Although these figures are on the whole not very large, the Committee has suggested that the true extent of harmful effects must have been much greater, since the information they have obtained is incomplete.

That psychological harm is much more serious than physical injury as a consequence of sexual abuse seems to be a common observation. Thus even if it is granted that child molesters or paedophiles are often not physically violent individuals, they are still held guilty of causing psychological damage to children with whom they have been sexually involved. One of the most often mentioned long-term psychological problems consequent on child sexual abuse is sexual maladjustment in adulthood. A recent study by Finkelhor (1984)[40] has produced results that point to long-term negative effects on the 'sexual self-esteem' of people with a history of childhood sexual abuse. Using a regression analysis, Finkelhor argued that his finding was independent of all extraneous variables, i.e. that the observed reduction in sexual self-esteem must be a 'true' effect of earlier abusive experiences.

Besides sexual maladjustment in later life, other long-term psychological disturbances have also been observed in individuals who have had experience of childhood sexual abuse. Lindberg & Distad (1985a) talked about sexual abuse victims as suffering from 'post-traumatic stress disorders'[41] even on average 17 years after their experience of abuse. Such stress disorders include affect disturbance, depression, guilt feelings, sleep problems, experience of depersonalisation, etc. Thus sexual contact between adults and children is seen as responsible for a wide range of undesirable effects on the victims, both immediately and in the long run.

Apart from these five recent studies, a large part of the existing literature on child sexual abuse has also documented the ill-effects of such abuse on children. Besides the obvious danger of injuries due to assault on the child, other physical danger includes unwanted pregnancies and congenital defects in incestuous offspring (British Medical Journal, 1981; Roybal & Goodwin, 1982), as well as vaginitis and gonorrhoea (De Jong 1985; Sgroi, 1977). More immediate psychological harm that has been documented includes inappropriate sexual acting-out (Litin, Giffin & Johnson, 1956; Pomeroy, Behar & Stewart, 1981; Yates,

---

[39] One notable feature of Table 7 is the relatively high proportion of girl victims who have sustained physical injuries as a result of sexual abuse. While the Report has not given any explanation, it is plausible to suggest that more boys were involved in consensual sexual activities with the 'perpetrators', and hence fewer of them were physically injured. It should also be noted that most physical injuries were, according to the Report, of a minor nature, such as bruising, scratches, or redness and inflammation. In the case of girls, vaginal discharge, broken hymen and pregnancy were included as 'injuries', which might have contributed to the observed higher percentages. Since victims with physical injuries required medical attention, it is not surprising that the Hospital Survey produced the highest percentages of such injuries.

[40] Finkelhor (1984), ch. 12.

[41] This is a DSM-III diagnosis.

1982), self-injurious and suicidal behaviour (L.S. Anderson, 1981; de Young, 1982c; Goodwin, 1981; Lindberg & Distad, 1985b), as well as hysterical seizures (Goodwin, Simms & Bergman, 1979; Gross, 1979).[42] With respect to longer-term ill effects, the following have been documented: subsequent prostitution (James & Meyerding, 1978; Silbert & Pines, 1981), drug and alcohol abuse (Benward & Densen-Gerber, 1975; Lindberg & Distad, 1985b), intergenerational 'transmission' of abusive or sexually inappropriate behaviour[43] (Goodwin, McCarthy & DiVasto, 1981; Groth, 1979; Longo, 1982; Sroufe & Ward, 1980), sexual maladjustment in adult life (Becker, Abel & Skinner, 1979; de Young, 1982a; Herman, 1981; Meiselman, 1978, 1980; Tsai, Feldman-Summers & Edgar, 1979), initiation into homosexual or lesbian activities (Finkelhor, 1981b; Goodwin & DiVasto, 1979), and post-traumatic stress symptoms (Hyde & Kaufman, 1984). Given the documentation of all these negative outcomes, it is expected that most professional practitioners see incest or adult-child sexual contact as very damaging to children.[44]

Sexual contact between adults and children which involves physical violence raises no disagreement among researchers or practitioners – it is universally condemned as criminal and unacceptable. However, with respect to psychological harm, specifically in cases where no coercion is involved, there is significant disagreement among researchers. It is obvious that there is a not unimportant distinction between 'being upset' by an abusive experience at the time of its occurrence and 'long-term harm'. Probably nobody will deny that any unwelcome sexual approach will elicit a negative reaction from the 'victim' – yet this is different from asserting that every incident of 'sexual abuse' will leave some indelible scar on a child. Moreover, the direction of the alleged causal relation is difficult to establish unequivocally. For example, some studies have shown that rather than sexual abuse resulting in the 'victims' engaging in delinquent behaviour, it might be the case that exposure to a 'delinquent' subculture makes some female adolescents more vulnerable to sexual abuse by older males in these circles.[45] The next two sections will discuss these problems more fully.

7.5.3 Controversy over outcome research

There are several review studies on the question of effects of childhood sexual experience with adults, which, while surveying more or less a similar pool of outcome research, have reached very different conclusions.

[42] While self-injurious behaviour and seizures are psychological effects of abuse, they obviously also lead to *physical* harm.

[43] That is, the victims would grow up either to be sexually/physically abusive parents (or they would tend to behave in sexually inappropriate ways with their own children), or to be prone to commit sexual offences outside the family, such as rape or child molestation.

[44] See surveys by James, Womack & Stauss (1978), LaBarbera, Martin & Dozier (1980).

[45] See Gruber (1984), Gruber & Jones (1981), Jones, Gruber & Timbers (1981), Wright & West (1981).

Brongersma (1980, 1984), in his review of over ten studies, mainly European and Scandinavian, arrived at the conclusion that no psychological damage was observed in children who were sexually involved with adults.[46] Traumatisation, if it did occur, was a consequence of the traumatising reactions from other people upon disclosure of the sexual relationship, rather than of the sexual contact itself. Thus, Brongersma made the following conclusion as the basis for his call for reform of the law:

> We have come to the conclusion that the term 'indecent' can no longer be used to include sexual behaviour which arises through *love, tenderness* or *affection* which is not carried out against the will of the child. (1980, p. 30, italics added)

It is clear that here Brongersma is talking about *consensual* adult-child sexual relationships rather than coercive sexual abuse – to him, the former will not, in itself, have an undesirable effect on the children involved. He has given three categories of adult-child sexual contact:[47]

(1) Abuse with violence – criminal law should apply.

(2) No violence, but the child dislikes the contact – criminal proceedings should be avoided, focus should be on helping the child to forget the event.

(3) Mutual loving relationships – criminal law should not interfere; while parents can use civil law to stop the relationship if they thought the adult would be a bad influence on the child, the judge must take into account the child's opinion.

It is to the defence of the last category that Brongersma devotes his effort.

A second review which has reached a similar conclusion is Constantine (1981a). After analysing about 30 outcome studies, Constantine made the following points:

(1) There is no inbuilt or inevitable outcome of adult-child sexual contact. Whether the experience leads to benefit or harm depends on factors other than the contact itself. Therefore, sexual relationship between adults and children should not *a priori* be ruled out.

(2) A four-factor model can be constructed to predict the outcome of an adult-child sexual encounter. These factors are:

(i) The child's freedom and consent.

(ii) The child's knowledge of sex and social norms.

(iii) Family reactions to the child's experience.

(iv) Society's reactions to the child's experience.

---

[46] Over the past decade, Brongersma has collected numerous case histories of consensual paedophilic relationship, but his studies are mostly published in Dutch. Nevertheless, a major study of his is to be published towards the end of 1986, and it will have an English edition (personal communication from Brongersma, 1986).

[47] See Brongersma (1984), p. 83.

Interaction of these four factors will produce different outcomes for a child involved in sexual contact with an adult. The 'best case' is where the sexual relationship is consensual, and the child has adequate knowledge about sex but not too bothered about social norms; the 'worst case' is where the contact is coerced, and the child has little knowledge about sex but is keenly aware of the social disapproval regarding such activity. In this latter case, both guilt feeling and anxiety will reach the highest level.

(3) The last two factors, family and social reactions, are pivotal in determining how the child will fare – like Brongersma, Constantine argued that it is the social reactions rather than the sexual contact itself that will traumatise the child.

(4) Such a four-factor model is not confined to adult-child sexual contact, but is applicable to any form of sexual relationship. That is, sexual relationships between children and adults are not particularly inducive to negative consequences. Given the same sets of unfavourable social reactions, the same lack of sexual knowledge and free choice, sexual contact between two adults will produce ill-effects similar to those observed in that between a child and an adult.

Another review, Powell & Chalkley (1981), has reached a conclusion similar to that of Brongersma and Constantine. It differs from the latter two in that the authors had themselves conducted a diagnostic exercise on all the published cases of adult-child sexual contact that they could find in the literature, and used this as a basis of their argument. Their conclusion is that although at the surface there is an observable difference between sexually abused children and non-abused ones in terms of diagnosed psychopathology, the association between occurrence of abuse and psychopathology is correlational rather than causal.

Powell and Chalkley then proceeded to review twelve outcome studies and arrived at the following conclusions:

(1) Some children did participate actively in sexual contact with adults.

(2) No long-term ill-effects were observed; no induction into homosexuality was found as a result of childhood sexual contact with adults.

(3) Children who were found to be disturbed after sexual contact with adults were those who were already disturbed before.

Nevertheless, they are careful not to dismiss the *possibility* of harm:

As the evidence stands, there is little ground for saying that a paedophile assault will damage a child. But catastrophic reactions *may* be shown by *particular* children under *particular* circumstances. Further research should concentrate upon pinpointing these children and circumstances. (1981, pp. 74-5, italics in original)

It is to be expected that many mainstream researchers and practitioners will vehemently oppose such an optimistic outlook on the effects of adult-child sexual contact. Groth (1982), in a review of the book in which the work of Powell & Chalkley (1981) is published, mounted a scathing attack on the latter's article:

> The most serious misinformation is promoted by Graham E. Powell and A.J. Chalkley in their chapter addressing the effects of pedophile attention on the child. They base their conclusion that such cross-generational sexual activity is predominantly innocuous or benign on a survey of impact studies which are grossly outdated. With one exception the sparse body of work they cite is between 20 and 40 years old. It has only been within the past 5 years that clinicians have begun to realize the extent of this problem and to rethink and revise outmoded psychoanalytic and psychiatric attitudes towards victimology. What Powell and Chalkley have done is to recycle myth and misconception, pertaining to the essential harmlessness of pedophilic activity. (Groth, 1982, p. 240)

Researchers who hold views similar to Groth's have published reviews which conclude that sexual contact between adults and children is harmful rather than benign. Mrazek & Mrazek (1981) have summarised the data of some 50 studies and pointed out that many more have demonstrated the harmful effects of adult-child sexual contact than have suggested otherwise. Similarly, Steele & Alexander (1981), in their review of long-term effects of childhood sexual abuse, have come to the conclusion that victims tended to remain badly affected even many years after the original trauma. Although they did acknowledge the contribution of factors other than the sexual activity itself, they suggested that 'the experience of sexual abuse seems to gain much of its potential for later damage by being the central core around which all other noxious experiences become organized' (pp. 232-3). Their argument is that even in cases where no obvious adjustment problems are seen, 'much pain and turmoil might exist beneath an outwardly normal or seemingly well-adjusted appearance' (p. 233).

There are two fundamental difficulties in any discussion of effects of adult-child sexual contact. First, there is the question how to define psychological harm; secondly, how to establish the link between adult-child sexual contact and psychological harm, particularly harm which only appears later in life. Steele and Alexander argue that childhood experience of sexual abuse constitutes the 'central core' around which other difficulties in the victim's life would become organised – the problem is that it is not easy to demonstrate any direct causal connection between such sexual experiences and other difficulties in a person's life, especially when these difficulties are only observed years after the alleged cause, namely sexual abuse, has occurred. Thus Steele and Alexander have to acknowledge that 'possibly there are relatively few late effects of abuse if there are not many other detrimental factors involved beyond simple sexual interaction' (1981, p. 232). In other words, they are not able to assert without qualification that the sexual contact itself will always produce long-term ill-effects. Perhaps one possible 'other detrimental factor' which Steele and Alexander have in mind is long-term coercion involved in the abuse. As discussed above, Brongersma and Constantine are not defending such coercive sexual abuse. Indeed, no researcher, however liberal, would want to suggest that coercion has no negative effect, whether short- or long-term.

The view of researchers like Brongersma and Constantine, as outlined above, is that the most detrimental factor is often the stigmatising and catastrophic reactions that the family and society show towards the child's experience. These researchers have argued that this is a far more significant factor than the sexual contact itself. Even if we do not adopt the pro-paedophile position of Brongersma or Constantine, it is still reasonable to suggest that perhaps the 'other detrimental factors' which Steele and Alexander mentioned might be independent of the abuse itself (e.g. family disintegration before the abuse), and that such factors also constitute part of the so-called 'central core' around which an individual's later difficulties are organised, in which case it is rather misleading to say that the adult-child sexual contact is the only, or major, cause of maladjustment in the child's later life.

The suggestion by Steele and Alexander of 'pain and turmoil underneath a seemingly well-adjusted appearance' illustrates the serious difficulty of defining the notion of 'effect' in relation to adult-child sexual contact. Admittedly one has to take into account the not-so-easily-observable aspects of a victim's life in order to assess the extent of suffering resulting from any trauma. The question is how 'deep' one needs to go into the inner life of the individual? Must one also consider suffering or pathology within the realm of the 'unconscious'? Is it necessary, or reasonable, to postulate ill-effects that the victim is not aware of? To postulate *hidden* ill-effects is to pre-empt the answer to the question of harm.

Both Mrazek & Mrazek (1981) and Powell & Chalkley (1981) have, in their respective reviews, mentioned many theoretical and methodological problems of most impact/outcome studies. Yet these two research teams have arrived at diametrically opposite conclusions. The difficulty is clearly seen when the two reviews used the same piece of research for *different* purposes. For example, the oft-quoted study by Bender & Blau (1937) has been reviewed by both Powell & Chalkley (1981) and Mrazek & Mrazek (1981). Whereas Powell and Chalkley have taken this study as illustrating the harmlessness of adult-child sexual contact, the Mrazeks have listed it under 'research showing ill-effects'.

A more recent review, which shares the same view as that of Steele & Alexander and the Mrazeks, can be found in Browne & Finkelhor (1986). In their review of some 26 studies, Browne and Finkelhor have used three parameters to organise their material: (1) initial effects of abuse, (2) long-term effects, and (3) factors contributing to effects. While acknowledging that many of these studies are methodologically inadequate, Browne and Finkelhor have nevertheless come to the conclusion that they did indicate at least some sexual abuse victims were suffering from initial reactions of fear, anxiety, depression, anger, hostility and inappropriate sexual acting out, as well as long-term effects of depression, anxiety, feelings of isolation and stigma, low self-esteem, self-destructive behaviour, substance abuse, sexual difficulties, mistrust of other people and a tendency towards revictimisation. These ill-effects were particularly marked if the abuser was the father, if genital contact was involved, if coercion was used, or if other family members were unsupportive. Their overall conclusion is therefore 'that a history of childhood sexual abuse is associated with greater risk for mental health and adjustment problems in adulthood' (p. 72).[48]

After affirming the view that childhood sexual experiences with adults are harmful, Finkelhor and Browne proceeded to organise these harmful effects in terms of a four-factor model (Finkelhor & Browne 1985).[49] They call these four factors *traumagenic dynamics*: (1) traumatic sexualisation, (2) betrayal, (3) powerlessness, and (4) stigmatisation. Although Finkelhor and Browne realise that these four 'dynamics' constitute a *conceptual* framework for categorising the effects of sexual abuse, and that each 'dynamic' is simply a name representing a clustering of negative effects with a common theme, their use of the four terms has confused the issue rather than clarifying it. The four 'dynamics' have become thing-like entities that could *cause* harm to children. For example, they talked of 'specific injurious dynamics' causing trauma, children 'suffering from a disempowering dynamic', or 'these dynamics altering children's cognitive and emotional orientation to the world', etc. Their uncritical use of the term 'dynamics' tends to give the impression that the ill-effects described are objective, concrete and powerful, and hence will reinforce their overall argument that sexual contact with adults is very harmful to children.

7.5.4 The difficulty of assessing effects

The discussion in the last section shows that different reviewers may reach very different conclusions with respect to the effect of adult-child sexual contact. In this section I shall unravel some of the difficulties involved.

First of all, the search for a *causal* link between sexual experience with adults and any subsequent effects, particularly long-term ones, might not

[48] Finkelhor (1980a, 1981a) did acknowledge that sexual activities involving siblings during childhood would not necessarily lead to harmful effects on the children involved.

[49] Browne & Finkelhor (1986), the review on effects, was first submitted for publication in October 1984, while Finkelhor & Browne (1985), the article that organises 'harmful effects' into a model, was submitted in February 1985. Thus it is probably the case that their four-factor model was worked out after they had completed their review on effects.

be a methodologically possible task. The use of correlational techniques can best produce results suggesting the tendency for social or psychological problems to be clustered in certain individuals, but not the causal relationship between one such problem (e.g. childhood sexual contact with adults) with another (e.g. sexual difficulties in adulthood). The use of control groups for comparison might not solve the difficulty because, as Courtois has found, statistical analysis of group differences may provide no firm basis for any conclusion regarding the link between abuse and other forms of maladjustment.[50]

The other problem related to the search for a causal link in the complex interaction among different variables in the production of 'effects'. Presumably a multivariate design might yield a more valid picture regarding causation. Even granted this, however, the likelihood of deriving firm conclusions from such analysis is still uncertain. Browne and Finkelhor (1986) have repeatedly remarked in their analysis that the existing literature shows contradictory results because of complex interaction among many factors. Although they are confident that a multivariate design will take care of this, the question remains whether the *personal* quality of human experience would not be lost amidst the numerous ANOVA F values and other statistical parameters.

Whether using simple correlational or t-test techniques, or more sophisticated multivariate methodologies, researchers who are keen to find causal links between child sexual abuse and maladjustment of the victims must finally rely on *post hoc* or *ad hoc* explanations, often couched in commonsensical terms, to *spell out* these links in an intelligible way. In so doing, a lot more is read into the statistical results than the latter actually allow – and the researchers are dependent on some tacit understanding of human life, which, however, is not explicitly discussed or adequately theorised. It is therefore more important to analyse conceptually these explanations, and the terms used, than to focus on the statistical significance (or otherwise) of the data. Take, for instance, the following passage from Finkelhor & Browne (1985):

> The anger stemming from betrayal is part of what may lie behind the aggressive and hostile posture of some sexual abuse victims, particularly adolescents. Such anger may be a primitive way of trying to protect the self against future betrayals. (p. 536)

The first statement in the quotation is based on studies which show that statistically more sexual abuse victims manifest aggressive and hostile behaviour than do non-abused individuals. The *postulated* link consists of the notions of 'anger', 'betrayal' and a desire to 'protect the self against future betrayals'. These notions are not provided by the statistical

[50] Courtois (1979, 1980) attempted to study the experience of incest and its aftermath by correlating 7 variables related to the experience with 8 'life spheres', but the 119 t-tests performed on the data were all found to be statistically not significant. Her explanation is that 'response to incest is too unique or idiosyncratic' (1979, p. 342).

results, but are rather derived from the commonsensical understanding that the researchers have regarding human experience. It would be much more fruitful if the *victim* had a chance to spell out in greater detail her personal construction of the experience and its effects, in her own words, so that what the researchers here refer to as 'anger' and a 'desire' to protect the self might be compared with the victim's own account. Instead of studying the victims by questionnaires, rating scales, or 'instruments specifically designed to assess the impact of sexual abuse',[51] a much more veridical type of material can be gathered through the collection of *narratives* from them. It is from these narratives that the researchers' inferences about 'anger', 'hostility', 'betrayal', etc., and the links, if any, between these notions and abusive experiences can be established.[52]

An important issue related to the study of the effects of childhood sexual contact with adults pertains to the definition of the notion of 'abuse'. Researchers who view every form of adult-child sexual contact as abuse tend to assume that such contact is inevitably injurious to the child, and so will orient their search accordingly; whereas researchers who are sympathetic to certain forms of adult-child sexual contact might focus on those cases where consensuality is present and social-institutional intervention absent, and thus might find no negative effects. The inclusion of all types of experience within the same study will confuse the picture – for example, accidental contact with exhibitionists tends not to produce any serious harm on children while the experience of rape will no doubt be very traumatic. Generalising from one type of experience to all experiences will bias the conclusion reached regarding the question of effects. It may therefore be the case that the question, 'Is childhood sexual contact with adults harmful?' is not a meaningful question in so far as it is put in a generalised form.

The problem of definition arises also in regard to the notion of 'effect'. Whether it is reasonable to define 'increased frequency of sexual activities' as 'promiscuity' (and hence 'ill'-effect) is debatable. The difficulty is compounded when sometimes '*decreased* frequency in sexual activities' is defined as 'dissatisfaction with sex life' and hence as 'ill'-effect as well. Taking increase or decrease in sexual activities as an 'ill'-effect involves making a value-judgment. This illustrates the necessity for the discussion of effects to be grounded on an explication of the ethical and value assumptions underlying the various studies.

The problem of an *a priori* value-judgment regarding the harm or otherwise of childhood sexual contact with adults also manifests itself in the choice of literature for review by a researcher. If a researcher has taken an ethical stand against any form of adult-child sexual contact, she

---

[51] Finkelhor & Browne (1985, p. 539) suggested that instruments specifically designed to tap the four 'traumagenic dynamics' are needed to improve both assessment of child sexual abuse cases and research on such abuse.

[52] It is possible that asking children to talk about their sexual experiences with adults, in a non-clinical and non-threatening setting, may yield information confirming the benign nature of at least some form of adult-child sexual contact (e.g. Sandfort, 1982).

might select only those studies that are favourable to her stand. Thus in the review of Browne & Finkelhor (1986), quite a number of earlier studies have been ignored,[53] all of which have either concluded that the sexual contact itself, if no force is involved, is not harmful to any appreciable extent, or that the children involved in such sexual contact are participants rather than victims. As the question of effect hinges on whether or not *consensual* contact is seen as possible, the answer seems to have been predetermined by the position that the researcher has taken regarding this possibility.

One final example of the difficulty involved in studies on effects can be found in Fromuth (1986). In a retrospective questionnaire study of a student sample, Fromuth attempted to correlate childhood sexual abuse experience with subsequent psychological maladjustment. After analysing her data statistically, she found that childhood sexual abuse accounted for less than 2 per cent of the variance of the respondents' scores on psychological adjustment. One of the fundamental problems involved is whether using such a paper-and-pencil 'test' can really yield valid information about a person's 'psychological adjustment', even if some 'statistically significant' findings had been obtained. Furthermore, while Finkelhor (1984) has concluded that individuals with a history of childhood sexual abuse tend to suffer from low 'sexual self-esteem' in later life, Fromuth's (1986) data have shown no difference between the abused and the control groups precisely on the *same* variable. However, even though she has arrived at many more statistically non-significant findings than significant ones, Fromuth still concluded that the 'no-harm' theory cannot be accepted. Her reasons are:

(1) The definition of sexual abuse used in her study was too broad (encounters with exhibitionists were included), which might have lower the correlations between abuse and subsequent ill-effects.

(2) The healthy individuals in the abused sample might have masked the effects on the severely affected ones.

(3) The time lapse between the abuse and the research was too short for its long-term effects to be more observable.

(4) Sexual abuse in itself might not be related to later maladjustment, but when in interaction with other factors, such as the lack of parent support, it might produce maladjustment.

These four points show that Fromuth's study is methodologically inadequate on her own admission – yet she clearly favours the conclusion of harmful effects despite this difficulty. Much more serious is her tendency to 'explain away' the negative findings by various illogical or *ad hoc* arguments such as (2) and (3) above. All this reflects the basic

[53] These studies are: Bender & Blau (1937), Bender & Grugett (1952), Bernard (1981, 1985), Burton (1968), Constantine (1981a), Ingram (1981), Lempp (1978), J.A. Nelson (1981), Powell & Chalkley (1981), Rossman (1979), Sandfort (1982, 1984), Virkkunen (1975, 1981) Weiss *et al*. (1955), and P. Wilson (1981).

problem of the debate on effects of adult-child sexual contact: each investigator's conclusion is somehow predetermined by the value-judgment she has made.

In a monograph on child sexual abuse and social work, Chesterman (1985) started with a review of a very selected sample of outcome studies and concluded that sexual contact with adults is always harmful to children. He then discussed the various obstacles to an effective social-work response and suggested that these obstacles resulted from a lack of professional concern for, and awareness of, the problem. This is his recommendation:

> I therefore tend to feel that until the 'private trouble' of incest is taken up by concerned professionals as a serious 'issue' there will be little significant widespread change. (p. 30)

This call for the transformation of private family life into an object of public scrutiny follows on from Chesterman's affirmation of the harmful nature of intergenerational sexual contact. In contrast, the review by Constantine (1981a), which concludes that adult-child sexual contact is not in itself a harmful experience, provides the basis on which its author has constructed a 'radical perspective' for the sexual liberation of children – giving back to children their sexual rights (Constantine 1981b). It seems that the answer to the question to what extent adult-child sexual contact is harmful depends very much on what use the researcher wants to make of it.

7.6 Adult-child sexual contact as a 'problem'

'Statistics' is 'the science of the state', the art of government – the collection and collation of 'truths' about the state's resources and its conditions. It constitutes an essential component of modern political rationality.[54] However, the 'deployment' of statistics in the control of the population is nowadays not always through the state apparatus. Rather, it pervades the whole social body through various channels, both official and unofficial. As mentioned earlier, prevalence statistics are most frequently used to show the seriousness of the 'problem' of adult-child sexual contact. These statistics are presented as evidence that in countries like Britain or the United States, hundreds of thousands of children are sexually abused every year, and that millions of people have been sexually abused one way or another during their childhood. Pubescent girls are seen as most 'at risk', but younger children and boys are by no means immune from molestation. The harmful effects of sexual abuse are serious, repercussive and long-lasting – it threatens the mental health of whole populations.[55]

---

[54] See Rabinow (1984), p. 16.
[55] Russell (1984a) talks about child sexual abuse, rape and sexual harassment as manifestations of the same male violence that threatens the 'well-being and survival of the

While the image of the child molester as a 'dirty old man' in a raincoat has been repeatedly pronounced an inaccurate myth, a new image is now being constructed in its place – the child molester is simply an *ordinary* man, who lives next door or even in the same family as the child victim, and incest is often treated as the most common variety of child sexual abuse.

Such a new image underlines the purported ubiquity as well as danger of child sexual abuse – it *is* a serious social problem of modern society. A passage from Forward & Buck (1978), a popular work aimed at the general public, well illustrates this construction:

> This is not so much a book about incest as it is a book about people – all kinds of people. There are probably more than *ten million* Americans who have been involved in incest, and they come from every economic, cultural, racial, educational, religious, and geographical background. They are doctors, policemen, prostitutes, secretaries, artists, and merchants. They are heterosexual, bisexual, and homosexual. They are happily married and four-times divorced. They are leading productive lives and they have been convicted of murder. They are emotionally stable and they have multiple personalities. In short, the people whose stories appear in this book have only one thing in common: incest.
>
> Incest is not some freakish perversion confined to the back alleys of Marrakech; it is a *fact of life* that has involved *at least* one out of every twenty Americans. (pp. 2-3, italics added)

This description is an alarming one – it is meant to be so. Incest is treated as *the* problem of modern family life.

There are, however, many complex problems related to these statistics. The first problem is the very definition of a 'case' of child sexual abuse.

As discussed earlier, different research studies have used different age criteria for the notion of a 'child', hence the various estimates of prevalence do not match. Any age criterion is arbitrary, as sexual maturity varies enormously from child to child, both physically and psychologically. Many researchers have extended the term 'child' to cover individuals up to age 18 or beyond because they argue that these young people are still socially and psychologically under the authority of adults (particularly powerful adults like fathers) and as such must be protected from the latter's sexual advances. Studies that have adopted such a view will inevitably produce high prevalence rates of 'child' sexual abuse.

While the notion of 'sexual abuse' implies both a sexual motive as well as the lack of consent, most surveys do not enquire whether the 'victim' *consents* to the contact. Consent is seen as impossible even if no overt coercion is involved. Any bodily-sensual contact between an adult[56] and a child is defined as a case of sexual abuse.

The problem with this assumption is that it may actually *create* cases of

_____

entire population of the United States' (p. 289).

[56] In some studies, teenage 'perpetrators' are also included in the statistics of prevalence of child sexual abuse.

abuse from experiences which are not seen as such by the parties concerned. A grandfather, quoted in Tucker (1985), said:

> I've always been very close to a grand-daughter. She's four years old. And when I put my arm around her, I touched her leg down in this area, and here comes this shield saying, you know, don't do that, don't do that, like there was something wrong with it. And it's the fear, I guess, in the country of some kook somewhere going to see me touch this child and press charges against me or something. (p. 97)

Here the grandfather certainly enjoys 'touching up' his granddaughter. Does that constitute 'sexual abuse'? Likewise, is a grandfather who always wants good-night kisses from his grand-children an abuser? Even if it is a *sensual* enjoyment, must it be socially and legally condemned as 'sexual abuse'?

In relation to this problem of a 'case', the question arises who the client actually is in reported child sexual abuse, or what the reason is for a parent to accuse her husband of molesting their daughter. Is it a matter of a marital row, of wanting a divorce, or a tactic to obtain exclusive custodial rights to the children? Could it be a matter of parent-child conflicts over the child's quest for independence? The child might not be maliciously lying, she might just be retrospectively construing some of her father's behaviour as sexual abuse in order to get away from his control.[57] It is not suggested here that a high proportion of sexual abuse reports are false or are intentional fabrication. The point is that motives for allegation of abuse are complex – it is possible that some activity, hitherto considered innocuous, has, during times of crisis, come to be *construed* as sexual abuse, for reasons not immediately tied to the 'safety' of the child 'victims'. Whether or not that activity is in itself abuse is another question – the object of the complaint might simply be, say, to obtain a divorce.

The over-enthusiasm of professionals in 'diagnosing' child sexual abuse might be responsible for the rise in prevalence statistics.[58] Faced with the claim that child sexual abuse is increasing, there are calls within the medical profession for greater alertness to this problem in the diagnostic assessment of children. For example, Cantwell (1983) recommends that vaginal inspection should become a routine part of medical physical examination of prepubertal girls. Besides the ethical problems associated with the procedure itself, uncritical reliance on such an examination as an infallible indicator of child sexual abuse will run the risk of producing

[57] Expert opinions are sometimes sought by the prosecution in child sexual abuse cases to affirm the credibility of the child's testimony. However, such 'credibility assessment' tasks are highly complicated and there might not be a clear-cut yes or no answer (Mann, 1985). If psychiatrists and psychologists work with the assumption that child sexual abuse reports and allegations are always true, their 'expert' opinions will undoubtedly be one-sided.

[58] In recent years, more than 65 per cent of cases in the annual incidence of child maltreatment in the USA turn out to be unfounded – this is a consequence of over-reporting and over-diagnosing (Besharov, 1985, p. 556).

false positive judgments, which, once the child protection machinery is set in motion, may lead to much injustice done to the families involved. The recent Cleveland child sexual abuse controversy, in which 121 children were diagnosed, within a 5-month period in 1987, by two paediatricians (whose diagnosis was supported by senior staff from the local Social Services Department) as having been sexually abused and consequently taken away from home and placed into foster care without the due process of law ascertaining the truth of the alleged abuse, illustrates starkly the danger of the tendency in some over-zealous professionals to construct cases of sexual abuse based on equivocal evidence. After months of enquiry and court hearings, 98 of the 121 children have now been returned home, and some parents are taking legal action to sue the doctors involved.

When the Cleveland crisis reached boiling point in the summer of 1987, the Secretary of State for Social Services set up a Statutory Enquiry, chaired by Lord Justice Butler-Sloss, to look into this volatile situation. A year later, Lord Justice Butler-Sloss published her enquiry report, which, while recognising the extent of the problem of child sexual abuse, is very critical of the ways in which the paediatricians and senior social workers had diagnosed abuse on inadequate evidence. Serious doubts have been thrown on the diagnostic method 'reflex anal dilatation' which was heavily relied upon by the two paediatricians. Certainly this controversy has jostled people into the realisation that the identification of child sexual abuse is not a simple straightforward matter.

Besides 'reflex anal dilatation', other controversial diagnostic techniques include the use of 'anatomically correct dolls' to interview the child. The use of these dolls, together with very leading questions, in the assessment of young children can easily produce false positives of child sexual abuse.[59] Once the paediatrician, child psychiatrist or social worker has decided, on the basis of an assessment carried out in the highly artificial setting of the consulting room, that the child in question has been molested, the family concerned might find the ensuing child protection procedures totally beyond their control. Even if they genuinely believed that sexual abuse had not taken place in their family, they would find it extremely difficult to convince the authorities that this is a false positive judgment – out of self-protection, the professionals involved would tend to look for confirming evidence and dismiss alternative explanations.[60] Recently, a group of parents in Britain have formed an

[59] The use of such procedures has aroused much criticism, particularly from defence lawyers. In two recent wardship cases involving sexual abuse allegations, an English judge has rejected 'evidence' obtained through the use of 'anatomically correct dolls' in a child-psychiatric interview as invalid (see *The Times*, 16 July 1986, p. 3 and p. 36.)

[60] Social workers and other professionals in the child care field are wary of making 'false negative' mistakes – the price to pay is too great, as can be seen in the Beckford case, in which the social workers involved were sacked, the social services director of Brent eventually resigned (*Guardian*, 16 August 1986), and the profession as a whole came in for some severe criticism from the public enquiry report (Blom-Cooper, 1985). The Rayner controversy (November 1987) is another case in point.

organisation called Parents Against Injustice (PAIN) to call for a code of practice that will govern the actions of child-care professionals in their intervention into alleged child abuse cases. Their aim is to prevent wrongful intervention into families, which, according to their experience, is not at all uncommon.[61]

The construction of a 'case' of child sexual abuse by professionals merits critical scrutiny.[62] Schultz (1981) has argued that 'the very labelling and intervention in child/adolescent/adult sexual interation may themselves by victimogenic or traumatogenic' (p. 29), because 'labelling the child a sex victim, or assuming a symptom complex may have self-fulfilling potential when coming from persons of expertise or authority' (Schultz & Jones, 1983, p. 104). Here Schultz is calling for caution against 'iatrogenesis'[63] – that is, the creation of a case of 'sickness' by the medical profession when the experience itself does not warrant such a construction. While professional practitioners might not be consciously or intentionally creating the atmosphere of alarm regarding the ubiquity of child sexual abuse to maintain their professional power, the effect of 'iatrogenesis' that Schultz talks about does reinforce the sense of an urgent need for more resources for, and greater professionalisation of, the 'management' of child sexual abuse. The affirmation of such a need makes practitioners feel justified in actively intervening into the life of families and individuals. Judging from the increasing number of treatment programmes, research projects, postgraduate dissertations, and more significantly popular publications and media coverage on child sexual abuse, particularly in the United States, it is apparent that a positive feedforward cycle has been operating here. More research and professional intervention will 'unearth' more 'cases', and more staggering statistics will be published, which will lead to the call for more intervention and funding for research or for the setting up of special programmes, and more professionals will flock to this field because it is a 'growth' area; thus even more research is done, and the problem is seen as more and more serious, and so on. The accumulation by professionals and researchers of 'statistics and information' about child sexual abuse makes them the 'experts' who can exercise power in various ways, not least in the construction of life histories of abusers or abusive families in the form

[61] PAIN is currently conducting a survey to find out how many parents have been wrongfully accused of physical or sexual abuse of their children. They have documented case histories of families broken up by state intervention (care orders, forced fostering, prosecutions, etc.) on the basis of dubious 'evidence' (personal communication from Mrs Sue Amphlett, organiser of PAIN). A similar organisation, Victims of Child Abuse Laws (VOCAL) has recently been set up in the United States.

[62] In relation to physical child abuse, some work has already been done (e.g. Besharov, 1985; Freeman, 1983; Parton, 1985). There is certainly a similar need for studies on 'the politics of child sexual abuse', as well as studies on the history of the emergence of child sexual abuse as a 'social problem'.

[63] 'While both psychiatrists and social workers have criticized law enforcement and the law profession for inducing legal process trauma, they have not critically examined their own interventions for possible victimogenesis, traumatogenesis or iatrogenesis' (Schultz, 1981, p. 29).

of psychological or psychiatric reports, which can often determine the fate of the individuals concerned.

Indeed, child sexual abuse 'cases' may not only be 'iatrogenic', but 'research/survey-genic' as well.[64] There is no way of telling whether or not survey respondents have only come to construe their past experience in terms of child sexual abuse while participating in the survey.[65] Retrospective surveys never ask respondents to provide their own definition of sexual abuse. Rather, a definition, sometimes so loose as to range from sexual intercourse to an obscene telephone call or exposure to pornography, is provided in the questionnaire. Such loose definitions will inevitably lead to the inclusion of many innocuous events as child sexual abuse, and consequently lead to an inflation of the prevalence statistics. If a respondent indicates that she has had an encounter covered by the definition, one positive 'case' has been 'identified'. Many people, including children, might not consider an encounter with a 'flasher' sexual abuse, but such encounters nevertheless go into the child sexual abuse statistics. Nowadays, with so much sexually explicit material in the mass media, as well as flirtatious 'sex-talk' in the social environment in which many children live, it is possible to argue that most children have been 'exposed to pornography'. The 'ubiquity' of child sexual abuse *could* be easily established, if the researcher *wanted* it to be so. But if the child did not feel that she was a victim, must we try to convince her that she was? Lost in these statistics is not only the possibility of a child consenting to engage in sensual-sexual interaction with an adult, but also the possibility that the adult has no intention of harming the child.

In this connection, it is interesting to note that although Schultz & Jones (1983) have acknowledged the presence of consensuality in the sexual activities reported by many of their survey respondents, and although they are aware of the possibility of 'iatrogenesis' of child sexual abuse 'cases', they nevertheless have to submit to the *Zeitgeist* and talk about their findings as showing 'child sexual abuse occurring *everywhere* in West Virginia',[66] and that they are not 'condoning adult-child sexuality'.

Wyatt & Peters (1986a, 1986b) have, after discussing the various problems and factors contributing to the discrepant findings in child sexual abuse prevalence studies, recommended a list of research strategies which aim at making the survey respondent more at ease and

[64] Erving Goffman has alluded to this possibility while discussing the creation of 'deviants' by social scientists (1963, p. 140, n.1).

[65] Certainly researchers can argue that such 'consciousness-raising' is one beneficial side-effect of the survey, and that it is good that the respondents have come to see their childhood experience as abuse. Such an argument, however, illustrates precisely the ideological nature of statistics: some surveys and statistical reports might have a hidden purpose – to make people see their experience as abuse, and to channel social resources to combat such 'abuse'.

[66] They conducted their retrospective study on a student sample in West Virginia. The description 'everywhere' is based on a prevalence rate of 43.8 per cent, which, however, covers all (including consensual) sexual acts, not just abusive incidents.

more willing to disclose experience of abuse.[67] Although not explicitly stated, the aim is to produce more 'accurate', i.e. higher, prevalence rates – the assumption is that, since child sexual abuse is ubiquitous, only higher rates are truly indicative of the magnitude of the problem. The possibility that a survey interview may become a process of persuasion is simply ignored by these authors.

Prevalence statistics are often used by feminists in their accusations of male sexual oppression of females. Russell (1984a)[68] has concluded from her survey of a sample of San Francisco women that *every other* female child (aged under 18) has been sexually abused (including indecent exposure). When rape, child sexual abuse and sexual harassment at work are taken together, 'the lives of *all* women are affected by at least one of these forms of sexual exploitation, either directly or indirectly' (p. 87, italics in original). Her final argument is as follows:

> If 90 per cent of the crimes of violence were perpetrated by a particular minority group or social class, that minority group or social class would be viewed as a distinct problem and treated accordingly. But despite the fact that 90 per cent of the ruling gender is responsible for such crimes [i.e. sexual violence to females], the fact of this collective responsibility is almost universally ignored. This demonstrates the ability of those in power to define what and who the problem is. (p. 289)

There is no uncertainty in Russell's presentation of her case. Child sexual abuse is rampant, it is continuous with rape and other forms of sexual exploitation of females by males, the 'ruling gender'. Thus child sexual abuse is a feminist issue; it is a matter of power imbalance between the sexes. It is interesting to note that Russell has made a slip in the passage quoted above. Instead of saying that '... the fact that 90 per cent of such crimes are perpetrated by the ruling gender', she has written, '... the fact that 90 per cent of the ruling gender is responsible for such crimes'.[69] Whether deliberate or not, this slip has the effect of giving the impression that nearly *every* male is an abuser – just as every female *is* a victim.

While Russell's work will probably not be read by the average person in the street, the mass media have come in to fill the gap by disseminating to the public information on prevalence statistics and conclusions drawn from these statistics, which will leave no doubt as to the seriousness of the problem of child sexual abuse. In a recent article in the *Sunday Observer*, Rance & Lloyd (1986) asserted that 'one in five women, and one in ten men have been sexually abused as children'. Alongside these statistics, the authors have made the following comment on a specific case:

[67] These strategies include using the interview method rather than questionnaire, asking more questions about specific abusive events, and rewarding the respondents' effort by giving them monetary reimbursement, etc.

[68] Russell claims that her book is the first one to 'document thoroughly and rigorously' sexual exploitation in a major US city (San Francisco).

[69] The 90 per cent referred to here is the average proportion of male perpetrators found in

> So now, a man like Alan who has brutally assaulted or killed children can
> leave prison on his earliest release date, into the anonymous bed-sit land of
> a new city, where he is free to offend again ... (p. 46, column 7)

Such juxtaposing of statistics and horrifying examples will have the effect
of associating the two in the mind of the public – every single case in
these alarming statistics would be thought to be similar to this example
of child murder, and the magnitude of the horror will thus increase
enormously.

One interesting feature in the English *Criminal Statistics* should be
noted. Throughout the 15-year-period 1970–1984, the proportion of
notifiable sexual offences never exceeded 2 per cent of all recorded serious
offences, with a highest rate of 1.9 per cent in 1973 and a lowest of 0.6 per
cent in the last three years of the period. Indeed, only six of the fifteen
years have a rate exceeding 1 per cent. Assuming that about half[70] of all
these sexual offences involved an adult perpetrator and a child victim,
the overall adult-child sexual offences would only amount to about 0.3-1
per cent of all recorded serious crimes. The major bulk of these serious
crimes consisted of theft and burglary (over 75 per cent of the total),
which would never get as much national media attention as the relatively
'rare' adult-child sexual offences. Moreover, if the estimate of Walmsley &
White (1979) of the extent of 'consensual' contact in sexual 'offences' is
applicable to sexual offences involving children, the incidence of *coercive*
child sexual abuse would be further reduced among the total crime rate.
Despite all these considerations, child sexual abuse cases will always hit
the headlines – the significance of adult-child sexual contact lies not in its
being very prevalent or otherwise, but rather in its deep impact on the
psychological structure of society.

---

studies of sexual exploitation of children. About 10 per cent of perpetrators are female.

[70] The analysis of criminal statistics by Walmsley & White (1979, 1980) shows that over
half of all notifiable sexual offences involve an offender over 21 and a victim under 16 years
of age.

8

Theoretical Models

Sexual contact between adults and children constitutes a very serious social problem – at least that is what many researchers are trying to show. The next question is how to account for the occurrence of such abuse – in this chapter I shall present some of the explanatory models that researchers and professionals have constructed.

8.1 The psychoanalytic perspective

8.1.1 Perversions

Within the broad spectrum of the different schools of psychoanalysis, there is general agreement on what is to be deemed 'normal' sexuality, the key features of which are attraction to an adult partner of the opposite sex, and genital orgasm as the ultimate goal. Deviant or perverse sexuality is defined as a sexual preference which departs from this accepted norm.[1] To the extent that adult sexual perversions resemble childhood pregenital activities, they are often understood in terms of either a regression to, or a fixation at, a pregenital (hence immature) stage of development. Some psychoanalysts argue for the normative nature of adult genital heterosexuality by referring to the supreme importance of procreation.[2] Any form of sexual activity which deviates from this biological aim is a paraphilia (i.e. a perversion).[3]

Since, to psychoanalysts, adult psychological maladjustment has its root in childhood experience, sexual deviations are always traced back to some developmental difficulty in childhood. Freud's notion of the Oedipus complex, which occupies a pivotal place in psychoanalytic theory, is often regarded as the source of most psychological problems, including perversions. Because the Oedipus complex is seen as a consequence of intense incestuous desire on the part of the child, perversions are interpreted as the pathological expression of the effort to contain this unacceptable desire.

[1] See e.g. Roche (1950), p. 4; Rosen (1979a), p. 30.
[2] See Karpman (1954).
[3] Even masturbation, strictly speaking, is a paraphilia because it does not contribute to procreation (Karpman, 1954, p. 349).

Psychoanalysis is not a homogeneous monolith, but rather an amalgam of many different theories and practices. Thus while Karpman (1954) views all paraphilias as 'a flight from incest', Storr (1964) has placed more emphasis on emotional immaturity and the inability to love as the dominant structure of sexual deviations. Rosen (1979b) stresses the function of perversions as a regulator of self-esteem, and Stoller (1974, 1976) interprets them in terms of hostility and revenge ('eroticised hatred').

8.1.2 Paedophilia

With respect to the origin of paedophilia, a number of specific formulations can be found in the psychoanalytic literature: unresolved Oedipus complex; psychic impotence; arrested libidinal development; weaning trauma leading to oral dependence, or to hostility towards mother, which in turn is displaced to a female child; castration fear resulting in autoerotic fixation; narcissistic compensation which is generalised to other children, etc.[4]

The theme of 'substitution' often appears in psychoanalytical writings on paedophilia. For example, Anthony Storr has made the following suggestions:

> The man who suffers from paedophilia as a true deviation does not do so from excess of sensuality, but rather because he has been unable to find sexual satisfaction in an adult relationship. It is not from a superfluity of lust, but rather because of a timid inability to make contact with contemporaries that a man generally finds that children form the focus of his sexual interest. ... A man who had not freed himself from the maternal tie tended to regard women as dangerous and potentially 'castrating'. One way of circumventing such fears is to substitute a child for an adult woman. ... When sexual impulses are denied their normal fulfilment in an adult love relationship they continue to seek expression in ways which are generally abandoned by those who have been able to reach a more mature stage of development. Very many people have been paedophilics in one sense; for very many people have had sexual contacts with children when they themselves were children. When adult sexual expression has never been attained, the desire for sexual contact with children may persist. When an adult relation has had to be abandoned, because of death, absence, or illness of a partner, the desire for sexual contact with children may re-assert itself. (Storr, 1964, pp. 102-3)

On the other hand, the formulation of the paedophile as a man who is narcissistically in love with his previous youthful self is also prominent in the literature of psychoanalysis. Fraser (1976) has attempted to construct a general theory of paedophilia around the motif of narcissism. The following is his account:

[4] Examples of these formulations can be found in Allen (1949, 1969), Caprio & Brenner (1961), Cassity (1927), Kurland (1960), Sword (1978).

The paedophile has, in the first place, been doubly deprived; his emotional attachment to his mother has been intense, but not fully returned, or not returned at all. His father has been absent, disliked, or despised. As a result, the dilemma which he reaches at the Oedipal stage is particularly cruel. To an extent, this crisis is common to all male children; a boy becomes aware of his father's role, and thus of the threatened loss to him of exclusive possession of his mother. The classical defence is 'identification with the aggressor', in which the boy takes his father as his behavioural model; by doing so, he hopes to absorb from his father the characteristics that will again capture his mother's affection. But what happens to the boy when his father is absent, or where there is some intense, or even subtle father-son aversion? The practical effect is that his father then cannot, of course, be the male model, and there is no 'aggressor' with whom to identify. Doubly frustrated, the boy turns back on the only love-object left – himself. Thus *narcissistic inversion* takes place and, as he grows older, he remains deeply in love with the child he was then. This is impossible, so he must project (i.e. transfer his affection outwards) on to other children of a similar age to this lost child, who thus become love-objects for him. (p. 20, italics in original)

Fraser has made the following remarks on the question of sexual attraction to girls:

Is it even possible that an emotionally-starved youth can see, in his mirror, the features of a little girl? Even though rarely, he can; the clue is that we are dealing here with *early* inversion – inversion at a stage when boys and girls are, after all, much more physically alike than they will be after puberty, when the 'secondary sexual characteristics' will be increasingly manifest. Sexual preferences are, as we shall see, blurred anyway in paedophiles – though quite obviously the growing invert is much more likely to see, mirrored in his pool, the face of a child of his own sex. But there are influences which may, so to speak, stir and ruffle the water – leading, if not to strange distortions, at least to the anomaly of projection on to a child whose sex is opposite to his own. ... 'Early' is really the key word. By the time that the Oedipal stage is reached most boys, by learning, by group identification, by parental reinforcements, have developed a sufficient number of traits of 'maleness' to define at least the features of a young boy – and thus to limit the extent to which inversion can occur. So, if perception of a father's inadequacy comes *late*, projection is on to the weighty muscleman beloved of adult homosexual magazines. Lewis Carroll's experience, however, lay at the opposite extreme; his intellectual precocity, proceeding years in advance of his gender identification, meant, as a result of father-son detachment, total inversion from the male and on to the person of a little girl. (1976, pp 43, 166-7, italics in original)

From these quotations, Fraser's formulation can be summarised in the following way:

(1) Paedophilia has its root in the lack of an external love-object during the Oedipal stage of a child's growth.

(2) This lack of love-object is due to both the Oedipal anxiety over the child's incestuous desire for the mother, thus barring the latter

from remaining a love-object, as well as the absence of the father, either physically or psychologically, for the child to identify with, as a resolution of the Oedipus complex.

(3) This double deprivation means that the only person in whom the child can invest his love is himself – hence narcissistic inversion occurs.

(4) Usually the person who suffers from narcissistic inversion would project his love to a child of his own sex because the latter represents best his former self.

(5) However, in the case of a very sensitive and intellectually precocious child, who experiences his double deprivation before the Oedipal stage, and hence before a firm gender identification is established, his love could be invested in a child of either sex.

Although Fraser has not explicitly stated his allegiance to any particular psychoanalytic school of thought, it is apparent from his work that a number of concepts originally developed by Jung have been given a prominent place. For instance, the concept of archetypes, of which the 'Child' is the one most heavily used by Fraser, forms a pivotal component in his formulation of narcissistic inversion. This archetype occupies a similarly significant role in another Jungian work – Kraemer (1976). In this collection of essays by four Jungian analysts, paedophilia is acknowledged as a normal part of human experience – the lapse into abnormality is neither spectacular nor confined to very unusual individuals. The theme of childhood abandonment and deprivation as a precursor of paedophilia is articulated. Also, the archetype of the 'Inner Child' or 'Divine Youth' is taken as the source from which a paedophilic narcissism can spring. The operation of such an archetype is not only to be found in the paedophile himself, but also in his parents, who tend to idealise their son, thus leading to his narcissistic development. Furthermore, 'replacing the whole with the part' is another prominent theme in this Jungian construction of paedophilia. Because paedophilic desire is not adult-genital, it is deemed to be 'non-whole', and because paedophiles are seen as incapable of relationships, paedophilia is not love either.

8.1.3. Incest

To the psychoanalyst, childhood incestuous desire is interesting in so far as it is the source of adult neuroses and perversions. Whether incest actually occurs in the life of a child is not as important as the role this fantasy plays in shaping future psychological maladjustment.[5] This attitude is precisely what feminists have found so objectionable in psychoanalysis – Freud and his followers are accused of not only ignoring

---

[5] 'As a matter of fact, in psychoanalytic practice we are not usually concerned so much with actual incest as with the part which unconscious incestuous interest plays in the formation of other paraphilias' (Karpman, 1954, p. 345).

the grotesque reality of incestuous abuse of children by parents, but also of biasing the view of other professions regarding the veracity of children's reports of incestuous assault by treating such reports as childhood fantasies.[6]

Within the framework that Freud has developed, incestuous desire on the part of the child does not need to be explained – it is the natural expression of the primordial *id* desire, which often makes children willing victims of incestuous abuse by parents (A. Freud, 1981). Incestuous acts initiated by a parent, presumably, can be accounted for in terms of unresolved Oedipal strivings operating in the reverse direction, or as a result of developmental failure.[7] Anna Freud (1981) postulated that the experience of actual incestuous relationship with parents during the Oedipal stage of psychosexual development would predispose an individual towards incestuous acting out after he had become a parent himself.

8.1.4 A brief critical note on psychoanalysis

Recent critiques of psychoanalysis have shown that it is much more a quasi-religious cult than a body of proven scientific knowledge.[8] Because of its nature as an exclusive 'guild', psychoanalysis rejects any scrutiny by 'outsiders' – only the practitioners of psychoanalysis are reckoned as having any access to 'truth'. The various systems of psychoanalytic thoughts have become firm systems of beliefs, and their practitioners, by virtue of their exclusive claim on 'truth', have become the 'secular priests'[9] of the new religion. Seen in this light, it is not surprising that the empirical content of psychoanalysis is difficult to establish.[10] Take, for example, the Oedipus complex. This is a conceptualisation of a certain stage in a child's development which Freud came to theorise on the basis of analysis of adult patients – it is extremely difficult to demonstrate the operation of such a complex in the *experience* of the infants themselves. Far from being universally valid, the notion of the Oedipus complex is very much a culture-bound concept, as various anthropological studies have shown.[11]

On the conceptual level, the notion of the unconscious, on which the

[6] Feminist critique of Freud can be found in e.g. Albin (1977), Ward (1984). Within psychoanalysis itself, some analysts are beginning to criticise Freud on this count as well, e.g. Masson (1984), Miller (1985), Peters (1976). Masson's work is particularly interesting – it is a documentation of events surrounding Freud's abandonment of the 'seduction theory' in favour of the 'childhood fantasy theory', and it has aroused serious controversy within psychoanalytical circles.

[7] See Gaddini (1983).

[8] See Gellner (1985), Szasz (1978).

[9] For the critique of the psychotherapeutic profession as a 'secular priesthood' see North (1972).

[10] Although certain claims of psychoanalysis, such as selective forgetting, are open to validation, many of its concepts and conceptualisations are difficult to verify empirically. A good review can be found in B.A. Farrell (1981).

[11] See e.g. Benedict (1935), Malinowski (1927), Mead (1949).

existence and operation of the Oedipus complex hinges, is very difficult to handle, since it controls its own manifestation as well as the evidence about itself, and it is purposive and cunning (Gellner, 1985, p. 221). It is doubtful that anyone, Freud included, could have broken through its 'defences' and come to grips with its nature. Harré (1979) has pointed out that the logical difficulty of Freud's notion of the unconscious is that 'from the point of view of the self the removal of material from consciousness, and hence from the possibility of control, is a defensive manoeuvre undertaken by that very self' (p. 253). Such an uncontrollable mechanism within the 'self' resembles the discredited notion of the *homunculus*. The all-pervasive emphasis on the unconscious in psychoanalysis does not accord with the experience of reflexive self-monitoring in practical living;[12] it also tends to neglect the significance of the interpersonal dimension in the development of personhood.[13]

While many authors have rejected Freud's work as 'unscientific', attempts have been made to resolve this difficulty by interpreting psychoanalysis as a practice which concerns itself with 'meanings' rather than, as the physical sciences do, with 'facts'.[14] The most important component of such a formulation is the notion of 'narrative intelligibility' – that is, the truth of psychoanalytic theories lies not in the empirical verification of objective facts, but in the attainment of hermeneutical validity of experience. A psychoanalytic interpretation can be regarded as true if it is consistent with the rules for decoding unconscious material, forms an intelligible narrative, and is therapeutically effective.

While the operation of psychoanalytic practices may be *internally* consistent with its own set of rules and evidentiary procedures, it is difficult for somebody who does not accept the basic tenets of Freudian theory to see the validity of these practices. The analysand's acceptance of psychoanalytic interpretations may be a result of increased suggestibility arising from the emotionally intense and power-imbalanced analytic relationship. The observation that Freudian patients tend to have Oedipal dreams while Jungian patients have archetypal ones illustrates this difficulty vividly. On the other hand, if the analysand rejects the analyst's interpretations, it is still possible, within the internal logic of psychoanalysis, for the analyst to interpret such rejection as 'resistance' – a pathological expression of the analysand's neurosis. There is no way that the analyst's interpretations can be called into question.[15] It is a

[12] See Giddens (1984), p. 50.

[13] Hsu (1971) has proposed a concept of personhood in terms of the interface between the individual and his immediate social circle. Within this conceptualisation, the notion of the unconscious is not given prominence.

[14] A reinterpretation of psychoanalysis in this manner can be found in the work of Paul Ricoeur, e.g. Ricoeur (1981).

[15] Jean-Paul Sartre once published a tape transcript of a 'psychoanalytic dialogue' he got from an analysand. This dialogue was tape-recorded during one of the analytic sessions (presumably the last!) by the analysand without the analyst knowing. When the analysand produced the tape-recorder from his pocket, the analyst at once refused to say anything

matter of the imposition on the analysand of a rigid scheme of interpretative constructs, which is taken by the analyst as universally valid. Thus the 'hermeneutics' is defined by the psychoanalyst alone, rather than, as in this present research, by the meaning-bestowing capacity of each individual person.[16] Any interpretation is a *creative* act – it is not an unearthing of the past, but an active bestowal of meanings on the present. The insistence of orthodox psychoanalysis on the universal and objective truth of its theories and categories, and its imposition of a rigid interpretative framework on the analysand's experience are difficult to defend.

One frequent criticism of psychoanalysis is that it has completely glossed over the patriarchal nature of Western society – its glorification of the male phallus, its focus on the development of the male child, and its theorising of female sexuality in terms of masochism are all taken as a reflection of its complicity with patriarchal oppression of females. While there are authors who have attempted to draw out from Freud's work a radical and subversive theory about society and sexuality,[17] orthodox psychoanalysis *is* conservative – it is never interested in, and is actually very antagonistic to, the articulation of the subversive potential in the Freudian corpus; it is especially hostile to any attempt, whether in the name of Freud or not, which questions its elitist establishment.

Given the many problems regarding the nature and practice of psychoanalysis, it is difficult to accept as valid its various formulations of paedophilia. However, while the technical details of psychoanalytic concepts such as the unconscious, the Oedipus complex, or narcissistic inversion are highly problematic, more 'commonsense' elaboration of psychoanalytic ideas, such as Storr's use of the 'substitution theme' quoted earlier, might prove useful.

8.2 The biological perspective

8.2.1 *The medical model*

Sexual abuse of children is a disease of sorts. We need to effectively diagnose and treat it. So very often it will be said that the best thing to do is nothing so trauma isn't caused by the courts, police, doctors, etc. When other diseases are handled in this manner, the disease spreads – sexual abuse of children is no different. (D. Anderson, 1979, p. 794)

The man who sexually molests a child and the man who sexually assaults or sadistically murders a woman are psychologically disordered persons; their acts are best understood as equivalent to symptoms. (Cohen, Groth &

other than demanding adamantly the immediate withdrawal of the analysand from the consulting room. Sartre's lively account of the analysand 'revolting' against his analyst and turning the analytic situation into a battle-ground for his individuality is a rare example of a challenge to psychoanalytic hegemony. (Originally the 'Psychoanalytic Dialogue' was published in *Les Temps Modernes*, April 1969. It was reprinted in Sartre (1974) several years later.)

[16] See Chapter 9.
[17] See Sayers (1985), Weeks (1985).

Siegel, 1978, p. 37)

There is evidence that paedophilia has a different age of onset and a different course, ... paedophilia is unlike the other paraphilias clinically. ... Twelve in-patients meeting all criteria were studied; five had non-paedophilic paraphilia; seven had paedophilia. (Gaffney & Berlin, 1984, pp. 657-8)

Sexual abuse is not similar to other forms of child abuse. It generally differs in causal factors, family dynamics, and treatment. However, sexual abuse and nonsexual abuse sometimes occur simultaneously in the same patient. ... If there is evidence of danger of further abuse, the child should be protected, by hospitalisation if necessary. ... Ideally, a coordinator for child abuse patients should be available for each case. (J.G. Jones, pp. 142, 143, 144)

Acts of paedophilia, rape, and incest are uncomfortable subjects that are underdiagnosed and underreported. Effective management involves a multidisciplinary approach that is difficult to achieve without a special program for sexually abused children. These children deserve all the time, skill, and research that are applied to any other serious and common medical problem. They are now beginning to get this attention. (J.G. Jones, 1982, abstract)

Paedophilia is not, *per se*, a mental disorder within the meaning of the Mental Health Act (1959) and may be regarded as a disease of the morals rather than a disease of the mind. (Power, 1977, p. 806)

These quotations illustrate how the medical model has shaped the thinking of many contemporary researchers and practitioners regarding sexual contact between adults and children.

(1) Such sexual contact in general, and paedophilia in particular, is taken as an objective disease entity, a medical problem, something that could be 'had' like a common cold or cancer. As a disease, 'it' resides within the 'disordered' people whose behaviour is understood as 'symptoms'.[18]

(2) Since it is a disease that can 'spread' (although not infectious like, say, malaria), it can be studied within the context of epidemiology.

(3) The format within which intervention is conducted is medical: involving concepts like 'age of onset', 'course', 'diagnosis', 'treatment', etc., and medical personnel are seen as the most suitable people to handle these cases. The children involved are sometimes also seen as 'patients' in need of medical attention such as hospitalisation.

The medical model is usually a pragmatic approach, with its focus on treatment of the 'medical problem'. The most drastic method of medical treatment of paedophilia is surgical castration, which involves

[18] While paedophilia is often taken as a mental disorder, this is less often the case with incest. Nevertheless, some authors do treat incest as a mental disorder. For example, one author started a paper by saying: 'the first surprise is that Diagnostic and Statistical

irreversible removal of the testicles.[19] However, the ethical difficulty involved is too great to allow it to be commonly used. Moreover, recent reviews have shown that it is not as effective as was previously thought.[20] Another form of physical treatment is drug therapy with anti-androgens such as cyproterone acetate or medroxyprogesterone acetate, which suppress sexual drive as well as ejaculatory capacity. Success in treatment of sexual deviation, including paedophilia, with these drugs has been documented in a number of studies.[21] Some work has also been done in developing stereotaxic neurosurgery in the treatment of paedophiles and other sexual offenders.[22]

8.2.2. The physiological approach

Many researchers have sought a biochemical or neurophysiological model to explain deviance, crime or the criminal 'personality'.[23] Since human sexual and gender behaviour is at least partially endocrinologically organised, the explanation is usually sought in some possible disturbances of the hormonal systems.[24] As homosexuality is taken as a disorder in gender differentiation, a lot of effort has gone into a search for a model of endocrine dysfunction for homosexuality. In recent years, particular attention has been paid to the possible role of foetal hormonal imbalance in the causation of primary male homosexuality, specifically the lack of a complete 'androgenisation' of the undifferentiated brain of the male foetus.[25] However, recent findings by a Dutch researcher[26] have cast doubt on the validity of the neuroendocrinological theory of homosexuality. Similarly, Prentky (1985), after an extensive review of the literature on neurochemistry and neuroendocrinology, concluded that it is difficult to attribute an unequivocal role to neurophysiological processes in the genesis of sexual aggression. Though he agreed that biological factors are important, he also stressed the powerful influence of social learning factors. His caution can be seen in his judgment that the effects of androgens are 'neither direct nor obvious' (p. 41).

Regarding paedophilia, or more generally adult sexual desire for children, little biochemical or neurophysiological research has been done. It may, however, be possible to extrapolate from endocrine studies on male homosexuality to the case of homosexual paedophilia (pederasty),

---

Manual of Mental Disorders I, II and III do not mention the word incest at all' (Renshaw, 1983, p. 1) – as if it is a grave mistake not to classify incest as a mental disorder.

[19] A classic study is Bremer (1959).

[20] See Heim (1981), Heim & Hursch (1979).

[21] See Gagne (1981), Ortmann (1980), Pinta (1978), Spodak, Falck & Rappeport (1978).

[22] See review by Freund (1980).

[23] See e.g. Eysenck (1964), Hippchen (1978), Lewis & Balla (1976), Mednick & Christiansen (1977), Mednick & Finello (1983), Mednick, Gabrielli & Hutchings (1984), Yeudall (1977, 1980).

[24] See e.g. Gladue, Green & Hellman (1984), Goodman (1983), Rada *et al.* (1983).

[25] See Feldman & MacCulloch (1971, 1980), MacCulloch & Waddington (1981).

[26] See Gooren (1986a, 1986b).

especially if paedophilia is classified as a homosexual disorder. Yet there is no study that attempts to integrate the two within a single model. Recently, a very preliminary study has been done on the question 'Is there hypothalamic-pituitary-gonadal dysfunction in paedophilia?' (Gaffney & Berlin, 1984). By correlating the sexual orientation of paedophiles *vs* non-paedophiles with their respective luteinising hormone response (LH response) to injected luteinising hormone-releasing hormone (LHRH), Gaffney and Berlin found that the paedophiles' LH response to LHRH is greater than that of other sexual deviants or normal controls. They concluded that a dysfunction of the hypothalamic-pituitary-gonadal (HPG) axis (which is responsible for hormonal balance) is implicated in the 'pathophysiological processes' of paedophilia. While this study differs from those conducted by MacCulloch and his colleagues in that no specific reference is made to *foetal* hormonal imbalance, it is nevertheless a study in the same direction.

There are at least two problems with the study of Gaffney and Berlin:

(1) Their results are based on correlational data, which do not warrant any attribution of causes.

(2) There is no clear *theory-based* postulation on which the observed hormonal differences could be interpreted in such a way that sexual desire for *children* could be *understood*. It is always possible to find a significant correlation between any two sets of variables – the essential thing is to have a theoretically derived hypothesis about such correlations. If taken in conjunction with the studies of MacCulloch and his colleagues, it might be possible to argue that the findings of Gaffney and Berlin support the neuroendocrine theory of primary male homosexuality, which could conceivably be extended to cover homosexual paedophilia. But the difficulty is that nearly all of their paedophile 'patients' are heterosexual and so cannot be 'primary homosexuals' as defined by MacCulloch and his colleagues.

While it is reasonable to argue that all human actions have some biological basis, and that abnormalities in the biological functioning of the body will increase the likelihood of anomalous behaviour, it is not possible to generalise this to every *specific* human act that is deemed abnormal or unusual, and to *reduce* all human experience to biology. As pointed out above, it is theoretically plausible that neuroendocrinological imbalances might contribute to unusual gender preference in the choice of sexual partner, or perhaps to the level of sexual activity that a person would want to engage in. There does not seem to be, however, any theoretically worked out relationship between the desire for children and neuroendocrinological anomalies.[27]

---

[27] It can conceivably be argued that neuroendocrinological anomalies might lead to a decrease in sex drive and hence to a disposition towards sex play with children rather than full sexual intercourse with adults. But neither Gaffney and Berlin, nor any other

It is interesting to note that Berlin and his colleagues, in advocating for a humanitarian treatment approach in response to paedophilia, have acknowledged that paedophiles might have a 'genuine concern for the well being of children', and that they might indeed 'fall in love with young boys or girls in an erotic, sensual way' (Berlin & Krout, 1986, p. 27). Perhaps this could be taken as a tacit admission that the *phenomenological* experience of the individual cannot be subsumed by the language of physiology.

8.2.3. The genetic/evolutionary model

The espousal of a physiological model often entails the adoption of some sort of genetic explanation for the anomaly in question, although this is not always the case. In his discussion of the 'biology of sexuality', Goodman (1983) has underlined the importance of the sex-linked factor, the HY-antigen,[28] in the regulation of the neuroendocrine system, which in turn controls the development of sexuality and its deviations. While there is very little theorising about paedophilia in terms of genetic aberrations,[29] the work of the following researchers is relevant to this question.

Rooth (1973) has postulated that exhibitionism and paedophilia are best understood as innately determined behaviour characteristic of an immature developmental stage. In a more sophisticated manner, Pinkava (1971) has constructed a 'logical model' of sexual deviance based on evolutionary and ethological data. He proposed that human sexual behaviour is continuous with the behaviour of animals and so the same general principles of *instinct* mechanisms apply. He employed the concept of 'innate releasing mechanism' (IRM), borrowed from ethology, as the basic paradigm to conceptualise human instinctual behaviour. Impairment of these genetically determined IRM systems, presumably at the neural level, will lead to faulty 'imprinting' of inappropriate sexual behaviour. In the case of paedophilia, Pinkava postulated an impairment of the IRM system resulting in the features of a baby or child,[30] which under normal circumstances would only elicit parental/nurturing behaviour from the adult, becoming the trigger for sexual attraction and behaviour.

The difficulty with Pinkava's model is that it is highly conceptual (couched in terms of formal logic) with no supporting *evidence*. He made a number of assumptions about IRM systems in the determination of

---

researchers, have theorised in this way.

[28] The HY-antigen is a genetic factor associated with one of the sex chromosomes, the Y-chromosome.

[29] Twin studies are often used in the pursuit of a genetic formulation of homosexuality. A review of this can be found in West (1977, pp. 78-84), and a most recent example of such research is Eckert *et al.* (1986). I am not aware of any study on paedophilia using twins.

[30] Features of babies and infants include disproportionately big head with short facial parts and thin neck, short fat limbs and clumsy movement.

human behaviour, and *postulated* various impairments to these systems with no corroborative data. Secondly, it is very doubtful that features of babies and infants are in any way near to those of *peri-pubertal* children, who constitute the 'love-object' of most paedophiles. Moreover, since imprinting is usually taken as a mechanism that shapes the behaviour patterns of *newly born* animals, its invocation necessitates the presence of children in the immediate environment of the would-be paedophile soon after his birth, as well as the hypothesis that all paedophiles would have experienced paedophilic attraction from a very early age on, since they would have been thus 'imprinted' at birth. While it might be possible to argue that *sexual* imprinting only occurs at puberty, the notion of imprinting to a set of babyish features remains very problematic. In sum, 'innate releasing mechanisms' might be a viable concept in ethological studies of lower animals, but its value in explaining human behaviour, which is much more than physiology and genetics, is very low.

John Money (1980a, 1983) has constructed the most detailed evolutionary-physiological model for sexual behaviour and sexual deviations. He has collated a large body of data from genetics, neurophysiology, ethology and other behavioural sciences on which to base his model. The key construct that he uses is 'gender-identity/role', which is a behavioural description of the complex interplay of phylogenetic and ontogenetic factors in the development of gender behaviour in individual members of a particular species.[31] Impairment to this complex system, e.g. neurohormonal dysfunctions of the kind discussed by MacCulloch and his colleagues, results in faulty development of the gender-identity/role, which might manifest in various forms of sexual deviations. Money (1983) pointed out that since paraphilic behaviour is often paroxysmal and trancelike, it is likely that brain dysfunctions are implicated even if no abnormal EEGs are observed.[32]

While Money has no doubt placed great emphasis on the genetic nature of paraphilias, he does acknowledge the contribution of non-biological factors such as 'deprivation of childhood sexual rehearsal play' (1983, p. 146). With respect to paedophilia, Money put forward no specific theory other than attributing it to faulty imprinting – in line with the postulation of Pinkava (1971).

More recently, Wilson & Cox (1983) have done a study of paedophiles following essentially the Eysenckian approach. Basing on data gathered by questionnaires (including the Eysenck Personality Questionnaire,

[31] Phylogenetic factors (those mediated through evolutionary development) determine the basic behaviour patterns while ontogenetic factors (those specific to the individual) are immediately responsible for the development of, and modification in, actual behaviour output.

[32] Papatheophilou, James & Orwin (1975) did find some EEG abnormality in a group of treatment-seeking homosexuals, and they concluded on that basis that a 'cerebral immaturity' hypothesis of homosexuality is plausible. Nevertheless, Money's observation about the 'trancelike' character of paraphilia might not be very useful because every form of sexual excitement, whether conventional or paraphilic, has a 'trancelike' quality to it.

EPQ), they attempted to built up a picture of the typical paedophile. Their conclusion is that:

> paedophilia would seem to be one of several alternative adaptations to the problem of lack of success (or perceived inability to succeed) in intermale competition for access to females. It has been often noted by ethologists that the males of any species are thrown into strong Darwinian competition with one another. Those that are most successful monopolise an unequal share of female resources, and the others have to make do with various substitute sexual outlets. Following this model, we would not expect to find any genetic predisposition toward paedophilia *per se*, but as with homosexuality and certain other sex deviations, some degree of heritability would be mediated by the constitutional basis of dominance versus submissiveness. In other words, paedophiles may inherit their submissive nature, which in turn makes for difficulties in establishing normal sexual roles. (p. 125)

While taking care not to attribute paedophilia to biology alone, Wilson and Cox have articulated a basically sociobiological-evolutionary model to explain adult sexual interest in children. To them, the EPQ data point to the paedophile's genetically determined proneness to failures in adult heterosexual competition, and his consequent turning towards children is interpreted, within a sociobiological framework, as a 'survival' strategy.

8.2.4 A critical note on the biological perspective

As a humane approach to those who before the eighteenth century would have been considered either morally degenerate or possessed by the Devil and thus either imprisoned or banished from human society, the medical model has no doubt made some contribution to the improvement of social attitudes to these distressed individuals. Yet the development of the medical model and its profession into a monolithic institutional structure, with power over many aspects of individual and social life in modern society (even in areas where no identifiable medical aspects are involved), has gone beyond its proper limits.[33] To talk about sexual abuse of children as a 'spreading disease' may be permissible as a metaphor, but we must not take it too literally.

Certainly all human actions and activities are associated with some physiological substrate – a group of angry demonstrators share a very high level of adrenalin secretion, yet the adrenalin as such has nothing to do with the demonstration – it cannot render the actions of the angry mob intelligible. In this regard, correlation between a particular physiological state, such as the HPG axis anomaly discussed by Gaffney & Berlin (1984), and paedophilic activities might not lead to any understanding of the human experience subsumed under the term 'paedophilia'.

Furthermore, the use of drugs to produce sexual incapacitation in

---

[33] Critique of the hegemony of the medical profession can be found in Bradshaw (1978), Illich (1975), Ingleby (1980), Szasz (1970, 1971, 1977), and van den Berg (1978).

paedophiles does not prove an organic aetiology for this 'condition'. Surely the most effective treatment, in terms of eliminating paedophilic behaviour, is the death penalty – but nobody would argue that the very fact that these paedophiles are *alive* constitutes the cause of paedophilic behaviour. While no doubt an absurd analogy, this illustrates the problem of inferring causation from the outcome of certain forms of treatment.

From the perspective of this study, the most serious problem in the biological approach to human experience is the danger of reification of theoretical concepts. It has already been pointed out that many authors who have espoused the medical model talk as if paedophilia is some*thing* that can be 'had', a 'disease' that 'spreads', and by implication an entity that can be eliminated by drugs. If not actually postulating a genetic configuration responsible for paedophilia, these authors argue that particular types of neural circuits responsible for paedophilic behaviour can be established by conditioning or imprinting. This reification of theoretical constructs that represent hypotheses rather than established physical entities and the attribution to them a 'thing'-like quality,[34] as well as the reduction to biology of the human experience of interpersonal relationships, are fundamental faults of the misuse of the biological model.

8.3 The behavioural perspective

Behaviourism was once associated with a fairly strict doctrine: 'Only the observable can be studied scientifically.' After over half a century, however, it has become much more flexible and includes a variety of approaches. Nevertheless, the basic features of a behavioural approach still consist of (1) emphasis on objectivity, (2) reliance on observable behaviour as the most important source of data, (3) stress on quantitative measurements, (4) preference for the hypothetico-deductive method in doing research, (5) use of concepts such as conditioning, learning and reinforcement, and (6) use of behavioural technologies in practical application, such as aversion therapy for the elimination of deviant behaviour. Very often, researchers or practitioners who espouse a behavioural approach also operate within a biological/medical model – this is particularly the case in the field of abnormal psychology or psychiatry.

8.3.1 Sexual deviations and paedophilia

The simplest behavioural model of sexual deviation relies on the concept of the conditioning of sexual responses to deviant stimuli through repeated association of the two. A sexually deviant experience which has

[34] Eysenck talks as if his constructs E, N, P are real entities represented by genes – 'a person develops neurotic disorders primarily if he is high genetically on neuroticism and introversion' (1980, p. 61).

produced sexual arousal and gratification can act on the subsequent behaviour of the individual through repeated fantasising of the original experience.[35] In terms of *operant* conditioning, the association of adult heterosexual experience with some unpleasant consequences is seen as underlying the diminution in frequency of heterosexual behaviour (aversive conditioning) and the development of alternative sexual practices. However, Freund and his colleagues have found in several studies that androphilic and pederastic men did not show aversive responses to the female body, female genitalia or depiction of heterosexual intercourse. They concluded that male homosexuality (including pederasty) cannot be understood as a phobic reaction to the non-preferred sex.[36]

With reference to paedophilia, a generalised and life-long inability to form emotional attachments to adult peers has been postulated as responsible for the initial acquisition of paedophilic tendencies, which are subsequently reinforced and maintained by repeated sexual contact with children (Feldman, 1977). While the cause of this 'inability to form emotional attachment to peers' is not explicitly theorised, it is not inconceivable that Feldman would agree with the genetic model proposed by Wilson & Cox (1983) discussed above.

In the past two decades, more and more researchers of the behaviourist persuasion have begun to realise the importance of cognitive factors in the development of behaviour. Emotions are far from purely physiological responses, conditionable to any and every external stimulus; rather they are found to be heavily influenced by cognitive appraisal of situations and subjective labelling of internal states. The same pattern of physiological changes can be differently interpreted depending on external cues and the attributional activities of the individual.[37] Recently, the role played by perceptual as well as cognitive processes in the development and maintenance of human sexual attraction is beginning to receive attention.[38] Howells (1979, 1981) suggested that cognitive labelling of sexual arousal is an important factor in the development of paedophilic tendencies. Whether a person feels sexually attracted to children is, at least in part, a function of how he cognitively organises his perception and conception of children in relation to his emotional responses to them. Paedophiles tend to perceive and construe interpersonal relationships in terms of superiority-inferiority or dominance-submission, and to construe themselves as incapable of controlling the social environment. On the other hand, children tend to be perceived as submissive and innocent, and hence are more approachable. Howells' findings suggest a hypothesis

[35] See McGuire, Carlisle & Young (1965); for a review of the contribution of fantasies to sexual deviations see G.D. Wilson (1978).

[36] See Freund (1967), Freund, Langevin & Zajac (1974), Freund *et al.* (1973), Freund *et al.* (1974).

[37] See for example the classic study on the labelling of emotions by Schachter & Singer (1962).

[38] See Tesser & Reardon (1981).

that paedophiles prefer children because the latter are less threatening. Whether this cognitive structuring of a person's relation to children is a consequence of the assumption of the paedophile role, or exists before that role is taken up, has not been clarified.

The cognitive-behavioural perspective has moved away from 'radical behaviourism' in that the human person is not treated as a 'black box' of which only observable 'input' and 'output' can be studied – the processes within the 'black box', such as perception, conceptual structuring, attribution of meanings to emotional experiences, etc., are now reckoned as not only legitimate, but indeed important, issues to be dealt with.

8.3.2 *Behavioural assessment and treatment of sexual deviations*

Within the behavioural perspective a number of quantitative methods have been developed to assess different sexual preferences. There are at least two broad categories of methods: rating scales and personality inventories, and physiological measurements. The first category will be discussed in Section 8.4 below, while the second will be discussed here.

Penile plethysmography. The measurement of changes in penile volume, as an index of penile erection, has long been taken as the fundamental method of assessing sexual arousal and its variation. This method has been called penile plethysmography, phalloplethysmography, or simply phallometric method. G.G. Abel, K. Freund and V.L. Quinsey have been closely associated with the development and use of this method.

Abel and his colleagues have used plethysmography in studying the patterns of sexual arousal in rapists and child molesters, as well as in constructing indices for the identification of 'dangerous' (violent) paedophiles.[39] Freund and his colleagues have also relied heavily on this method to study the 'structure of erotic preference' in 'nondeviant' males, homosexuals as well as paedophiles.[40] Some researchers have used phallometry in conjunction with other physiological measurements in a multi-channel polygraphic set-up for the assessment of paedophilic offenders.[41] Quinsey (1973, 1977, 1979) has reviewed and discussed the methodological issues surrounding penile plethysmography, and concluded that despite problems such as 'faking', this method remains the best index for the assessment of sexual arousal.

Based on the finding of similarity in plethysmographic responses between paedophiles and heterosexual incest offenders, Abel *et al.* (1981) concluded that incest offenders could actually be seen as a subcategory of paedophiles. However, since paedophiles are found to base their sexual preferences mainly on age rather than gender (Freund, 1967), whereas the majority of incest offenders are involved with their daughters, it might be more useful to keep the two groups separate. The key to the

[39] See Abel & Blanchard (1976), Abel *et al.* (1977), Abel *et al.* (1981), Abel *et al.* (1978).
[40] See Freund (1967, 1971, 1976, 1981), Freund & Costell (1970), Freund *et al* (1975).
[41] See Field & Williams (1971).

problem lies in distinguishing physical sexual arousal (which can be measured by phallometric method) from sexual preferences or relationships. To label an individual 'paedophilic' just on the basis of his penile response to pictures of nude children might be too hasty – not only because of the problems of 'faking', but also because of the diffuse nature of human sexual responses. Since 'nondeviant' males do show some arousal to stimuli of nude female adolescents or children,[42] it is not surprising that incest offenders show similar responses.

Psychoanalysis, hypnotherapy, group psychotherapy and supportive group work have all been claimed to be successful in treating individuals who have committed sexual offences against children,[43] but behavioural treatment is undoubtedly the most widely adopted strategy in the management of sex offenders, including paedophiles and child molesters. It basically involves modification of the deviant sexual behaviour pattern by means of various conditioning procedures.[44]

Behaviour modification. Perhaps the best known behavioural treatment method for sexual deviation is aversion therapy. The basic idea of aversion therapy is to associate an unpleasant consequence (e.g. an electric shock) with the sexual response to a deviant stimulus (e.g. penile erection to the picture of a nude child), such that in the course of time the deviant response becomes suppressed. A complementary component to aversive conditioning in a treatment package is 'orgasmic reconditioning' – the developing of an association between the individual's sexual arousal and a socially acceptable stimulus object (e.g. an adult figure), so that the elimination of the individual's deviant sexual preference will not leave him in a vacuum. The basic premise of such techniques is that since deviant sexuality is a consequence of 'faulty' conditioning, a process of deconditioning coupled with reconditioning will eliminate the fault. Various forms of behaviour modification procedures applied to the treatment of paedophilia include aversive deconditioning with orgasmic reconditioning,[45] covert sensitisation,[46] satiation treatment,[47] and even *in vivo* sex therapy using the Masters and Johnson techniques for reconditioning to arousal to adults.[48]

Social skills training. As behaviourally inclined practitioners become more aware of social and interpersonal influences in the shaping of an individual's behaviour, the 'social skills' model has gained increased acceptance as a theoretical and therapeutic approach in the management

[42] See Freund *et al.* (1972).
[43] See Fox & Weaver (1978), Hartman (1965), Karpman (1950), Scott (1977), Shaw (1978a, 1978b), Weaver & Fox (1984).
[44] Review of behavioural treatment of sex offenders can be found in Bancroft (1974), Brodsky (1980), Crawford (1981), Dengrove (1967), Feldman & MacCulloch (1971, 1980), Gelder (1979), Hawton (1983), and West (1980).
[45] See Marshall (1973), Nolan & Sandman (1978).
[46] See Barlow & Wincze (1980), Brownell, Hayes & Barlow (1977), Callahan & Leitenberg (1973).
[47] See Marshall & Barbaree (1978).
[48] See Kohlenberg (1974).

of sex offenders.[49] Not only is the reconditioning of arousal patterns to adult partners an important component in the treatment of paedophiles, social skills training is also essential since deficit in social skills is seen as underlying the paedophile's difficulties with adult relationships.

8.4 The trait/typology approach

8.4.1 *The search for typical profiles*

As mentioned before, behaviourally inclined researchers and practitioners tend to use nomothetic questionnaires, personality inventories and rating scales to construct 'objective' profiles of sex offenders. Offender typologies serve the functions of categorising individuals into neat pigeon-holes, enabling the professional to feel a sense of understanding regarding the problem at hand, and providing the practitioner with a direction and prescription for the handling of these offenders. Attempts to arrive at typical profiles of sex offenders have been made using the EPQ,[50] MMPI,[51] or a simple correlation of recorded offender characteristics such as age, race, alcoholism, psychiatric status, etc.[52]

8.4.2 *Typologies of paedophilia*

Effort has been put into classifying paedophiles into different types. The dimensions used vary from one scheme to another.

Offence characteristics typologies

Gebhard *et al.* (1965), in their well known study on sex offenders, delineated eight types of paedophilic offenders according to the four offence dimensions of gender preference, degree of violence, victim age, and consanguinity: (1) heterosexual offenders *vs* children, (2) heterosexual offenders *vs* minors, (3) heterosexual aggressors *vs* children, (4) heterosexual aggressors *vs* minors, (5) incest offenders *vs* children, (6) incest offenders *vs* minors, (7) homosexual offenders *vs* children, and (8) homosexual offenders *vs* minors. In terms of personality profiles, these eight groups of men are quite similar to each other – apart from the group of 'incest offenders *vs* minors', who are described as 'nondescript', the rest are all said to be characterised by deprived childhood and bad relationships with parents, as well as an impulsive tendency to seek immediate gratification. Since the study of Gehbard and his colleagues was conducted with prisoners, it is expected that they would be dealing with a relatively more homogeneous sample of people drawn mainly from

[49] See Alexander & Johnson (1980), Becker *et al.* (1978), Brodsky & West (1981), N.B. Edwards (1972), Rice & Quinsey (1980), Tasto (1980).
[50] See Eysenck (1976), Gosselin & Wilson (1980), Wilson & Cox (1983).
[51] See Howells & Wright (1978), Rader (1977).
[52] See Ellis, Doorbar & Johnston (1954).

families in the lower strata of American society, with all the attendant features of deprivation and anti-social behaviour.

Groth and his colleagues have constructed a typology based on the single offence characteristic of the degree of coercion involved: sex-pressure cases *vs* sex-force cases.[53] In the latter type, more overt coercion, usually physical, is involved. These two types have been further divided to yield four subtypes: (1) sex-pressure enticement type, (2) sex-pressure entrapment type, (3) sex-force exploitative type, and (4) sex-force sadistic type. The first two types involve bribing, persuading, and cajoling the child, or making the child feel indebted. The difference between the last two types is that in a sadistic case, the physical violence committed on the child is an end in itself rather than a means of subduing the child for sexual purposes. It is clear that this is the most pernicious type of sexual abuse of children.

Personality traits classification

There is apparently some agreement in the finding that paedophiles are characterised by an MMPI scale 4 elevation (Pd – psychopathic deviate), while rapists (whether of adults or of children) are characterised by a 4,8-elevation (Pd and Sc, i.e. psychopathic deviate and schizophrenia).[54] In the case of rapists of children, since their MMPI profile is essentially the same as that of rapists of adults, it has been suggested that the immediate availability of the child victim, rather than a specific preference for immature partners, is the crucial factor.[55] As far as the overlap between the rapist and the paedophile groups in the 'psychopathic deviate' scale is concerned, Panton (1978) pointed out that rapists are characterised by the 'social alienation' component of the Pd scale, whereas paedophiles are characterised by the self-alienation component. The conclusion is that rapists are much more anti-social and psychologically disturbed than paedophiles. While this conclusion agrees with some non-MMPI comparative studies based on case records and clinical material,[56] the association of particular MMPI profiles with specific offence categories is not always found.[57]

Within the category of sexual offenders against children, a number of subcategories have been delineated.[58] There is much overlap in the typologies constructed by these different investigators, and the three most commonly agreed categories are:

[53] See Groth (1978), Groth & Birnbaum (1979), Groth & Burgess (1977).
[54] See Armentrout & Hauer (1978), Panton (1978), Toobert, Bartelme & Jones (1959).
[55] See Panton (1978).
[56] See Henn, Herjanic & Vanderpearl (1976), Pacht & Cowden (1974).
[57] See Anderson, Kunce & Rich (1979).
[58] See Cohen, Seghorn & Calmas (1969), Fitch (1962), Groth (1978), Groth & Burgess (1977), Virkkunen (1976).

(1) The fixated offender – sexual offence with children is a result of immature, arrested psychosexual development.

(2) The regressed offender – sexual offence with children is a result of experience of frustration in adult relationships.

(3) The sociopathic offender – sexual offence against children is part of an anti-social, aggressive, and sometimes sadistic criminal behaviour pattern.

It is clear that a person who feels sexually attracted to children will not be treated as 'normal'.

8.4.3 Comparison with homosexuality

In relation to the search for a typology of paedophilia, there are several questions regarding its relationship to homosexuality:[59]

(1) Is pederasty (paedophilia with boys) one form of homosexuality?

(2) Are homosexuals who are attracted to men also attracted (and hence 'dangerous') to boys?

(3) Will childhood sexual contact with adult males turn a boy into a homosexual paedophile?

(4) Will childhood sexual contact with adult males make a boy homosexual subsequently?

While there is some evidence which might suggest an affirmative answer to question (3),[60] it is often argued that sexual orientation is determined long before puberty,[61] and so childhood sexual contact with adults, which normally occurs when the child is around puberty, would not influence later sexual orientation. Some studies have concluded that homosexuality and homosexual paedophilia (pederasty) tend to be mutually exclusive.[62] Similarly, West (1983a, 1983b, 1984b) has argued that homosexuals do not constitute a danger to children because they are attracted to sexually mature males who have a strong physique. Thus, Groth & Birnbaum (1978) have concluded that 'homosexuality and homosexual paedophilia may be mutually exclusive and that the adult heterosexual male constitutes a greater risk to the underage child than does the adult homosexual male' (p. 175).

---

[59] The question arises because paedophiles who are more vocal, and who have formed themselves into pressure groups tend to be attracted to boys, and so giving the impression that paedophilia is a 'homosexual' orientation. Moreover, there is a tendency within some professional circles to treat paedophilia as one form of homosexuality.

[60] Freund *et al.* (1975) found that homosexual paedophiles tended to have a history of childhood seduction by older males, a result which could be interpreted as indicating a link between such seduction and subsequent development of pederasty.

[61] See Marmor (1980), Money (1980b), West (1977).

[62] See Curran & Parr (1957), Jersild (1967), Groth & Birnbaum (1978), Newton (1978), Schofield (1965b).

8.4.4 *The difficulty of establishing a typical profile*

In the Clarke Institute of Psychiatry in Toronto, Ron Langevin has attempted to build up a general framework within which to sort out the complexity of the spectrum of sexual preferences in men. In his most recent work (1985), Langevin and his colleagues have constructed profiles for different types of sexual anomalies using an organising model with the three constructs of 'erotic preference', 'gender identity' and 'aggression'. They consider these three dimensions crucial to the classification (and hence understanding) of deviant sexual practices. With respect to the dimension of erotic preference, Langevin's earlier work (1983) has established the use of a 'stimulus-response matrix' to categorise various sexual preferences.

Using much questionnaire data collected from paedophiles,[63] Langevin and his colleagues have come to the conclusion that these individuals are not particularly peculiar in their profiles in terms of the three dimensions of their model:

> Paedophiles remain an enigma. ... They equate the child sexually in many ways with the adult; in body characteristics and desired responses. Moreover, paedophiles do not seem especially unassertive nor to have an aversion to the adult female. In fact, *the paedophile may be characterised by a failure to inhibit conventional albeit weaker sexual responses that the average man has toward children*. In other respects they are unremarkable. (Langevin, 1985, pp. 278-9, italics in the original)

Langevin and his colleagues had to conclude that paedophilia remains an 'enigma'. Perhaps the crux of the problem lies in the over-reliance of researchers on nomothetic methods, which tend to obscure the complexity and uniqueness of the experience of the individual.

8.5 The family system theory perspective

Family system theory is currently the most popular paradigm adopted by researchers and practitioners dealing with sexual abuse of children.It is often stated in the literature that sexual abuse of children most frequently takes place within a family setting, even if the abuser is not a blood relation to the victim. Many authors have indeed expanded the definition of incest to cover almost every type of intrafamilial adult-child sexual contact.[64] With an expanded definition, the following are also

---

[63] Langevin and his colleagues have developed the 'Clarke Sex History Questionnaire', which is   very detailed on the sexual practice and experience of the respondent.

[64] See e.g. Browning & Boatman (1977), Cooper (1978), De Young (1982a), Finkelhor (1979a), Forward & Buck (1978), Herman (1981), Justice & Justice (1980), Kempe & Kempe (1984), Meiselman (1978), Mey & Neff (1982), Renvoize (1982). But Sagarin (1977) has argued for distinguishing between *consanguine* incest from other forms of non-consanguine intrafamilial child sexual abuse, because such a distinction has important aetiological and treatment implications. One of the differences is the observation that the rate of sexual

included in the category of incest: non-penetrative and homosexual activities, contact between non-consanguineous persons such as adopted or step-relatives, and even contact between a child and its parent's live-in partner – the important elements are the authority status of the adult perpetrator and a family-like set-up.

Another reason for the upsurge in popularity of family system theory is that there is nowadays a general swing in theoretical orientation among professionals from a model of individual psychopathology to one that takes interpersonal relationships and interactions into account. To study child sexual abuse in terms of a family system perspective is in agreement with this movement away from the individual-pathology type of thinking.

Although there are many anthropological studies on the incest taboo,[65] they have not attracted the attention of practising professionals because of their lack of 'treatment value'. The family system perspective, on the other hand, not only provides a model by which child sexual abuse can be understood, but is also a strategy for treatment and intervention.

One of the earlier studies suggested that incest has its origin in subcultural permissiveness (Lukianowicz, 1972), while another highlighted paternal alcoholism as an important contributing factor (Virkkunen, 1974). More recent reviews and studies tend to look at incest as a result of family disintegration.[66] However, this 'family approach' should not be taken as a totally new development. Earlier studies did not ignore the contribution of family disorganisation in the genesis of incest.[67]

8.5.1. Basic features of the family system perspective

The fundamental tenet of system theory is that within any homeostatic system all elements are interrelated in such a way that any movement or change in one element will affect the others. The stability of the system is ensured by a dynamic balancing of all the effects of changes in the elements. Applying this concept to the family, it is possible to argue that the elements within a family, its members, are in constant adjustment and readjustment with each other as the family goes through its life cycle.

---

abuse by *stepfathers* is much greater than that by natural fathers (Russell, 1984b).

[65] See e.g. R. Fox (1980), Lévi-Strauss (1969), Mead (1935), Shepher (1983), Westermarck (1891), and also the review by Lester (1972).

[66] Most researchers nowadays will look at incest as occurring in the context of family dysfunction, even if they do not explicitly espouse a family system perspective. Examples are: Bluglass (1979), Brant & Tisza (1977), Browning & Boatman (1977), Canepa & Bandini (1980), de Young (1982a), Forward & Buck (1978), Herman (1981), MacFarlane (1978), Mayhall & Norgard (1983), Meiselman (1978), Mey & Neff (1982), Rist (1979), Renvoize (1982), Rosenfeld (1977, 1978), Rosenfeld et al. (1977), Selby et al. (1980), Singer (1979). Even a psychoanalyst, J.J. Peters (1976), has produced a more or less family system formulation of child sexual abuse.

[67] See Maisch (1973), Weinberg (1955). Both have discussed family disorganisation as an important factor in the development of incest.

Any shift in position of one element (e.g. a son leaving home) will create an instability in the system (e.g. the mother becoming depressed), which can only be corrected by changes in some other parts of the system (e.g. the father spending more time with his wife). This concept of 'dynamic equilibrium' can provide a framework for connecting together the various observations about sexual abuse inside the family.

Within this perspective, the 'family dynamics' that are responsible for incest (or equivalent sexual relationships between an authority figure and a child inside a family) revolve round the concept of 'dysfunctional pattern of relationships'. The parents are estranged from each other for various reasons, chief among which is the mother's rejection of sexual relations with the father; this leads to the reversal of roles between mother and daughter, as the latter is pushed into a spouse/caretaker role for the father; the father, whose resources for dealing with emotional difficulties are limited since he tends to be a socially isolated individual, turns to the daughter for emotional as well as sexual gratification; this intimate contact creates a high level of ambivalence in the daughter, who on the one hand wants to be emotionally close to the father and to take care of him, but also feels on the other hand the devouring quality of the furtive relationship she has with him. The intense need, for all members involved, to maintain the family intact, which very often is their only source of emotional comfort, makes it virtually impossible for this incestuous secret to be disclosed. This incestuous relationship fulfils the function of easing the tension in the parental relationship, and some form of stability returns to the family. The equilibrium thus achieved is not exactly the same as before – the whole system, that is, the relationship network among members of the family, has changed. So there is within the family system an inherent tendency towards yet another crisis – for instance, when the daughter begins to have boyfriends, her relation to her father may become very strained, creating a serious instability in the whole system again. If there are other younger daughters in the family, they may be pushed into a 'replacement role' to offset the imbalance created by the moving away of the elder daughter, and thus the vicious circle of incestuous relationships is maintained.

8.5.2 Typologies

Some researchers have tried to provide a better understanding of child sexual abuse within the family by constructing typologies descriptive of observed patterns of family interaction. The three most commonly mentioned are endogamous, paedophilic and sociopathic incest.[68]

Wells (1981) and Will (1983) have used the term 'chaotic family' to describe the overall disorganisation within the 'sociopathic' incestuous family. Not only is there a blurring of generational boundaries and roles, even the daily activities and the essential functions of the family are in

---

[68] See e.g. Weinberg (1955).

disarray. Incest is simply one manifestation of this general disorganisation. Anderson & Shafer (1979) have used the concept of 'character-
disordered family' as a diagnostic label for the 'chaotic family', which as a
unit exhibits characteristics of the character-disorder syndrome. The lack
of impulse control, judgment ability, guilty conscience, ability for
interpersonal intimacy, and the presence of anti-social traits, manipula-
tiveness, self-indulgence, etc., are said to be not only traits of the
father-perpetrator, but are also observed to varying degrees in other
members of the family.

Another type of incestuous family is called the 'endogamous' family
(Rosenfeld, 1979; Will, 1983), in which incest is concealed under a cloak of
social respectability – there is no history of criminality, deviance, or other
social welfare problems.[69] The chief characteristics of such a family
include impaired marital relationship, overt paternal domination,
maternal abdication of responsibility, and fear of family disintegration. It
is called endogamous because there is a tendency within it to resolve
internal tension through intrafamiliar sexuality – the father tends not to
seek outside sexual relationships when there are sexual problems
between himself and his wife; he would rather turn to his children for
intimacy.

A subdivision within this endogamous category has been made (Ciba
Foundation, 1984): the conflict-avoiding versus the conflict-regulating
family. This subdivision provides a perspective within which differences
in parental relationships can be systematically classified. In a
conflict-avoiding family, the mother is observed to be more independent
while the father is very dependent on and demanding of his wife for
emotional support and sexual gratification. Incest occurs because the
father feels sexually frustrated by his wife but cannot break away due to
his own emotional immaturity. Problems, including the incestuous
relationship, are not discussed but denied, not least by the mother herself
(hence, 'conflict-avoiding'). The conflict-regulating family, on the other
hand, is described as one with an authoritarian father who abuses his
children, and a weak and dependent mother who, while close to the
children, is unable to protect them from his abuse. Incest occurs as a
regulator of conflicts: the tension in the parents' relationship is 'resolved'
through the formation of the father-daughter incest bond.

The most elaborate typology is the 'spectrum of parent-child sexuality'
proposed by Summit and Kryso (1978). Altogether ten types of
parent-child sexuality are described:

(1) Incidental sexual contact – contact not explicitly or deliberately
planned, but either accidental or subconsciously motivated, with only
superficial or play-like activities.

---

[69] For example, Julian & Mohr (1979) found from a US national sample of
father-daughter incest cases a profile of the perpetrator as a financially responsible,
law-abiding, intelligent and fairly educated person.

(2) Ideological sexual contact – permissive parents encouraging free sexual expression in the family.

(3) Psychotic intrusion – sexual contact resulting from mental illness, similar to Bagley's (1969) 'pathological incest'.

(4) Rustic environment incest – similar to Lukianowicz's (1972) subcultural incest.

(5) True endogamous incest – the paradigmatic case of the dysfunctional pattern of the incestuous family.

(6) Misogynistic incest – incest committed by men with an intense fear and hatred of women, often accompanied by physical abuse.

(7) Imperious incest – committed by extremely chauvinistic males, with a combination of elements from the ideological, rustic and misogynistic types.

(8) Paedophilic incest – where specific erotic fascination with children is involved.

(9) Child rape – committed by a chronically antisocial man whose victims might be the children of the woman that he is living with.

(10) Perverse incest – pornographic practices beyond any social limits of decency.

While the so-called 'incidental sexual contact' and 'ideological sexual contact' in the Summit-Kryso spectrum may be excluded from the classification,[70] the remaining eight can be collapsed into five categories: psychotic incest; subcultural incest ('rustic environment incest'), endogamous incest ('endogamous', 'misogynistic' and 'imperious' incest), paedophilic incest and psychopathic incest ('child rape' and 'perverse' incest). Such a typology more or less matches those proposed by other researchers described earlier.

8.5.3 The intergenerational 'transmission' of incest

A common theme in family theories of incest is that mothers of incestuous families have often been victims of child sexual abuse themselves. The pattern repeats itself not only in the sense that females who have been abused are unable to protect their own children,[71] but also that they tend to get married to males who are likely to become sexual abusers. Similarly, experience of child sexual abuse is also said to be characteristic of the life history of abusers themselves.[72] Besides the probability of sexual abuse repeating itself from one generation to another, there is also the problem of sexual abuse of successive generations of children by the *same* abuser. Information culled from cases of grandfather-

---

[70] It can be argued that these two are not necessarily 'abuse'.

[71] These women are seen as having been psychologically traumatised to such an extent that they tend to ignore unconsciously any signs of abuse in their current families.

[72] 'Sexual abuse in the family is essentially behaviour that was learned by the parents when they were children and is perpetrated with their own children in times of stress or crisis' (Jorné, 1979, p. 289).

granddaughter incest[73] shows that some grandfathers had not only abused their granddaughters, but had also abused their daughters when the latter were young. These cases illustrate the inability of sexually abused females to protect their own children from the same abuser.

Cooper & Cormier (1982) talk of the intergenerational 'transmission' of incest as a pattern that demands much more professional attention. According to their analysis, mothers in incestuous families 'may be unconsciously copying the parenting model they received as children, a model which permitted a father to turn towards his daughter for sexual gratification'. They also suggest that the victimised daughter might recreate the incest situation in her family of procreation to 'vicariously experience the incest again in order to regain her childhood, or to seek revenge against her mother who is symbolised by the daughter, or to make her husband over into her father's image' (p. 234). This formulation shows that:

(1) The term 'transmission' refers to a complex set of psychodynamics which leads to the repeating of behavioural patterns conducive to sexual abuse – it is a psychological, not a biological, issue.

(2) The mother is portrayed as playing a significant, albeit unconscious, role in the creation of the abusive situation, even though she is not blamed for playing this role.

(3) While the family system model provides an overall framework for the conceptualisation of intrafamilial child sexual abuse, there is no constraint placed on the incorporation of other theoretical constructs into the explanatory scheme – especially in terms of the formulation of the specific 'family dynamics' responsible for upsetting or restoring system equilibrium. Cooper and Cormier have evidently employed a number of psychoanalytic concepts in the proposition quoted above.

8.5.4 The question of physical abuse

Avery-Clark, O'Neil & Laws (1981) have attempted to integrate intrafamilial physical child abuse with intrafamilial sexual child abuse under the same conceptual framework. After a detailed comparison, they concluded that the sexually abusive family shares a number of common characteristics with the physically abusive family, such as parental inadequacy, parental alcoholism, pathological family interactions, poor living conditions, marital conflicts, social isolation, histories of abuse in the childhood of parents, and the tension-reduction function of the abuse. They suggested that the two phenomena may be viewed as unitary under the construct of 'aggression' since sex and physical violence are often linked together as, for example, in the case of sadism.

However, as Finkelhor (1982) has argued, sexual abuse in the family, despite superficial resemblance, is distinct from physical abuse in that it

---

[73] See Goodwin, Cormier & Owen (1983).

is a problem of masculine socialisation while physical abuse is a problem of parenting. Frude (1982) has also argued that the sexual need of the father is the fundamental factor around which other variables relevant to child sexual abuse are organised. He observed that the non-sexual factors took on a sexualised significance at the psychological level for the father during the development of incest. For instance, financial difficulties have negative repercussions on the father's gender identity, heightening a sense of impotence in him which might in turn affect the marital relationship. Thus, to Frude, the basic social configuration of the incestuous family consists of a sexually frustrated male seeking gratification from an attractive daughter over whom he has power. The apparent similarities between the incestuous family and the physically abusive family are only incidental. In the case of physical abuse, *both* the father and the mother may be involved in the abusive acts, whereas it is nearly always the case that in sexual abuse the father is the perpetrator.

8.5.5 Treatment of sexually abusive families

The focus of treatment has recently shifted from the individual paedophile to the child victim as well as the dysfunctional family which produces child sexual abuse. The professional's first task is to identify and monitor the occurrence of child sexual abuse. There are many publications, including practical manuals, which aim at providing workers in the caring professions with the skills to identify and treat child sexual abuse cases.[74] Practitioners are urged to be particularly alert to 'masked presentation' of child sexual abuse in the form of behaviour, learning or psychosomatic problems.[75] Procedures for physical examination of victims,[76] innovative methods such as using the children's drawings as diagnostic indicators,[77] and crisis intervention techniques[78] have been developed to tackle the crisis arising from the disclosure of child sexual abuse in a family.

Family therapy

Family system theory is as much a treatment approach as an explanatory model. Most proponents are practitioners involved in treatment programmes for incestuous families run along family therapy lines.[79] The following is a brief account of the principles of a family approach

---

[74] See e.g. Burgess *et al.* (1978), Goodwin (1982a), Mrazek & Kempe (1981), Schlesinger (1982), Sgroi (1982).

[75] See Hunter, Kilstrom & Loda (1985).

[76] See Cantwell (1983), Paul (1977), Woodling & Heger (1986).

[77] See Goodwin (1982b), Yates, Beutler & Crago (1985).

[78] See Evertine & Evertine (1983).

[79] Discussion on family therapy with incestuous families can be found in Ciba Foundation (1984), Deaton & Sandlin (1980), Forseth & Brown (1981), Furniss (1983), Giarretto (1976, 1977, 1978, 1981), Giarretto, Giarretto & Sgroi (1978), Jorné (1979), Latham (1981), J. Lloyd (1982), NSPCC (1984a) and Tierney & Corwin (1983).

treatment model:

(1) Treatment of incestuous families must be integrated with, and backed up by the criminal justice system.

(2) Treatment is an inter-agency effort, so harmony and colla-boration between agencies must be properly co-ordinated – one essential component of this co-ordination is the multi-agencies case conference in which division of labour and treatment strategies are designed and progress monitored.

(3) Professional intervention into the family should proceed in a step-wise fashion, with top priority given to the protection of children.

(4) Therapy for the family should be multi-modal, with individual, conjoint, group and family therapy appropriately arranged along a carefully constructed time-scale. Special skills for therapeutic interaction with children are emphasised.

(5) The fundamental objective of these various therapy modalities is to help the father-perpetrator admit his guilt and accept his responsibility. The mother must also come to terms with the part she has played in the development of the abuse, and learn alternative patterns of behaviour. The child-victim, on the other hand, is helped to realise and accept that she is *not* to be blamed in any way, and to develop her ability to resist inappropriate sexual advances from adults. Family therapy sessions are used, wherever possible, to bring the father-perpetrator face-to-face with his family, so that the whole experience can be dealt with openly in front of all the members. Group therapy, in the form of parents' group or child victims' group, is conducted to reduce the sense of isolation of individual families, and to foster mutual support among families going through similar crises.

(6) While it varies from case to case, the reunion of the family is the goal of therapy, when the parents, particularly the father-perpetrator, have shown commitment to take up their proper parental responsi-bility towards their children.

While such multi-modality, multi-agency comprehensive treatment programmes are said to be particularly effective in dealing with the aftermath of disclosed cases of intra-familial child sexual abuse,[80] there are a number of problems that might hinder therapeutic progress: collusion between the family and one sector of the professional system, conflicts between different agencies, discrepancy in treatment objectives, or the family opting out of treatment, etc.[81] One specific problem arises

[80] In America, Giarretto and his colleagues reported a high success rate for their programme in terms of family readjustment and low recidivism. This is also confirmed by the review of Kroth (1979). However, it must be borne in mind that since there is a very stringent set of criteria for the selection of 'suitable' families for treatment in the Giarretto programme, its 'success' might be as much a result of the high motivation of these families to reunite as of the effectiveness of the treatment procedures.

[81] See Bander, Fein & Bishop (1982), Coulter *et al.* (1985), Furniss (1983).

when the incestuous abuse is disclosed many years after its occurrence – the question is whether professional intervention into the family is appropriate. MacFarlane & Korbin (1983) have discussed this problem with reference to a case study, and concluded that if adequate planning was done, and back-up resources secured, confrontation with the abuser might 'facilitate the process of healing, and integrate the disjointed pieces of their collective pasts' (p. 236). Such intervention is seen as necessary particularly in cases where the abuser might further abuse other children in the family.

Not only are there treatment programmes which directly intervene into families where child sexual abuse has occurred, diverse preventive programmes have also been developed. Such preventive work includes telephone information services and community awareness programmes,[82] as well as training of children's awareness of the problem of child sexual abuse.[83] Specific training programmes for 'human services workers' as well as law enforcement officers have also been developed.[84]

While the family theory perspective is a useful model, particularly in understanding the contribution of intricate interpersonal relationships to the development of incest, it is important to note the role that patriarchal traditions have played in shaping family relationships.

8.6 The feminist perspective

8.6.1 Patriarchy as the root of all evil

Sexual contact between adults and children, as feminists see it, is always a matter of patriarchal oppression – this is consistent with the general feminist view that social life, as it now stands, is in every aspect organised in terms of male domination. Children, whether girls or boys, are always seen as part of the 'female' world, and hence always under the control of males.[85] Within this formulation, every incident of adult-child sexual contact, including incest, is 'abuse', 'assault' or 'rape'.

This is how Herman and Hirschman introduce the feminist perspective:

> Our survey of what has been written about incest, then, raises several questions. Why does incest between fathers and daughters occur so much more frequently than incest between mothers and sons? Why, though this finding has been consistently documented in all available sources, has no

[82] See Thomas & Johnson (1979).
[83] See Brassard, Tyler & Kehle (1983), Conte *et al.* (1985), Elliott (1985), Wolfe *et al.* (1986).
[84] See Siegel (1981), Stone, Tyler & Mead (1984).
[85] Boys are said to be learning the habit of 'sexual assault' on girls from school age onwards (London Rape Crisis Centre, 1984), and feminists see them as men-in-the-making – they are the 'reservists' of the dominant male 'army' (Ward, 1984). However, the more moderate stream of feminism tends to see boys as, together with girls, potential victims of adult male oppression.

previous attempt been made to explain it? Why does the incest victim find so little attention or compassion in the literature, while she finds so many authorities who are willing to assert either that the incest did not happen, that it did not harm her, or that she was to blame for it? We believe that a feminist perspective must be invoked in order to address these questions. (1977, p. 739)

This exemplifies the feminist articulation of the 'problematic' of incest: incest is a *paternal* crime, yet this fundamental feature of the phenomenon is ignored by researchers, and incest victims (females) usually get the greater share of the blame. Given the general framework of feminism, both intrafamilial and extrafamilial adult-child contact are interpreted as similar phenomena brought about by patriarchal sexual oppression. Since the 'family' is traditionally the starting point of the feminist critique of patriarchy, intrafamilial sexual abuse, more specifically father-daughter incest, has become the paradigm case for feminist analysis.

8.6.2 The 're-claiming' of female experience

In feminist theorising, 'naming' and talking about one's *own* experience is the first step towards liberation. Thus feminist writings tend to begin with stories of personal experiences.[86] The following quotations illustrate how these personal experiences are *named*:

In defining child sexual abuse we do not like to use the word 'incest'. This is because separating off incest from the sexual abuse of women and children blurs the fact that the location of power in men/fathers allows them to abuse women/children in all situations whether in society or the family. It is also a term which implies mutuality and participation by the girl being abused. (Hamblin & Bowen, 1981, p. 6)

When I began the research that is the subject of this book, I used the term 'child sexual abuse'. That quickly changed to 'incest', since the vast bulk of child sexual abuse occurs within the family and the largest single group of offenders is comprised of natural fathers. However, the more I read, and the more that women talked to me about their experiences, the more it became clear to me that not only was I looking at father-daughter rape, but also at a phenomenon of epic proportions, which could only be named by the capitalised form: Father-Daughter Rape. (Ward, 1984, p. 3)

Besides the articulation of personal experience and naming it as 'rape', feminist works also stress the following:

(1) Virtually all perpetrators of child sexual abuse are male.
(2) The majority of victims are young girls.
(3) The perpetrators always use physical violence, threats,

[86] For example, both Fairtlough (1983) and Ward (1984) start with narratives of personal

enticement, or a combination of these to coerce the child into submission, as well as to force her to keep the secret.

(4) In a majority of the cases, the abuse lasts for a long period of time, sometimes many years, especially if the abuser is a father-figure.

(5) Most victims suffer from serious harm, both physical and psychological.

(6) Most victims do not dare to complain – even if they do, they are either disbelieved, or blamed, or both.

(7) Most mothers in families where child sexual abuse takes place are themselves abused in various ways and powerless to protect their daughters.

(8) Most victims receive no adequate help or support from the criminal justice system or the caring professions even if they are able to report the abuse.[87]

One important element in feminist theorising is that sexual abuse of children is part and parcel of the male attitude that females and children are men's property. As Susan Brownmiller (1975, p. 281) argues, the patriarchal philosophy of sexual private property constitutes the underlying structure of the widespread phenomenon of male sexual oppression of females. In this connection, an asymmetry has emerged in that the taboo against son-mother incest is much stronger than that against father-daughter incest, because the father possesses the 'property right' over the females in his household whereas the son does not (not yet). The residual taboo against father-daughter sexual union, according to this analysis, is only for safeguarding the economic-exchange value of the daughter who must serve as a commodity for profit in future marriage. Given this patriarchal property rights attitude, mother-son incest is a challenge to the father's property rights and hence a greater anathema.

8.6.3 Feminist critique of the family system approach

The feminist focus on men's culpability and full responsibility for child sexual abuse leads to a rejection of family system theories, which, as some feminists see it, tend implicitly to put the blame on mothers for not satisfying their husbands sexually, who therefore turn to their daughters for gratification.

> The concept of 'family dysfunction' is now widely used to put the blame and responsibility for sexual abuse not on the man who commits the crime but on the mother and daughter. We have seen the way the girl is blamed.

---

experience of incest victims.

[87] In a survey of practising professionals, Attias & Goodwin (1985) found that the male respondents were more sceptical about incest allegations and less ready to handle such cases than their female counterparts. More seriously, de Young (1981) has documented cases of male therapists sexually exploiting their female clients after the latter's disclosure

Mothers are held responsible in a number of ways. The main argument is that the couple have a bad sexual relationship which creates unrelieved sexual tension in the fathers/abusers. The implication of this is that men have a right to have their sexual needs met by women, if necessary by their daughters. ... It is not families who sexually abuse children. We must ask who is responsible for the real injustice? Our starting point must be that the person responsible for the crime of sexual abuse is the man who commits it – no one forces him to do it. When he does it, it is an expression of his power. (Hamblin & Bowen, 1981, p. 31)

The fact that the overwhelming proportion of offendes are male, and their targets female, shows how incest, as a phenomenon, reproduces the power and control men hold over women in society at large as well as within the family unit. Explaining incest in terms of the 'dysfunctional family', the dominant explanation at present, ignores this fact. (Stanko, 1985, p. 32)

Family theory proponents are not unaware of this criticism, but they point out that to view incest as just patriarchal oppression is an over-simplification of a complex reality.

... feminists at first saw incest as an example of men subjugating women ... But the truth cannot be so simply expressed without blurring the *actuality of the experience*. A further aspect of the way women frequently were, and are, blamed for the occurrence of incest, is that it was often assumed women drove their husbands into their daughter's arms by being frigid, and also were blamed for refusing to listen to their daughter's pleas for help. Women in the feminist movement are understandably unhappy to accept any truth in these last two statements, and yet repeatedly we hear exactly these two accusations from male offenders and their daughters. The facts seem to be that very often the mother herself has been an incest victim, so that it is not surprising if she has sexual difficulties in her marriage (bearing in mind that the father also most probably had his own childhood problems) and is unwilling or unable to face the possibility that the same pattern may be happening to her own daughter. (Renvoize 1982, pp. 40-1, italics added)

It is clear that Renvoize does not agree with the feminist position – she argues that 'the actuality of the experience' of incest points to a family dysfunctional state, to which the mother has indeed contributed her part. Feminists, however, interpret these 'facts' differently – they argue that there is no reason why wives *should* be responsible for satisfying the sexual needs of their husbands, and no reason why men's sexual desires must always be gratified. To adopt this feminist stand would be to reject the idea that mothers in incestuous families are 'abdicating from their responsibilities'. To be fair to family theorists, however, it should be stressed that while they do see mothers as playing a role in the genesis of incest, they are not *blaming* them, as feminists have alleged. Rather,

of childhood incest experience. These are taken by feminists as clear evidence of the pervasive influence of the patriarchal mentality among professionals, or even as proof of the collusion between male professionals and the patriarchal society in oppressing females.

their objective is to help the mother take up her responsibility in the rehabilitation of the family.

8.6.4 Differences among feminists

While there is a consensus within feminism to blame patriarchy as responsible for causing child sexual abuse, individual feminists have different emphases in their analysis.

One particular feminist group has espoused a very radical attitude towards patriarchy. A typical example can be found in the work of Elizabeth Ward (1984). The hallmark of this radical wing of the feminist movement is its 'separatism': patriarchy, and with it the conventional family structure, are deemed to be beyond salvaging, and a rejection of patriarchy must take the form of a rejection of the family set-up as it now obtains in western society. Women must join together to construct a totally different social order within which they can lead their own lives. It is an integral part of this strategy to choose lesbianism voluntarily as a political stance declaring the rejection of male domination in general and male sexuality in particular.

In the context of such an extremist view, all men, regardless of whether they have sexually abused their daughters, are accused of exploiting their daughters in various ways. Ward (1984) is eloquent in her condemnation:

Father-Daughter relations vary along a continuum from rape to complete disinterest. The disinterested end of the spectrum, however, is lightly weighted compared with the sexual and/or emotional connection between most Fathers and Daughters. In the vast majorities of families in which there is no Father-Daughter rape, there is, instead, an emphasis on the Father-Daughter tie, within the family constellation of relationships. Most Father-Daughter relations are characterised by an exchange: he gives her validation of her femininity (i.e. female sexuality as defined by male supremacist culture), and she gives him emotional support in the form of validation as a patriarchal figure (at least overtly – she may bitch about him covertly). This exchange, apparently mutual, is actually determined by the power balance between them: the father gives her validation *in return for* the emotional comfort she bestows on him. She thereby becomes 'a good girl'. Most Fathers set a high price on their Daughter's sexuality: she is only a good girl if she does *not* fool around with boys. The implicit demand of most Fathers is that their Daughters be seen as attractive, sexual, and, paradoxically, hard-to-get, chaste. When a Daughter does manage to fulfil this image, other men will flatter the Father with remarks, or looks, that appraise *his* property; she's a good-looker, but it's Hands Off. ... In the typical patriarchal family, then, most Daughters are being prepared, overtly or covertly, for stereotypical femininity – which is based on dislike of women and aggrandisement of men. The patriarchal family constructs Daughters who are ready, willing and able to co-operate in male supremacist society. Father-Daughter rape is merely a phenomenon at one end of the spectrum of the means by which this construction is achieved. (pp. 196-7, italics in original)[88]

While many female researchers in the field of child sexual abuse tend to espouse a feminist perspective in their analysis, most of them would not feel at ease with the kind of extreme position propounded by Ward. One very important element in this moderate feminist position is the desire to reform the family structure along non-patriarchal lines rather than to reject it completely.[89] The last paragraph of Judith Herman's book, *Father-Daughter Incest* (1981), is clearly written with this hope in mind:

> As long as fathers retain their authoritarian role, they cannot take part in the tasks or the rewards of parenthood. They can never know what it means to share a work of love on the basis of equality, or what it means to nurture the life of a new generation. When men no longer rule their families, they may learn for the first time what it means to belong to one. (Herman, 1981, p. 218)

The assumption underlying Herman's position is that it is possible to make the family an ideal place for love and nurture between different generations of human beings. Unlike the radical feminists, who regard the family as not worth salvaging, Herman takes it as the aim of the feminist movement to make the family habitable once more.

This 'taking the family seriously' has other ramifications for Herman's analysis of the nature of intra-familial child sexual abuse. She has pointed out that only when one looks at the significance of family relationships can one begin to understand the finer emotional complexities involved in such kind of sexual abuse – to that extent, she feels that feminists like Brownmiller have simplified the picture to the detriment of the victims of the abuse. In her words,

> Susan Brownmiller, in her study of rape as a paradigm of relations between men and women, refers briefly to father-daughter incest. Stressing the coercive aspect of the situation, she calls it 'father-rape'. To label it thus is to understate the complexity of the relationship. The father's sexual approach is clearly an abuse of power and authority, and the daughter almost always understands it as such. But, unlike rape, it occurs in the context of a caring relationship. The victim feels overwhelmed by her father's superior power and unable to resist him; she may feel disgust, loathing, and shame. But at the same time she often feels that this is the only kind of love she can get, and prefers it to no love at all. The daughter is not raped, but seduced. In

[88] Clearly, Ward does not allow for the possibility of an equal and mutually caring relationship between a father and a daughter – she looks at every relationship within the family very much in terms of a kind of 'male conspiracy' theory. It is, therefore, rather surprising to find that she has thanked her own father in the 'Acknowledgements' of her book for giving her 'unending support'! The problem of reflexivity is perhaps very acutely illustrated here.

[89] See e.g. Fairtlough (1983), Herman (1981), Herman & Hirschman (1977, 1981), MacFarlane (1978).

fact, to describe what occurs as a rape is to minimise the harm to the child, for what is involved here is not simply an assault, it is a betrayal. (Herman & Hirschman, 1977, p. 748)

The work of Herman clearly shows that espousing a feminist perspective does not entail the rejection of the family system approach – the two can be combined in both analysis and practice.

8.6.5 Strategies for feminist action

The strategies that feminists have adopted in response to male patriarchal sexual oppression include family therapy, rape crisis centres, women's refuges and separatism. The more moderate feminists do not shy away from collaborating with men in their effort to provide therapy for sexually abusive families, to develop educational programmes for female self defence and to work for a more effective legal system for dealing with child sexual abuse.[90] The more extremist feminists, however, tend to avoid co-operating with men – their mistrust of males is so great that they feel only women and girls can truly work together for their own protection.[91]

The feminist perspective provides a timely corrective to male-dominated theorising in the area of human sexuality. However, it is perhaps unwise, both theoretically as well as from the point of view of practical reforms, to adhere to an extremist stance like that of Elizabeth Ward. While patriarchal biases and prejudices are prevalent in Western society, a sweeping 'male-conspiracy' type theory would only make such prejudices more difficult to overcome.

Nature is endowed with the pervasive presence of the two sexes, which, presumably, must collaborate in order to further the survival of life as we know it. 'Separatism', as a general and rigid principle for the organising of a 'new' social order, will be more destructive than constructive.

Thus it seems more reasonable to treat Ward's position as a kind of antidote to 'shock' researchers and practitioners, especially male ones, into vigilance against their patriarchal biases. For practical purposes, the moderate perspective exemplified by feminists such as Judith Herman will make a better contribution.

---

[90] See Fairtlough (1983), Herman (1981), Nava (1984).

[91] 'Those men who say they want to "help", could most pertinently demonstrate this by working for and with all the men in the world who see women as rape-bait, who use women in sexually abusive way. Just as women have formed support environments and groups for the victims of sexual and physical abuse, so caring men could form re-education groups, de-programming groups for their brothers who cannot see beyond the actions demanded by their own alienated masculinity.' (Ward, 1984, p. 195). Ward is telling men that women and girls do not welcome their intruding into their own effort of self-liberation – if they (men) are really sincere in their wish to amend their 'sin', they should do so by changing the attitudes of other men.

8.7 The multifactor perspective: the work of Finkelhor

While there have been efforts to produce typologies of both paedophiles and incestuous families,[92] and to identify 'family characteristics correlates' of child sexual abuse,[93] only David Finkelhor has consistently worked towards building up a 'multifactor' model that aims at covering all cases of child sexual abuse.

In an early paper, Finkelhor (1978) identified from existing research evidence six causal factors responsible for creating an incestuous family situation: (1) incestuous personality of the father-perpetrator, (2) role confusion within the family, (3) sexualised family interaction, (4) family history of abandonment and fear of abandonment, (5) isolation and subcultural permissiveness, and (6) opportunity factors such as mother's ill health. On the other hand, he has also derived from his own survey data eight 'risk factors', which, when taken together, constitute a predictor of the likelihood of a child being sexually abused (Finkelhor, 1980b). The list is: (1) living with step-father, (2) living without mother, (3) lack of close relationship with mother, (4) mother with poor education, (5) mother is sexually repressive and punitive, (6) lack of affection from father, (7) low family income, and (8) lonely childhood.

With respect to social-institutional contribution to paedophilic behaviour, Finkelhor (1982), in agreement with a moderate feminist perspective, has suggested patriarchy as a fundamental factor. There are four aspects to this factor:

(1) Men are socialised to view sexual success as essential to the maintenance of their male gender identity.

(2) Men are socialised not to seek emotional satisfaction or affection, and when they do, they pursue this in sexualised form; whereas women are prepared for a nurturing role which provides legitimate channels for expressing and obtaining emotional intimacy, including physical contact with children.

(3) For men, sex can be isolated and reduced to physical pleasure, while women are socialised to focus on relationships of which sex is only one component.

(4) Men are socialised to seek younger and physically smaller sexual partners while women seek older and bigger ones.

Regarding the origin of paedophilic behaviour, Finkelhor has suggested a 'four-factor' model which has its focus on the individual paedophile in the context of patriarchal socialisation (Finkelhor & Araji, 1983). These four factors are:

(1) Emotional congruence – the paedophile finds sexual involvement with children gratifying because it fits his emotional development.

[92] See Sections 8.4 and 8.5.2 above.
[93] See Gruber & Jones (1983), Martin & Walters (1982).

(2) Sexual arousal – when a person has become sexually arousable by children because of social or psychological reasons, he becomes more likely to commit paedophilic acts.

(3) Blockage – when there is some blockage, be it developmental or situational, to a person's developing peer relationships in adulthood, it is likely that he will commit paedophilic acts.

(4) Disinhibition – when conventional inhibitions against sexual contact with children are overcome, a person can more easily become sexually involved with children.

In an attempt to integrate these various findings and theories into a general model of child sexual abuse, Finkelhor (1984) has constructed a 'Four Precondition Model'. These four preconditions, which are considered explanatory of the occurrence of all types of child sexual abuse, are as follows:

(1) The perpetrator's motivation to sexually abuse – this precondition subsumes the first three factors of the four-factor model of paedophilia, i.e. emotional congruence, sexual arousal and blockage; it also subsumes the factor of patriarchal socialisation as contributory to abuse motivation.

(2) The overcoming of internal inhibitors – this subsumes the fourth factor, disinhibition, of the model of paedophilia; it refers to both the social and psychological conditions that enable the perpetrator to disregard the ethical conventions that he has learned.

(3) The overcoming of external inhibitors – this precondition subsumes some of the 'risk factors' as well as 'causal factors' described earlier, such as absence of mother, social isolation of the family, etc.; the presence of this precondition means that there is no external constraint that might prevent the occurrence of the abuse.

(4) The overcoming of the child's resistance – this precondition also subsumes some of the 'risk factors' such as the victim being a lonely child; the overcoming of the child's resistance may simply be an application of physical force, which is the clearest expression of patriarchal power.

While Finkelhor's effort is commendable in so far as it represents an attempt to put some order into the mass of material produced by research studies and theorising, it is important to point out that his desire to build up *one* single general model that can subsume all theories and be applied to all cases of adult-child sexual contact is not necessarily a useful objective. It has been pointed out above (Section 7.5.4) that some researchers have found it difficult statistically to systematise incest experiences because they are 'too unique or idiosyncratic'; it has also been noted that elaborate typological studies by the Langevin team in Toronto have reached the conclusion that paedophilia remains an 'enigma' Section 8.4.4 above). As Howells (1981) has argued, paedophilia, and more generally sexual contact between adults and children, is not a unitary phenomenon, but rather consists of very different types of relationships and encounters. It is doubtful whether a 'grand theory' is really possible.

8.8 Common characteristics of theoretical models

Apart from perhaps the radical feminist perspective, all the theoretical models discussed in this chapter affirm the normative status of adult heterosexuality, although as far as rehabilitation of paedophile offenders is concerned, behaviourists or even psychoanalysts are prepared to accept attainment to adult homosexuality as a desirable treatment goal (for paedophiles attracted to boys). The corollary of this affirmation of a normative standard is the espousal of the notion of 'abnormality', whether couched in terms of individual pathology, deviant conditioning or family dysfunction. Classification schemes or multifactor theories are introduced to systematise the data produced by research, so that appropriate management strategies can be devised.

Most of the theorists discussed are working within the mainstream professions. They are part of the state apparatus which aims at controlling deviant elements in society. The management and control strategies take the form of 'treatment', whether of the individual or the family.[94] Such treatment programmes, particularly those involving behaviour modification techniques, or family therapy backed by court orders, constitute a powerful regime to which individuals and families concerned must submit. Although professionals may not be insensitive to the needs of individual 'cases', their work is of necessity bound by the normative standards of acceptable sexuality and family life that their theories have stipulated, either explicitly or implicitly.

Through this therapeutic, rehabilitative work, data are generated, records created, and knowledge of child sexual abuse accumulated. This knowledge is further recycled, expanded and affirmed by the continuing practice of the professionals. Official records, research findings, explanatory theories and treatment programmes are not treated as problematic, rather they are taken as the reality by which the life of an individual person or a family is judged. Effort towards constructing a neat and comprehensive grand theory, such as that undertaken by David Finkelhor, reinforces this belief in the professionally/academically constructed 'reality'.

---

[94] Treatment programmes are increasing in number, particularly in the USA. Many are big projects which involve a large administrative and bureaucratic machinery, and are characterised by a clear ideology of systematic control of the individual person. Review of such programmes can be found in Annis (1982), Brecher (1978) and Knopp (1984). It is worthy of note that the treatment ideology exemplified in some programmes take the form of *schooling* the deviants into a socially acceptable mould, as reported by Knopp (1984): 'a few programs offer final written examinations and award certificates to those who have completed the module [of positive sexuality]' (p. 51).

It is not my intention, however, to dismiss totally these theoretical models. Some are certainly useful in describing aspects of adult-child sexual contact: the family system theory can clarify the interpersonal relationships underlying the occurrence of incest in some families, and the feminist perspective has rightly raised important questions pertaining to a wider context, such as male domination over females in our society. Granted this, however, it appears that most professionally/ academically constructed models of intergenerational sexual contact have not given much consideration to the personal construction made by the 'perpetrator' himself. To that extent, it is questionable whether these models are adequate to subsume the experience of the central actor of the drama – the adult person involved in the sexual contact. It is hoped that the present work will contribute towards closing this gap.

9

Theoretical and Methodological
Considerations

Some researchers in the social sciences believe that 'social facts', be they love and hate between individuals, or alliances and wars between nations, are objectively 'out there' to be studied by the social scientist, just as a tree is 'out there' in the field to be 'botanised' by a biologist. Research into the social world is thus a purely empirical activity, one that attempts to discover social reality 'as it is'.

This positivist view has been severely, and rightly, criticised by authors who are aware of the hermeneutical nature of human experience and the ideological nature of 'social facts'.[1] It has become increasingly apparent that 'facts' are theory-bound rather than objectively 'given'. All facts are human interpretations, as every act of observation is informed by some theory, albeit implicit in most cases. 'Facts' are produced by the person who 'goes out' to 'collect' them. It is therefore imperative that the theoretical assumptions underlying a piece of research be clarified at the outset so that the process of the production of 'facts' can be evaluated.

9.1 Human agency

The first theoretical assumption of the present work is that the human being is an active, self-monitoring and self-directing agent.[2] This is captured by Harré & Secord's (1972) rule of thumb: 'For scientific purposes, treat people as if they were human beings.' (p. 84) This seemingly banal reminder is most important – its upshot is that people are *not* machines or merely evolutionarily advanced animals. Treating people as human beings raises the question of what the essential characteristics of human existence are – and in answer to that question,

[1] Many sociologists, psychologists and philosophers have conducted critiques of the positivist-empiricist tradition in the social sciences, and have proposed alternative paradigms for theorising and research; examples are: Berger (1963), Berger & Luckmann (1967), Gauld & Shotter (1977), Giddens (1976), Harré (1974b, 1977b, 1978a, 1979), Harré & Secord (1972), Harré, Clarke & de Carlo (1985), C.W. Mills (1959), Shotter (1970, 1975, 1982b), Trigg (1985), Weber (1947, 1971), Winch (1958).

[2] The concept of 'agency' has been discussed by many authors, e.g. Giddens (1976, 1979), Harré (1983), Shotter (1982a), C. Taylor (1977).

the subjective 'I', to which all action-descriptions such as intention, reason, plan, purpose, feeling, desire, etc., are predicted, must be taken as the starting point. Human beings *act* in a meaningful fashion, rather than responding mechanically to external stimulation. A human person intends, desires, reasons, plans – and acts. Through these 'active impingings' on the world, he is giving form to his life. He construes and reconstrues reality, and acts according to his constructions in a hypothesis-testing fashion.[3] As a person grows and accumulates experience, he will evolve a specific style of construing, and his constructions may coalesce into some sort of a system, which can be called a 'personal construct system', 'implicit theory', or 'theory-in-use'.

The concept of *action* is pivotal to the notion of human agency: human actions are goal-directed, purposeful and meaningful. A hand moving up and then dropping down might constitute the action of 'waving one's hand', which might in turn constitute an *act* of greeting in certain circumstances and one of farewell in others. Hence human actions must be understood hermeneutically – that is, their *meanings* have to be interpreted for them to be intelligible. The meaning of an act-action sequence is jointly produced or negotiated by at least two actors in a culturally specific context. It is not possible to talk of waving a 'farewell' to nobody, although it is possible that the other 'actor' is imaginary or metaphorical (saying 'good-bye' to a city, for instance). This tendency towards meaning is the most fundamental feature of human existence. It is inherent in all human acts, including day-to-day practical activities as well as specialised ones such as 'research'.[4]

The self-regulatory quality of human action can be conceptualised in terms of the notion of 'rule'[5] or 'routines'.[6] A person acts according to an experience of internal orderliness, as if he is following some well-defined procedures. On the collective level, human actors have created various rules for social action, some explicit, such as religious liturgies or marriage ceremonies, some implicit, such as dinner-table etiquette, or behavioural codes in the world of soccer fans.[7] Human beings are not only rule-following, they are also capable of creating rules.[8] This concept of

[3] The language of 'personal construing' and 'personal construction' has been most consistently employed and elaborated into a coherent theory of human experience in the work of an American psychologist, George Kelly (1955, 1969, 1978). Such structuring of the world through bestowing meanings is not confined to the social realm, but pervades the whole of human 'lived experience', including the physical and temporal-spatial aspects of life (see Harré, 1978b).

[4] Whether this tendency towards meaning is biologically given, or socially evolved in the development of human societies, is a question beyond the scope of this discussion.

[5] See Collett (1977), Harré (1974a, 1977a, 1984).

[6] See Garfinkel (1967), Giddens (1984).

[7] In the work of Harré, liturgies and ceremonies are called formal episodes, i.e. where an explicit set of formal rules are operative, while those that are not explicitly rule-governed, such as the behaviour of football fans on the soccer terraces, are called 'enigmatic'. The latter are analysed in terms of the rule-following model so that its structure can be explicated, as in the analysis of football fans by Marsh, Rosser & Harré (1978).

[8] See Shotter (1981), pp. 161-2.

rule-creation-rule-following has a strong affinity with what Giddens (1984) has called 'practical consciousness'. An actor acts with reflexive capability of self-monitoring, but he does not usually think about this on the level of 'discursive consciousness'. Only when asked to account for his actions will he articulate the implicit rules and structures underlying his actions.

Rules underlying human action embody meanings, define goals and specify steps. Yet a rule is not a binding force rigidly scheduling every minute detail of a person's actions. As Brenner (1982) has demonstrated, 'people *must* develop choices as they cannot simply rely on rule-following in their actions. ... Action in situations other than 'closed' ones relies on active goal-pursuing, bargaining and the negotiation of situational definitions, the expression of skills and self-fulfilment, among others, and not just following rules' (p. 226). 'Rule' is an analytical concept descriptive of human agency – human actions are *approximations* to rules.

Hermeneutical analysis of human actions involves delineating intentions, reasons, plans, desires, purposes, etc. – categories which form the predicate of a subjective 'I'; it also involves applying the 'rule model' to the regularities of actions. Through such analyses, the meanings of human actions are explicated – i.e. made intelligible. As human experience is predicated to the 'I', the descriptive concepts that are commensurate with such experience are not always publicly determinable – there is a certain degree of solipsism inherent in human existence – and hence the actor's account constitutes an indispensable source of information about his actions. Although it has been argued that understanding the meaning of a human act is not the same as explaining its occurrence,[9] there is general agreement among social scientists who do not adhere rigidly to positivist empiricism that intentional descriptions provided by human actors are admissible as at least part of a scientific explanation of human action.[10] Indeed, Giddens (1982b) has argued strongly against the separation of 'understanding' from 'explaining', and has concluded that both concepts are essential to an adequate social science.

9.2 Reflexivity

A person is self-monitoring: he is capable of thinking of how he thinks, he has the power to intervene into his own actions. Reflexivity – the ability to be an object unto oneself – is a fundamental aspect of human experience. To be reflexive in research means to include oneself in one's conceptualisation of the social world. The researcher is only a special case in the general conceptualisation of human beings as active agents construing their worlds. There are theoretically an unlimited number of alternative ways of construing the world. Each of these alternatives can

[9] See e.g. Walker (1977).
[10] See e.g. Pettit (1976).

be a personally meaningful construction. Social research is the active pursuit of alternative constructions of reality, and it takes into account the constructions made by the human actors under study.

The type of work a researcher does reflects the type of theory he holds about the world. Since I construe the reality of human existence in the way outlined above, it follows that my research will place emphasis on the active nature of the human person, as well as the hermeneutical tendency inherent in human actions – not only in my own actions, but in the actions of those people within the domain of my research as well. This perspective leads to an understanding of the research situation as one in which not only is the researcher actively construing what is going on, but the 'subject'[11] is also actively construing what the researcher is trying to do. This reflexive stand leads to a respect for the individual person as an equal participant with the researcher in the research enterprise; it also leads to an emphasis on *negotiation* between the researcher and the participants.

The aim of research on human experience, following this formulation, is to attempt to achieve an understanding of each individual's personal representation of reality, rather than pursuing an unitary, objectively real world and the 'causes' of human activities within this 'real world'. Because reality, and our personal experiences within it, are in constant flux, the categories with which we make sense of the world cannot remain static. To be creative in research, one must be constantly aware of the diverse possibilities within the realm of human actions, and take them into account. Any research 'findings' can never claim universal validity – they are only particular renderings of the world.[12]

9.3 The world as phenomenologically experienced

The stress on the intentional nature of human action, and on the human person as actively construing reality and constructing a meaningful world, is at the heart of the phenomenological tradition – phenomenological analysis is concerned with 'how the objective is subjectively constituted'.[13] However, to say that the objective is subjectively constituted does not mean that the world is but a phantom of the mind. Rather, phenomenology insists on a complete *enmeshing* of the person with the world. To talk of a 'person' necessarily implies a 'world' in which the person is located; likewise, to talk of a 'world' entails the presence of a 'person' to whom the world is a world. This emphasis on the enmeshing of

---

[11] It is ironical that in traditional positivist psychology, particularly in experimental studies, the individuals whom the researcher studies are called 'subjects'. While the usage of this term in that specific context implies a passive, manipulable and 'naive' individual, the word 'subject', as illustrated in phenomenological or existential writings, actually means an active, self-monitoring and knowledgeable agent to whom all action-predicates refer.

[12] The issue of 'reflexivity' poses serious problems to philosophy and the human studies, which cannot be adequately dealt with here. A recent discussion of the topic can be found in Lawson (1985).

[13] Quoted from Bolton (1979), p. 161.

the person with the world can be clearly seen in daily examples – one sees the loneliness of the evening *in* a bottle of wine bought for a now cancelled date; one sees anger or irritation *in* the movements of a friend's body. Far from being a 'projection' of an intra-psychic 'something' onto an object 'out there' in the physical world, the experience (e.g. of loneliness) is established within the subject-object *Gestalt*.

In phenomenological analysis, reality is not objectively 'out there', but emergent in the interaction between a person and the world. In order to understand human experience, that experience itself must be studied as it phenomenologically appears to the person concerned, rather than reduced to a series of lower-order 'objective' components. As John Shotter has argued, we must start phenomenologically, with an analysis of the social psychological processes as we experience them: 'we must deal with that which in each and everyone's *experience* makes it possible for us to live our daily lives in processes of exchange with both one another and our physical surroundings'.[14] A good example of human experience described phenomenologically is provided by one informant of the present study – Nick is talking about his experience after a beloved boy left him after a three-year relationship:

> (A long pause of over a minute – weeps – sighs) Christ! Nothing is the same after he left – you know – just like, (long pause) just like the world has lost its colour – every, everything was different. (Nick)

Nick's world *had* changed – the first step towards understanding is to accept that to Nick the world had indeed changed.

C.S. Lewis, talking about his experience after his wife died, had expressed a similar sentiment:

> I see the rowan berries reddening and don't know for a moment why they, of all things, should be depressing. I hear a clock strike and some quality it always had before has gone out of the sound. What's wrong with the world to make it so flat, shabby, worn-out looking? Then I remember. (Lewis, 1961, p. 30)

In the words of the Dutch phenomenologist-psychiatrist, J.H. van den Berg (1972), Nick and C.S. Lewis were experiencing the changing of the world in a 'pre-reflective' manner. If pressed, Nick might possibly admit that the world did not literally lose its colour, and C.S. Lewis might also, on reflection, acknowledge that the 'flat, shabby, worn-out looking' quality of the world was a figure of speech. Nevertheless, their *immediate* experience told them otherwise – the world *had* lost its colour, and *had* become flat, shabby and worn-out. Reflection could not take away their pre-reflective experience that the world had changed. As Romanyshyn (1982) has demonstrated, psychological life is metaphorical in essence – it is the personal capturing/construing of the world through the vehicle of

[14] Shotter (1978), p. 40.

metaphors that human experiences are appropriated, understood and lived.

The task of phenomenology is to establish a description of the subjective world of the individual. Such a description will furnish material for an understanding of the meaning of a person's experience, and will become, to that extent, the basis for an explanation of his actions.

9.4 The social constitution of subjectivity

Although the above discussion has emphasised that the human person is an active agent, this does not preclude the operation of social forces in the constitution of individual subjectivity.[15] The enmeshing of the person with the world means that the source of subjectivity cannot simply be located in some intra-individual realm. The human person does not live in an isolated vacuum – he is necessarily part of a collective. If we are to take this into account, we cannot hold a purely essentialist view of human nature, a view which divorces 'the personal' from 'the social'. It is to the credit of Marxists (social structures precede individual consciousness) and feminists ('the personal is political') that nowadays social scientists, including psychologists, have begun to realise that an individual person must be seen as partly a 'product' of social structures and processes. At the interpersonal level, an individual's sense of being a subject arises from, and is maintained through, interaction with other people: a baby develops into personhood through a process of 'intentional socialisation' involving primarily the parents;[16] and the person maintains a sense of identity through a recognition of himself in other people's construction. The constitution of the interpersonal realm rests on mutual construing.[17] Although this is complex and prone to misunderstanding, as Laing, Phillipson & Lee (1966) have demonstrated, it is nevertheless the material that makes up the goings-on of the social world.

While the source of human subjectivity is not just intra-individual, neither is its constitution entirely conditioned by society. Human agency shapes social processes, which in turn provide the context within which human subjectivity arises. The intimate relationship between the personal and the social is best captured by the concept of 'duality of structure'.[18] Human activities constitute and reconstitute the social world, yet the structures of this world are beyond the control of any individual person. It is human action that creates the social realm, yet it is the social realm that provides the conditions of possibility for the meaningful execution of human action. That is, human action is both structured and structuring (hence 'duality') – 'by acting we can create the conditions for further action'.[19]

[15] 'Subjectivity' refers to the experience of being an individual 'subject', of being an 'I'.
[16] See Shotter (1973b, 1974).
[17] See the 'sociality corollary' in Kelly (1955).
[18] On the concept of 'duality of structure', see Giddens (1979, 1984), Shotter (1983, 1984).
[19] Shotter (1984), p. 196.

9.5 The construction of sexuality

Sexuality, one of the key components of a person's subjectivity, is not a biological given, but a socially constituted dimension of human life. Within the constraints imposed by the human body, there are numerous possibilities for sexual expression. A person's sexuality is a product of learning – development and changes are possible even after it has taken a relatively stable form. A person is always in the process of 'becoming', in all aspects of his existence, including the domain of 'the sexual'.

This learning, however, is not a type of mechanical conditioning, rather, it is learning within the context of a social world – the learning of the symbolic meanings that the collective has bestowed on bodies, organs, activities and sexual identities.

Such a conceptualisation of the notion of 'sexuality' has been articulated by interactionists since the mid-seventies. Plummer (1975) started from the premise of the phenomenological nature of human experience[20] and derived from this premise an interactionist/labelling account of sexuality and sexual deviance. His basic argument is that sexuality is a matter of socially constructed symbolic meanings – it is never merely a physical release of 'libidinal' energy. Within such an analysis, sexuality is not always or only concerned with physial 'sex' – the 'sexual' is embedded within the whole spectrum of the 'social'. Rape, for instance, can be seen as organised around themes of power, masculinity, and aggression,[21] while homosexuality can be interpreted in terms of counter-cultural movements and subversive politics,[22] and heterosexuality in terms of the institutions of procreation and the family.

The interactionist account puts much emphasis on social contexts and cultural constraints in the 'making' of sexuality.[23] While the physical-sexual act can be pictured as a matter of the relative positioning of bodies and their movements, such a physical event is always given a cultural symbolic contour which maps it onto the domain of the human. There are superimposed on our natural bodies many layers of 'unnatural' cultural artefacts, chief among which is the notion of 'normality'. Sexual normality depends on juxtaposing the right bodies at the right time in the right space. This process of social definition is formally established in the

[20] Plummer (1975) has argued that phenomenologically the world is a subjective, symbolic, processual reality wherein the individual carves out an existence through interactions with other people.

[21] See Plummer (1984).

[22] See Gagnon & Simon (1967).

[23] The rules and meanings that define social contexts regulate the experience of sexuality, and, in the terminology of Gagnon & Simon, provide the material for the 'scripts' with which sexual encounters are enacted. It is when the scripts followed by participants of an encounter do not match that problems arise, because 'the sources of arousal, passion or excitement (the recognition of a sexual possibility), as well as the way the event is experienced (if, indeed, an event follows), derive from a complicated set of layered symbolic meanings that are not only difficult to comprehend from the observed behaviour, but also may not be shared by the participants' (Gagnon & Simon, 1974, p. 23).

institution of the law – transgressing the legal proscription regarding what is sexually permissible in terms of age, gender, and kin relationship between persons will be treated as 'crimes against nature'.

To argue for a conceptualisation of sexuality as social construction does not, however, entail the conclusion that private-individual sexual identities and practices are isomorphic with collective sexual cultures. While human action is structured by the collective, it is also structuring the collective in return. The interplay of institutional resources and constraints with human agency leads to individualised diversities within the sexual domain. Thus within the normative domain of adult heterosexuality, there is still the possibility of individual variation, and as the result of the action of some groups of individuals the orthodoxy of heterosexuality has nowadays been modified to some extent, and homosexual relationships have become more socially acceptable, albeit within the confines of certain heterosexual standards such as love and fidelity.

Within the interactionist framework, cultural diversity and value plurality form the basis for relativising the concept of 'normality', and sexual deviance is theorised in the following way:

> There is no form of behaviour, sexual or nonsexual, that is intrinsically deviant. ... A form of behavior becomes deviant when it is defined as violating the norms of some collectivity. ... Thus deviation, as a social act, must be conceived in terms of social structure, social situation, and the character of specific actors rather than in terms of a fixed and seemingly immutable set (or sets) of moral postures. (Gagnon & Simon, 1967, p. 2)

The interactionist perspective is not too concerned with the *origin* of particular forms of sexuality. It is much more concerned with the *development* of sexual identities or 'careers' through interactional processes between individuals and society. It is the contention of the interactionist position that the labelling of a particular form of sexual expression as deviant, whether by society or by the actor himself, will lead to qualitative changes in the experience of that sexual behaviour, and eventually produce stable categories of identities. However, it must be stressed that 'labelling' is not necessarily a phenomenon of *overt* oppression of minorities by society. A person may actively label himself or his actions with the categories supplied by the dominant discourses of society without feeling oppressed. The adoption of a sexual identity is a subtle process, and the individual may experience it as part of his natural subjectivity.[24]

9.6 Understanding human action: towards a methodology

The present research project is focussed on 'understanding' adult sexual experience with children. In the ordinary sense of the word, when a person says 'I understand', what he means is that he 'knows what it is

[24] While this early work on the social construction of sexuality was largely focussed on

like'. There is the connotation of an 'as if' quality to the claim made in the phrase 'I understand' – 'as if I have had the same sort of experience'. In the context of trying to understand how an adult experiences sexual contact with children, it is impossible for the researcher actually to enter into such sexual contact.[25] Nevertheless, an understanding can be achieved by listening with empathy to how a paedophile accounts for his sexual experiences. It must be acknowledged, however, that human experiences are, in the final analysis, ontologically solipsistic. One can never really *share*, in the literal sense of the word, the pain (or joy, for that matter) experienced by another person.

Thus human experiences have to be communicated through metaphors, which mediate between different individuals, bringing about some measure of 'common-ness' in the 'shared' existence of being human. To that extent, the 'as if' quality is unavoidable in interpersonal understanding. One can never understand what it is like to be a paedophile, unless of course one is a paedophile oneself – indeed, even among paedophiles, the feelings of one differ from those of another. This much is pointed out by a paedophile with whom I had some contact but whom I was not able to interview:

> I really do not see how you can really hope to gain an understanding of the nature of paedophilia if you do not share the feelings of people whose sex drives take this particular direction. No amount of listening to detailed descriptions of instances of mutual love between adults and juniors, seductions, mutual masturbation, spankings etc., can have much academic significance. (Charles)

While it is very difficult for a non-paedophile to understand paedophilic feelings in the sense of 'having the same experience', I disagree with Charles's dismissal of the use of listening. To me, 'listening' is the first step, and one of the most important steps, towards building up an 'as if' understanding between persons. Therefore, this research can be seen as a sort of 'listening exercise' – listening to what paedophiles and people who have had sexual contact with children have to say; letting them speak for themselves; presenting their personal construction of their experiences. The emphasis on the immediate experience of an individual as his reality forms the basis of a descriptive methodology for research.

The analysis of human action begins at the level of specific episodes, such as a customary act of greeting, an argument or an experience of sexual intercourse. These episodes, of specific social 'happenings', form the 'building blocks' of social life. Analysis of them will furnish information on the underlying structures of human social (inter)action, in

---

homosexuality, there is some recent work, based on the same theoretical framework, on paedophilia (e.g. Plummer, 1979, 1981a).

[25] Even if one is willing to try out 'paedophilic' activities, it might not be psychologically possible because of the absence of such a desire, which means when actual contact is attempted, it would not be the same as in the case of someone who desires it.

terms of both individual intentional structures as well as their social-institutional substrates. Actual observation and recording of such episodes, particularly with video techniques, is desirable for the detailed teasing out of the action patterns and rules embedded in the social events. However, this ideal research strategy of actual recording is obviously impossible to carry out in many situations, where the actions involved are by nature private to only the individuals concerned, e.g. episodes of actual sexual contact between an adult and a child. In such situations, the way to go about doing research is to have the actor(s) give an *account* of the episode for analysis.

Talking is a basic feature of social life.[26] The study of human experience, therefore, must begin with how people talk about their lives. In keeping with the constructivist view, Kelly (1955) advocated what he called 'the credulous approach' in psychological research, an approach which treats the narrative of each of the research participants as the most important source of information. Similarly, Harré & Secord (1972) propose a research attitude that treats individuals as capable of accounting for their actions. Giddens (1984), referring to ethnomethodological studies as examples, also argues for the view that actors can, when asked, discursively explain their 'practical consciousness'. The basis of this reliance on a person's accounting is the notion of 'privileged knowledge' – a person has privileged access to information about his own activities.[27]

In this connection, it is important to point out that a person's accounting is not a 'report', but a 'telling'.[28] A report implies a third person observation stance, whereas 'telling' refers to the active first-person narrative of involvement. The participants in this research were not asked to produce 'introspective reports' of what goes on 'inside' their mind – they were asked to account for their actions as they normally do in the conduct of their day-to-day life. Within such a context, the researcher is not a third person, but a *second person* to whom the account is *addressed*.

In order to achieve a proper understanding of adult-child sexual contact, it is necessary to capture the experience of such contact from the personal perspective of the individuals involved.[29] Ideally speaking, research effort should be directed towards letting both parties (i.e. the child *and* the adult) articulate their experience in such a way that a negotiated account could be obtained from their respective narratives.

However, in the present study, practical constraints have prevented the accomplishment of the ideal paradigm of 'joint accounting'. Refusal from child protection agencies made access to children impossible, and so

[26] Human existence is so intimately bound up with talk that Harré has remarked that 'the fundamental human reality is a conversation' (1983, p. 20). Also, Wittgenstein (1953) has referred to the speaking of a language as constituting the essence of a 'form of life'.

[27] See Polanyi (1958, 1966, 1969), Shotter (1982a).

[28] See Shotter (1981).

[29] Research in this direction is rare – Sandfort (1982) is a notable exception.

the research focus has to be on the adults. Although far from ideal, the collecting of *personal accounts* from adults with paedophilic desire constitutes an important part of the 'documentation' process in the study of adult-child sexual contact. While some previous research had used accounts provided by adults who had sexual involvement with children, they tended to impose a particular model of *pathology* on the material.[30] The present study attempts to present the participants' *own* construction of their sexual experience, so that the personal meanings of the experience can be highlighted.

9.7 A note on definition

While some researchers have included all persons under the age of 18 as 'children', most others use the age of 16 or 14 as the criterion. On the other hand, puberty has often been used as a dividing line in the study of paedophilia, but since puberty spans a period of time and the time of its onset varies enormously from individual to individual, it is not possible to say exactly what age 'puberty' corresponds to in general. Regarding the nature of the contact, some authors define all adult-child sexual contact as *abuse*, while others think it is important to take into consideration the possibility of consensuality.

For the purpose of this research, no rigid definition is used because any age criterion is simply an arbitrary boundary line adopted to map out a more or less distinct domain of concern under the heading of adult-child sexual contact. Much more important perhaps is the age gap between the parties involved. While obviously the greater the age gap, the more certain that the sexual contact can be considered as of the adult-child variety, the minimum age gap of five years, used by many researchers, is a reasonable criterion. However, one must not be too rigid about this – each relationship has to be considered individually, for example, it is conceivable that 'normal' heterosexual courtship is possible between a 15-year-old girl and a 20-year-old man. I have therefore not adopted a rigid 'screening' procedure in selecting informants. Any adult man[31] who has a sexual desire for young persons before or around puberty could be included, even if this is not his exclusive sexual orientation.

There are two considerations regarding the term 'sexual contact':

(1) It is used neutrally to include both coercive or abusive incidents, and consensual relationships.

(2) The word 'sexual' is difficult to define – some authors tend to

---

[30] See e.g. Bell & Hall (1971), McCaghy (1967), Ortiz y Pino & Goodwin (1982), Wilson & Cox (1983).

[31] While it is debatable whether paedophilia, or more generally adult sexual interest in children, is confined to men, I have restricted myself to a male sample because of the virtual impossibility of getting in touch with female 'paedophiles' either through official or unofficial channels. In this connection, it should be pointed out that throughout the text, the pronoun 'he' is used to refer to a person in general, not out of conformity to male 'sexism', but

include any bodily contact ranging from a sensual good-night kiss to full penetrative intercourse within the same realm of 'the sexual', while others apply the term only to the more explicitly genital activities with orgasm as the ultimate goal. The criterion adopted here, however, is a personal-constructivist rather than a behavioural one. That is, the focus is on the *intentional* pursuit, on the part of the adult, of pleasures that are to him associated with sexual excitement and gratification (not necessarily orgasmic). This no doubt still leaves the word 'sexual' undefined and hence problematic. But as can be seen later, the informants in this study have their own ways of construing what constitutes the realm of 'the sexual', and it is better to leave the term less defined so as to allow room for personal construction.

Lastly, the term 'paedophile' is used here in the loose sense to describe an adult who has a sexual interest in children – no reference to specific aetiological theories or to exclusivity in sexual preference is implied; it is simply used as a convenient short-hand label in place of the clumsy phrase 'an adult who has had, or who desires to have, sexual contact with children'.

9.8 The research process

9.8.1 The informants

Difficulty in getting informants

I applied to the Home Office Research Unit for permission to interview sex offenders in prisons. I had also contacted several child guidance and child protection agencies, some probation services departments, as well as a few psychiatric clinics for help in getting in touch with the appropriate informants. Of all these I had some success only with the psychiatric clinics. The others either turned down my request straight away, or did so after some negotiation with me. In the end, I turned to other sources for help.

Sources of informants

There were three sources through which I came into contact with men who have had, or who desire to have, sexual contact with children. I was able to interview 20 of them. The three sources were:

(1) Psychiatric clinics. With the help of several psychiatrists, I was able to interview 9 men who were undergoing psychiatric treatment because of sexual desire for, or activities with, children. Usually these interviews took place in the clinic, but sometimes at the home of the

---

because it is usually the male paedophile that is the person in question.

informant. In all 22 interview sessions were conducted, over 36 hours altogether. Of these 9 men 8 gave permission for tape-recording and altogether 35 hours of tapes were collected.

(2) A paedophile organisation. I contacted the executive committee of a paedophile organisation and asked them to consider assisting me by introducing me to their members. Although they were very suspicious about 'research', they did put me in touch with three of their members. However, this assistance was very soon withdrawn, and I only gained three informants from this source, with 4 taped interview sessions totalling 8½ hours. The interviews took place at the informants' homes.

(3) *Forum* magazine. In 1984-5 I put an advertisement in this magazine four times: 'Psychologist researching on paedophilia needs volunteer informants. Confidentiality guaranteed.' A total of 31 respondents responded to the advertisement. Six just sent a letter describing some of their sexual experiences without leaving a contact address. Of the remaining 25, 14 stopped further correspondence with me after I had sent them a first letter explaining the objectives and method of my study – a second letter also elicited no response. The rest were willing to help, but I was only able to interview 8 of them; the others discussed their experiences only in correspondence. Altogether I conducted 11 interview sessions with the 8 informants, totalling 27 hours; 2 of them refused permission for tape-recording, so only 24 hours of tape were obtained. The interview was conducted either at the informant's home or at my home.

Names of informants

The names of the informants used in this present work are all fictitious to conceal their identities. Informants from source (1) are Adrian, Andy, Fred, Keith, Matthew, Nick, Patrick, Robert and Vincent; those from source (2) are Daniel, Eugene and George; and those from source (3) are Ben, Bruce, Edward, Jack, Joe, Martin, Simon and Tom.

9.8.2 *The interview setting*

In terms of the setting of the interview, the informants could be divided into two groups: those who were introduced to me by the psychiatrists (the 'clinic' informants), and those I contacted through other channels (the 'volunteer' informants). In the former group, the interview usually took place in the clinic, although I did interview some (who were no longer patients of the clinic) in a home setting. In the case of informants contacted through other channels, I conducted the interview either at my home or at the informant's home. While undoubtedly the home setting was much more relaxed and conducive to free conversation, I did not find the 'clinic' informants, *as a group*, particularly affected by the more formal setting of the clinic.

When I met an informant for the first time, I always gave him a detailed explanation of my research:

(1) The objective of my research – that I wanted to collect personal accounts of people who had had sexual experiences with children so as to attempt an understanding of what such experiences meant to them.

(2) What his participation in my study meant – that it was a totally free choice on his part, he did not *have to* agree to be interviewed by me; and if he was a 'clinic' informant, that his participation in my study would in no way affect his relationship with his psychiatrist or other staff of the clinic, or affect his legal situation if he was involved in a court case.

(3) That I would ensure the confidential nature of his participation in my study – I had no relationship whatsoever with the court, the police, or other government organisations; I was an independent academic researcher connected to a university; he did not need to mention names or identifying characteristics while discussing his experiences; all material that I might obtain from him would be kept strictly confidential and anonymous, and nobody but myself would have access to the material; I would not feed back information to the psychiatrists or other staff of the clinic if he was a 'clinic' informant; when I wrote the report of my research I would disguise any material I might use in such a way that the informant's identity would not be known.

The method that I used to gather information in the interview was tape-recording. When I negotiated with the clinics for permission to conduct interviews there I discussed the issue of tape-recording with them, and obtained permission to do so on condition that: (1) permission was given by the individual informant, and (2) I erased the tapes after transcribing the interview.

After I had explained in detail the purpose of my research, I then discussed with the informant whether or not he would agree to let me tape-record our conversation. I explained to him that the recording was used only as an aide-mémoire so that I would not have to write notes during the interview, and our conversation could run smoothly without being interrupted. I also made it clear that he was not obliged to give permission for the tape-recording and that he was completely free to make up his mind. I told him that the tapes would only be accessible to myself and nobody else, and that they would be wiped after I had transcribed them, but I did not go any further to persuade or pressure him to accept my request. Most of the informants agreed to let me tape-record our conversation (3 disagreed). After thus explaining my research to the informant, I usually asked him if he had any queries so that I could clarify further. In other words, I tried my best to make the interview as intelligible to the informant as possible.

9.8.3 The conduct of the interview

I adopted an open-ended, spontaneous, conversational style in conducting the interview. Throughout my contact with each informant, I strove to maintain a receptive, listening posture. This, together with my assurances about confidentiality and anonymity, helped to reduce the anxiety engendered in the informant by the interview. The non-threatening atmosphere I tried to produce in the meeting enabled me to establish adequate rapport with the informant. Even in the clinic setting most informants did not appear to feel that they were being coerced into an unwelcome situation.

Although I had a list of questions and issues to be discussed with each informant, I usually followed fairly spontaneously the informant's lead in discussing various issues. Having said that, I should point out that not all informants were eloquent or talkative, and so often it was I who played the major part in moving the interview forward. Also, because I had to collect material with respect to certain questions, I tended to structure our conversation accordingly, but I did so in accordance with the mood of the informant as well as with the appropriateness of the moment. I encouraged the informant to talk about himself in as spontaneous a manner as possible, and I tried my best to avoid turning the interview into a question-and-answer 'interrogation'. If the informant agreed and if circumstances permitted, I usually arranged at least two or three meetings with him, so that our conversation could proceed at a pace that would not put pressure on him. In this way, I could also feed back to him my construction of his account in the following session, and engage in a process of negotiation with him to arrive at a more refined construction.

The list of issues that constituted a guideline or structure for the interview is as follows:

(1) How did the informant view himself as a person? This issue pertained to the notion of self-identity – whether or not he organised his life consciously around the self-ascription of a paedophile identity, and how he characterised himself as an individual. In this connection, I would ask the informant to talk about his parents, his childhood, family life, marriage, when and how he came to realise that he was 'paedophile' (if he did), and so on.

(2) How did he explain the origin and development of his sexual desire for children? This question represented the central concern of the research – how the informant construed his sexuality, what his experiences with children meant to him, and how he compared children with adults. In this connection, I would ask the informant to talk about specific encounters with children, without divulging identifying details, to illustrate his construction of adult-child sexual contact. Sexual experiences with adults were also discussed whenever appropriate.

(3) How did he cope with society? This included his daily life, employment, problems with the law or other official agencies, and so on.

Although I tried to maintain a flexible as well as empathetic stance during my conversation with all informants, one of them (Patrick) did show some anxiety about the discussion. While he was not unwilling to talk about how he explained his paedophilic orientation, and also his view about society's repression of sexuality, he did not want to talk in detail about his offences because he was fed up with having to repeat the stories to many professionals. He did not think that by repeating his story people like himself would be helped – as the fault lay not with these people, in his view, but with society. I did not press him unduly, but let him talk in whatever manner he felt at ease.

With informants whom I met more than once, I followed this strategy:

(1) I listened carefully to the tape of the previous meeting, transcribed the conversation verbatim, then attempted to make a coherent picture of the informant's life as well as of his construction of his sexuality.

(2) I started the following session with a recapitulation of what was discussed in the previous one, and invited the informant to comment on my construction of his account, to clarify what was doubtful, or to add what he felt had been left out, and then proceeded to explore further with him issues that had not been touched on so far.

At the end of our contact, I would briefly summarise what we had done, and expressed my gratitude for the informant's help, as well as reassuring him of my undertaking to keep all the material confidential.

9.8.4 The response of the informants

As indicated above, most of the informants had no problem exploring and discussing their experiences with me. On the whole, detail about sexual encounters did not pose any difficulty for our conversation. As far as the source of informants was concerned ('clinic' *vs* 'volunteer' sources), no appreciable difference was observed in terms of the informants' willingness to engage in an exploration with me of their life and sexual experiences. In retrospect, however, there does seem to be some difference between the 'clinic' and the 'volunteer' group in that quite a number of informants in the latter group used sexual pluralism and ethical relativity as justification for their paedophilic desire, while only one or two 'clinic' informants can be said to have produced such an argument. Nevertheless, not all 'clinic' informants had expressed agreement with a negative ('pathology') view of adult sexual desire for children, nor did all 'volunteer' informants give a rosy picture of their sexual orientation. My sample of informants is too small to form an adequate basis on which to establish any generalisation about the influence of the clinic setting, if any, on the accounts that the informants produced.

With respect to the decision to participate in my study, probably each individual informant had his own reasons and motives. Certainly these motives might have shaped the way he talked about his experiences during the interview, but the question 'how' could not be answered given the limitation of the present study (perhaps this problem is inherently impossible to solve). Nevertheless, I will make some speculations regarding the informants' motives:

(1) Since no money was involved as a reward for any informant, their participation could not be a result of a pursuit for material gain.

(2) Some of the 'clinic' informants might have wanted to please their psychiatrists when they decided to take part in my study. If this was true, however, it did not produce any uniformity in the kind of accounts they produced.

(3) There were some informants, from both the 'clinic' and the 'volunteer' group, who appeared to need to talk to some sympathetic listener about their experiences. They may have been feeling lonely, or it may be the case that their 'secret' had caused tension in their mind. By talking at length with me, they had found somebody to share their feelings, without having to submit to any pressure to change themselves.[32] Again, if this was true, it did not produce uniformity in these informants' accounts.

(4) While some informants appeared to have an urge to talk about their sexual experiences as a relief of tension, others actually became interested in exploring various issues about their experiences. Although this may not have been the original motive that prompted them to agree to take part in the study, it may have maintained their willingness to go further with me and to persist in the second, third, and even fourth session.

9.8.5 The production of accounts

The interview was the setting where the informant's account was produced. However, as I was also a participant in the interview, I inevitably contributed something to the production of his account.

(1) I had used open-ended questions as far as possible to avoid 'leading' the informant to a particular way of construing or describing his experiences.

(2) I had done my best to maintain a non-imposing and receptive style in interacting with the informant, to encourage him to speak freely.

(3) As the object of my study was not a matter of testing any hypothesis, I was not looking for any particular type of accounts.

(4) It can be said that given my open and receptive attitudes, the informant might have taken me as a supporter of paedophilia, and hence provided an account that aimed at reinforcing this sympathy. Yet it could also be argued that such receptive attitudes would not arouse in the informant the need to present a defensive account.

---

[32] Some 'clinic' informants indeed indicated that I was a better person to talk to than their psychiatrists because I was not trying to 'treat' (change) them.

After the interview with an informant was completed, I wrote up a 'life story' of the particular individual, following as closely as possible his own narrative. I also sorted out his accounts under several headings: description of self, explanation of sexual desire for children, relationship with adults, childhood experiences, parents, marriage, etc. Under each heading, I put all the verbatim quotations that were directly related to that particular topic. I also went through paedophilic episodes described by the informant by intensive reading and re-reading of his narrative, and then attempted to discern the underlying structure of the activities embedded in each episode. As I was accumulating material from one informant after another, I began to compare the analysis I had arrived at in each case with others, and to tease out similarities and patterns in their accounts.

One problem related to the production of accounts is the question of the validity of the material produced. It can be argued that the material that I have gathered is subjective and unquantifiable. There are two parts to this challenge: (1) whether the informants were reliable sources of information, i.e. whether or not they were telling me what they actually thought, and (2) whether what they had told me, even if they were honest with me, represented their 'real' situation.

The answer to the first question must be that I cannot *guarantee* the reliability of my informants. However, I do not think that I was in a worse position compared to other studies. Even in objectively controlled situations, such as laboratory experiments using plethysmographic measures, the participants could still confound the results by deliberate effort. If a person wants to keep his feelings and views from other people, no research strategy can prevent him from doing so. To the second objection one could argue that the question of 'what is reality' is not a question about 'objectivity' if the term 'objectivity' is taken to mean 'something out there independent of the human observer'. To an individual person, reality is what he construes to be real. What the informant told me in the interview represented his account *situated in this particular context*, and as such constituted the material for my study. It could be argued that at best this account was the informant's *rationalisation* of his own behaviour. This, however, might prove to be an argument in favour of, rather than against, my work. If we take 'rationalisation' not in the positivist sense as 'false' or 'unreliable', but in its etymological sense of 'related to reason/meaning', then we could accept, indeed we have to say, that the informant's account constituted his effort to give reason and meaning to his experience[33] and this is precisely what this work sets out to *document*. The situation in which the informant's account was produced was one in which I asked him to reflect on, to explain, to justify, or if you like, to 'rationalise', his sexual desire. The situation was *not* one in which the informant ran the risk of

---

[33] Such a 'tendency to meaning' is the fundamental feature of human life, as argued above.

incriminating himself by what he might say; it was not a police interrogation in which he had to defend himself – to that extent, I expected that his 'rationalisation' would be more likely to represent what he *believed*, and hence what I wanted to understand. Even when what he had told me represented more of his fantasies than his actual experiences, this material still reflected his understanding of his desire.

The account presented here is *my* construction of the informants' accounts in so far as they are written by me, although I have taken the step of using verbatim quotations from their accounts as frequently as space permits. In this sense, it is true that my theoretical position with respect to not only the nature of social sciences, but also the subject of paedophilia, has contributed to the production of the account that forms the present work. My justification is that no account, of whatever issue, particularly those concerning human experiences, can claim an absolutely neutral stand. Every account is a situated point of view. The point of view represented by this study is situated within a critical approach to the socially constituted nature of human sexuality.

There are other possible points of view on this subject, some of which have been documented in Chapters 7 and 8. Children who have had sexual contact with adults might produce accounts different from mine or from those of my informants.[34] Furthermore, it is plausible to suggest that other paedophiles not interviewed in this study might produce accounts totally at variance with the ones I have collected. One such group of people are those adults who enjoy *violent* molestation of children. Probably this group of people would be very much less inclined to take part in my study, even if I could get in touch with them. The self-selected nature of my small sample of informants precludes any claim of generalisability. But since generalisability is *not* the objective of this study (*documenting* the experiences of *some* people is), this defect is not a fatal one.

9.9 Ethical problems encountered in this study

9.9.1 'Criminal' information

The problem of research in human activities that are defined by society as 'criminal' poses a dilemma between the researcher's duty as a responsible member of society, and the demand of professional ethics on the researcher to keep confidential all material gathered from individuals participating in the research. In my study, this problem arose whenever the informant discussed with me specific episodes of sexual activities with children. My solution was to take my responsibility to the informant as a greater priority because it was on the understanding that I would

---

[34] It is possible to say that because it lacks any discussion of children's accounts of sexual contact with, or abuse by, adults, this work suffers from a serious defect. However, as pointed out before, practical circumstances prevented me from gaining access to such children, hence I had to focus on the adults' accounts alone.

keep all information provided strictly confidential that he had agreed to participate in my study in the first place. Although I felt that on the whole the rapport between me and the informants was good, I could not be perfectly sure that what each informant had told me concerned events that had actually happened. What I had got was the *personal construction* of each informant concerning his desire and experiences. I was not trying to establish the 'objective' truth or otherwise of events that the informant talked about – I was not in possession of unequivocal 'evidence' about illegal activities.

Furthermore, my research proposal and interview protocols had been scrutinised by various committees of the psychiatric clinics in which I conducted my fieldwork. After an elaborate process of vetting, the respective ethical committees of these clinics had given me formal approval to conduct my research under their auspices. It was agreed that I would keep strictly confidential all the material that I had obtained from the informants – I would not feed back any information about the informants to the psychiatrists or other staff of the clinic. In other words, the format and content of my study had 'official' recognition. I took this to mean that the nature and method of my research were deemed acceptable within the ethical guidelines of established institutions in this society.

9.9.2 Exploitation of the informants

While all research involving human 'subjects' can be criticised as exploiting the participants involved, admittedly mine seems much more exploitative because of the very private nature of the research topic – sexual experience – and the vulnerability of the informants in discussing with me their 'illegal' activities.

Faced with this problem, I do not think there is any neat solution. Unless we decide to give up all hopes of attempting any *intersubjective understanding* of human sexual experiences in a systematic way, we have to accept the fact that strictly speaking, however well-intentioned, our research work can always be said to be exploiting our informants. Even if we provided remuneration for the effort that the informants had made (I had not done so in my study), it would still be possible to argue that the informants were no less (indeed even *more*) exploited. Having said that, however, I do feel that I did manage to take steps to minimise any possible exploitation in my study:

(1) I explained to each informant in detail the nature of my study – I did *not* use any deception in my research strategy.

(2) I stressed that the informant was completely free to decide whether or not to take part in my research. Particularly with informants introduced to me by the psychiatrists, I made sure that they understood that they were *not* obliged to help me. Obviously I cannot guarantee that, even given my clarification and emphasis on the voluntary nature of participation, the informant's decision to help

me was necessarily a truly free one. Nevertheless, it can be safely surmised that whatever motives they cherished, those informants whom I contacted through unofficial channels were in no way under any coercion to participate in my study.

(3) I took care to ensure the confidentiality of the material I gathered, and to let the informants know that I had done so.

(4) I respected the mood of each informant during the interview, and did not press him if he did not want to discuss any particular point at a particular moment.

However, even so, I still cannot claim that I have not exploited my informants. While I have not used the accounts to obtain any material gains such as money (selling the accounts to the *Sun*, say), I cannot deny that I have made an important gain through using their information – I have gained a PhD degree. However, in the process of completing my research I have not intentionally caused harm to my informants. Instead, I have tried my best to make the meeting between myself and the informant beneficial to him as well:

(1) Given my clinical psychology background, I was keen to make the interview an occasion for the informant to gain some *self-understanding*. While my aim was to gather information in relation to my research questions, I felt that this was not in conflict with the possibility of the informant coming to a better understanding of himself. I was not trying to impose my view on him, rather attempting through the negotiating process of the interview to provide him with the opportunity to construe and reconstrue his experiences and to arrive at a clearer picture of himself. Whether such self-understanding is a *benefit* can be debated, but some informants actually said that it was through our meetings and discussion that they began to reflect more seriously about their experiences, and thereby came to a clearer understanding of themselves.

(2) It seemed to me that quite a number of my informants were fairly lonely people – they did not have the opportunity to talk to people about their experiences. This loneliness was to some extent reduced through our meeting and discussion (in a context in which the informant could feel safe and free). Indeed several informants indicated that the interview with me provided the first occasion they had ever had to talk about their experiences and feelings freely to somebody who was sympathetic.

(3) In trying to make the interview a process whereby understanding can be achieved, I put before the informant the views of mainstream society and invited him to comment on them. This discussion might alert the informant to the necessity of taking into consideration the wider context of society in his reflection.

It could conceivably be argued that an increase in self-understanding would only help the informant persist in his 'illegal' activities, perhaps in a more sophisticated manner. Alternatively, increase in self-understanding might make the informant become more content and settled in his paedophile identity. Furthermore, while sympathetic listening to the informant's accounts might help temporarily to relieve him of the tension of a lonely secret existence, it had not really provided him with any long-term benefit – our contact inevitably stopped after I had completed my fieldwork, and the experience of having had a sympathetic listener might actually create a greater dissatisfaction in the informant concerning his lonely existence. Moreover, the experience with a sympathetic listener might foster in the informant a false hope that society was much more accepting than it actually was. Nevertheless, it is necessary to point out that, as discussed towards the end of Chapter 10, not all informants in this study were lonely, withdrawn, or insecure people. About half seemed to me to be confident in themselves and were leading an independent life. Thus perhaps it is not necessary to dwell on the possible negative effect that an encounter with me might produce in their lives. Many of the informants were quite resilient people, and I have to bear in mind that my existence only constituted a very tiny part of their experience.

There is, however, the question of possible harm now that I have completed this work and it is accessible to the public. To prevent any possible harm to the informants, I have endeavoured to disguise the accounts so as to mask the identity of all the informants. It is not my intention to defend paedophilia, nor to arouse public hostility to those who feel sexually attracted to children. My wish is to contribute, albeit in a small way, to a better understanding of the experience.

In retrospect, however, two points can be raised:

(1) Does my work with these informants belong to the tradition of the institutions of 'confession' which, from the medieval Catholic confessional to contemporary psychoanalytic practice, constitutes a powerful tool of oppression? While I had tried my best to respect the autonomy of each informant, the very question that I asked – how he explained his sexual desire for children – was an implicit judgment that *that* was something to be investigated, rather than, for instance, the alternative question of why society was so oppressive towards paedophilia. Although some informants had expressed a critical view of society's hostility towards paedophiles, the central concern of my study was still the individual informant's explanation of himself. Thus there is a tension in my work: I have argued against the categorisation of paedophiles into a fixed sexual identity, yet my interviews with the informants seem to have reinforced such an identity.

(2) Knowledge is power. I have produced 'knowledge' about my informants, yet I have not taken the step of feeding back this knowledge to each of them in an effort to make our encounter an 'emancipatory' one. This neglect is in a way inherent in the

'evolutionary' nature of the project – I did not fully develop my 'thesis' until I had written the whole work, and by that time I had already ceased all contact with my informants.

Despite these doubts, I have conducted my study with a clear conscience – I only hope that in future work I may be able to resolve some of the problems discussed here.

10

Personal Accounts

As discussed in the last chapter, this is not a hypothesis-testing type of study. Rather, it is an attempt, through collecting and analysing personal accounts, to look at how paedophiles understand their sexuality. This chapter will present the personal accounts provided by the individual informants. Common factors in their construction will be analysed in this and the next chapter.

10.1 Personal explanation

Because of lack of space, the 'life story' of each informant will not be presented in full here. Only a brief description will be given, with the focus on how he explained his sexual desire for, and encounter with children.

Adrian

Adrian was a 48-year-old divorcee. He lived with his aged mother, along with his elder sister and her husband. He worked as a labourer and had quite a stable work record over the last thirty years. However, he had been arrested many times for sexual offences against children, and had been imprisoned for six months.

In Adrian's narrative, sex is construed as a basic necessity in life – just like other biological needs such as feeding:

> They [i.e. sexual activities] give me a great feeling inside, when just before a meal time, your stomach feels empty, you go and have a meal, and you feel lovely and, full up. ... If I had a woman, I could get what I wanted any time I want it, more or less. Not every two minutes of the day, you know, every night, and that would satisfy my stomach – well my sex drives.

This feeding imagery is embedded in the context of a sense of deprivation: from infancy onwards, Adrian had experienced much ostracism because of his poor physique,[1] and he felt that he was preventd from growing up

[1] He was less than five foot tall, allegedly a result of premature birth.

as his peers did. Since women were not interested in him, he turned to children:

> I think, the lack of the real thing – lack of intercourse. ... As I said before, 'cause I can't get the real thing, see, as far as I'm concerned, I tried to get girls, from a very very early age, but I have been advised – sort of guided the other way – and while I'm looking, they're gone, got a steady boyfriend, married and got a family, you see, leaving me still, still down the bottom. ... I think, I'm deprived, and I think to myself, why should I be deprived of my sex life, *every* animal, *every* human being has got a sex drive. If you can't get one, you're going after the other.

Mixed with this deep sense of deprivation, however, is a fatalistic optimism about divine providence:

> Everything I do or say, is arranged by God. Everything you do or say, or whatever, is arranged by God. ... Well I find God, you know, perhaps he leads me to – er – some place – there'd be a bloke there to masturbate – or who wants me. ... I think God's given – let me do this, particular thing [i.e. sex with children], one to satisfy me, to not let me suffer too much, and secondly, to – mm – keep me happy until he get – such time he gets me a woman.

Andy

Andy was a 34-year-old unemployed man. He had spent most of his childhood in children's homes and over ten years of his adult life in a special hospital because of sexual offences against boys. He described his sexual desire for children as a consequence of this lengthy institutional experience.

> Unfortunately my family had to split, well, now I went to the children's home, full of boys – mm – and this is when I started to get the issue of grubby sex, you know, I got the idea of grubby sex. What I mean to say by grubby sex is that you begin to learn habits that you shouldn't learn, you know, like masturbating each other off, see, that's the way I learned. I was in a children's home and you couldn't get out of it. There're the older boys doing it, and the younger boys used to watching it, and so, I picked it up. And then I went back to my parents, and then I was again took to a children's home, full of boys again, and you get to know what – mm – each did with other boys – er – what's the word for it (pause) excuse my language – bum each other, right, then I was, took out, took back to home again. When my Mum, when my Mum died when I was 13, my Dad left, I was put into a children's home, and there'd be hundred or more boys, about eight staff. There, this particular staff used to go round picking up boys, taking to his room, and having sex with them. And, by this time, you get to know, I got to know more about having sex with boys than I did with girls, so, that's what started me off, on the wrong course. ... The kids, they start off when they are in a boarding school, approved school, and children's homes, that's the main thing, children will pick up, they will learn sex with other boys, do

it to each other, and this is what I found out, they do it to each other. And when you get older, you still fancy smaller kids, because in your age, you haven't really made up your own mind, your previous experiences when you first started. So what I'm saying is you may be fifty odd, right, but you still fancy small children because the men haven't actually grown up, grown out of the sexual ways when they were kids themselves, I think this might be the problem. The kids, still in their kiddy minds, fancy other kids, and I think this is really what is is – it is with me. ... What I was saying here – mm – I think, as I grew up, I don't, I don't think sex come along with me at the same time, I learned that at a much later date. ... I learned sex when I was about 19, I was ignorant of sex except I was going round interfering with children – but I was ignorant of actual sex, I didn't learn it in school.

Andy's understanding of his own sexuality can be summarised as follows:

(1) Institutionalisation had produced in him the habit of having sex with other boys.
(2) Such a habit persisted even after he had grown up, and he felt he still fancied boys.
(3) Because he had only had sexual experiences with boys from childhood onwards, he was ignorant of 'actual sex', and all he could do was 'interfering with children', which completed the vicious circle by leading to further institutionalisation.

For Andy, it is never a question of sexual 'relationships', rather, all his experiences were of the nature of sexual 'events' – one-off encounters with boys.

Ben

Ben was a businessman in his thirties. He lived alone. Sexually he was drawn towards pubescent boys, and had considerable experience of sexual contact with them. So far he had not been arrested for any sexual offence. This is how he described his experience:

Most important thing I look for, I suppose, is a loving relationship with a boy, and (pause) although I've had physical relationships with, probably, I don't know, maybe a hundred or more boys over the years, I can only point to four or five true relationships over that time, and, when I said 'time', I was talking about a period of about twelve to fifteen years.

Ben indicated that while he had done a lot of thinking, he was unable to explain why he had become sexually interested in boys. Nevertheless, from the following quotation, it appears that he was more inclined towards an 'inborn' explanation:

I suppose I can identify an interest in boys right back to when I was a child, ten or even younger. I'm not sure if one had a choice, because as I say the interest in boys definitely dates back to my own childhood and in a little bit of first experience at age 10. I think perhaps the question of, of choice, or, experimenting or experiencing other forms of relationships, other sexual relationships – er – come out of, in part – er – curiosity, and in part, wanting to conform to the norm. What one sees, all round, has been acceptable and therefore good. Er – you don't discard that until at least you'd tried it, and (pause) I don't think there was in reality a question of choice, of making a choice. That's something I would like to investigate myself. As I see it now, I don't think there's a choice available. The way I see it now is that either it's there at birth or it's created perhaps via one's environment in very very early years.

While Ben was not absolutely sure about the origin of his paedophilic desire, he was certain about the type of boys he had relationships with:

You see, there is, one can draw a generic picture of the boys that I get involved with, they all fit within certain parameters, and, whether it's that or not is certainly interesting, is that my own childhood, to a degree, fits within that same generic pattern. Now, er – the parameters are (a) either single parent upbringing or divorce and remarriage, and (pause) (b) here it varies, because I differ from the boys if you like, the boys come from generally what one would describe as a social welfare background, unemployment, and dependence on social welfare income and so on, whereas I didn't – er – (c) is they're all of reasonable or slightly above average intelligence, and yet all gross underachievers academically.

When asked about the significance of these 'parameters', Ben had this to say:

The major reason for a child to establish a loving relationship with an adult has got to be the lack of that facility in his own immediate environment. In other words, that outside adult provides something that is missing in that child's life, OK? Without that being the case, it doesn't happen, OK? Because if the kid is getting all the love and attention he needs at home, he's not going to look for it outside.

Although Ben would not avoid casual encounters with boys, it was a stable relationship that he was looking for, not simply a physical encounter:

I do not like, I mean there are boys who are – mm – constantly around men, yea? Those boys are 13, 14 who, for money, or whatever reasons, are always around. That type of boy doesn't interest me. And I think in every case I have been the boy's first contact sexually. Or you know, he may have tried something with his mate at school, and – not, you know – if I have intercourse with a boy – er – I wouldn't like the idea that he'd done that with somebody else before, OK? So in terms of innocence, yes, that's a very important feature to me. But – mm – if the boy is able to discuss interesting topics, be it politics or whatever – that I would enjoy.

To Ben, his relationship with a boy was mutual – the meaningfulness of his experience lies in the understanding that both parties in such a relationship were deriving emotional and physical satisfaction from it. He was looking for a loving relationship with another person, as he said, it only happened that he preferred that person to be physically a 13-year-old boy.

Bruce

Bruce was a 36-year-old man who owned a thriving home computer business. Ever since his early twenties, he had experienced a growing sexual desire for peri-pubertal girls. While he did not have any actual sexual contact, as an adult, with children, he fantasised a lot about young girls even though he had sexual relationships with women. The following quotations show how he construed his paedophilic tendency:

I feel that there must be some connection between my ongoing interest in children and the fact that, for nearly 19 years, my only experience of direct contact with a female's genitals was the episode with Theresa.[2] My repeated re-living of that experience in daydreams and masturbation fantasies must have contributed to my paedophilia. The fact that I didn't have proper sexual experiences in my teens and twenties must be attributed to my parents' attitude towards social relationships generally and sex in particular giving me a very ignorant and inhibited approach to relationships with others of my age group.

One of the things that pushed me at that time into an overt interest in young girls was that I found myself a bit socially out of my depth even with the 17, 18 year olds when I was 23. ... I wonder now in my own mind, whether my whole interest in this direction is a wish to give children around this stage of their sexual development sex education that I never had. ... We're men, it's more difficult for us to understand a female viewpoint than it is to understand a male viewpoint, and therefore I suppose it follows that logically the majority of the teaching about sex needs to be done by the opposite sex, to teach them what the opposite sex's viewpoint is.

The scarcity of the opportunity of having the young girl, would steer me towards the young girls, it's part novelty part rarity. Because I'd missed out on relationships with girls when I was sexually maturing myself – mm – I've always then been trying to get back to having a girlfriend of about 12, 13, so that I then had the experience of having a friend of the opposite sex who was maturing.

From these accounts, the following schematic representation was constructed, which Bruce found acceptable as an accurate description of the development of his paedophilic desire: strict upbringing + lonely childhood + 'Theresa trauma' → inhibition → no proper sexual experiences during teens and twenties → feeling out of depth while

---

[2] At the age of 12, Bruce attempted to have sexual intercourse with a 10-year-old girl (Theresa) who lived next door – he succeeded in partially penetrating her. When his parents found this out, they punished him severely.

socialising with peers → re-living Theresa encounter → feeling having missed out on relationships with a maturing girl during his younger days → wanting to make up for this → wanting to give such a girl the sex education that he himself had missed → repeated fantasies of pubertal girls → rarity and novelty of such a possible experience → all these add up to an intense desire for, and excitement about, paedophilic relationships.

While Bruce felt satisfied with his previous as well as current adult sexual relationships with his woman friends, he was nevertheless very keen to get back what he had 'missed' – sexual experience with pubescent girls. He felt that his paedophilic desire could co-exist with his adult relationships, because it was not a substitute for the latter, and neither was the latter a substitute for his desire for young girls. In sum, Bruce wanted to have both, and felt that he could and would enjoy both.

Daniel

Daniel was in his mid-forties. He had a degree in mathematics and had worked as a computer programmer, then a school teacher before becoming unemployed in 1973. He had been hospitalised for nervous breakdown due to pressure of work, and had to take medication for one or two years, which he felt was responsible for making him impotent with his wife. Their relationship subsequently deteriorated, and finally his wife divorced him and obtained custody of their three children. He had been living on his own ever since. Two years after the divorce, Daniel was arrested and convicted of indecent assault on three underage girls (his daughter, a niece and a girl living next door: all six years old). He had since joined a paedophile organisation, and felt definite that he was a paedophile.

Daniel explained his sexual involvement with children as a consequence of his difficulties with women in general, and his wife in particular:

I think I kept the same fear of women, well, girls my own age, even though the age group is changing, I'm still nervous about anybody my own age, any woman my own age.

I think she [i.e. his wife] had left at that time, which means my sister would have died as well,[3] yes, possibly I was feeling emotionally insecure, I was feeling emotionally starved really – mm – possibly I was looking extra hard for a sexual partner, and perhaps this, sort of, pushed me to break the barriers of the conventions.

I'm a little shy of marriage, because of the social difficulties, having to be tied to another adult – mm – with the possibilities of, break-down of the relationship, and, the trauma that produces, a bit shy of that, of going to – permanent relationship.

[3] Daniel's sister died in an accident in the same year in which his wife left him.

As he was settling down into a paedophile identity, Daniel had constructed a somewhat sociobiological interpretation of paedophilia, from which he was able to derive meaning and validation for his experience:

> Perhaps, when men become too old, or perhaps, they just don't happen to have sexual partners, it may be beneficial for them to care for – er – to care for related children, it's a possibility there. ... There were some primates, it might be natural for the less dominant adults to assume the role of paedophiles. ... There was the possibility that the least dominant male may take on the role of looking after children. ... I mean, in an extended family situation, it could be there is a positive role for uncles looking after related children – er – could be beneficial to the survival of their genes, couldn't it? They haven't got a natural mate of their own, for some reason, perhaps by looking after related children, children of their sisters, brothers – mm – they could help propagate their type. ... On thinking about it, perhaps, well I mean, it is sort of obviously beneficial, it seems to me to be beneficial to children, to have a good relationship with an adult. I mean you find the parents haven't got time for all the children, the parents are too busy, and I mean it's beneficial for the children, to have alternative adult friends. [Researcher asked: Does that require a sexual relationship?] No, but the sexual relationship bonds the friendship. The relationship is stronger if there's a sexual element in it – mm – I certainly found this, the child enjoys the sexual relationship, it doesn't prevent the child from growing up as it has been frequently said because, the sexual relation, the sexual part only occupies a small part of the day, the rest of the day the child was playing like any other child. The fact that the child has an adult friend could be beneficial to the child's survival.

From these quotations, it can be seen that the logic of Daniel's argument for paedophilia runs as follows:

(1) Non-dominant males are suited to play the role of care-taker of the young by virtue of their lack of an adult partner.

(2) While taking care of children they can find sexual satisfaction through paedophilic activities, which are also beneficial to the children because these activities would strengthen the protective bond and hence ensure the children's survival.

(3) The overall effect is the increase of the probability of propagation of the genes of the community.

(4) Since he was a non-dominant male who had lost his partner, Daniel felt that a paedophile role suited him best.

Edward

Edward was a 51-year-old unemployed man. He had worked for 20 years in the army before being sacked for homosexual behaviour. Thereafter he lived with his mother and worked in several places. A year after she died he became unemployed. He had been living alone ever since. Although

Edward had a strong sexual desire for boys, he had so far had sexual contact with only one boy.

Edward had portrayed the emergence of his paedophilic interest in the context of difficulties with women. He spoke of 'feelings of inferiority to women and of sexual inadequacy'.

> Right from when I was young I was a – er – dreadful stutterer. Now, that could have been a contributory factor in my shyness. I found it rather difficult to (long pause) er – mix with girls and women. I was just plain scared of girls – mm – they, they were so different, that, I just didn't know – mm – how to behave with them. ... If I had a brother or a sister, either older or younger, it, it would probably have made a big difference to, to me. If it'd been a sister, it probably would have made me more – er – attuned to women, because I would have been used to having a woman about the place. If it'd been a brother – er – it might have made me less, might have made me less shy.

> I have never, in the past, looked for an explanation for my sexual outlook. At the beginning it could be put down to my loneliness caused by my bad stutter. This kept me apart from other children and enhanced the stutter which increased the isolation, until eventually a kind of 'shield' grew around me. When the pranks and jokes of other children began to plague me, I could retreat into my shield and try to ignore them. Girls were an alien race to me. They frightened me, and to a certain extent, they still do. Therefore the explanation for me being a homosexual can be traced back to my childhood stutter, the isolation, be it self-imposed, and the resultant shyness. The shyness never left me, I am still shy of meeting people. I don't like parties, pubs, clubs, and on top of all that, as I have said a number of times before, I am scared of meeting women. I can work with them, but I am afraid of socialising with them, which had ended up with me being attracted to other men. This attraction has not changed much over the years. Up until the late 60s, I had not regarded boys as sex objects. I had been aproached two or three times in cinemas by boys, who had made very clear the sexual motives for their approach. I refused them, because at that time it was easy for me to do and I was still unsure of myself. In the early 1970s I quickly became aware that a vast majority of living-in recruits were younger than me. It was about then that my present outlook on my sex life and future started. I started to fear the future. I was alone, I had nobody close I could share joys and sorrows with. I had spent so many years alone that I had forgotten how to make 'contact' with other people, other adults. It was about then I started to buy the 'boy' type picture books mainly because, at least to me, they were beautiful, and also because they looked so controllable. By that I mean, that if there was anybody I could control from a position of authority, it was a child, preferably a boy.

To summarise:

(1) Edward's life-long problem of stuttering had rendered him deeply fearful of social interaction and social situations.

(2) Being an only child, he felt he had no opportunity to learn how to relate to people, particularly to the opposite sex.

(3) He became very shy and socially isolated, and very frightened of females.

(4) He therefore turned to men for sexual gratification.

(5) Eventually he found himself attracted to boys since he felt they were the ones he could dominate.

Eugene

Although Eugene was only 22 years old, he had already identified himself as a paedophile. Throughout his late teens, he had had three heterosexual relationships with peers, all of which did not last beyond several months. He felt that on each occasion he and his partner were not really compatible with each other. After the last of these, with a woman of 20, had ended, Eugene felt lonely, and it was at this point in time that he began relationships with young girls.

In his view, however, his paedophilic relationships were not a second-best substitute, but rather what suited him most. He felt that his 18-month relationship with a 10-year-old girl was 'just like an adult heterosexual relationship' and that he was 'very emotionally devoted to her' – the feelings were so intense that he felt he could draw no other conclusion than that he was 'in love with a small child'. This experience led him to conclude that all his past relationships with female peers were not enjoyable at all. In his words:

A grown-up woman is very independent, she can make decisions, and, you know, young girls can't make any decision really, a young girl, got to be looked after and cared for, and – I think that's where the emotional feeling comes in. ... I love to have a girl of 9 years old to live with me, and I will care for her and look after her. ... I am not saying that I want to be the dominant one, but, I mean I went out with a girl when I was 20, she was very mature for her age, and I was trying to make decisions, but she, she seemed to have a better decision than me, and I used to feel like a bit, more like a son, you know, she's a bit more like a mother to me. She was very independent, and I sat back. I felt a lot for her. I just felt that I was denied my duty really. I thought, I got a girlfriend, I'll be able to look after her and do this and that. She started being, taking all the decisions, and I, I felt put off really, you know.

From what he said, it appeared that Eugene had found his ex-girlfriends too dominant, a situation which he disliked. In contrast, relationships with young girls offer him the opportunity to fulfil the 'duty' of taking care of his partner.

Fred

Fred was a technician in his mid-thirties. He was married and had three daughters. He had been convicted of and imprisoned for indecent assault on his eldest daughter. But subsequently he had reunited with his family.

Fred construed his sexual involvement with his daughter as a result of the deterioration in his relationship with his wife under the pressure of work.

> See, nothing really happened in the sense of – mm – intercourse or anything like that, I suppose in a way I was just taking my sexual frustration out on my daughter. ... I was doing two jobs – mm – I was going home 5 o'clock at night, going out at six, till about eleven at night, you see, and I think, I just worked to the utter extent. I think what it was, I was working too many hours, and we [i.e. he and his wife] didn't have much time together. When we did the children were there anyway, but then you're going to say you still found time to have sex with your daughter – er (long pause) I don't know really, it's a mess, it was a mess.
>
> I think it was to get rid of my sexual frustration, more than anything. ... There's something lacking in the marriage – mm – I suppose everybody goes through it in a way. I think the excitement of marriage, and, sort of (pause) it needs something to shake it up again, to really know what you've got, what you don't want to lose, and I certainly found that. Well, there wasn't hardly any relationship with my wife for – er – two or three years back – well, that's my fault, I was, I suppose workaholic.

Fred insisted that he had no particular desire for children – his understanding of his sexual offence was in terms of using the daughter to compensate for what he could not get from his relationship with his wife.

George

George was a Welshman in his mid-fifties. He had been a manual worker in various trades, but had been unemployed for nearly twenty years because of conflicts with trade unions. Ever since his mid-teens, George had been sexually involved with pubescent girls, and had gone to prison because of such activities.

To George, his paedophilic desires were very much a part of himself, something that he must have been born with:

> Paedophilic feelings do not arise. They exist already. Girls fascinated me before my fourth birthday. They still do fifty and a half years later. ... I am not sure if one's feelings are sharp at birth, but one does have a full emotional range, including the sex emotion. I meant simply that as far back as I can recall, my interest has been in girls. No decision had to be made, I was already 'girlified'.

Although it is fairly clear that George took his paedophilic desire to be inborn, he was nevertheless very specific about the *beginning* of this desire: when he was barely four he had been watching throughout one summer with keen interest the daily chasing-and-spanking play between a woman neighbour and her three young daughters, he felt from then on he had developed a strong desire to spank young girls, a desire which gradually came to constitute his sexuality. His current practice consisted of mutual fondling and spanking with girls.

> The most significant sexual experience I had in childhood, was the one previously described, with the woman chasing her daughters around the lawn, and whipping them. It is still significant over fifty-one years later. ... The power of my first sexual experience, was not obvious to me, until later years, but from that moment I have always wanted to spank girls, and have been fascinated by their underwear. A glimpse of a petticoat puts me in torment even now, and the excitement of touching the girl, of handling her, is always new and vital.

George's desire for girls was set in the context of an intense hatred for adults. He particularly hated his family, and had stopped all contact with them for a long time. This is how he described his parents:

> If those parents were average, then I think every parent should be stood against a wall and shot; and I don't mean may be! They were not brutal people physically, but they and their relatives were experts in mental cruelty, particularly towards children. ... I hated their nasty, sneering attitude, and they hated me. Love was never lost, it was never there in the first place.

To summarise, George's construction of his sexuality is: fixation to a 'sexual' experience in early childhood, with a progressively intensified rejection of the adult world reinforcing his solitary lifestyle, and strengthening his attraction to young girls.

Jack

Jack was in his mid-fifties, widowed and with three grown-up children. He was a long-distance lorry driver before becoming unemployed. He was now doing a degree with the Open University and was active in the local art school. Throughout his adult life, Jack had had sexual contact (from fondling to full intercourse) with quite a number of pubertal girls, including his own daughter, but was only arrested once.

Jack described his sexual experiences with children in this way:

> We [i.e. he and his wife] had a very good sex life together, she had a very strong sex drive and she was adventurous and always willing to experiment and try new ways to improve our sex life. We were very compatible, we both enjoyed oral sex and anal sex as well as straight sex. Throughout our married life I always looked for young girls to go with. They were mostly only quick casual affairs, but now that I am alone, I can devote more time to get to know them and form longer relationships and use the privacy and comfort of my home. ... I don't quite know how I came to be attracted to children. I have always felt this way about them. May be it is because I find them so gentle and truthful I find I can be myself with them. I find no need to protect myself from them.

Sex with children is very nice, there's something about sex with a child which you don't get from an adult. You're not in competition, you don't have to prove anything at all. It's when, when the girl gets to the age, maybe fifteen or so, that she becomes an adult, that is the time when she begins to use her sex – mm – in luring a man if you like, and when she gets to that stage, then the child ceases to have an appeal for me.

I think I am looking for a little extra pleasure with a young girl because her vagina is smaller and tighter. Most people believe that the youngest and freshest are the sweetest and most value.

Jack found sex with young girls physically and emotionally enjoyable. But he pointed out that he had had a very good sex life with his wife throughout their marriage. Thus to him, paedophilic contact was not a substitute arising from an unsatisfactory adult relationship, rather it was a desirable experience in itself. This positive portrayal of sex with children has to be looked at in the context of Jack's libertarian views on sex in general. He felt that a permissive attitude regarding sexual matters was the best way to bring up children – he always encouraged his children to be frank and not to be ashamed of sex. He attributed his permissive attitude to his own adolescent sexual experiences with a middle-aged woman, who had experimented with him and taught him a great deal about sex.

Jack saw adult-child sexual contact as a positive experience for both the adult and the child – it is refreshing to the former and educational to the latter, and hence is a legitimate part of normal human sexuality. To him, paedophilia does not have to be an exclusive form of sexuality – it can be integrated into the sex life of any individual.

Joe

Joe was a businessman in his mid-fifties. He was married and had three grown-up children. Like Jack, Joe had articulated a libertarian view on adult-child sexual contact. He felt that sex, without coercion, could never be wrong. As long as affection was involved, sex would be a 'natural expression of friendship', and there was no need to find any special explanation for paedophilia.

Joe attributed the development of this ('the only rational') attitude to his upbringing – his father was a very liberal man and had encouraged him to have sex with his mother; his father also taught him not to accept tradition but to question it critically. Joe had now espoused a very permissive attitude to sex – he had had sex with his daughters and his wife had had sex with their son; they also taught their friends' children how to engage in sexual activities should they be willing to learn. To Joe, this was 'practical sex education in the true sense of the word'. It is important to note that Joe did not feel exclusively attracted to children. Rather, he had a lot of different sexual experiences such as spouse swapping.

To summarise, Joe construed human sexuality in terms of a libertarian ethics – sex is for the enjoyment of every human being, including the aged, the handicapped and the young. No boundary should be drawn (not even blood ties) except the prohibition of coercion. Within this scheme of things, adult-child sexual contact ceases to be a problem.

Keith

Keith was an unemployed man in his mid-forties. He was single, and had been taking care of his ailing parents for many years. He had developed a strong sexual interest in children since his own childhood days. In the past twenty years, Keith had been convicted several times of sexual offences against children, and had been sent to prison twice.

To Keith, his desire for children was continuous with the sexual activities he had while he was young:

> When I was very young, and, as I say, I liked the idea, you know, I enjoyed it, so therefore I tried to carry on. ... When I was going to school, I always looked at girls, because they, I mean I knew, I knew what I'd got, I mean I knew what boys got, so I was curious to find out what girls got, and when I got older, and found that girls weren't available, then boys came along, you can go for boys, as a friend, you see, and you do things.

Keith portrayed the development of his sexuality in the context of a solitary upbringing – he recalled being a loner who, from an early age on, had developed a tendency to talk to himself, to toys or to imaginary friends; whenever he felt insecure he would resort to solitary self-talking and masturbation. His current sexual practices included enacting tape-recorded sexual fantasies or written stories he himself produced, in addition to the occasional actual contact with children whenever he got the opportunity.

Keith had also talked about his feelings of sexual inadequacy – he felt that people always looked at him as the 'village idiot', that he could not converse, especially with women, and that his penis was laughably small. These feelings heightened his social isolation, and while he did have some sexual experience with both men and women, he always preferred children. Besides physically more attractive, children were different from adults to relate to:

> If you masturbate with a young girl, they tend to fight you a bit, because they know they are not allowed to do or you are not allowed to do that so they fight, you see, but at the same time they are curious, and they want to find out what it's all about, but at the same time they resist – now that's good because if a person resists you a little bit, then it's more – mm – stimulating for yourself. But if you, say, with a woman to have sex, she just lay there, I mean, you gonna have sex, and there's no fight whatsoever, you know, I mean, the more, the more illicit it is, the more – mm – exciting I think.

To summarise, Keith had come to understand his sexuality as a continuation of his childhood experiences, in the context of feelings of inferiority and a solitary life.

Martin

Martin was a businessman in his mid-fifties. He separated from his wife in 1981, but they remained business partners. Now he was living with two mistresses together – one was 35, the other 17. He had three grown-up children.

Like Jack and Joe, Martin had also expressed a libertarian view regarding sex. To him, given knowledge and free choice, any sexual encounter was permissible, provided that one's own offspring and very young children were excluded. Regarding incest, Martin reasoned that sex in the family would spoil parent-child relationships; regarding young children, he felt they do not really understand sex: 'a 6-year-old girl doesn't bloody know, they wouldn't know what it is, they want affection, not sex', he said.

While not exclusively attracted to children, Martin had had many sexual encounters with pubertal girls. As in his view intercourse was essential to sex, he would not go for very young girls. However, any girl who was physically mature (or maturing) could become his partner – 'when they are big enough, they are old enough' – and he had no respect for any arbitrary age of consent. To him, children were sexual beings who were keen to 'test their own sexuality and their sexual power'.

> This sounds big-headed I know but they [i.e. girls] seem to be drawn to me in spite of my age. They visit me voluntarily even when I say 'go away'!

It is relevant to point out that Martin had suffered from speech difficulty during infancy, but with a strong determination he had overcome it and had since become a volunteer speech therapy helper. Because of his volunteer work, he had developed good communication skills with children, and had the opportunity to interact with them.

Martin summarised himself in this way: 'I suppose I'm just an immoral sod – I just don't say "No" to any attractive female.'

Matthew

Matthew was 53. He had married twice – the first marriage ended in divorce after 14 years; the second one, while not without its ups and downs, was on the whole satisfactory. He had been living with his second wife from 1968 up to now, together with the two children from *her* previous marriage. Matthew had been arrested twice for sexual offences against children[4] – the first time was shortly before his divorce from his first wife, when he was feeling extremely frustrated with the difficult

---

[4] These offences involved indecent touching of children he met in parks and playgrounds.

relationship he had with her; the second time was a few years ago, when he was suffering from impotence, and could not have intercourse with his second wife.

Matthew construed his offences as a consequence of the difficulties he experienced with his two wives:

> It seems that when I'm able to have sex with my wife, whichever wife – the first or the second – everything was fine, I didn't want to touch children. But as soon as for one reason or another I can't have sex – mm – I seem to start on the young children. ... My problem, I mean, I can't get an erection, that is what I look on as my problem at the moment, but – er – how having anything to do with children should make up for that, I just can't say, it just seems to come at a time, when my love life is, I suppose, a little inadequate.

The difficulties on the two occasions were not the same – in the first case, Matthew could not have sex because his first wife refused to; in his second marriage, however, it was his impotence that prevented sex. Apparently his impotence was associated with the obesity of his wife as well as the row they had after each had had an affair with somebody else.

Besides marital-sexual difficulties, Matthew also attributed his sexual offences to a liking for children in general:

> I always liked children, and it started off with talking to children, just in the normal sort of way. ... I think I was shy with adults, but I was never shy with children. ... I think it's more – fatherly, I mean I don't, I don't want to do the girl any harm, and I don't want to make love to her, but, I just want to have – contact with her. ... I suppose it wouldn't have mattered if I touched her hair, her face, put my arm round her, or touched her on her sexual parts, I don't think it would make any difference – I just enjoyed the feel of children I suppose.

An encounter with a girl was a source of satisfaction to Matthew especially in times of emotional instability. While touching up young girls could not solve his sexual problem, it was satisfying to him all the same:

> When playing with the little girl, it was sexual feeling, but it was a completely different sexual feeling to the one I would have if I was making love to my wife. I suppose it's just the thought of something new, exciting, same as when I'd had the affairs, that was more exciting because it was something different. ... Really it was such a minor sort of touching, that – er – it didn't seem to be that much wrong, it was more of a loving touching than sexual touching if you know what I mean. ... I mean even just talking to the children was a satisfaction, what satisfaction I'm not quite sure, but, after I've talked to the child, I didn't really want to do the same thing over and over again on the same day. ... Once I had my little chat with the child, you know, I was happy.

The construction that Matthew has provided shows that his sexual contact with children is not a substitute for adult sex in the strict sense –

the act he committed was very mild. It can be understood in the context of a need to communicate with and to be close to another person, especially when he is troubled by a deep sense of impotence (as a person and as a sexual partner) – being a loner, Matthew tended to express this need by approaching children, with whom he felt much more at ease.

Nick

Nick was a 33-year-old construction worker. He had a history of property offences as well as a record of violence both inside and outside prison. While he had had much sexual experience with children, he had only been arrested once for such an offence.

Nick came from a very deprived and broken family, and was placed in a children's home at the age of 3. Like Andy, he talked about his early and lengthy institutionalisation as the origin of his paedophilic orientation. However, unlike Andy, Nick did not portray the development of his sexuality in terms of 'habit', rather he linked his strong love for children, specifically boys, to an intense hatred for adults:

> That's all they [i.e. adults] want me for – it's my money. They don't want me for myself. ... My earlier hate for the adult person, just sheer hate. ... I wanted my father to be there, but my father wasn't, ... he should have kept in touch, you know, instead of shirking his responsibilities. ... She [i.e. his mother] used to abandon us, her kids, you know, very young kids, without food, she was a bad woman anyway, she pissed off, she wasn't a mother at all, to any of us, you know, she pissed off, and left us high and dry. ... I felt rejected, I felt lil e people didn't give a shit for me.

It is in this context of hatred for adults that Nick's strong love for children took shape:

> For me, without, without the spirit of children around, I'm alone. (weeps) I have to look – this is difficult – I have to look, for things worth living for. ... Spirit is the charisma of childhood, that is – mm – childness, just the fun, the innocence – sex isn't the main thing, the main thing is, being wanted I suppose. ... I like kids because, I didn't have any other, real, great experiences with adults when I was a kid. ... You can't learn to be paedophiliac, it's something that happens, it's a form of growth, growth that makes you a paedophiliac – it's the way you're brought up, experiences you had, experiences of being unloved, experiences of having difficult relationships with adults. There'd always be paedophiliacs, as long as you got, the attitudes people got.

Although according to his criminal and prison records Nick was a violent person, he was actually very eloquent in expressing his love for children – it was this 'starvation of love plus anti-adult feelings' that turned him into a paedophile.

Patrick

Patrick was a 57-year-old unmarried engineer. He lived with his parents until they died some years ago. Since then he had lived alone. He had been convicted once for sexual offences against boys.

While submitting to psychiatric treatment for paedophilia, Patrick was actually very resentful towards society because of the ostracism he had to suffer as a result of his sexual orientation. He was constantly depressed – he felt caught between a desire to fight against society and a sense of total resignation – and he had thought about suicide.

When asked about his explanation for his sexual interest in boys, Patrick insisted that his desire was not caused by anything – upbringing or otherwise – it was simply a matter of constitution ('it's just the way I am'). He pointed out that he 'had done no harm to children', and that what he had done would not have caused any stir fifty years ago – he argued that society was 'nearer to earth' in the past and was thus more tolerant of adult-child sexual activities. To him, paedophilia was not a medical problem, but a sociological one in that society rather than the paedophile was at fault – society had become so repressive sexually that people like himself were unjustly persecuted and stigmatised. He felt that no explanation was needed for his activities, even though society demanded one.

Robert

Robert was a 37-year-old musician. He was single but had sexual relationships with several women. Because of a strong desire for boys, which made him feel very guilty, he started therapy with a psychoanalyst and was still in analysis at the time of this study.

While Robert had never had any actual sexual contact with boys, his desire to do so was strong. In talking about the origin of this desire, he could not really account for his experience satisfactorily – his impulses seemed to be an 'arbitrary thing' which just happened to him. After therapy had started, however, Robert gradually came to see his sexual desire in terms of his socially secluded childhood and his guilt-ridden upbringing, which resulted in interpersonal difficulties, especially with the opposite sex. On the other hand, Robert felt that because of his restrictive and repressive upbringing, he had not been able successfully to resolve his earlier homosexual tendencies which were part of normal adolescent development. Consequently he became sexually 'fixed' to this adolescent homosexual phase, which tended to become for him an escape route away from problems of adult life.

I'd wondered whether in fact that I had what may well have been a quite normal homosexual phase, feelings at the time when I'd been about 14, or 15, and never did anything about it, and the fact that I didn't have any sexual relation with anybody at that time. ... The most obvious explanation to me is that sort of having discovered at the age of 14, or 15, the excitement of sexual feelings towards boys, that I didn't want to leave go of that at all – I mean it's too exciting. ... They [i.e. his parents] had probably unwittingly fuelled my sense of guilt about sex in general. It's been a problem to establish any lasting involvements with women – mm – I think that has been one of the reasons, and I can identify certain periods where, very definitely I had, you know, my impulses were predominantly heterosexual, and then other moments predominantly paedophilic.

From his account, it seems likely that Robert's understanding of his sexual attraction towards boys is influenced by the views of his therapist to a considerable extent. The central theme of this understanding is a linking up of two factors – repressive upbringing leading to heterosexual difficulties and fixation to an adolescent homosexual phase.

Simon

Simon was a 74-year-old retired salesman. He separated from his wife in his mid-fifties because she could not accept his sexual activities with boys. He had a grown-up son, who was married and had children of his own. According to Simon, he got married simply to get away from the possessive grip of his mother – he felt that he could never relate to any woman sexually, and throughout his marriage he had only had sexual intercourse with his wife a few times.[5]

Simon had given an account of his life in terms of the numerous paedophilic (sometimes affectionate but non-sexual) encounters that he had throughout his long life. He had been arrested a number of times for his sexual activities with boys, and had spent nearly two years in prison at the age of 65.

To him, his sexual love for boys was a normal, integral part of his whole life as he felt he was born like this (in his words, 'a fact of nature'). While admitting that he had difficulty relating to women sexually, he maintained that he had no problem in social relationships with them, and that his paedophilic orientation was his primary sexuality rather than a substitute. This inborn paedophilic orientation developed fully through habitual childhood sexual activities with other boys in an 'all male' environment (no sister at home, and boys' boarding school).

Tom

Tom was a 25-year-old businessman from a fairly well-off family. From adolescence onwards, he had gradually come to realise his strong sexual desire for young boys. He felt he could only attribute this to an innate

[5] During the third year of their marriage, Simon's wife had a miscarriage, and the subsequent medical complications necessitated the surgical removal of her uterus. From then on, his wife stopped all sexual activities. That suited Simon best since he was never interested in sex with a female.

disposition as there was nothing in his life that could be identified as responsible for changing his orientation. So far he had not acted out his desire for fear of the consequences. Except for a brief period of homosexual experimentation with a classmate during his early teens, he had had no sexual contact with any other person.

To Tom, his sexual attraction towards boys was very much a natural part of himself:

> I can offer no explanation of my feelings, it is just inherent in me, it is just something that comes naturally to me. ... I think, it'd always been in me, I don't think it's sort of one stage that happened that converts me over to that. I say, I think I would have been inbred. As far as I know, in my family, there's no other causes of that either. [Researcher asked: You used the word inbred –?] Well, yea, I felt it was innate, it's not something that happened in my life that changed me totally, from that to something else. It's always been there. [Researcher: Yes, but how about the realisation? Is the realisation –?] Er – it's really just come on gradually. I mean when I was at school, I found I was attracted to couple of boys, and, it's just sort of gone on from there. I mean it's nothing, as I said, it's nothing that happened that made me to be like that.

While Tom did not feel that his paedophilic interest was a result of any developmental problem, he did mention shyness, especially in relation to the opposite sex, as a characteristic feature of his personality:

> I find, sort of in the presence of girls and women I seem to be very self-conscious. I find it hard to make conversation. As I said, by nature, I'm a shy person anyway, and – er – I feel sort of shy, more shy in the company of women than I do with men and boys.

Although Tom construed his sexuality as an innate disposition and hence perfectly normal, he was still ambivalent sometimes:

> As far as I'm concerned I don't feel there's anything wrong with this, it's just sort of society and the way society works, that's all. But – er – I wouldn't certainly, I wouldn't tell my mother and my father sort of I am the way I am. ... I don't sort of feel in myself that I'm doing anything wrong, but, I know, it's not normal to be the way I am, but – er – like I say, it just comes naturally to me.

Vincent

Vincent was an accountant in his mid-twenties. He came from a well-to-do family – both his father and his elder brother were professional engineers. He was single and lived with his parents. From his late teens up to now, Vincent had been convicted three times of sexual assault against, or indecency with, young girls. He was receiving psychotherapy at the time of this study. This is how he accounted for the occurrence of these offences:

I think a lot of the problem does stem from the fact that I've not been able to make relationships with girls. Although I went to a co-educational school, I didn't mix with the girls. Not having done so, I don't really know how to approach women. Mm – certainly I only commit these sorts of offences when I have met a woman who I'd like to get to know better sexually, but, being unable to approach her, I then go away, I go round areas where I think that girls are likely to congregate, I'd look for girls, not necessarily to have a sexual relationship with, but just to be with them, because I find that being with young children, you get a lot of release of tension, as I do personally because they have a lot of, well, I call it love – er – it's affection, they can be terribly affectionate to anybody. ... In the presence of younger children, you can feel the warmth and affection they have towards you, you see, and that makes me feel much better in myself – mm – that, you know, that there's still people out there who care for me, albeit in a childish sort of way, and that does make me feel happier.

Thus to Vincent, his attraction towards girls is a result of frustration in peer heterosexual relationships, particularly in times of stress. In each of the three occasions on which he had committed a sexual offence, he could identify this frustration:

(1) First offence – pressure of O-Level examinations, and failure to start a relationship with a female classmate.

(2) Second offence – pressure of accountancy examinations, and failure to make progress in a relationship with a woman friend.

(3) Third offence – uncertainty over professional future because of his previous offence, and failure to establish a relationship with two young women he chatted up on a train.

With respect to his inability to establish close relationships with female peers, Vincent offered this explanation:

I didn't see my parents behaving in a social way, or socialising, I should say, with other people, and therefore I didn't come to know how to do it myself, which is obviously a problem. ... I was never really brought up to express my feelings to anybody, so even if I wanted to, I don't know if I would have done – mm – and that obviously was difficult for me.

It was to this inability to relate to people in general, and the opposite sex in particular, that Vincent attributed the development of his paedophilic tendencies.

10.2 Commonality in construction

While it must be stressed that each informant of this study has a unique story to tell, and each has made a specifically personal construction of his sexuality, some similarities are still discernible. Four broadly defined patterns can be identified in the accounts of the 20 informants. These categories are not meant to be mutually exclusive – some informants' construction can be put under more than one category; nor are they to be taken as narrowly defined – the experiences subsumed under the same category still differ from each other.

10.2.1 Sexual desire for children as inborn disposition

Of the 7 informants who are exclusively attracted to boys or young males, 4 have described their orientation as inborn – they can see no particular precipitating events or experiences that might have led to the development of their paedophilic desire. They are Ben, Patrick, Simon and Tom.[6] The *leitmotif* of their accounts is 'this is me', or 'just the way I am'. It is not a matter of conscious choice, rather it is the unfolding of an innate constitution.

Since this paedophilic proclivity is construed as natural, these informants feel that their desire is normal as far as they are concerned. Yet sometimes they do experience an anxious ambivalence because their desire is socially unacceptable.

> I do not consider it to be a perfectly normal situation because if it was – er – it would have to be more socially acceptable. Obviously, from my point of view, it would be very nice if the world accepted me as I was. Life would be so much easier. (Ben)

Added to this anxiety of self-doubt is the actual punishment (legal or otherwise) that society has imposed on these individuals, and they feel that they are suffering for what they *naturally* are. Patrick's stoic exclamation that 'every day is hell' illustrates vividly the condition in which some of these people find themselves.

In addition to these four, one other informant, who is attracted to *girls* only, has also attributed the origin of his paedophilic desire to an inborn disposition – George. However, George has pinpointed a particular event in his early childhood as responsible for making him aware of his sexuality. Subsequently, this event had become in his mind the most significant childhood experience that he had, which he always referred to when talking about the beginning of his paedophilic desire.

10.2.2 Sex with children as part of normal sexuality

There are four informants (all heterosexual) who not only have shown no ambivalence or anxiety towards sexual activities with children, but have actually construed such activities as a perfectly normal part of human sexual experience, not just for themselves, but for *everybody*: they are Bruce, Jack, Joe and Martin. These four men are not exclusively attracted to children, they simply do not feel it necessary to exclude children from their sex life. They believe that the free expression of human sexuality could release much suppressed human potential. Not

---

[6] The other three informants who are attracted to boys only are Andy, Nick and Edward.

only is consensual adult-child sexual contact harmless, it can actually be beneficial to the children and society as a whole. It is 'practical sex education in the true sense of the word' (as Joe has remarked), which would help the growing generation avoid much future difficulties as they mature into full adult sexuality.

> If everybody could have an experience at an early age, some kind of experience, people would not have nearly as many problems as what they do have, and I think that's why, sex with children, I think it's an extension of that – er – learning them what I've learned. But it got to be done in a nice, pleasant way, you can't force anybody. (Jack)

To these informants, the free expression of sexual desire is natural, it is only because society has been so repressive that people are held back from spontaneous sexual interaction with children, who are by nature interested in sex. There is no need to find an explanation for sexual attraction between an adult and a child, just as there is no need to find any explanation for similar attraction between two adults.

It is interesting to note that these four informants do not belong to any paedophile organisation. Moreover, they come from quite diverse backgrounds: Joe from a sexually permissive family; while Bruce had rather strict parents; Martin is a self-made builder; Bruce has had college education and is running a computer business; while Jack is an unemployed lorry driver; all four have had satisfying adult heterosexual relationships – Jack is now widowed, Martin divorced while Bruce is single; Jack, Joe and Martin have grown-up children but Bruce has never been a father; Jack is an amateur painter, Bruce's hobby is sailing, while Martin does volunteer work in speech therapy with children. All of them feel that paedophilic activities do not affect their adult sexual relationships in any negative way. Despite their differences in terms of occupation, interests and family background, the commonality in their view of adult-child sexual contact is marked.

10.2.3 Sex with children as continuation of childhood sexuality

A third type of construction is identified in the accounts of six of the informants, who have all attributed their current sexual orientation to childhood habits – they are Adrian, Andy, George, Keith, Nick and Simon. They started to be sexually involved with children when they were children themselves, and have remained so ever since. These childhood activities are construed as either providing a context for the development of an innate disposition (George and Simon) or serving in themselves as a major force in determining subsequent sexual orientation.

Four of these informants (Adrian, Andy, George and Nick) have described their attachment to children in the context of deprivation or difficulties with adults during childhood. As mentioned before, Andy and Nick had actually spent the greater part of their childhood in institutions.

Adrian, while giving a summary of his life, had recounted his sexual encounters with children, one episode after another, as if these experiences constituted the core of his life – he ended with the quip, 'So that's more or less the line of my life.' In the case of Andy and Nick, the lengthy institutionalisation that they had undergone during their childhood, a period in which their sexual habits with children were formed, was seen to be the origin of their paedophilic orientation. In the case of George, on the other hand, a very specific experience (watching a mother spank her young daughters) was construed as pivotal in influencing his subsequent development. Whatever the specific form of these childhood experiences, each of these six informants has identified a direct continuity between his childhood and adult sexuality, a continuity that is stable and firm.

10.2.4 *Difficulty in adult relationships*

More than half of all the informants expressed the view that difficulty in relating to adults is either the origin of their sexual involvement with children or a significant factor contributing to the development of such an orientation. Within this broad category, several finer patterns can be distinguished.

(1) Marital problems (sexual, emotional, or both): Daniel, Fred and Matthew have mentioned some links between their sexual involvement with or desire for children, and their dissatisfaction with their marriage.

(2) Inability to approach females: for various reasons Adrian, Bruce, Daniel, Edward, Keith, Matthew, Robert and Vincent felt that they had great difficulty establishing intimate relationships with the opposite sex, even though some of them had got married, or had relationships with women. In general, they tended to have had a rather lonely childhood, and had become shy of social interaction. More specific reasons given are: puritanical or repressive upbringing (Bruce, Daniel, Robert and Vincent), problem of stuttering (Edward), and inferiority complex (Keith).

(3) Incompatibility with adult females: Eugene explained his preference for young girls in terms of the incompatibility between himself and his ex-girlfriends. The latter were seen as too independent and dominant. Eugene felt that it was only when his girlfriend was dependent on him that he could fulfil his 'duty'.

(4) Hatred for adults: Both George and Nick have developed a strong hatred for adults from a young age on. The source of this hatred lies in their experiences with their respective families, which in time generalised to other adults. Because of this hatred, George and Nick did not like to relate to adults, and tended to seek the company of children.

Among the 20 informants, only four had had sexual contact with their own children – Daniel, Fred, Jack and Joe.[7] In the case of Jack and Joe, such sexual involvement was portrayed as consensual and mutually enjoyable, and their daughters were said to be happily married now. With David, his daughter was too small (6) to take an active part, so it was more a matter of him fondling or licking her. Nevertheless, he had described how his daughter showed signs of enjoyment, which made him feel satisfied. Only in the case of Fred did the contact fit the family system theory description of the endogamous incestuous relationship: it arose in the context of marital difficulty between Fred and his wife, with the daughter pushed into a substitute-wife role, and the abuse was disclosed when the daughter tried to run away from home.

With respect to preference for boys *vs* girls, a trend can be discerned. Those informants who are attracted to boys tend to construe their sexuality as either inborn or continuous with their childhood activities (e.g. Ben, Patrick, Simon, Tom), while those who are attracted to girls construe it more as a result of difficulty in adult relationships (e.g. Daniel, Matthew, Vincent). Those informants who explain their involvement with children in terms of a libertarian view of free sex tend also to be attracted to girls rather than to boys (e.g. Bruce, Jack, Joe, Martin). Regarding the age of the children, it appears that informants who are seeking a relationship tend to be involved with pubescent partners (e.g. Ben, Eugene), while those who feel the need for some sort of human contact as an antidote against feelings of insecurity go for younger children (e.g. Daniel, Matthew, Vincent). Informants who focus on physical sex, on the other hand, seem to welcome any child (e.g. Adrian, Andy, Keith, Simon).

10.3 The world of the 'paedophile'

It is commonly thought that adults who have become sexually involved with children are either socially incompetent or grossly pathological individuals. Yet in this study, the 20 informants have presented a very diverse picture regarding the kind of person they think they are. Each has his particular way of building up a world of his own, in which he finds meaning for his life. They are not 'abnormal' in the sense of being totally different from other 'ordinary' people – their lifestyle is often not exceptional. Yet on the other hand, each of them has a unique story to tell – but then every person, paedophile or not, always has a unique story to tell. Perhaps only a biographical approach can bring out all the rich complexity of a paedophile's life (or any person's life, for that matter).[8] This discussion can therefore be only very brief.

---

[7] The other informants who had been married were Adrian, Martin, Matthew, and Simon. According to their accounts, they never had sexual contact with their own children.

[8] T. Parker (1969) and P. Wilson (1981) contain short biographies of some paedophiles. Unfortunately this kind of work is rare.

10.3.1 Variation among informants

(1) The informants came from diverse family backgrounds, including poor, deprived families, broken homes, single-parent homes, children's homes (institutionalisation), ordinary working-class families, well-to-do families, religious families, libertarian families, etc.[9]

(2) Their age range is from early twenties to mid-seventies.

(3) Their education level varies from secondary school to university or professional training.

(4) Their occupations range from manual jobs, to clerical, technical, and private business, to professional careers like accountancy and music. A few were unemployed or already retired.

(5) In terms of hobbies and interests, the range is again quite wide: photography, woodwork, building car models, painting, music, philately, sailing, darts, reading (science, history, biography, travelling, archaeology), massage, computers and first aid (St John's Ambulance Brigade work was Andy's 'only hobby').

(6) Political beliefs: Daniel was a member of the Communist Party, George a Welsh nationalist, Jack called himself a humanist, Joe supported the Conservative Party.

10.3.2 Self description

While the popular image of the 'paedophile' as a shy and ineffectual person does find some support from this study, it must be stressed that this is by no means the only valid characterisation. The following discussion will illustrate the broad range of self-description that the informants have provided.

Insecure, timid, socially inadequate

About one-third of the informants have described themselves as timid, shy and fearful of social situations – they tend to lead a solitary life. For instance:

> When I was younger I spent all my time reading books, I didn't acquire any social skills. When I wanted to communicate with other people, I didn't have the necessary skills. ... I'm not sure whether I fit into any of the conventional groups – mm – I think I would like to be dominant, but I can't manage it – I tend to be too timid. (Daniel)

> I think I was shy with adults, but I was never shy with chldren. I was more at ease with children, you know, than I was with adults. The whole of my life I've been able to talk to children more than I could talk to adults. (Matthew)

---

[9] It must be stressed that this shows the *diversity* in people who feel sexually attracted to children – it is not meant to reinforce the assertion about the *ubiquity* of child sexual abuse.

I was extremely shy when I went to college, I think it's partly as a result of that I never went off my family unit for social contact. ... I didn't go out with girls in my teens at all, even in college I didn't – I went to music college – and the social contact, you know, with girls I'd always found the most difficult. ... I haven't had many, sort of, three heterosexual relationships, but again, it's been the difficulty of approaching women, which is part of my normal social difficulty, having no history of approaching women, asking for dates – mm – which is, sort of, difficult for me to, even make the first approach. (Robert)

Solitary lifestyle

As pointed out above, those informants who feel themselves socially inadequate tend to be lonely individuals. But there are also some informants who *choose* to lead a life isolated from other people. For example, Fred described himself as a 'one-person chap' who liked 'just to keep himself to himself'. George had also pointed out that social isolation was to him a matter of choice:

I'm alone, not lonely – I'm a loner by nature. I'm a person who likes to be alone, I don't seek company normally.

In the case of Vincent, who was an accountant, working with people was unavoidable, but he also tended to be a loner:

I suppose I'm a bit of a recluse really. I don't like people to pry into me, and I'd almost do anything to stop him doing it – I'm really sort of beating around the bush, but, you know, I've always been very introverted really, I suppose. I mean I'm not sort of out-going, egoistical a person who, you know, sort of makes a great show of himself and tries to make himself known, you know, but then I, I don't go to the other extreme, sort of, hide behind the curtain sort of thing, you know, I try to get somewhere between the two.

Another example of a lonely existence – quite a vivid one – is the case of Keith. Indeed he felt he was 'living in a fantasy world'. From an early age on he had developed the habit of talking to himself, to toys or to imaginary friends; he fantasised having sex with these imaginary characters when he felt insecure or lonesome. Even after he had grown up, Keith continued to derive gratification from his fantasy world: he wrote many stories about his erotic adventures with children, tape-recorded them and listened to them while masturbating. He had remained a solitary individual.

Double life

Very often the choice of leading a solitary life is made so as to avoid getting into trouble because of a socially unacceptable sexual orientation. The fear of being discovered has forced some of these informants into a kind of double-life: with a public persona for operating within society, and a secret existence with respect to sex.

Ben is a good example of this split. In business circles, he was known to be divorced (in fact he had never got married) – a reasonable explanation for the lack of a woman in his life. He characterised himself as a 'typical gregarious salesman' in business situations, who 'plays a very social animal'. While he said that he 'enjoys the acting', it is clear that his private life was quite different:

> Happiness comes in, very, very short sharp bursts between long periods of loneliness, and I think that applies equally to most gay people as it does to most people involved with kids. ... It is very difficult to see what the future might hold when a relationship comes to an end. The future looks extremely bleak, and by virtue of that I can say to you that over the last ten to twelve years, I have only had four or five true relationships. Obviously, there are long periods in between these relationships, especially when I say the current one, which lasts over two years, is the longest lasting ever, and none before really gone anything over a year or so, and, so there, you know, there're very long stretches of desert between the oases.

The self-confident group

As pointed out before, the popular image of the paedophile as a socially incompetent individual is not always valid. About half of the informants in this study had in one way or another expressed clear confidence in themselves.

(1) Success in career: Bruce has a thriving computer business; Robert is a busy performing musician; Martin owns a profit-making building firm; and Vincent is confident of becoming a successful accountant.

(2) Outward-going activities: Jack is active in adult education (as a student) and the local art scene (as an amateur painter); Martin is a volunteer trainer of children with speech difficulties; and Simon was very active in community work.

(3) Strong personality: George resisted successfully pressures from trade unions to force him into membership while he was working, and recently was trying to take on the local police for harassment; Jack has been very resilient after the death of his beloved wife, and is rebuilding his life through involvement in adult education and community activities; Nick was extremely demanding on himself in terms of learning fighting skills: he wanted to excel over everybody else and was very proud of his physical prowess.[10]

(4) Confidence in social relationships: Bruce maintained that while

---

[10] While Nick could be aggressive and violent, particularly in situations in which he felt he had to defend his rights – his record of physical violence against policemen, prison officers and other prison inmates attests to the fact that he does not fit the paedophile stereotype of a timid and shy person – yet it must be stressed that he could be very gentle and child-like in the company of children. Indeed, he broke down weeping during several of the interview sessions I had with him, when he was talking about his parents, and about his separation from a boy he loved.

difficulties in relating to the opposite sex did contribute to the origin of his paedophilic desire, he has long since overcome such difficulties and has no problem in heterosexual relationships, even though his desire for young girls remains. Jack, Joe, Martin and Simon have an active and successful social life. Indeed, Martin is proud of his physical attractiveness for women as well as for pubescent girls. Simon is very proud of his status as a leader of his local community; he said people repeatedly told him that he 'commanded a lot of respect in this city' – he was 'a good listener', he 'could talk', he 'never had any complex, was never shy'.

(5) Intelligence: a number of informants, such as Bruce, Joe and Martin had explicitly expressed confidence in their judgments and reasoning. They were proud of being rational and independent in their thinking.

It can be seen from the above discussion that both those individuals who feel exclusively attracted to children (George, Nick and Simon) as well as those who enjoy sex with both children and adults (Bruce, Jack, Joe and Martin) have characterised themselves as very different from a 'timid and shy' stereotype of a 'paedophile'.

10.3.3 The establishment of a paedophile identity

Some informants, when giving a description of themselves, had provided material about the process of identity formation that they had gone through. Daniel's account is discussed here as it illustrates this process most clearly.

Personality compatibility. As referred to above, Daniel described himself as a timid person who did not have the necessary social skills for interpersonal relationships. He felt vulnerable in the adult world, and was much more at ease with children, particularly younger ones. In the case of informants who are not as shy or timid as Daniel, there is still a reference to a particular liking for, or ability to interact with children (e.g. Bruce, Martin, Simon).

Immediate emotional crisis. Daniel had construed his difficulty with, and subsequent separation from, his wife as the immediate context for the clear emergence of his paedophilic interest. As he said, he was feeling 'emotionally starved' and had a great need for human contact. This need led to his breaking the conventional age barrier of sexual behaviour.

Stepwise realisation. Given the emotional needs that Daniel had experienced, and his inability to build up intimate relationships with women, he felt increasingly drawn towards children. But this was a progressive process: he talked about his interest in an 18-year-old girl, a 16-year-old, a 12-year-old, and then a 9-year-old:

The realisation that I was paedophile sort of grew gradually. I became sexually attracted to this 18-year-old babysitter. Previously I regarded her, I think I had a sort of mental block that she was too young, and therefore I didn't regard her as a possible sexual partner – mm – we're in a pub, she sat on my lap for some reason, and playing around or something, I think my wife said give Daniel a cuddle, so she sat on my lap, I stuck my hand up her jumper, feeling her breasts actually, by this means I broke through the barrier and realised that she was a plausible sexual partner. ... After the incident with the 18-year-old – the next girl I was sexually attracted to is 16. I think I was in love with the 18-year-old, then I swapped my affection to the 16-year-old girl – mm – we're both studying geography at a local school, I was studying it as a mature student, she was there as a sort of normal sixth former – mm – but again my attention embarrassed her. Whether she would have been more receptive to my attention if I could have manoeuvred things so she wasn't embarrassed by my attention – that's sort of, social manoeuvring involved again, I couldn't cope with things, I didn't bother, really bother about the fact, you know, I didn't sort of think that it's so unusual, 'cause after all 16 is legal. Anyway, I then noticed that I was looking up the legs of a 12-year-old, who used to come round to play with my kids, and this probably, I thought to myself immediately, I shouldn't be doing this, you know, I shouldn't be wanting to look up her skirt. ... The 12-year-old had a 9-year-old sister, who actually got a much nicer personality. The 12-year-old was nice to look at, but she didn't have a nice personality, she had a sort of slightly vicious, you know, unpleasant streak to her. But the 9-year-old was very sweet. She was fairly plump – I said I like looking at a thin girl, but plumpness doesn't deter me. I was very fond of the 9-year-old and by this time I start fantasising about her. ... I had a sort of shock, and I realised I was in love with a 9-year-old girl, and, I mean, it's quite a surprise apparently when I was in love with a 16-year-old girl. When I found I was in love with a 9-year-old girl, I had sort of, to do some serious thinking about this.

Yielding to social pressure. When Daniel got into trouble with the law because of his sexual activities with underage girls, he accepted psychiatric treatment for his 'sexual deviation'. However, he only agreed to have social skills training; he refused to undergo aversion therapy.

Seeking support. Rather than going along with society's demands, Daniel tried to find a better way out. He read relevant books, hoping to gather information on the subject of paedophilia. In time, he had developed a sociobiological interpretation of the role of paedophiles in human society, which provided him with a sense of coherence and meaning for his experience, and helped him to accept his situation positively.

Confirmation of identity. In the course of seeking support, Daniel came into contact with a paedophile organisation and joined it. This step was an important one since it confirmed his identification with the cause of the paedophile: he felt that there was a legitimate place for paedophiles in society, and wanted to participate in the paedophile liberation campaign.

Psychological integration. The confirmation of identity involves not only the outward action of joining the paedophile organisation, but also an inward psychological integration – a building up of a *personal* identity. As the following quotation shows, Daniel was in the process of achieving such integration:

272   *II. Adult Sexual Experiences with Children*

I felt, I've been shipwrecked – because I was in all these legal problems, so I accepted treatment. I mean, I'd decided, that now I landed on this shore, quite a pleasant shore, I'd much rather stay there, instead of trying to get up into uncharted waters – to me it seems to be uncharted waters of adult heterosexuality. ... I mean, perhaps sort of having found myself on this shore, I mean, I think the mistake is to regard it as shipwreck. Perhaps – mm – I suppose I regard it as a landing.

Based on an analysis of Daniel's account, a broad scheme of the identity formation process can be constructed as follows:

(1) Disposition: personality styles, upbringing, or difficulties that might either steer a person away from adult sexual relationships towards children, or enable him to relate to children easily.

(2) Precipitation: events or experiences that are immediately responsible for the emergence of a desire for, or sexual involvement with, children.

(3) Recognition: a gradual or sudden realisation of persistent sexual feelings towards children.

(4) Uncertainty: a state in which the person wavers over whether to conform to social norms or to reject such demands; it may be a situation in which formal social pressure (such as legal sanction) is acutely experienced.

(5) Seeking confirmation: when the person decides to at least query society's demands, he will search for alternative explanations (e.g. cultural relativism) and alternative value system (e.g. sexual liberation) with which to make sense of his feelings and experiences. Joining a paedophile organisation is the most overt form of seeking confirmation of a person's sexual attraction towards children.

(6) Self integration: a stage at which the individual has come to accept the identity of a paedophile, and begins to structure his life accordingly.

In Chapter 8, Finkelhor's attempt to build a mutifactor model for child sexual abuse, and also for paedophilia, was discussed. The description presented here regarding the process of identity formation in a paedophile differs from Finkelhor's model of paedophilia in one major respect – whereas Finkelhor's theory is explicitly based on a notion of psychopathology, the 'model' developed here avoids making such a judgment – it is more a descriptive account which, I hope, highlights the pattern in some of the informants' narratives.[11]

It must be pointed out that not all informants in this study, and certainly not all paedophiles, go through exactly the same process of

---

[11] In this regard, this discussion can be taken as a preliminary attempt to sketch the 'moral career' of the paedophile (who, under current social conditions, must try his best to manage a *stigmatised* existence) more in the spirit of the work of H.S. Becker (1963), Goffman (1963) or Plummer (1975).

identity formation as outlined here. This scheme is simply a model for interpreting possible patterns. Take, for instance, the case of Bruce. While he felt a 'disposition' towards sexual relationships with young girls, there were no specific precipitating events which were immediately responsible for the emergence of his desire. Rather it was a process of realisation shaped by various experiences throughout his development. He did not feel uncertain about his desire, and was under no social pressure to conform. He found confirmation in the ideas of the relativity of sexual ethics and the culturally conditioned nature of human sexual behaviour. Being successful in his career and adult relationships, he could integrate his paedophilic desire as a normal part of himself.

On the other hand, in the case of Edward, disposition (solitary life, stuttering) and uncertainty (fear of the law) can be observed. No precipitating event or confirmation-seeking effort is apparent. Nevertheless, he had a firm view regarding himself as an individual who could only play a totally submissive role in an adult relationship. He felt that a relationship with a boy would satisfy him, but did not dare to seek one out. Regarding his self-realisation of paedophilic feelings, it was a gradual process, from the fear of the opposite sex, through homosexual experiences with men, eventually to fantasising about boys.

For Simon, his identity was firmly established from his teens – it was 'dispositional' in the strict sense of the term – he could identify no immediate precipitating event. While he *had* experienced a lot of social pressure in the form of police arrest, prosecution and imprisonment, he felt no uncertainty about his paedophilic disposition – the pressure only made him more discreet about his activities.

One last example can be found in Tom O'Carroll's autobiographical story (1980). He talked about the persistent attraction he experienced towards boys, the gradual realisation of his being a paedophile, the period of uncertainty in which he avoided any opportunity for sexual contact with boys, his doomed effort to try heterosexual relationships and even marriage, his troubles with the law after his desire for children was found out by the school authorities (he was a teacher), and his effort at vindicating the goodness of his love for boys. His book is not only the product of the process of seeking confirmation, but also an eloquent statement of self-justification.

10.3.4 The pursuit of a meaningful life

Like any other person, a paedophile has to make his life meaningful – sex with children is not what every paedophile thinks about all the time. For individuals like Bruce, Joe, Martin, Robert, Tom or Vincent, who have a stable career, life is meaningful by virtue of their pursuit of success in their work. For others, special effort has to be put into *making* life worth living.

Andy, who was from a very deprived background, and was unemployed after being released from lengthy institutionalisation, managed to train as a first-aider. From then on, volunteer first-aid work had become 'very important' to him. Daniel had taken up a political cause: the liberation of paedophiles. Simon, who was in his seventies, and had suffered unemployment as well as imprisonment in his old age, was still very active in creating a meaningful and enjoyable life by immersing himself in volunteer community work. Keith, who was also unemployed, had literally built up a 'world' of his own. A visit to his room revealed to the visitor the richness of his world – numerous car models, vehicle paraphernalia, small wooden furniture he himself made, gramophone music records, books, pictures of children cut out from magazines, pasted on paper and carefully bound together into many volumes. These were the things that occupied his waking life – it was his world, in which he found fulfilment and satisfaction.

Perhaps the experience of George can summarise how these people were pursuing, indeed building, a meaningful life:

> Unemployment changed all that. I had to take an interest in something, and find some way to pass all the time previously spent in work. Visits to the cinema were on when I could manage them, but what to do in between whiles? I had to think, plan, act, and it was new to me. I had to find some method of living, and to try to obtain a modicum of enjoyment out of life. In 1958, I began to study Welsh history, and later, about 1968, I began to study the etymon of various Welsh place names. All this meant hard work, and little understanding, but it passed the time, and taught me to think, spasmodically at first, but continuously in time. Wales, always my first love, became even dearer to me, and my life took on meaning, and value began to assert itself. No more the humdrum work to bed routine, for now I was living, and enjoying life. (George)

As Nick remarked, 'sex isn't the main thing' – to many of these informants, sex does not constitute the whole of their life, although it does form part of it. Like every 'ordinary' person, these 'paedophiles' are trying to construct a meaningful existence out of the material that they find available in life.

11

Further Analysis

In the last chapter, an account is given of the various patterns of personal construction that the informants have provided regarding their sexual involvement with children. That discussion is on the whole conducted at a descriptive level – it is the individual informant's *own* construction that is the focus of the presentation. The analysis is confined to teasing out similarities so that patterns of construing are discernible.

In this chapter, the analysis is carried forward in a more interpretative direction. It is divided into three parts; (1) episode analysis, through which the rule structures involved in specific episodes of sexual encounter with children are identified; (2) model construction, through which these rule structures are integrated into coherent hermeneutical models; (3) discourse analysis, through which the 'discourses of sexuality' embedded in the informants' construction are explicated.

11.1 Episode analysis

After going through the specific adult-child sexual episodes provided by the informants in detail, a number of distinguishing features can be identified.

An encounter with a child is often experienced as much more satisfying than sexual contact with adults because the child is more affectionate and physically more attractive. The encounter frequently begins with looking, specifically looking at the child's underwear and then the exposed genitalia. Sometimes the 'contact' would not go beyond such looking – even so, the excitement can be very intense.

In some of these encounters, the (sexual) interactions follow a particular routine – more or less initiated by the adult, but sometimes actively shaped by the child as well. This routine involves either explicit rules of conduct for the interaction between the informant and the child, or some pattern which the informant follows in approaching children. While orgasm often constitutes the goal of these encounters, some informants have insisted that 'sex isn't the main thing' – indeed the conflict of love versus lust is articulated clearly by one particular informant. Such a conflict can be understood in terms of a desire to establish a relationship with the child, rather than merely obtaining sexual release.

11.1.1 The special appeal of children

Over half of the informants have mentioned specific characteristics in children which they find particularly appealing. Paedophilic relationships are seen as *in themselves* more satisfying than sex with adults – these relationships are often the informants' first choice, rather than a substitute when adult sex is lacking.

In the informants' accounts, children are portrayed as gentle, truthful, broadminded, affectionate, perceptive and with an 'enquiring mind', whereas adults are described as narrow-minded, selfish and lacking any depth of feeling. Children possess 'spirit' and 'innocence', while adults are preoccupied with material gains. Children are warm, generous and easy to communicate with – there is no need to put up a front when interacting with them.

More specifically, Ben had elaborated on the particular appeal of a boy in the pubertal stage of development:

> It's a very exciting and worrying time for the boy. His body and his mind are going through very very rapid changes. He's starting to have feelings that he doesn't understand and yet that excite him. So because of those feelings, because he's starting to masturbate – er – he's starting to think about sex, with those experiences and with those feelings, he's more likely to want to experiment in some type of sex, or even given a particular social situation, to enter into a relationship that involves sex. ... Boys, as they grow up, would experiment. I would say, I don't know, but I would think certainly more than ninety per cent of boys would experiment in some way with other boys, and that would normally happen around 12 or 13. So, if I'm available, in certain situations where, you know, if a child is at that stage where he wants to experiment, he would experiment with almost anybody that's available, provided that he wasn't repulsed by that person for some other reasons. That's in some way what makes it the most interesting age to me – mm – that the child is interested out of curiosity, that the child is responsive physically and emotionally – mm – you only (laughs) you only got to put your hand on a boy's belly, without touching his genitals, you only stroke his belly and he would get an erection. It's a very very special period of a child's life, he's intensely curious and he's becoming a young man, no longer a child, and becoming a young man. Puberty creates a different person.

On the other hand, some informants have placed special emphasis on the physical attractiveness of children. This ranges from an adoration of the form of the male body, or a fascination with boys' penises,[1] to an idealisation of young girls' genitalia.

The contrast between children and adults is, to some of the informants, a serious indictment against society – all the good qualities that children possess inevitably evaporate away once they have entered into the adult world:

[1] For example, Adrian had made the following remark, 'I'm attracted, I want to see boys' penises. Now they say, everybody says, all boys are the same – now they are *not* the same. Some've been circumcised, some have little ones, some have big ones, some have long ones, fat ones, thin ones, I want to see them.'

Children are immeasurably perceptive, but by the time they have grown up, society has dealt them a deadly blow, and their perception has fled for all times. ... Girls have a tremendous depth of feeling, and sense of responsibility, even the most irrational of them, and are also very broadminded. All this is lost when they grow up. (George)

They are warm and generous and it is only when they get older and they learn the ways of the world and ask what's in it for me or what is it worth. When that happens they lose all their charm and enchantment. (Jack)[2]

11.1.2 The excitement of looking

A number of informants in this study have expressed the feeling that looking at children, particularly at their private parts, by lifting up skirts or lowering knickers, is a very exciting experience. In the narratives of specific episodes, some informants have spelled out this 'looking' at length. The following is a description from Vincent:

There were several children involved in the last case I was involved with, where the oldest of the girls suggested we play doctors and nurses to the youngest girl, and it was the oldest girl who then exposed the youngest girl to me, that was completely without me actually prompting them to it. It then developed from there, and I said, you know, would they all like to do it, which they did. It's something I didn't *want* to happen, but having happened the first instance, which, you know, it was such an enjoyable experience for me, I just couldn't really stop myself from asking to go further. [Researcher: How did you feel?] Well, I felt excited, and – mm – sickened, because, I felt excited this was going to happen, and also I felt sickened from the fact that I didn't really want it to happen, you know, this was something that I've been trying to stop from happening, but since it was going to go ahead, I felt that I couldn't really stop it, you know, I felt elated, I was on a high, but I knew it was wrong, and for that reason, I felt sickened in the stomach – mm – like butterflies, you know, a very peculiar feeling, to have both, both experiences at the same time. ... Although I'm quite happy, to – er – not actually have the exposure itself, but to sort of go round and see girls playing, and then to catch a glimpse of the lower portion of their knickers, while they're playing sort of thing, you know, if their skirts are raised, that would also give me – hmm – a sexual relief. ... [Researcher: You said you didn't do anything, you just look?] Yes. [Researcher: What did the looking do to you?] Well, as I said, it gives me sexual gratification, I'll have an erection, and I'll have an elation, I'll be feeling quite light-headed and high, you know, just got drunk without actually having to take lots of beer, or to smoke pot. [Researcher: Do you have to examine the girl's vagina?] No, no, that as I say would involve some form of physical contact with the girl, of a sexual nature. [Researcher: So in a way, you would not be able to look at it carefully, or closely?] No, no. [Researcher: It's just, quite a superficial –?] Oh, it's *very* superficial. I mean, the sort of events would probably take less

---

[2] It is important to pursue further the question of how such a contrast has come about, and what part, if any, the adult world plays in the constitution of this contrast. But that has to be another project.

than 30 seconds from start to finish – er – the actual sexual part of it, whereas I might be sort of chatting to the girls for half an hour or even an hour, before the sexual event may happen, or I may, as in the last case, carrying on playing with them for 20 or so minutes after the sexual activity had taken place. ... I imagine that I was, more interested in the girls first – mm – that maybe even because I have not seen the woman's sex organ close to, sort of thing, that I made these initial approaches towards girls, in the first place, to find out, what the sex organ was like, and then to sort of progress up, but, that is not what actually happened, because I'd sort of stopped at the one level, I'd stayed with the young girls, I haven't sort of done anything more than look at them, you know, I haven't attempted to, to sort of, part the lips of a vagina, and to sort of see, what's beneath, or anything like that.

From this long quotation, the following pattern can be observed:

(1) Just looking at a young girl's genitalia is already a sexual experience for Vincent.

(2) The excitement produced by this looking is intense ('elated, high, light-headed, drunk'); once started, the excitement would prevent Vincent from stopping.

(3) However, the looking would also produce a guilt feeling ('sickened, butterflies in the stomach, knowing that it is wrong'); but the excitement is stronger than the guilt feeling.

(4) It is a very tentative kind of sexual approach to girls. It goes no further than seeking to look at girls' genitalia briefly. Initially Vincent thought this might be a first step in his attempt to relate to the opposite sex, but he found that he had not progressed beyond this act of 'superficial' looking.

While Vincent did not go further than just looking at young girls' exposed genitalia, for a number of other informants, looking only constituted the first of a series of acts which would bring sexual excitement and release, for example:

When I'm in the company of a girl, a young girl, I must see her underwear. I must see – that's the initial start – must see her underwear, you see, then I have to see, what's inside the underwear. ... If you see a young girl, or a woman in bathing costume, you know what she's got underneath, but you can't see it, and you want to see it. But when you see her on the beach naked, then you say, well, that's what she's got, that's it, it's nothing that gets the imagination, you know. (Keith)

It is not simply the actual looking at a girl's genitalia that is exciting, but a *progressive* 'discovery' from looking at the knickers, through fantasising about what is *hidden* underneath, and then slowly revealing the girl's private parts – it is this *process* that is so captivating.[3]

[3] The sexual excitement produced by looking at a naked or semi-naked body is of course not confined to paedophilia, but is a feature common to all forms of sexual activities.

11.1.3 A set routine

Looking is often the start of a more or less routine series of actions that will bring about sexual fulfilment for the paedophile. Sometimes this routine is *jointly* executed by both the adult and the child. The following episode is provided by George:

I think it was June, two months before her eleventh birthday, but I am not quite certain on that. She called, as usual, and I let her into my bedroom; she wore a brown skirt, blue jumper, black shoes, white socks, ankle length, a full petticoat, white, and blue cotton knickers, no vest. I sat on the bed, made her bend over my knee, face down; had to push her head down, and she argued about that, in fact she loved objecting to anything, so I simply hauled her further over my knee to lift her feet off the floor, poor girl. She then objected to her hands touching the floor, so I had to adjust for that. I lifted up her skirt and petticoat as she lay still, and spanked her, hand first, then stick, on her knickers. She of course objected furiously, I was hitting her 'too hard'. When I stopped and pulled her knickers down below her knees, she grinned happily and turned her head round to look up at me, so I could see her laugh, and with her eyes sparkling too! I then spanked her naked buttocks soundly, as before, and she was blushing furiously when I let her up, and placed her back on her feet. I then turned away to strip off except for my knickers,[4] and when I turned back, she was lying back on my bed grinning wickedly at me. On a sudden impulse I said, 'Can I undress you, take all your clothes off?' 'Yes!' she said. I started to do so, she had a lovely body, and when I pulled her knickers back down her legs she said 'No!' I stopped, and after some debate on the situation was given permission to pull her knickers all the way down her legs; 'But don't take them off,' she told me. I drew them down to her ankles, and turned them inside out at that point. When I took hold of her petticoat, she said 'No! Don't take it off.' 'Yes!' I said. 'No!' She said, 'Don't!' 'Well', I replied, 'I will just lift it up,' so pulled her petticoat up to her chin, all of it, and had a look at her. She smiled happily, and drew her legs apart. She let me place my hands where I wanted to go on her body, and also between her legs. I then sat on her stomach, gently, and rubbed my hand along in front of my knickers, her eyes followed me avidly. 'I'll part your legs,' I told her. She smiled happily and studied the ceiling as I drew them apart, and touched her in between. She seemed surprised when I told her to pull her knickers up, and to get up. It was now her turn to spank me, so she ordered me to get down on my knees, and to face the wall, then I had to bend over just right, which took a lot of adjusting, and I was told to keep my head down. She took her time, so I glanced around at her, and was immediately ordered to turn around and to lower my head. Having embarrassed me as far as she could, she thrashed me with the same stick I had used on her and, as my knickers were thin, it hurt woefully. I was soundly whipped by her, and then when she let me get up, I had to bend over while she pulled my knickers down to examine my bottom.

From the above account, and also other descriptions George had given,

[4] George had the habit of wearing knickers.

it is clear that his interaction with his girl friends followed a particular pattern:

(1) He preferred to meet two of them together at a time. This was more exciting.

(2) He wanted them to wear a skirt or frock because he wanted to lift up a skirt to see.

(3) He always treated his girl friends as equal partners, who could claim a fair share of the fun, and who could make their own choice. Sometimes George argued and 'fought' with them over what he could do – this reflected the playfulness of their interaction.

(4) Their activities were mainly spanking and fondling. In the past, George used to let the girls spank him first, and then he spanked them in return. Because of a complaint from one girl that he spanked her too hard and that she had no opportunity to 'get her own back', he reversed the order of the game: now he would spank the girls first, and then let them take their revenge.

(5) Besides spanking, he would also touch the legs or the body of the girls, and each girl 'has the right to extend her activity in any way that pleases her'.

(6) The spanking activity followed these steps:

(i) He would either bend the girl over his knees, or have her lie on the ground.

(ii) He would lift up her skirt and petticoats to have a good look.

(iii) Initially he would smack the girl's bottom by hand or with a stick, with her knickers on, then would lower the knickers and spank her bare bottom.

(iv) Usually he would not undress the girl except lowering her knickers for the spanking.

(v) Occasionally, he would give a girl a 'punishment spanking' with her permission, to make her cry and then to soothe her himself. He only did this with older girls.

(7) He had discussed these activities with his girl friends when they asked him to. Some girls had tried to get him to have sexual intercourse with them, but he would say no by using the excuse of being impotent.

(8) He had established quite a long-term relationship (two or three years) with several girls in their early teens. He gave them presents or pocket money, and whenever a girl had taken a 'punishment spanking' from him, he would give her some money as reward.

While in the case of George the sequence of events were brought about by the *collaboration* of himself and the girls, for Matthew the pattern was much more a one-sided routine on his part, and involved a much more superficial kind of contact:

(1) Matthew tended to feel vulnerable and 'less than a man' for not

being able to have sexual intercourse with his wife because of his impotence.

(2) When he was idling at home with nothing to do, this sense of vulnerability was especially intense, and he had to go out looking for the company of young girls.

(3) He would talk to the girl he met in the park or playground, and might touch her hair, her face, or put his arm round her, or sometimes touch her on her private parts.

(4) The urge to touch the girl only arose after they had been chatting for several minutes about the girl's life. Matthew might talk to her about her clothes or her body before touching her.

(5) Whether or not there was any touching involved, he would feel happy and emotionally settled after the encounter with a girl.

It should be pointed out that not every informant was always, or was always aware of, following a routine when relating to children. The above discussion aims at capturing the pattern of actions in some of the informants' experiences. The notion of routine is useful as it reveals what is psychologically significant in terms of regularity of actions.

11.1.4 Simple physical release

A close reading of some of these adult-child sexual episodes reveals that the actions of some informants are governed by the pursuit of mere physical-sexual release. The following account given by Adrian illustrates this observation:

This young boy was only about 10, probably 11, and he's just been, what you call – er – circumcised. I said, oh, I've never seen anybody been sort of circumcised, let me see it, and he had no hesitation and showed me. And every time, I said oh, let's see how it's getting on, and he'd show me. And while we were staying there, we met his nephew [sic], 'cause he's about 12 years old, he changed in the car, and I saw he had a nice one – not big one, normal, you know, same size, and that excited me, and he let me feel it. And, he moved away from [this town], oh, to [another town], I went to see his parents, he took me up the attic, and he let me feel it again, very nice. And then, the second time I went there, he was 13, I think, he's a teenager, and his father was there, but in a different room. He went to get me a drink, 'cause it was a public house, you see, while he was getting my drink, I went in there and touched him, got it out, sucked it, and kissed him. He came back, he laid on a settee, and I felt it, really hard then. Then his father came in, we didn't say nothing, father went out again. I stood up, he started wanking me off – that was that boy. The other boy that was circumcised, I saw him again, about three or four months after, at the swimming pool, and he was fully developed then – oh, he had a very long one, and I'd been with him four or five times I should think, and he kisses me, sucks me off, and I did the same to him.

As mentioned in the last chapter, Adrian had described his experience in terms of a feeding imagery – sex with children provided fulfilment for a biological need just like having a meal. It was usually with a stranger boy, and lasted only several minutes (the duration of mutual masturbation to orgasm). There was no conversation as such, just the physical act. It followed this pattern:

(1) Adrian would find an excuse to look at the boy's penis, the looking was exciting to him.

(2) He would feel the boy's penis, if the boy did not object. Apparently the boys he met also found their activities exciting and pleasurable.

(3) The climax of the encounter involved mutual masturbation and fellatio to orgasm – the only goal of the encounter.

Another example is Keith:

If I was messing about with any kid, or anybody, if I don't ejaculate with them then it's defeated, you see. Oh, fair enough, I can later think about what I've been doing and have a, you know, masturbation, myself, but, having ejaculation while you are in the company with a person is more thrilling, you know. ... On several occasions, I've been in the company of children, and I've been able to fondle them, especially the girls. They've been sitting on my lap, and I've got an erection. All the time I was, you know, feeling them, you know, and ejaculated in my pants, and then pushed the child off. Well, she said, what you push me off for? 'Cause you know, when you've, it's like you having sex with a girl, well, once you had sex with them, you want to get off, finished, you don't want to lay there for ever, you see, 'cause you got to wait until you're ready for sex again, you see.

Adrian and Keith represent one extreme end of the physical-emotional continuum. In the case of other informants, the emotional element involved was more prominent even if the dominant motive structuring the interaction was still the pursuit of sexual satisfaction. Orgasm does constitute the ultimate goal for some, but it is not always so for others.

11.1.5 'Sex isn't the main thing'

Nick is not the only informant who has expressed this sentiment – sex is not the main thing they want, it is a 'loving relationship' with a child that they desire.

Most important thing I look for, I suppose, is a loving relationship with a boy, and (pause) although I've had physical relationships with, probably, I don't know, maybe a hundred or more boys over the years, I can only point to four or five true relationships over that time. (Ben)

I didn't seem to need an orgasm myself at the time, I was quite pleased that she [i.e. his own daughter] had an orgasm, it seemed to me very satisfying the fact that I'd been able to give her this pleasure. (Daniel)

Another example is Matthew. As mentioned before, Matthew would feel satisfied just in the company of children, chatting with them, and watching them play. He did not need to touch the children – even if he did touch them, he often did so on their head or arm, it was only occasionally that he touched their private parts. In his words, it was a 'loving touching' rather than a sexual one.

On the other hand, George had this to say:

> To me a sexual act is simply any activity which provides the individual with sexual enjoyment. For me, the most desirable is to spank a girl, and to be able to be spanked by her. Ejaculation is not the most enjoyable part, handling the girl's knickers, or her legs, as I spank her is. My enjoyment has increased since ejaculation has become almost non-existent. ... Sexual enjoyment is caused by the excitement that flows through me when I meet a girl. Ejaculation neither adds nor detracts, erection was a nuisance, and ejaculation likewise.

It is clear that sexual fulfilment is a *personal* construction. Ejaculatory orgasm is not necessarily the most important element in the paedophilic relationships that the informants of this study have experienced.[5] Nick's remarks remain the most eloquent articulation of such an experience:

> It's not just sex, I enjoyed their company. Lots of things come into it. Sex, to me, sex is a very small part, you know, in a relationship with a boy, sex is, you know, the smallest part. ... The answer lies in, in being wanted, being needed, being able to give, being able to take, in a child-adult relationship. ... Sex isn't the main thing, the main thing is being wanted I suppose.

11.1.6 *The establishment of a relationship*

'To be wanted, to be able to give, to be able to take' is to be involved in a relationship – a loving relationship with the child is often looked upon as the most important thing by some adults sexually involved with children. The establishing of a relationship is a prominent *motif* in the narrative of some informants. The following quotation from Ben illustrates this:

> If it becomes a relationship rather than a one-off experience, then it's because I'm filling a role that is not available elsewhere in [the boy's] life. ... Now, I have spent many many many hours in my life standing or doing something or watching or doing things that I never interest in whatsoever, but, standing, or watching or doing them, purely because that's what the boy wants to do, yeah? Mm – I mean, I stood at many go-kart tracks watching kids, you know, round and round on go-karts for hours on end which they absolutely adore, which is an incredibly boring thing to watch after the first three minutes – mm – trips to the zoo, trips to the movies, the films and things in which I've absolutely no interest. I don't physically want

[5] Indeed, non-ejaculatory sexual pleasure is not confined to paedophilia or other 'deviations', but may be a part of any sexual relationship. Sexual feelings are diffuse and not just genital.

to do it, but because it's incumbent upon me to do things that the child would enjoy because I want the child to be happy. I mean, when the boy is here, we will need two television sets, because we have totally different interests, yeah? Er – I want to watch an interesting documentary, he wants to watch a comedy, (laughs) so, you know, if my boy stays here for a fortnight, I'm likely not to see the news on television for a fortnight, right? [Researcher: How then can an emotional bond develop when intellectually you're so far apart?] The bond develops out of a mutual need for love and affection. The bond is nurtured and develops further out of both of us doing things for the other person even we're not necessarily particularly interested ourselves, yeah? Mm – now, it's not the case with the one at the moment because he enjoys the sex as much as I do if not more. But I know that in the past, there may have been occasions, I mean, once the relationship is established, where the boy would – I have to differentiate this from force or whatever – but I mean there may have been occasions where the boy would make love because I wanted to, all right? Mm – he may have been actually ready to go to sleep, all right? That's the other side of the coin to me watching the go-kart for three hours, OK? We all become trained, not Pavlovian, but trained to a degree that we know that somebody wants something recognised, and we recognise it, yea? Not because it interests us, but because we know that they want it recognised. The thing that's mutual, is the love and the affection, all right? Out of that affection, we do things for each other.

The relationship is based on mutual affection, and the fulfilling of each other's needs. The interaction involved is not just sexual, but consists of a whole range of activities that can be found within any intimate relationship – activities jointly carried out because of a recognition of each other's needs.

Furthermore, a paedophilic relationship is not explicitly contracted or methodically established – the two parties involved do not stand back and make detached observation or calculation, they are preoccupied in the act of relating to each other, which is spontaneous and subtle.

The reference to love can also be seen in a situation where the pursuit is simply physical release. Edward realised that what he wanted from the boy he met was sex, yet he felt very guilty about this, so he tried to convince himself that love was involved:

I tried to delude myself that I was in love with him. I remember at one time telling him as he left, I said I love you, but (pause) I didn't, I didn't love him, not him as a boy, all I did love was him as a body, it was a body I loved, not him. And so, in effect, what I felt was just sexual lust, not love. [Researcher: Why did you need to delude yourself – you used the word 'delude'?] Yes, it was – er – it was to – if, if I (pause) if I once admitted that, to myself, that it was his body I wanted, then I would probably had taken, I might have actually gone further than I wanted to go, so by telling myself that I actually loved him, I was, I was imposing (pause) a certain amount of self-control, because without that amount of self-control, without the love being sort of in the forefront and not lust, it would have been, I would probably have – I didn't push the matter to the point, where I actually got in a position that I was actually between his legs, about to commit rape. ... If I admitted to myself that all my reactions, all my feelings towards the boy was pure lust, then that respect towards him as a person and that gentleness that love presupposes would have been lost, and that it would have been (pause) it would have made the rape that would have occurred earlier even worse.

11.1.7 'It doesn't happen unless the child needs it'

Nearly all of the informants of this study have stated that they would not force children to have sex. The child's willingness is a very important component of the encounter, particularly for those who wanted a 'loving relationship'.

'I don't believe you can have a crime if you haven't got a victim, right? And if the child is willing he's not a victim. ... There cannot be any sense of doing against the child's will. That would negate it for me completely. (Ben)

What drew Pat and I together? Well, I liked her, fancied her, and desired to smack her bottom, and also feel her legs. Pat liked to be the centre of attention, and she knew I would always welcome her. Friendship just sprouted between us. ... Pat and I had a very good relationship, and saw no reasons to keep things under wraps. (George)

I think she enjoys it, because she was moaning, groaning, showing signs of pleasure. (Jack)

Let me get this quite clear, I don't go out seeking boys for my pleasure. I don't go out encouraging boys for my pleasure. I only encourage boys who come to me and want me to have a bit of sex play with them, and that has always been my angle. I have never ever forced a boy. (Simon)

In this connection, the issue of consent arises. Some quotations from the informants will show how *they* understand the notion of 'consent':

They have – mm – they have to be consenting. Hmm – I use the word carefully, because – er – even at 13 or 14, a boy cannot verbalise his consent. It's something one has to sense. Because, you went to a boy of 13 and said, do you want to have sex with me – er – it would be a very rare occasion where the kid said yes, because he would feel wrong to say yes, even if he wanted to. So it has to, it comes out of an instinctive understanding of the child's feelings, it has to be mutual. (Ben)

My personal opinion is that a girl of 12 is capable of giving consent to intercourse, and that younger girls are capable of consenting to petting. Any deep self-criticism which the girl might feel later is, I believe, a product of the values of western society being thrust upon her, rather than anything absolute. (Bruce)

From these quotations it is clear that some of my informants see their sexual activities with children as part of a continuing relationship. As in the case of an adult-adult relationship, the partners do not need to discuss explicitly 'informed consent' before engaging in sex with each other, so these informants feel that sex comes spontaneously as a natural part of their paedophilic relationships.

While most of my informants have explicitly affirmed that their involvement with children is always consensual, they are not unaware of the occurrence of child molestation in society. Andy, Nick and Vincent admitted that they had forced themselves on children on some occasions, but insisted that this was not their usual pattern of behaviour. When Nick realised that he might hurt a boy he tried to grab for sex, he 'came to his senses' and asked himself:

> What the fucking hell am I doing – destroying the very thing I love? You know, it's just fucking crazy.

Indeed, he regretted terribly what he had done, and at one time felt very suicidal.

In the case of Edward, he realised, as mentioned earlier, that his feelings toward the boy he fondled were more a matter of lust than love, and he knew that the boy only complied because of the money he regularly gave him. The kind of ambivalence that Edward felt can also be seen in other informants. Thus, although his desire for boys only remained on the level of fantasies, Robert had nevertheless experienced so intense a guilty feeling that he had to seek psychotherapy, and this is the conclusion he has come to:

> I sometimes examine the possibility that this is the case, you know, that perhaps people are making a big fuss about it, you know, that the boys aren't really hurt. But on balance, I think I just have to admit that, perhaps even because one doesn't know what the effect would be, and that in itself is probably sufficient to say one oughtn't to do it, even if the parties seem to be willing.

Matthew had also experienced similar ambivalence:

> I feel rather disgusted with people who are trying to make legal sex with children – it's a silly thing for me to say, because I'm (laughs) borderline myself, but I still feel very disgusted with people who want to have sex with children.

While being remanded in prison for sexual offences against children, Matthew met a number of men who had committed similar offences, and his perplexity was heightened:

> They are just normal people. I think people like me and like them, we must have a split personality because we can be normal in our working lives, but when it gets on to sex, there was something different from other people.

Nevertheless, Keith felt that whether an activity was abusive or not might be difficult to judge:

You see, there's a very, very thin border line between what is legal and what is illegal. Now you can get a family, and maybe the husband's job to bathe the children. Now the husband can undress the little ones, of about 5 or 6 or perhaps younger, in the bath and give her a wash, and he can rub round her, rub her all over, you see, now he was not doing anything wrong, but if I come along, and bathe the little girl, and rub her, I'm breaking the law, because I'm not a father. But I'm doing no more than he's done. ... If I got a little girl on my knees, and I got my hand in her pants, I'm just stroking, not trying to put my fingers in, I don't see anything wrong in there. I mean, we had people living with us over the years, with children, and I've seen the mother kiss the little girl's privates, got the little girl in the bath, and lift her up, you know, kiss the girl, or the little boy, that's all part of maternal.

From these examples, it can be seen that the informants in this study do not simplistically take for granted that all kinds of adult-child sexual contact are acceptable. Sometimes they feel ambivalent, sometimes guilty, and sometimes even outraged by what they themselves or others have done to children. Having said that, however, it must be repeated that most of them have affirmed the consensual and mutual nature of their involvement with children, and see it as benign and beneficial.

11.2 Analogy, metaphor and model

Language constitutes the basic reality of human experience. We use language to organise our activities, to make sense of the goings-on in the world, and to construct some overall order for our existence. Reality, phenomenologically speaking, is construed through the use of language. A specific language is the fundamental substrate of a particular 'form of life'.

A language continually evolves by virtue of human creativity. Words, phrases and sentences are not static in meaning – the meaning of a word is in its use. One of the distinctly human qualities of language use is the creation of metaphors and analogies. An average member of a language community is capable of grasping the meaning of even non-conventional, *ad hoc*, metaphorical language, e.g. it will not be difficult nowadays to understand the quip: 'He's got a computer in his head, that's why he always win!' The use of metaphors and analogies enriches human experience. Without them, a large part of human experiences and feelings cannot be elaborated, conveyed, apprehended, and assimilated. Metaphors and analogies are indispensable 'vehicles' for human understanding and communication.[6]

[6] Here, the terms 'metaphor' and 'analogy' have not been distinguished from each other. While indeed they are similar in meaning, it is still possible to identify a difference between the two: an analogy is a form of language use in which the 'as if' quality of the correspondence between a particular phrase and its referent/meaning is made explicit, whereas in the case of a metaphor, this 'as if' quality is not explicitly acknowledged. 'He swims *like* a fish' is an analogy while 'he *is* a fish in water' is a metaphor. For the purpose of this discussion, however, 'metaphor' and 'analogy' will be used interchangeably – the most important point is that both concepts involve an 'as if' quality. This is what underlies the

The concept of 'model' used here must be understood in terms of 'analogy' and 'metaphor'. A model is a coherent scheme of using particular metaphors or analogies – it is a framework in which there is a correspondence between its elements and those of the phenomenon it describes. Some ecologists have used the 'illness' model to describe the plight of the Earth – it is suffering from the 'ailments' of pollution, unlimited exploitation, etc., its 'health' is being destroyed by human greed and recklessness, it is displaying 'symptoms' of exhaustion, and so on. The use of a model in the construction/description of reality is a graphic way of conveying meanings.

The informants of this study communicated their experience through the medium of language. Often they talked in terms of metaphors and analogies, which do cohere into discernible models. It is not suggested here that an informant is consciously applying a particular model while carrying out his actions. The point is, these actions are conducted in such a way that when the informant accounts for them he tends to use certain metaphors or analogies which can be organised into a coherent model. In this section I attempt to organise the material discussed so far into appropriate models.

11.2.1 The external control model

There are, as discussed in the last chapter, a number of informants who feel that their sexual proclivities towards children are inborn characteristics over which they have no control. It should, however, be noted that the attribution to 'external control' by these informants pertains to their sexual *orientation*, not specific acts of sexual contact with children. Their innate disposition represents a need which they cannot fulfil in any other way, yet they are able to choose when, where, how, and with whom to fulfil this need. They cannot control the formation of their paedophile nature, but they are capable of reflexively monitoring their action in relation to children.[7]

Attributing paedophilia to an innate disposition is not the only way to express the 'external control' quality of such an experience. Adrian had expressed a kind of optimistic fatalism: he felt that God was behind everything he did, and that God would always lead him to somebody for sex so that he would not suffer too much from deprivation.

Indeed, fate seems to be the operative principle underlying some of these informants' understanding of their sexuality. It is an outside force, an external order which obtains in their existence, that has predetermined how their sexual proclivities would turn out to be. Perhaps the issue of human freedom and responsibility should have been

---

discussion.

[7] It is interesting to note, in this regard, that there is some evidence showing that sex offenders tend to explain their offending behaviour as something beyond their voluntary control, and that such explanations appear to be more acceptable to magistrates (L. Taylor, 1972).

pursued further with these informants – but maybe this is too philosophical a question to be tackled in this work.

11.2.2 The play model

Play is a childhood activity, or more accurately, the form which most childhood activities take. The essential characteristic of play is that it is a form of activity which is *not necessary for the conduct of life*.[8] Play is not serious, it is fun; play is not a must, there is scope for freedom to act otherwise; play is risk-free, it does not impinge on the actuality of human living. Childhood play is a precursor of adult ritual/rule-following behaviour.[9]

The immediate problem of looking at adult-child sexual contact in terms of play is the possible objection raised by paedophiles that their desire and activities are *serious*, that they constitute an *end* rather than a 'precursor' of something else.

This objection can be accommodated by making it clear that the proposition that play is not serious involves a *retrospective* value judgment – people can be very serious *during* play. Children *are* serious about play, to them play is not 'make-believe' – it *is* belief. Moreover, while play is not necessary for the conduct of life, it does not follow that it has no place in the development of the individual human person or the social fabric of human communities. To the extent that play is the precursor of adult rule-following behaviour, it has an important contribution to make in the psychosocial development of the individual. Not only does play help the child to develop a command of rules and action patterns;[10] its 'surreal' nature enables the individual to escape from the continuous tension of real living: a person who cannot play, or who cannot assume a 'playful' attitude must at all times be subject to the tremendous pressure of realistic living.

Play is 'surreal' – it does not involve the tension and pressure inherent in the adult world. As such, it might prove to be a form of activity in which shy and diffident people, such as Daniel and Matthew in this study, can find human contact without experiencing the pressure of the adult world.

Childhood sexual play spans a wide spectrum, including undressing, looking, touching, manipulating, urinating, spanking, etc., all of which can be found in the activities that the informants of this study engaged in with children. Some informants have talked about how they played with children in conventional childhood games such as 'doctors and nurses', through which they obtain sexual satisfaction. For example, Vincent chatted with young girls in parks and playgrounds, watched them play, and participated in their games. The opportunity to watch these girls lifting up their skirts or lowering their knickers was something highly exciting to him. While the desire to look at and find out about each other's

---

[8] See Shotter (1973a).

[9] See Harré (1974c).

[10] Or in Shotter's terms, the development of 'personal power' (Shotter, 1973b, 1974).

bodies is a common phenomenon among children, Vincent's excitement over similar activities was no doubt overlaid with an adult's sexual fantasies. On the other hand, there are informants who got involved in games with children not for sexual pleasure, but because such involvement constitutes the kind of relationship they desire. For instance, Nick loved to be with boys because they had the 'spirit of youth'. He often played with his nephews and their friends: they played rough-and-tumble games, they played football, they went camping and searching for adventures and mischiefs, they visited amusement arcades, they looked for fun. Nick was not keen on seeking sex with the boys he went out with. He recalled fond memories of boys who did not agree to have sex with him, but that did not detract from the fun and enjoyment he had with them.

In applying the play model to understand adult-child sexual contact, there is the question of whether it is play from the child's view or from the adult's. Since this study is concerned with the subjective experience of the adults involved in such contact, its focus will be that of the adult's view. Nevertheless, it appears that children involved in sexual activities with adults might indeed take these activities as a matter of play. The following quotation from Daniel provides some hints on this:

> During the first year she responded quite well at first to my caress, and then, and then she won't let me touch her again, and I think her mother had been speaking to her or something, I really don't know what her mother had said, but I suspect she said something to her, and she said Mummy said I mustn't, not till I'm 7. She must have been 6 at the time. So I said, well, can't we pretend you're 7? She said, O.K., and so we pretended she was 7, and she used to mount the bed and lift her nightie up for me, and her sister asked me to do the same to her once or twice, but she didn't seem particularly keen, so I didn't pursue the matter. ... They didn't do anything to me – well, they used to unzip my trousers, and say let's have a look at his willie, and unzip my trousers, and pull my penis out, and put it back again – didn't do anything, you know, more than that – it's just – er – curiosity. [Researcher: Did they enjoy it?] Well, the older sister asked the younger one what was it like, and she said all right, but the tone of her voice was definitely one of pleasure, the phrase all right can mean a variety of things, the way she said it tells me that it means it was good.

George talked about his spanking activities with his girl friends as 'play' – it was all 'good-natured fun'. He talked about the girls being amused and excited, as well as pleased that they were the ones he wanted to *play* with. As spelled out earlier, their sessions often followed a clear pattern – a set of 'the rules of the game'. The episode quoted in Section 11.1.3 above illustrates the playfulness of the interaction, from both George's as well as the girl's view – they argued and fought over the detail of the proceedings, and carried them out in a style akin to the conduct of a ritual, which was all part of the fun.[11]

[11] It is important to note that to George, these spanking activities with his girl friends

The following quotation from Keith summarises the fascination that childhood play can arouse in some paedophiles:

> Children get involved in sex with each other, because they don't feel it's wrong, you see, now you can meet a child and you can say to a child, should we play doctors and nurses or whatever, and they know what you're talking about, and they do it to each other, sometimes they are willing to do it with an adult. ... I suppose, you can say that I'm slightly immature, haven't lost my childhood, ... childhood is a very very short sort of time in your life, goes too quickly, and it's very sweet, you know, it's all innocent. ... You know, you do things which you don't do as an adult, I mean, if you're a child, you can take your clothes off and plunge into a river, to swim, you're quite free, you have no inhibitions, but if you strip off, as an adult, you get arrested.

As this quotation from Keith shows, the experience of playful sexual contact with children may be associated with a desire to remain in childhood. A related observation is that growing up into the adult world is condemned by some informants as a process through which innocent children become selfish individuals, after which spontaneous human relationships become impossible (see Section 11.1.1 above). Indeed some informants expressed the feeling that they have not, and do not want to be, grown up, for instance:

> I'd never grown up. Sexually I have remained in childhood, but have never once regretted it. I'd always been a child in that sense. (George)

11.2.3 The hedonism model

The cardinal feature of the accounts subsumed by the hedonism model is the seeking of pleasure. While it is possible to argue that every human activity is pleasure-seeking (if not explicitly, then in the long run or indirectly), the notion of hedonism is used in the present context to refer to the seeking of immediate physical-bodily pleasure – the pleasure of sexual orgasm. Within this hedonism model, two varieties can be construed: substitute sex, and sexual liberation.

Substitute sex

A number of informants in this study admitted that their sexual involvement with children was purely a matter of substitute sex for physical release – they wanted children because either the latter were more easily available or peers proved difficult to relate to.

Contact with children which can be subsumed under this model tends to show the following characteristics: (1) a matter of using the child's body as a means of obtaining sexual release: (2) ejaculatory orgasm as the

---

were in themselves fully satisfying to him – he did not need to masturbate or ejaculate either during the session or afterwards.

ultimate goal; (3) a substitution for adult sexual relationships which could not be obtained – a matter of 'easy sex'.

A vivid example of this mentality can be found in Adrian. To him, his desire for children was the same as his desire for food when he was hungry. He could not get women, but children were just as good. Masturbation with children gave him the feeling of being satisfied, like a full stomach after a meal.

Sexual liberation

As mentioned before, there are informants in this study who have articulated a libertarian view on sexual activities with children – sex is for pleasure, and children can have such pleasure with adults, so there is no reason why they should be excluded. While Jack and Joe had explicitly articulated an 'educational' justification for adult-child sex, Bruce and Simon had pointed out the culturally or historically conditioned nature of human sexual practices, and used this as the legitimation for their sexual involvement with children. These informants condemned the sexually repressive atmosphere of western culture, and rejected the conventional norm of adult heterosexuality. Bruce, Jack, Joe, and Martin are not paedophile in the sense of being attracted to children exclusively. Sex with children is part of their permissive sexual lifestyle – they enjoy sex with children as they do with adults. Their anti-repression stance is clear: free sex should be free for all.

Perhaps Martin's remark can best sum up this hedonistic view: 'I suppose I'm just an immoral sod, I just don't say "no" to any attractive female!'

11.2.4 The love model

Many of the informants in this study talked about the experience of love, affection, or closeness with children. The sense of emotional contact with another human person is as important as, if not actually more important than, the excitement of sex. In this context, three varieties of 'love' can be discerned: a broadly defined sense of emotional bond, the fascination with teenage love, and a fully-fledged notion of romantic love similar to that of conventional heterosexual courtship.

Emotional contact

Daniel talked about his feeling of emotional deprivation after his wife left him, and his strong need for an emotional bond with somebody. He felt he was 'in love with' younger and younger girls, from a 16-year-old, to a 9-year-old and eventually to some 6-year-olds. Matthew had also talked about his need to be in the company of children when he felt that his 'love life was inadequate'. To him, even just chatting with a child was already very satisfying, he had no need to touch children sexually. If he did touch them, it was not a sexual touch that could provide him with the kind of satisfaction that intercourse would give, rather it was a matter of being close to someone. Similarly, Vincent had talked about the wonderful feeling that children's affection could give him – a feeling of 'being needed'.

These three informants were in search of close human contact – although such a quest was the result of relationship problems, it was not a matter of sexual substitution, but an expression of emotional needs. Children are affectionate, they often make these emotionally starved adults feel wanted and happy.

Parental feelings. This need for emotional contact is sometimes expressed in terms of parental protectiveness, fatherly love, or even 'maternal' feelings. For example, Matthew had talked about feeling 'fatherly' when he wanted to touch a girl.

Although Ben's paedophilic relationships can best be characterised by the courtship model (see below), he has nevertheless also expressed a feeling of being 'parental' to his boy partners:

> My attitude towards my boys is a combination of the two things, the two parents. On the one hand, I can see from my mother's side that I'm possessive and perhaps over-protective, and from both of them really the fact that I do like cooking, cleaning and all the parental things, I want to display the fact that I'm doing things for them, I want to look after them.

Even Keith, whose attraction towards children was more a matter of pleasure-seeking, did talk about some sort of parental feeling for children:

> You see, there's an adult, and there's a child, you can pick the child up and you can cuddle it, and you can do a lot more with it, sort of, sort of a maternal thing, you know, with an adult you can't, I mean you can't. ... With a woman you can't baby-talk, I mean you can talk to a child, you know, talk to the child, like a father.

In the case of Simon, he was actually very proud of being seen as a father-figure by many of the boys he had sexual contact with. He was proud of his ability to provide them with what they could not get from their own fathers:

> Very, very few boys can relate to their father. There are very few boys that have a good honest relationship with their father. They haven't got the relationship with their father to tell him anything and everything. But they would come to a stranger, or a friend, and this is where I come in. I can talk, and I never talk down to a boy. I always talk to a boy on his own level, as far as it's humanly possible. And gradually, those boys would come to trust me, and they do realise that if I say, or promise a thing, or promise not to do a thing, then they know they can trust me – the building up of that trust is very, very important.

One last example is Daniel. Daniel construed paedophilia in terms of evolutionarily advantageous surrogate parenthood. He felt it is possible for a man to make such a contribution:

> I think men are intrinsically more gentle than they might pretend to be. ... I think men can be as gentle as women. Men can also care for babies – mm – apart from the fact that men haven't got the necessary attribute to feed young babies, men can still care for them.

Regarding his own feelings, he said:

> Some children I may, I may feel sort of caring – er – would wish to protect them and care for them more than I wish to have sex with them – mm – but there was a tendency to sort of start feeling sexually aroused to the child.

Thus to Daniel, and these other informants, paedophilic activities are intimately *enmeshed* with their parental feelings towards children.

Young love

As discussed in the last chapter, Nick's explanation for his paedophilic orientation is 'starvation of love plus anti-adult attitude'. He could only experience love when he was relating to boys. However, although he felt he was homosexual, he nevertheless wanted to see a boy and a girl make love, and to join in to partake of this love, because, in his words, 'young love is the most beautiful'. This sentiment was shared by Bruce, whose desire for a relationship with a young girl can be characterised by a yearning to return to the stage of a teenager, and to go through a period of adolescent romance which he had missed when he was growing up. His current fantasy is a romantic-erotic encounter with a 12-year-old girl (a 'Lolita'), despite the fact that he has a woman sexual partner. He described his feelings as no different from that of an adolescent boy who was involved in a love affair.

Romantic courtship

Young love is romantic, but still it has the connotation of being an 'experiment'. Courtship, however, is serious and evokes the image of a long-term relationship. From the various descriptions given by these informants,[12] the following features are identified, which can best be subsumed by the model of romantic courtship:

(1) Paedophilia is a relationship or partnership, not a casual encounter.

(2) Love and affection constitutes a central component: intense emotions are often involved, such as a sense of beauty or a feeling of 'falling in love'.

---

[12] These descriptions have already been discussed earlier in this and the last chapter, see

(3) There is a mutual recognising and accommodating of each other's needs – an altruism to do things for each other to foster the growth of love.

(4) The partners have the ability to sense and understand subtle feelings or cues from each other.

(5) Faithfulness to the partner is valued; sometimes this is associated with a desire for 'virginity' or feelings of jealousy.

(6) The interaction is characterised by spontaneity and a lack of self-consciousness.

(7) Sex is not the only ingredient but a very important one.

(8) It is a relationship with a *particular* person, not a class of individuals.

However, in applying the courtship model to understand particular instances of adult-child sexual relationship, the following caveats have to be kept in mind:

(1) While sex is not the only ingredient in such a relationship, it is sometimes the case that non-sexual activities are not always fulfilling, e.g. Ben found that he could not always communicate with his boys on a level that was commensurate with his own intellectual capacity, thus his fantasy of a partner with a mind of a 30-year-old but the body of a 13-year-old. Although this was only a spur-of-the-moment fantasy, it did convey the strain in adult-child love relationships despite the rosy picture of romantic courtship.

(2) While the adult may experience the relationship as courtship, the child might not see it this way. A paedophile telling a boy that he loved him could confuse the boy because to the boy the relationship might simply be an extension of the sort of things he was doing with his friends. Bruce acknowledged that while he wanted a love relationship with a pubescent girl, the girl might approach the relationship only out of curiosity. But even so, these informants felt that this would not detract from their relationships the experience of mutual affection and love.

11.3 Discourse analysis

While the four models discussed in the last section are constructed for the interpretation of the informants' experiences on a personal-psychological level, they can also be articulated in the form of social discourses that pervade modern society.

A discourse is here defined as a complex of social practices and statements about these practices which have the power to shape people's consciousness, their daily life, and the social production of what counts as knowledge/truth. In the following discussion, the relevant parts of the

---

particularly Section 11.1.6 above. Quotations will not be repeated here.

informants' accounts will be systematised to illustrate the discourses which form an organic whole as the complex of social practices that are subsumed under the notion of 'sexuality' – a complex that effects the social regulation of the human body. This discourse of sexuality provides the socio-cultural context in which the explanatory accounts of my informants have developed.[13]

11.3.1 The male sex drive discourse

The *primacy* of the male sex drive has been clearly articulated by a number of informants. For example, Adrian insisted that he *had* a sex drive that must be satisfied – if not one way, then another. A similar view was expressed by Matthew:

> The last eleven years of my life with my first wife – I didn't have any sexual experiences with her at all. Being a normal sort of person at the time, I went elsewhere for my pleasures, and I had a few affairs, which she didn't know very much about, but I wasn't particularly worried whether she knew or not, because I wasn't getting my sex at home, so I went elsewhere for it. I was in my late 20s, early 30s – that was the time when I needed to have sex.

> When you're making love to another woman who you're having an affair with, it doesn't matter a damn whether you satisfy her or not, as long as you satisfy yourself.

Matthew had made it clear that 'as a normal person' he needed his 'sexual pleasures' – as Adrian said, he would not let himself be 'deprived of' such pleasures. Implicit in this conception of the male sex drive is the primacy of orgasmic *ejaculation*. For instance, Keith remarked that the 'ultimate thing' of sex is to ejaculate, without which its aim would be defeated.

The conception of the male sex drive as something natural, something that must be satisfied, and something that is 'unstoppable', has permeated the consciousness of a lot of people in our society.[14] Although it is not possible to postulate a causal link between this discourse of male sex drive and adult sexual interest in children, it is no doubt that such a discourse has provided a context in which some adults can justify their paedophilic involvement.

11.3.2 The masculinity discourse

Closely associated with the conception of the primacy of the male sex

---

[13] This discussion is an attempt to highlight the socio-structural substrate of the informants' construction – to that extent, it will overlap considerably with what has been said in the last section.

[14] See Hollway (1984).

drive is the 'macho' image of masculinity.[15] 'Being male' means to be the boss. The other side of the same coin is 'being male' is to be able to perform sexually. Such a requirement has put great pressure on many men:

> I feel that I owe it to [my second wife], to make love to her, to give her a full sexual life. I think I do miss having sex with her, I mean, we still go through the motions, and play together, you know, but when it comes to having intercourse, that's not possible. I don't feel I'm doing my job, (laughs) I'm – er – just playing with my hands, I feel inadequate. Though my wife said she's satisfied, I still feel that – er – I'm less than a man if I can't. (Matthew)

The demand for a man to be sexually capable is focussed on his penis – it is no good producing orgasm in the partner by hands, the 'authentic' organ has to be involved.[16] Matthew had commented that his two years in the army were the best time of his life, and he regretted not having pursued it as a career. He liked very much the discipline and the tough training of army life, and had an abiding interest in weaponry. Probably the army, as a symbol of 'the masculine', has had a lasting effect on Matthew's perception of himself.

Another aspect of this masculine image is that a man must be depended on by females. Because Eugene felt he could not fulfil his 'duty' of looking after his girlfriend, since she was too independent, he turned to pubescent girls, with whom he could find fulfilment in this regard.

11.3.3 The discourse of normative heterosexuality

Heterosexuality is to most people the only normal form of human sexual behaviour. As pointed out in Chapter 8, such a discourse underlies most of the academic work on sexual deviance. The pervasiveness of this discourse can be observed even in a paedophile exclusively attracted to boys – Ben:

> Whatever else you see it, you have to see it as an aberration, if only because, no matter what society, or at what state of history you look at, OK, there are many many instances of sex with boys, but they are never the life-long or conclusive experiences of people, yeah? Mm – even in societies and even at times of history where sex with boys has been acceptable, socially acceptable, it has generally only been as an intermediate stage before marriage, yeah? And if you look at history, if you read Roman and Greek history and mythology, if you consider the attitudes of Arabs, Turks, Afghans, some portions of the Far East, where at various times or at various places, sex with boys was acceptable, it's only acceptable within certain limitations, not as a life-long condition, OK? So that certainly, I consider it,

[15] In a study of men's erotic fantasies, Crépault & Couture (1980) found that sexual power and aggressiveness constitute a dominant component of their respondents' sexual fantasies.
[16] Keith's anxiety about the size of his penis can also be understood within this masculinity discourse.

in the context of being a life-long condition, to be an aberration. ... Let's face it, it necessitates, it is the human condition that necessitates heterosexual relationships, otherwise the human race comes to an end, right? Therefore, the natural activity must be heterosexual.

The normative status given to the biological imperative of procreation is, as illustrated here, the basis of the discourse of heterosexuality. It is also what underlies the concept of sexual normalcy propounded by some psychoanalysts.[17] The normative demand of heterosexuality is so deeply rooted in people's consciousness that quite a number of my informants feel that because they have paedophilic leanings, however natural these feelings are, there must be 'something wrong' with them.

11.3.4 The romantic love discourse

Romantic love and courtship is a persistent ideal which generation after generation of young (and not-so-young) people are pursuing. As discussed earlier, the accounts of some informants in this study can best be understood in the context of this romantic courtship discourse.

In the experience of Edward, the effect of this discourse proved to be strong enough to produce a conflict of 'love *vs* lust' in his conscience. The following quotation shows how he portrayed the 'ideology of love':

What is love? I do not think it is anything I felt for John.[18] As I said before my feeling for John was lust. Of that I am sure. Love would be something else entirely. What? I do not know. If I did love John then I would not have wanted to harm him in any way. I would not have taken his clothes off and played with his organs. In fact if I did love John then I would have kept my hands off him and tried to get him to see me as a friend and, with hope, try to turn his friendship for me into love, so that in time he would have been the one to make the first sexual advances when he was ready, and knew what he was doing. ... What is love? I do not know. I know one thing, no matter how long the waiting, true love would not invade a person's privacy, no matter how much you want to have sex with him or her, you would not do so if the other had said 'no'. Therefore because I persisted in being intimate sexually with John, even after he had asked me to stop, means that I could not have truly loved him. I am not implying that love and sex are not one, when both partners love each other, then sex is one aspect of that love.

The discourse of love sanctions against lust. The corollary of this, however, is that love justifies a sexual relationship, even that between an adult and a child, as some informants have argued. Thus we can see the discourse of love acts in two directions: it discourages paedophilic involvement in some people, but encourages it in others.

---

[17] See discussion on Karpman in Section 8.1.1 above.
[18] John was the 12-year-old boy Edward had sexual contact with.

11.3.5 The discourse of 'the permissive society'

Opposite to the discourse of love is the discourse of permissiveness, where *pleasure* is the norm. A permissive and libertarian view on sex has been articulated by a number of informants in this study. The key arguments are cultural plurality and ethical relativism. The slogan of this position is anti-repression and sexual liberation of every individual. Sex is good, in whatever form and between any partners, provided that they engage in it willingly. This is construed as the only rational and intellectually respectable position to adopt. This discourse of 'the permissive society' has shown itself in the sexual revolution of the 'swinging sixties', and the thriving sexological industry in the western world. The following quotation from Bruce is an *apologia* for paedophilia constructed on the basis of this 'permissive society' discourse:

> My contention is that an adult can have a relationship with a child in a way that does not harm, and indeed helps, the child. I consider myself to be an adult capable of such a relationship. Other adults might be more selfish in an adult-child encounter and end up harming the child. By banning and stigmatising adult-child encounters, our society has ensured that such instances as do still occur are almost always of the bad kind, so giving the active opponents of child-adult encounters an argument for even heavier clampdown. If adult-child sex was commonplace, the majority of it would surely be good for both participants and, therefore, not something to be discouraged. Indeed, because the adult would be able to teach the child from an informed standpoint, many of the childhood misunderstandings about sex that come from child-child encounters would be avoided. I would regard child-child sex as being less preferable to child-adult sex, provided the present stigma were removed from the latter. ... To discuss role confusion resulting from a father-daughter relationship, I find I have to come back to the question of norms and values. Of course it will be harmful if everybody starts off with the belief that it is bad. However, if all concerned were to regard it as normal, then the stress would occur if it *didn't* happen! It is essential to realise the importance of the cultural norm in all these situations. I hate to labour the point, but, just as with my comments above, the 'problem' is created by our society's present attitude.

Bruce is not unaware of the occurrence of child molestation in society – he acknowledges that some adult-child sexual contact is harmful and 'bad'. Nevertheless, he insists that this should not rule out the possibility of beneficial adult-child sex. Indeed, he has attributed the prominence of the 'bad' cases to precisely the suppression of adult-child sex by society. Complete permissiveness is taken to be the solution to the problem.

11.3.6 The locus of action of discourses

The material gathered in this study is not sufficient for the identification of the locus of action of the sexuality discourses that shape the accounts of the informants. Nevertheless, one locus of operation that can be identified is the institution of professional therapy.

The psychoanalytic therapy that both Robert and Vincent have received seems to be responsible for shaping their interpretation of their sexual desire for children. Their tendency to 'psychologise' their desire in terms of repressive upbringing and unresolved adolescent complex has been observed. The underlying assumption of such psychoanalytic explanations is the normativeness of adult genital heterosexuality, which both Robert and Vincent are working towards through therapy.

The influence of non-psychoanalytic psychiatric practice can be seen in the case of Andy. In the following quotation, Andy is talking about his experience with aversion therapy:

> I'm really trying to cut boys out and going on to girls, but it's a hard fight. ... I'd probably see a boy of about 10 or 11, and I'd say to myself – mm – he's all right, but I'm thinking, if I did anything – this is what I think it out, so I don't recommit a crime – if I touched him, I'd go back to prison,[19] so from that point of view, prison is at the back of my mind all the time. ... I said I don't want to know the boys, I don't want pictures of little boys [in aversion therapy], I want pictures of big boys, he [i.e. the psychiatrist] goes why, and I explain to him that, the way I'm going, you know, if I get ready to leave prison, you know, it's been no good for me because I've been just thinking of little boys all the time, I said if you give me the pictures of men only, and see how that affects me. I was doing this course about two years, and it worked, when he did show me pictures of small boys, I got no reaction at all. ... So, anyway, that way worked, now when I left prison, and come here, I'd done relaxation courses, so if I did feel over-wrought – 'cause when I first left prison I began to feel over-wrought and I wanted to do it with kids – when I say kids I mean kids, and I knew that I was doing wrong, I told [the psychiatrist] this, then I went up and I saw a psychologist, and he gave me a tape-recorder to listen to, so when, when I did feel over-wrought, I could do a relaxation course, and it worked perfectly. Now I got no trouble, no trouble at all. I may think about it every now and then, but I quickly switch it off – like this, four boys walking down the road, I just thought no, don't, and just switch it all off, and walk, and carrying on walking – it worked.

The example of Andy shows the power of social institutions like psychiatry in forcing a change, even if it might just be short-term, in an individual's construction of his sexuality. It is through such social institutions that discourses of a normative sexuality find their expression.

11.4 Towards a broader perspective

Sexuality is not only concerned with the body and physical pleasure, but also with various social institutions, customs and mores, such as reproduction, parenthood, the family, health, and even aesthetics. The

---

[19] Andy had spent many years in a special hospital in England for the custody of offenders committed to psychiatric treatment.

emergence of the taboo on sex was intimately tied to the broader development of society from the medieval period to the modern era.[20]

Foucault (1979) has used the concept 'discourse of sexuality' to describe the complex of social practices that emerged in nineteenth-century Europe in relation to the 'disciplining' of the human body.[21] According to his analysis, sex, far from being meticulously repressed, had actually emerged as the dominant theme in nineteenth-century social life in Europe in the form of this sexuality discourse. Through the work of the medical profession, this discourse took on the respectable cloak of *scientia sexualis*, the science of sex. Knowledge on sex was produced, accumulated and became accepted 'truth', which in turn shaped the practices of the people. The discussion on sex, specifically the control of children's and women's sexuality, preoccupied both the educated elites and the common folk. Childhood sexual activities, especially masturbation, were considered a source of physical and moral, as well as individual and social danger; hence parents, teachers, doctors and psychologists were entrusted with the task of preventing them. Their efforts, closely related to the deployment of the school (with its rigid time-table, rules and discipline) in the organisation of children's life, constituted a 'pedagogisation' of children's sexuality.[22] On the other hand, the female body was seen as saturated with a 'pathological' sexuality, which was nevertheless integrated into the social fabric through childbearing and motherhood. The woman was denied a sex life. Yet the view that the female body was saturated with sexuality also enabled the emergence of the dichotomised image of 'Eve *vs* Madonna', and the practice of the double standard of allowing widespread prostitution for the service of the nineteenth-century gentleman. As the female body was 'hysterised' to the sole function of childbearing, so was sexual behaviour (at least within the matrimonial bedroom) 'socialised' in accordance with the fluctuating need to increase or decrease the birth rate. The regulation of procreation and of the size of the population became part of the 'science of the state' – statistics.

The medicalisation of sexuality is most clearly seen in the 'psychiatrisation' of perverse pleasure, whereby deviations from genital heterosexuality were 'pathologised' and classified under elaborate nosological schemes, and the medical practitioner called in to effect cures

---

[20] In this connection, the most frequently cited work is Ariès (1962), which shows that during the Middle Ages, the concept of childhood as a special developmental period was virtually non-existent, and children participated actively in adult social life. Sexuality was not a taboo subject, and sex play between adults and children was neither uncommon nor always scandalising. However, with the advent of rationalism and moralism in the seventeenth and eighteenth century, the gentry class in Europe began to build up a concept of childhood as a period of innocence and moral vulnerability, to be defended against the corrupting influences of adult life, among which sex was a most dangerous one.

[21] The theme of the 'disciplinary' society has been more fully discussed in an earlier work by Foucault (1977).

[22] This discussion of Foucault's analysis is based on Foucault (1979), as well as the exposition of Foucault's work by Sheridan (1980).

for such maladies. Psychoanalysis, with its preoccupation with sex, began to establish a system of 'truths' about human sexuality, through the production of knowledge in the form of case histories constructed by the analyst after interminable hours of 'analysis' with the patient. Such a method of knowledge/truth production belongs to the same *genre* as the Catholic confessional through which the penitent has to recount in minute detail his or her every thought, feeling and act related to sex (the sin of pleasure), thereby receiving absolution from the priest – in much the same way as a patient receives supposedly curative interpretations from the psychoanalyst. This technique of confession was not confined to the psychoanalytic profession and Christendom, but spread to a whole series of relationships – parents and children, teachers and students, doctors and patients as well as officials and delinquents. Far from being put out of sight, sexuality was in fact made highly visible in the nineteenth century.

According to Foucault, the control of the masses by the powers that be had hitherto been in the form of the threat of death – an application of naked force to kill. But beginning in the seventeenth and eighteenth century, a different set of strategies began to evolve – the machinery of discipline (the school, the prison, the military, etc.) and the machinery of sexuality (the control of the body). The pedagogisation of children's sexual behaviour, the hysterisation of the female body, the socialisation of procreation and the psychiatrisation of perverse pleasure were the four 'strategies of sexuality' constituting the disciplinary and control network over the human person (body). The law and the medical profession were partners in the pathologisation of sexual activities other than adult heterosexuality, rendering them within the purview of the criminal justice system, penal management agencies and treatment professionals. Sexual deviance was objectivised, named, given an aetiology and eventually associated with crime. Not only is 'sexual deviance' thus constituted as a distinct, 'real' category, the taken-for-granted 'truths' about sex, such as masculinity-femininity, the primacy of the male sex drive, or the normative nature of heterosexuality, have also emerged through the discourse of sexuality, within which individual persons are defined and confined.

The analysis of Foucault shows that sex was not repressed in the nineteenth century, rather, it was transformed by a discourse of sexuality. What then is the reality of the sexual revolution of the twentieth century, if there is no sexual repression to revolt against? The present-day boom in the sexological industry (self-help guides,[23] sex therapies, training workshops, etc.) can be traced back through Masters and Johnson, Kinsey, Havelock Ellis, Reich, and finally to Freud. On the surface, it is a reaction against Victorian prudery and repression, but actually it is a continuation of 'the course laid out by the general

---

[23] Examples of sexological self-help manuals: Cauthery, Stanway & Stanway (1983), Comfort (1972, 1974), Meeks & Heit (1982), Read (1979) and Zilbergeld (1979).

deployment of sexuality'[24] and as such, is an expression of the disciplining of the human body *via* the discourse of sexual revolution. In his analysis of the twentieth-century sexual revolution, Stephen Heath (1982) has argued that instead of liberating men and women from the supposed repression they have inherited from the previous century, this 'revolution' has actually subjected the human person to a new tyranny – the tyranny of the orgasm. The sexological enterprise, with its myriad stock of techniques and remedies, proclaims itself, in the context of the permissiveness discourse, the saviour of the 'sexually frustrated', the 'sexually repressed' and the 'sexually ignorant', and offers them a life of sexual bliss. In addition to the four strategies of sexuality identified by Foucault, the twentieth-century sexual revolution has added a fifth – the idealisation of the orgasm. In the last century the problem was 'you have a sex life'; in this century the problem becomes 'you lack a good sex life' – but no worry, sexology can fix it. Indeed sexology has 'fixed' it – it has created a sexual order within which every individual or every sexual act is fixed according to the hierarchy headed by the highest norm, the orgasm. Everybody must get his or her orgasm, this is a natural right. One should try various techniques, partners, positions, accessories – indeed anything or any activity that might turn one on. No one should be deprived of a share of the goal of life – orgasm. In exchanging the 'chains of repression' for 'sexual freedom', the sexologically inspired revolution has created another form of tyranny over the human body.

Seen in the context of this analysis, both the personal accounts of the 'paedophile' informants discussed above and the academic theories on child sexual abuse summarised in Chapter 8 can be understood as different manifestations of the sexuality discourse. The discourse of *heterosexuality* has not only provided a normative basis for the orthodox view of 'paedophilia as pathology', but also shaped the articulation of personal construction by individuals who want to justify adult-child sexual relationships. Although some of these individuals attempt to break away from the norm of heterosexuality, their libertarian hedonism is still governed by the logic of the sexuality discourse, albeit a 'permissive' one, and will therefore play a part in the control of the human body.

[24] Foucault (1979), p. 157.

12

Conclusion: the Question of Ethics

12.1 Recapitulation

This study is concerned with adult sexual experiences with children. It tries to describe the world within which men who feel sexually attracted to children conduct their lives. Its central aim is 'to give voice to the viewpoint of the paedophile'[1] – we must first of all listen, then we can attempt to build up an understanding of these people's lives.

As discussed in Chapter 10, sexual desire for children is construed by the informants of this study as:

(1) an inborn disposition,
(2) a part of normal human sexuality,
(3) a continuation of childhood sexuality, and
(4) a consequence of difficulty in adult relationships.

While most of the informants' explanations do not contain the assumption of abnormality or pathology, that is not to say that their accounts are all positive and optimistic – some informants' accounts convey a sense of ambivalence, particularly those who saw their sexual involvement with children as a consequence of difficulty in adult relationships.[2] Nevertheless, even in these cases, the informants did not feel that their desire for children was abnormal. For instance, Daniel affirmed that to him paedophilia was a positive and beneficial adaptation, Bruce argued that it was *in itself* a desirable form of human sexuality, and George, Nick, Edward as well as Keith, while acknowledging difficulty in relating to adults, had nevertheless expressed the view that involvement with children was what suited them best and what they wanted most.

In contrast to the biological models constructed by academic researchers, those informants who felt that they were born this way did not see their disposition as a biological anomaly, but rather as something

[1] Plummer (1981b), p. 132.
[2] Their accounts resemble the 'substitution' hypothesis put forth by Storr, they also seem to agree with the observation made by Howells that paedophiles tend to perceive children as more approachable (see Chapter 8 above).

304

natural and hence normal.[3] Of the five informants who hold this view, only Ben and Tom have expressed some doubt about the normality of their disposition, and that was a result of social pressure.

In contrast, all the academic/professional models discussed earlier see adult-child sexual contact, including paedophilia, incest and child molestation, as pathological. The psychoanalytic, biological and behavioural perspectives tend to construe it as an individual or intra-psychic aberration, while the family system approach and Finkelhor's multifactor model extend the notion of abnormality to cover networks of relationships. The feminist perspective, while treating adult-child sexual contact as always an expression of patriarchal oppression and exploitation of females and hence a political issue of power imbalance between the sexes, also implies that it is one form of pathology, not of an individual, but rather of all male individuals and their social institutions. The construction of adult-child sexual contact in terms of abnormality and pathology dominates both academic research and professional practice. More liberal views such as those advocated by Bernard (1985), Brongersma (1984), Plummer (1981a, 1981b), or Ullerstam (1967), although all respectable professionals, can only occupy a marginal place in the growing literature on the subject, not to say the work of professed paedophiles such as Moody (1980) and O'Carroll (1980).

However, the personal accounts and the academic accounts are not entirely disparate. One common factor lies in the discourse of the normative status of adult heterosexuality. Implicit in virtually all academic-professional models is the notion that adult heterosexuality is the standard of sexual normality. The effect of this discourse can also be observed in the informants' accounts: quite a number of them have construed their sexual interest in children either as a result of *failing* to achieve this heterosexual standard, or as a form of courtship *resembling* heterosexual love.

From the analysis of the informants' accounts, I have put forward the thesis that these individuals are, like the rest of us, trying to build a meaningful world in which to place their existence, that they are not necessarily obsessed with sex, and that they are, again like the rest of us, subject to the discipline of the sexuality discourse. The ideal world for the 'paedophile' is one in which adults are not excluded from childhood play, romantic love not confined to age-peers, and pleasure as well as permissiveness are the guiding principles. Perhaps some researchers can find in the personal accounts collected in this study evidence to 'pathologise' the individuals concerned, but the effort to reduce a person's life to a diagnostic category will mask the complexity of human experience.

The picture painted here is inevitably circumscribed by the kind of

---

[3]Even in the case of Daniel, whose 'sociobiological' account resembles that proposed by Wilson & Cox (1983), paedophilia is seen as *adaptational* rather than pathological.

informants obtained in the study. Since I have not interviewed any violent offenders who have assaulted, raped, or murdered children, my construction might tend towards a more positive depiction of paedophilia. The statistical picture presented in the literature, as discussed in Chapter 7, points to a very different conclusion. By virtue of the nomothetic nature of statistics, it is expected that personal experiences, such as those analysed here, will become masked by the frightening figures of incidence and prevalence rates. These statistics are used to support the construction of 'dangerousness' of the phenomenon of child sexual abuse as a whole as well as of *every* individual 'child molester' – as one recent report in the *Sunday Observer* suggested, 'child molesters cannot be left alone' (Rance & Lloyd, 1986).

Statistics tend to blur the difference between violent assaults on children and consensual paedophilic activities. The question of whether or not adult-child sexual contact is ethically acceptable hinges on a clarification of this difference.

12.2 The debate on ethics

As a comparison of two opposite positions regarding the question of the ethical acceptability of adult-child sexual contact, the work of David Finkelhor and of Tom O'Carroll will be discussed here.

12.2.1 The 'inability to consent' argument

The following points constitute the crux of Finkelhor's (1979b, 1984) argument:

(1) Children and adolescents do not possess the necessary knowledge regarding sexual relationships, so they cannot make any informed decision about such relationships.

(2) Children and adolescents are not truly free in relation to adults since they are always taught to obey adults from infancy onwards – they are unable to resist demands from adults.

Given these two assertions, children must of necessity be looked upon as incapable of giving free and informed consent to engage in sexual contact with adults[4] – and as consent is the foundation for any sexual relationship, sexual contact between adults and children must of necessity be regarded as unethical and wrong. This 'inability to consent' proposition is formulated in such a way as to make the rejection of adult-child sexual contact independent of the empirical question of whether or not such contact is harmful to children.

The first difficulty with Finkelhor's proposition is that whether

---

[4] 'Children, by their nature, are incapable of truly consenting to sex with adults. Because they are children, they cannot consent; they can never consent' (Finkelhor, 1979b, p. 649). In his 1984 book, Finkelhor has included adolescents within this formulation.

children and adolescents have knowledge about sexual relationships is precisely an empirical question. Children do not turn into adults overnight, they develop gradually and continuously. It would be irrational to define categorically all children and adolescents as lacking in knowledge about sexual matters. Information about sex accumulates as the child grows up, rather than being bestowed upon him when he reaches an arbitrary age of consent. How much sexual knowledge an individual (whether child or adult) has is a question that cannot be settled by any *a priori* principle. Moreover, there is a related difficulty of how much knowledge one needs to have before one is permitted to engage in sexual relationships. Probably many ordinary adults do not have much knowledge about sex, but nobody would want to restrict their sexual freedom.

Likewise, whether children and adolescents are always subservient to adults is an empirical rather than a logical issue. It is necessary for researchers to venture into the childhood world to find out if children are sometimes able to circumvent what adults are trying to do to them. Of course it is not suggested here that all children are capable of resisting adult demands, the point is rather that not all children are *incapable* of resisting adult encroachment. In short, Finkelhor's two arguments are neither necessarily nor logically true. Far from succeeding in disentangling the ethical question from the kind of empirical contingencies that he wants to avoid, Finkelhor has only incurred more empirical problems by his proposal.

While there is common agreement that the notion of 'consent' should form the basis of sexual relationship between two people, it must be pointed out that even in adult relationships, consent is rarely explicitly disussed, let alone the question of the adequacy of each partner's knowledge of sex. Rather, an intimate relationship involves a great deal of intuition and tacit understanding.[5] A related problem is that even in many adult relationships, the ideal of informed consent simply does not obtain. While acknowledging this difficulty, Finkelhor asserts that children 'as a class' are powerless, and so for them special protection, in the form of a benevolent paternalism, is needed.[6] The question is, however, whether power is necessarily associated with the commission of unethical acts. It is conceivable that a powerless person can commit a wrongful act towards a powerful person – the 'wrongfulness' of the act has nothing *inherently* to do with the possession (or otherwise) of power. The argument that children as a class are powerless vis-à-vis adults and hence in need of special protection from sexual activities with the latter is only tenable if such activities are *assumed* to be either wrong or *found* to be damaging to the children concerned. To make the first assumption begs the question because the present discussion is precisely on whether such activities are wrong. The second possibility concerns an empirical

---

[5] As some informants of this study have argued, the notion of consent in paedophilia has to be understood in the context of continuing relationships, see Section 11.1.7.

[6] See Finkelhor (1984), p. 19.

issue which Finkelhor does not want to include in his moral position. Thus his difficulty of having to *assume* the wrongness of adult-child sexual contact remains.

Furthermore, Finkelhor argues that because sex is so emotion-laden a domain in human life, sexual contact with adults will lead to long-term stigmatisation of the children involved. This is complementary to the argument put up by Abel, Becker & Cunningham-Rathner (1984) that if the child is aware of the sexual standards of society and the likely consequences of his decision, he will not truly consent to engage in sexual activities with an adult. The assumption here is that current sexual standards of society and social reactions to adult-child sexual contact are proper and should not be challenged. However, many paedophiles have argued that such stigmatisation arises precisely because society has mystified sex and has reacted to paedophilia irrationally and hysterically, thus turning sex into an unnecessarily emotion-laden subject. The observation about stigmatisation could thus be used as an argument for liberalisation, contrary to Finkelhor's position. While the question about the child's knowledge of the likely social consequences of his or her sexual involvement with an adult is an important *practical* question, it does not logically rule out the possibility of consensual paedophilia.

Finally, there is a certain circularity in Finkelhor's argument, which can be depicted as follows: wrongness of adult-child sex assumed → children in need of special protection → paternalism desirable → socialisation under paternalism desirable → children lack knowledge/ freedom with respect to sexuality → inability to consent → therefore adult-child sex is wrong. Finkelhor has not considered the possibility of actually teaching children about sex and giving them the freedom to choose if they want to become involved with adults sexually. To reject this possibility, Finkelhor has to claim either that such sexual involvement is damaging to the child's development or that it is intrinsically bad, or both – that is, he has to resort to the circular argument again.

12.2.2 Paedophilia: 'the radical case'

The pro-paedophilia position often makes use of two arguments: childhood sexuality and cultural relativism.

Since sexual behaviour is cross-culturally diverse, and since adult-child sexual contact is not uncommon in many cultures, such contact cannot, so the argument goes, be taken as intrinsically pathological.[7] If human

[7] The most frequently quoted work on cross-cultural analysis of human sexual behaviour is that of Ford & Beach (1952) who made use of the vast Human Relation Area Files of Yale University to study sexual activities in nearly 200 human societies, most of which were non-western, non-industrial, tribal communities. They found that there are many societies which differ markedly from western countries in sexual ethics as well as sexual conduct. There are cultures in which pre-marital homosexuality is virtually normative or where aggressive, painful stimulation during intercourse is erotically desirable and practised by both males and females, or where adolescent and childhood sexual activities are encouraged. While western societies tend to restrict pre-adolescent and adolescent sex-play,

sexual behaviour is diverse, it is not surprising that there are permissive subcultural groups even within restrictive societies. B.M. Berger (1977, 1981) has documented childhood sexual behaviour in some counter-cultural communes in the midst of a highly industrialised society (USA). He observed that children living in these communes are exposed to sexual experience at an early age as they are living close to adults, that discussions about sex in the communes are open, that child-child sexual play as well as adult-child sexual activities are socially accepted as long as they are consensual. The hallmark of such communes is the absence of a rigid age-grading system, and children are well integrated into the adult world.

The phenomenon of childhood sexuality, ever since the Kinsey surveys, has been repeatedly documented.[8] Schofield (1965a), in a survey of English young people, found that in his samples of nearly 2,000 adolescents, 82 per cent of the boys and 94 per cent of the girls had experienced kissing by the age of 16, and about half (both boys and girls) had experienced heavy petting, and 14 per cent of the boys and 5 per cent of the girls had experience of sexual intercourse. Children before the age of 12 had also had sexual experiences such as kissing, breast stimulation and petting, albeit to a lesser degree. In a later study, C. Farrell (1978, 1980) found in her sample of 1,500 teenagers that by the age of 16, 31 per cent of the boys and 12 per cent of the girls had had experience of intercourse. The rise in adolescent intercourse found in this study (compared with Schofield's data) is probably due to increasing permissiveness as well as the easy availability of contraceptives. A number of contributors to the volume on *Children and Sex* edited by Constantine & Martinson (1981), citing evidence from studies with pre-school children and pre-adolescents in various cultures, have made the observation that 'the child must be seen as a sexual being, in whom sexuality is a dynamic force in total personality development' (p. 59), and that 'pre-adolescence as a period of latency has been overstressed' (p. 92). While sexual education of children was very poorly developed twenty years ago,[9] the adult world is now becoming more aware of the need to recognise children as sexual beings, and the call to encourage and guide

---

adults in some non-western societies actually engage in sexual stimulation of infants and young children. Davenport (1976) has also documented the variation of sexual behaviour in different societies, from the highly permissive Polynesian communities to the strongly conservative Inis Beag villages in rural Ireland. He concluded that 'in man the inherited aspects of sex seem to be nearly formless, only by enculturation does sex assume form and meaning (p. 161). Beach (1976) has also concluded that 'we cannot seriously entertain the theory that exclusive heterosexuality represents the only "normal" or "healthy" form of sexual interaction for *Homo sapiens*' (p. 165).

[8] According to the survey conducted by Kinsey and his colleagues (1948, 1953), orgasm can be observed even in very small infants, and such orgasm is behaviourally similar to that experienced by adults except in the case of a male child ejaculation is absent. Masturbation also occurs at an early age; and sexual play, both heterosexual and homosexual, is very common among pre-adolescents.

[9] See Gagnon (1965b).

children towards a free and full expression of sex is beginning to be heard.[10]

O'Carroll (1980), drawing on the two lines of argument discussed above, has put forward what he calls a 'radical case' for paedophilia. His view can be summarised as follows:

(1) Children are by nature sexual beings – there is no sexual latency period in a child's development.

(2) Children need affection and would seek it – they would not avoid affectionate contact with adults. In this connection, affection and sex should not be dissociated but should be treated as natural complements of each other.

(3) In many non-western cultures, and in previous historical periods (such as classical Greece), sexual contact between adults and children is not problematic. Present-day western culture is irrationally repressive regarding human sexuality, and such repression is responsible for producing neuroses and psychological maladjustment.

(4) Paedophilic activities not only will not cause any harm to children, but will actually help them avoid future maladjustment.

(5) Society's traumatising reactions to paedophilic activities, rather than the activities themselves, are responsible for causing harm to children.

(6) Children could and would consent to sexual activities with adults, if left to their own devices. The notion of consent must simply be defined as a 'willingness' to participate in an activity – the requirement of full knowledge as well as a developed awareness of what is involved is a red herring.

In a nutshell, O'Carroll's position is that consensual activities can never be harmful to a child who has the desire and the need for sexual expression, and there is no good reason why such harmless sexual expression cannot be engaged in with a caring adult.

12.2.3 Difficulties of the pro-paedophile case

First of all, the argument from childhood sexuality raises several questions:

(1) The evidence cited usually deals with children's sexual activities among themselves, rather than with adults. The phenomenon of childhood sexuality does not *entail* the acceptability of adult-child contact.

(2) Granted that children are sexual beings, the question still remains whether they are 'sexual' in the sense that adults are.

(3) The healthy development observed in children living in

[10] See Jackson (1982), Martinson (1977a, 1977b), Yates (1978).

communes must be attributed to the whole atmosphere of freedom and general permissiveness in communal life rather than specifically to their early sexual experience.

The argument that sex should not be dissociated from affection is rather simplistic. In daily life, one tends to experience much more often just affection for other people, without any necessary association with sexual desire. O'Carroll might say that this is precisely an undesirable result created by a repressive separation of sex from affection. However, there is no evidence that even in a sexually permissive society, affection necessarily coincides with sexual desire. Even O'Carroll himself would probably admit that he would choose whom to relate to sexually – not just everybody that he is fond of.

Regarding the argument of cultural relativism, the following caveats must be considered:

(1) In most so-called permissive cultures, paedophilia, as an exclusive sexual orientation, is rare. It is more a matter of permissiveness in sexual expression in general. Moreover, sexual contact between adults and children in these cultures is often an expression of certain cultural-religious beliefs, such as initiation rites. The meaning of 'sex' in such situations is probably very different from that in western-industrial societies, and the activities observed are not 'paedophilic' in the sense we understand the term.

(2) The oft-quoted model of Greek love[11] must also be looked at with caution. For instance, DeMause (1974) argued that this Greek practice was actually a matter of sexual exploitation, not love. The general theme of DeMause's exposition is that child sexual abuse was much more rampant in ancient times – the notion of a bygone permissive age is deemed an overly romantic idea. Similarly, Karlen (1971, 1980) argued that Greek love as an educational, caring relationship between a man and a boy was a romanticised myth. Rather it was a matter of misogyny and Greek upper-class male decadence. To the Greek 'free men' who practised pederasty, boys were simply part of the 'non-men' world who could serve as sex objects. Homosexuality and pederasty as a fixed condition was viewed as abnormal and did not receive much social approval. Even Eglinton (1971), a strong advocate for Greek love as a model for present-day man-boy relationships, insisted that he was not defending an exclusive form of homosexuality. His model is rather that of a *heterosexually* satisfied mature man helping adolescent boys go through the latter's sexual development, and in the process enriching his own heterosexual repertoire.

In an innovative study of the 'use of pleasure' by the Greeks in classical times, Foucault (1986) argues that man-boy sex was not fundamentally different from man-woman sex – they were forms of

---

[11] For an exposition of Greek love see Dover (1978), Eglinton (1971).

pleasure that had to be subject to an 'ethical' practice of self-possession and rational morality. The focus of the Greek discourse on sexuality was the 'strategy of moderation', which defined the timing, quantity and opportunity of the use of sexual pleasure. The ethical model was the man of self-mastery, not one given to pleasure.

All these considerations indicate that to take the Greek love model out of its historical context and equate it with pederasty/paedophilia as practised nowadays is not warranted.

(3) Furthermore, why should the values of practices of other cultures be preferred to those currently in force in western societies? In order to justify such a preference, it has to be shown that these values and practices could produce much more social good. As mentioned above, the so-called 'sexual permissiveness' of the past has been interpreted by some researchers as more a phenomenon of sexual exploitation of children – the social good produced by this permissiveness has yet to be demonstrated. O'Carroll has argued that sexual repression in western societies is the source of neuroses and psychological maladjustment. But it is difficult to demonstrate (a) that objection to adult-child sexual contact is necessarily the same as sexual repression, (b) that neuroses are indeed more widespread nowadays than in the past, and (c) that such increase in neuroses, if true, is a result of sexual repression, and that the link is specifically with the suppression of adult-child sexual contact.

Whether or not adult-child sexual contact is, as O'Carroll has argued, in itself harmless and whether any harm that arises is due solely to society's adverse reactions is a complex issue that is far from settled (see Chapter 7). Nevertheless, given existing conditions, the effects of adult-child sexual contact are inevitably embedded in the whole social situation that obtains after the disclosure of such activities. To that extent, if a paedophile does not want to dwell in the utopia of instant revolution, he must take into account this practical issue in his evaluation of the effect of his involvement with children. Thus, the argument that knowledge about the social consequences of sexual contact with adults should be included in the definition of a child's 'informed consent' must be reckoned with.[12] This is not to say that society's current attitudes or statutes are sacrosanct, only that reforms and changes can only be achieved slowly and carefully, and often compromises have to be made.

Regarding the notion of 'informed consent', O'Carroll has argued that knowledge and awareness are irrelevant – as long as a child participates willingly in the sexual contact, consent should be assumed. There are some serious problems in this argument:

---

[12] This argument is put forth by Abel, Becker & Cunningham-Rathner (1984). See Section 12.2.1 above.

(1) Willingness' may not be a sufficient criterion for endorsing an action. For example, can one approve of a child taking heroin if he wanted to?

(2) Even assuming that 'willingness' can be an acceptable definition of consent, there remains the problem of how to define 'willingness', and to ascertain its presence in a child's acts. If it is simply defined behaviourally in terms of the child's involvement in the sexual activity, it cannot rule out the undesirable possibility of deception, bribery or seduction.

(3) To say that when left to their own devices children would be willing to engage in sexual activities with adults is to ignore the context of children's life. Children never live in a vacuum — they are never 'alone', they are always living under a certain set of circumstances. If they are not under the influence of their parents, they would be under the influence of other adults. To argue that parents should leave children alone to make up their own minds regarding adult-child sexual contact means that parental influences should give way to other people's (the paedophile's?) influence.

(4) Granted that children might seek sexual contact with adults if given the freedom to do so, the question of how to justify the paedophile's initiative in approaching a child still remains — since if children do not seek out adults actively it could be taken to mean that they do not want such contact. O'Carroll could counter by saying that the paedophile's initiative is needed because of existing repression. Yet the logical deduction from O'Carroll's argument that children left to their own devices would seek out adults is to attempt to create an environment of freedom for children, and see if they indeed will initiate such contact, rather than to let the paedophile impose his initiative on them.

(5) Another problem related to whether children will seek out adults for sexual contact if given freedom is the difficulty of ascertaining what the child is actually seeking. Is the child seeking 'sex' in the sense that the adult understands it — or is it something different?[13]

From this discussion, it seems that O'Carroll has not succeeded in establishing a strong defence for paedophilia. Nevertheless, his effort does reflect the fact that there is an urgent need to distinguish between those adults who use force to obtain sexual contact with children and those who do not, as well as between those children who just endure what is done to them and those who actively participate in sexual relationships with adults.

---

[13] As discussed in Section 11.2.4 above, some informants of this study have acknowledged that children involved in paedophilic relationships might not understand the relationship in the same way as that of their adult partners. What the child is actually 'consenting' to must be clarified.

12.2.4 The middle ground

To Finkelhor, the phenomenon of adult-child sexual contact poses no moral dilemma in that it can be categorically rejected. In effect, he is arguing that children and adolescents should be *defined* as unable to freely enter into any sexual relationship with adults. It would be simple, after adopting this definition, to formulate a policy regarding intervention into such sexual relationships and 'treatment' of individuals involved.

To O'Carroll, on the other hand, the issue is also clear – that sexual activities, including those with adults, would never in themselves be harmful to children, provided that the child is participating willingly in the activities. Any harm observed is due to the punitive reactions of society to a natural and pleasurable encounter between a loving adult and an affectionate child.

While it is not the main objective of this study to provide a solution to the ethical debate on adult-child sexual contact, the following points are listed here as a compromise between the two views discussed above:

(1) Any adult-child sexual encounter in which force or coercion is involved must be regarded as unacceptable.

(2) Pressure or deception should also be seen as unacceptable, but it has to be recognised that there are definitional problems here that require further research.

(3) Seduction by the adult, though undesirable, is not easily ascertainable since it would be difficult to distinguish self-serving seduction from 'normal' sensual interactions within a consensual relationship.

(4) The notion of consent, while relevant, is difficult to define – while it is not acceptable that a child's willingness, defined behaviourally, is taken as 'consent', neither is it appropriate to define categorically all children as unable to consent to sexual activities. Perhaps a more flexible and situation-specific approach is needed.

(5) There is the possibility that some adult-child sexual relationships are neither coercive nor in themselves damaging to the children involved. Rather than rejecting *a priori* all forms of adult-child sexual contact as abuse and hence morally wrong, it might be more fruitful to study the *continuum* of adult-child sexuality, bearing in mind that there is a considerable grey area in this continuum.[14]

Since adult-child sexual contact poses many difficult questions, it is to be expected that no legislative response will be universally accepted. What is important to recognise, in this context, is that the law is only a

[14] In this connection, there is a great need for more studies on how children who have been sexually involved with adults construe their experiences, such as the one conducted by Sandfort (1982).

practical arrangement for the peaceful co-existence of individuals living in a community. It does not have, and should not be endowed with, a kind of absolute moral status. In the realm of human sexuality, the operation of the law must take into account the socially constituted nature of the very concept of 'sexuality'. Although it is beyond the scope of the present work to tackle the question of legislative reform, some suggestions are made here as a basis for further investigation. First of all, any legislation relating to sex between adults and children should differentiate between coercive contact and consensual activities. This is especially important in view of the possibility of a long preventive custodial sentence being meted out to a person diagnosed as a 'paedophilic child molester'. If 're-offending' is taken as the only criterion of 'dangerousness', there is the likelihood of injustice done to paedophiles whose attraction to children is persistent but whose activities with the latter are always consensual. Secondly, any age of consent stipulation should take into consideration the variation in sexual maturity in children and teenagers, the question of their sexual rights, and the need for equal treatment of heterosexual and homosexual activities. Finally, it is my view that state intervention into families and the private life of individual citizens, particularly through the criminal justice system, should be kept to a minimum.

12.3 Some concluding thoughts

Ever since the medicalisation of sex, paedophilia has been pathologised and controlled as one form of sexual deviation. At present, the law is still vigorously condemning all sexual contact with children as criminal. In the effort to maintain a sexual order – patriarchy, age-grading and heterosexuality – it is inevitable that society outlaws the paedophile together with the violent child molester. The conceptualisation of the phenomenon of sexuality presented here should not be taken as one form of crude labelling theory. Rather it is an attempt to locate the concept of sexual deviation, of which paedophilia is an example, in the context of a critical analysis of the disciplinary strategies of society. It is also not a simple conspiracy theory – the state is just one 'nodal point' through which the human body is controlled, other nodal points include the school, the family, and the person himself. There is no one single 'oppressor' – the expression of power over the life of the individual is at once diffuse and not traceable to a single 'mind'. If a unitary notion is required, perhaps the concept of the 'internal logic' of modern disciplinary society may be used.

No doubt adult sexual contact with children, as a form of erotic experience, has an individual-personal dimension to it, as this study has shown. Yet as it is also a form of sexual deviance socially defined and outlawed, it also has to be examined in the context of the discourse of sexuality which constitutes a society's understanding of the 'truth' about sex. To see the criminalisation of paedophilia as merely a repression of childhood sexuality or the deprivation of the paeophile's right to fulfilment by orgasm may lead the movement of resistance in the direction of 'sexual revolution', which, as pointed out earlier, would only conform to the internal logic of modern society – the disciplining of the individual through fixing the body to a sexual order, albeit a 'permissive' one. As Giddens (1982a) has remarked, we need to strive for a liberation *from* sexuality rather than through sexuality. Or as Heath (1982, p. 168) has put it, 'we need to claim and realise against sexuality the possibility of being as concrete individualities and not as identities'.

The discourse of sexuality has provided the conditions for the emergence of categories such as 'the homosexual', 'the paedophile', 'the lesbian', 'the multiple-orgasmic woman', 'the pervert', 'the impotent man', etc., which mediate the expression of certain relations of power within modern society. Liberation will take place through resistance to such categorisation of individuals into fixed sexual identities. Through affirmation of the diffuse nature of human sexuality, and the plurality of sexual expression, the monolithic edifice of 'sexuality' can be subverted.[15]

Such a project of decategorisation is commensurate with the trend of recent works which aim at explicating the social constitution of the very notion of 'the subject'.[16] Foucault has talked about two senses of the word 'subject' – subject to someone else by control and dependence, and subject to one's own identity by a conscience or self-knowledge.[17] As shown in this study, paedophiles are trying to build a world of their own and to construct a meaningful life. But very often they are playing unawares into the hands of the discourse of sexuality, and have put themselves into the category of 'the paedophile'. They are 'subject' in both senses of the word, as elaborated by Foucault. Foucault's suggestion for resistance against this control of the individual via the notion of the 'subject' is to 'refuse what we are', and to 'promote new forms of subjectivity'.[18] Whether (and how) this suggestion can be put into practice within the confines of current power structures that obtain in our society, is a question too large to be pursued here.

[15] See Plummer (1981c), Weeks (1985).
[16] See e.g. Henriques *et al.* (1984).
[17] Quoted in Rabinow (1984), p. 21.
[18] Ibid., p. 22.

Bibliography

Abel, G.G. & Blanchard, E.B. (1976). The measurement and generation of sexual arousal. In M. Hersen, R.M. Eisler & P.M. Miller (eds), *Progress in Behavior Modification*, Vol. 2. New York: Academic Press.

Abel, G.G., Becker, J.V. & Cunningham-Rathner, J. (1984). Complications, consent, and cognitions in sex between children and adults. *International Journal of Law and Psychiatry* 7, 89-103.

Abel, G.G. *et al.* (1977). The component of rapists' sexual arousal. *Archives of General Psychiatry* 34, 895-903.

Abel, G.G. *et al.* (1978). Differentiating sexual aggressives with penile measures. *Criminal Justice and Behavior* 5, 315-32.

Abel, G.G. *et al.* (1981). Identifying dangerous child molesters. In R. Stuart (ed), *Violent Behavior*. Mazel: Brunner.

Adams-Tucker, C. (1981). A socioclinical overview of 28 sex-abused children. *Child Abuse and Neglect* 5, 361-7.

Albin, R.S. (1977). Psychological studies of rape – a review essay. *Signs* 3, 423-35.

Alexander, B.B. & Johnson, S.B. (1980). Reliability of heterosocial skills measurement with sex offenders. *Journal of Behavioral Assessment* 2, 225-37.

Allen, C.V. (1980). *Daddy's Girl*. Sevenoaks, Kent: New English Library.

Allen, C. (1949). *The Sexual Perversions and Abnormalities: A Study in the Psychology of Paraphilia*. London: OUP.

Allen, C. (1969). *A Textbook of Psychosexual Disorders*. London: OUP.

Allen, D.M. (1980). Young male prostitutes: a psychosocial study. *Archives of Sexual Behavior* 9, 399-426.

American Psychiatric Association (1980). *Diagnostic and Statistical Manual of Mental Disorders*. 3rd ed. Washington D.C.: American Psychiatric Association.

Anderson, D. (1979). Touching: when is it caring and nurturing or when is it exploitative and damaging? *Child Abuse and Neglect* 3, 793-4.

Anderson, L.M. & Shafer, G. (1979). The character-disordered family: a community treatment model for family sexual abuse. *American Journal of Orthopsychiatry* 49, 436-45.

Anderson, L.S. (1981). Notes on the linkage between the sexually abused child and the suicidal adolescent. *Journal of Adolescence* 4, 157-62.

Anderson, W.P. Kunce, J.T. & Rich, B. (1979). Sex offenders: three personality types. *Journal of Clinical Psychology* 35, 671-6.

Annis, L.V. (1982). A residential treatment program for male sex offenders. *International Journal of Offender Therapy and Comparative Criminology* 26, 223-4.

Ariès, P. (1962). *Centuries of Childhood*. London: Jonathan Cape.

Armemtrout, J.A. & Hauer, A.L. (1978). MMPIs of rapists of adults, rapists of children, and non-rapist sex offenders. *Journal of Clinical Psychology* 34, 330-32.

Armstrong, L. (1978). *Kiss Daddy Goodnight: A Speak-out on Incest*. New York: Hawthorne Books.

Attias, R. & Goodwin, J. (1985). Knowledge and management strategies in incest cases; a survey of physicians, psychologists and family counselors. *Child Abuse and Neglect* 9, 527-33.

Avery-Clark, C., O'Neil, J.A. & Laws, D.R. (1981). A comparison of intrafamilial sexual and physical child abuse. In M. Cook & K. Howells (eds), *Adult Sexual Interest in Children*. London: Academic Press.

Badgley, R.F. (1984). *Sexual Offences against Children*. (Report of a committee appointed by the Minister of Justice and the Attorney General of Canada.) Ottawa: Government Publishing Centre.

Bagley, C. (1969). The varieties of incest. *New Society*, August 21, 280-2.

Baker, A.W. & Duncan, S.P. (1985). Child sexual abuse: a study of prevalence in Great Britain. *Child Abuse and Neglect* 9, 457-67.

Bancroft, J. (1974). *Deviant Sexual Behaviour: Modification and Assessment*. London: OUP.

Bander, K., Fein, E. & Bishop, G. (1982). Child sex abuse treatment: some barriers to program operation. *Child Abuse and Neglect* 6, 185-91.

Barlow, D.H. & Wincze, J.P. (1980). Treatment of sexual deviations. In S.R. Leiblem & L.A. Pervin (eds), *Principles and Practice of Sex Therapy*. London: Tavistock.

BASPCAN (1981). *Child Sexual Abuse*. London: BASPCAN.

Bayer, R. & Spitzer, R.L. (1982). Edited correspondence on the status of homosexuality in DSM-III. *Journal of the History of the Behavioral Sciences* 18, 32-52.

Beach, F.A. (1976). Editorial preface to 'Homosexuality' by M. Hoffman. In F.A. Beach (ed), *Human Sexuality in Four Perspectives*. Baltimore: Johns Hopkins University Press.

Becker, H.S. (1963). *Outsiders: Studies in the Sociobiology of Deviance*. New York: Free Press.

Becker, J.V. Abel, G.G. & Skinner, L.J. (1979). The impact of a sexual assault on the victim's sexual life. *Victimology* 4, 229-35.

Becker, J.V. *et al.* (1978). Evaluating social skills of sexual aggressives. *Criminal Justice and Behavior* 5, 357-68.

Bell, A.P. & Hall, C.S. (1971). *The Personality of a Child Molester: An Analysis of Dreams*. Chicago: Aldine/Atherton.

Bell, A.P., Weinberg, M.S. & Hammersmith, S.K. (1981). *Sexual Preference*. Bloomington: Indiana University Press.

Bell, S. (1988). *When Salem came to the Boro*. London: Pan Books.

Bender, L. & Blau, A. (1937). The reaction of children to sexual relations with adults. *American Journal of Orthopsychiatry* 7, 500-18.

Bender, L. & Grugett, A.E. (1952). A follow-up report on children who had atypical sexual experience. *American Journal of Orthopsychiatry*, 22, 825-37.

Benedict, R. (1935). *Patterns of Culture*. London: Routledge & Kegan Paul.

Bentovim, A. *et al.* (1988). *Sexual Abuse in the Family*. Bristol: John Wright.

Benward, J. & Densen-Gerber, J. (1975). Incest as a causative factor in antisocial behavior: an explanatory study. *Contemporary Drug Problems* 4, 323-40.

Berger, B.M. (1977). Child-rearing research in communes: the extension of adult sexual behavior to young children. In E.K. & J.D. Oremland (eds), *The Sexual and Gender Development of Young Children: The Role of the Educator*. Cambridge, Mass: Ballinger.

Berger, B.M. (1981). Liberating child sexuality: commune experiences. In Constantine & Martinson (eds), *Children and Sex*.

Berger, P.L. (1963). *Invitation to Sociology: A Humanistic Perspective*. Harmondsworth: Penguin.

Berger, P.L. & Luckmann, T. (1967). *The Social Construction of Reality*. London: Allen Lane.

Berlin, F.S. & Krout, E. (1986). Pedophilia: diagnostic concepts, treatment, and ethical consideration. *American Journal of Forensic Psychiatry* 7, 13-30.

Berliner, L. (1977). Child sexual abuse: what happens next? *Victimology* 2, 327-31.

Bernard, F. (1975). An enquiry among a group of pedophiles. *Journal of Sex Research* 11, 242-55.

Bernard, F. (1981). Pedophilia: psychological consequences for the child. In Constantine & Martinson (eds), *Children and Sex*.

Bernard, F. (1985). *Paedophilia: A Factual Report*. Rotterdam: Enclave.

Besharov, D.J. (1985). 'Doing something' about child abuse: the need to narrow the grounds for state intervention. *Harvard Journal of Law and Public Policy* 8, 538-89.

Blom-Cooper, L. (1985). *A Child In Trust. The Report of the Panel of Inquiry into the*

Circumstances Surrounding the Death of Jasmine Beckford. London: London Borough of Brent.

Bluglass, R. (1979). Incest. *British Journal of Hospital Medicine*. August, 152-7.

Bolton, N. (1979). Phenomenology and psychology: being objective about the mind. In N. Bolton (ed), *Philosophical Problems in Psychology*. London: Methuen.

Bradshaw, J.S. (1978). *Doctors on Trial*. New York & London: Paddington Press.

Brady, K. (1979). *Father's Days: A True Story of Incest*. New York: Seaview Books.

Brant, R.S.T. & Tisza, V.B. (1977). The sexually misused child. *American Journal of Orthopsychiatry* 47, 80-90.

Brassard, M.R., Tyler, A.H. & Kehle, T.J. (1983). School programs to prevent intrafamilial child sexual abuse. *Child Abuse and Neglect* 7, 241-5.

Brecher, E.M. (1978). *Treatment Programs for Sex Offenders*. National Institute of Enforcement and Criminal Justice, US Department of Justice.

Bremer, J. (1959). *Asexualization*. New York: Macmillan.

Brenner, M. (1982). Actors' powers. In M. von Cranach & R. Harré (eds), *The Analysis of Action: Recent Theoretical and Empirical Advances*. Cambridge: CUP.

British Medical Journal (1981). Children born as a result of incest. *British Medical Journal* 282, 250.

Brodsky, S.L. (1980). Understanding and treating sexual offenders. *Howard Journal* 19, 102-15.

Brodsky, S.L. & West, D.J. (1981). Life-skills treatment of sex offenders. *Law and Psychology Review* 6, 97-168.

Brongersma, E. (1980). The meaning of 'indecency' with respect to moral offences involving children. *British Journal of Criminology* 20, 20-32.

Brongersma, E. (1984). Aggression against pedophiles. *International Journal of Law and Psychiatry* 7, 79-87.

Brongersma, E. (1987). *Loving Boys: A Multidisciplinary Study of Sexual Relations between Adult and Minor Males*. Amsterdam & New York: Global Academic Publ.

Browne, A. & Finkelhor, D. (1986). Impact of child sexual abuse: a review of the research. *Psychological Bulletin* 99, 66-77.

Brownell, K.D., Hayes, S.C. & Barlow, D.H. (1977). Patterns of appropriate and deviant sexual arousal: the behavioral treatment of multiple sexual deviations. *Journal of Consulting and Clinical Psychology* 46, 1144-55.

Browning, D.H. & Boatman, B. (1977). Incest: children at risk. *American Journal of Psychiatry* 134, 69-72.

Brownmiller, S. (1975). *Against Our Will*. London: Secker & Warburg.

Brunold, H. (1964). Observations after sexual traumata suffered in childhood. *Excerpta Criminologica* 4, 5-8.

Burbridge, M. & Walters, J. (1981). *Breaking the Silence: Gay Teenagers Speak for Themselves*. London: Joint Council for Teenagers.

Burgess, A.W. (ed) (1984) *Child Pornography and Sex Rings*. Lexington: D.C. Heath.

Burgess, A.W., Groth, A.N. & McCausland, M.P. (1981). Child sex initiation rings. *American Journal of Orthopsychiatry* 51, 110-19.

Burgess, A.W. *et al.* (1978). *Sexual Assault of Children and Adolescents*. Lexington: D.C. Heath.

Burns, J. (1984). A safe place for children. *Victimology* 9, 23-65.

Burton, L. (1968). *Vulnerable Children*. London: Routledge & Kegan Paul.

Butler-Sloss, Lord Justice Elizabeth. (1988). *Report of the Inquiry into Child Abuse in Cleveland, 1987*. London: H.M.S.O.

Callahan, E.J. & Leitenberg, H. (1973). Aversion therapy for sexual deviation: contingent shock and covert sensitization. *Journal of Abnormal Psychology* 81, 60-73.

Canadian Committee on Sexual Offences against Children and Youths (1984). *Sexual Offences Against Children*, Vol. 1 & 2. Ottawa: Canadian Government Publishing Centre.

Canepa, G. & Bandini, T. (1980). Incest and family dynamics: a clinical study. *International Journal of Law and Psychiatry* 3, 453-60.

Cantwell, H.B. (1981). Sexual abuse of children in Denver, 1979: review with implications for pediatric intervention and possible prevention. *Child Abuse and Neglect* 5, 75-85.

Cantwell, H.B. (1983). Vaginal inspection as it relates to child sexual abuse in girls under thirteen. *Child Abuse and Neglect* 7, 171-6.

Caprio, F.S. & Brenner, D.R. (1961). *Sexual Behavior: Psycho-legal Aspects.* New York: Citadel Press.

Cassity, J.H. (1927). Psychological considerations of pedophilia. *Psychoanalytic Review* 14, 189-99.

Caudrey, A. (1985). Save the children? *New Society*, December 13, 449-50.

Cauthery, P., Stanway, A. & Stanway, P. (1983). *The Complete Book of Love and Sex.* London: Century.

Ceresa, D. (1981). Sex under sixteen. *Spare Rib* 108, 32-5.

Chaneles, S. (1967). Child victims of sexual offenses. *Federal Probation* 31, 52-6.

Chesterman, M. (1985). *Child Sexual Abuse and Social Work.* Norwich: University of East Anglia.

Christopherson, R.J. (1981). Two approaches to the handling of child abuse: a comparison of the English and Dutch systems. *Child Abuse and Neglect* 5, 369-73.

Ciba Foundation (1984). *Child Sexual Abuse Within the Family.* London: Tavistock.

Cohen, M.L., Seghorn, T. & Calmas, W. (1969). Sociometric study of the sex offender. *Journal of Abnormal Psychology* 74, 249-55.

Collett, P. (ed) (1977). *Social Rules and Social Behaviour.* Totowa, New Jersey: Rowman & Littlefield.

Comfort, A. (ed) (1972). *The Joy of Sex: A Gourmet Guide to Lovemaking.* London: Modsets Securities Ltd.

Comfort, A. (ed) (1974) *More Joy: A Lovemaking Companion to 'The Joy of Sex'.* London: Mitchell Beazley.

Constantine, L.L. (1981a). The effects of early sexual experiences: a review and synthesis of research. In Constantine & Martinson (eds), *Children and Sex.*

Constantine, L.L. (1981b). The sexual rights of children: implications of a radical perspective. In Constantine & Martinson (eds), *Children and Sex.*

Constantine, L. L. & Martinson, F.M. (eds) (1981). *Children and Sex.* Boston: Little, Brown & Co.

Constantine, L. (1983). Child sexuality: Recent developments and implications for treatment, prevention and social policy. *Medicine and Law* 2, 55-67.

Conte, J.R. *et al.* (1985). An evaluation of a program to prevent the sexual victimization of young children. *Child Abuse and Neglect* 9, 319-28.

Coombs, N.R. (1974) Male prostitutes: A psychosocial view of behavior. *American Journal of Orthopsychiatry*, 44, 782-9.

Cooper, I. & Cormier, B. (1982). Inter-generational transmission of incest. *Canadian Journal of Psychiatry* 27, 231-5.

Coulter, M.L. *et al.* (1985). Conflicting needs and interests of researchers and service providers in child sexual abuse cases. *Child Abuse and Neglect* 9, 535-42.

Courtois, C.A. (1979). The incest experiences and its aftermath. *Victimology* 4, 337-47.

Courtois, C.A. (1980). Studying and counseling women with past incest experience. *Victimology* 5, 322-34.

Crawford, D.A. (1981). Treatment approaches with paedophiles. In M. Cook & K. Howells (eds), *Adult Sexual Interest In Children.* London: Academic Press.

Crépault, C. & Couture, M. (1980). Men's erotic fantasies. *Archives of Sexual Behavior* 9, 565-81.

Curran, D. & Parr, D. (1957). Homosexuality: an analysis of 100 male cases seen in private practice. *British Medical Journal* 1, 797-801.

Currier, R.L. (1981). Juvenile sexuality in global perspective. In Constantine and Martinson (eds), *Children and Sex.*

Davenport, W.H. (1976). Sex in cross-cultural perspective. In F.A. Beach (ed), *Human Sexuality in Four Perspectives.* Baltimore: Johns Hopkins University Press.

De Francis, V. (1969). *Protecting the Child Victim of Sex Crimes Committed by Adults.* Denver: American Humane Association.

De Jong, A.R. (1985). Vaginitis due to *Gardnerella vaginalis* and to *Candida albicans* in

sexual abuse. *Child Abuse and Neglect* 9, 27-9.
De Jong, A.R., Hervada, A.R. & Emmett, G.A. (1983). Epidemiologic variations in childhood sexual abuse. *Child Abuse and Neglect* 7, 155-62.
DeMause, L. (1974). The evolution of childhood. In L. DeMause (ed), *The History of Childhood*. London: Souvenir Press.
De Mott, B. (1980). The pro-incest lobby. *Psychology Today* 13, 11-16.
De Volkstrant (1985). New legislation on morality in view. *De Volkskrant*, 5 November. Netherlands (English translation).
De Young, M. (1981). Case reports: the sexual exploitation of incest victims by helping professionals. *Victimology* 6, 92-101.
De Young, M. (1982a). *The Sexual Victimization of Children*. N.C.: McFarland & Co.
De Young, M. (1982b). Innocent seducer or innocently seduced? The role of the child incest victim. *Journal of Clinical Child Psychology* 11, 56-60.
De Young, M. (1982c). Self-injurious behaviour in incest victims: a research note. *Child Welfare* 61, 577-84.
Deaton, F.A. & Sandlin, D.L. (1980). Sexual victimology within the home: a treatment approach. *Victimology* 5, 311-21.
Delin, B. (1978). *The Sex Offender*. Boston: Beacon Press.
Dengrove, D. (1967). Behavior therapy of the sexual disorders. *Journal of Sex Research* 3, 49-61.
Densen-Gerber, J. & Hutchinson, S.F. (1979). Sexual and commercial exploitation of children: legislative responses and treatment challenges. *Child Abuse and Neglect* 3, 61-6.
Dixon, K.N., Arnold, L.E. & Calestro, K. (1978). Father-son incest: underreported psychiatric problem? *American Journal of Psychiatry* 135, 835-38.
Doshay, L.J. (1943). *The Boy Sex Offender and his Later Criminal Career*. New York: Grune and Stratton.
Dover, K.J. (1978). *Greek Homosexuality*. London: Duckworth.
Eckert, E.D. *et al.* (1986). Homosexuality in monozygotic twins reared apart. *British Journal of Psychiatry* 148, 421-5.
Edwardes, A. & Masters, R.E.L. (1970). *The Cradle of Erotica*. London: Odyssey.
Edwards, N.B. (1972). Case conference: assertive training in a case of homosexual pedophilia. *Journal of Behavior Therapy and Experimental Psychiatry* 3, 55-63.
Eglinton, J.Z. (1971). *Greek Love*. London: Neville Spearman.
Eisenberg, N. & Glynn-Owens, R. (1987). Attitudes of health professionals to child sexual abuse and incest. *Child Abuse and Neglect* 11, 109-16.
Elliott, M. (1985). *Preventing Child Sexual Assault: A Practical Guide to Talking with Children*. London: Bedford Square Press.
Ellis, A., Doorbar, R.R. & Johnston, R. III (1954). Characteristics of convicted sex offenders. *Journal of Social Psychology* 40, 3-15.
Embling, J. (1986). *Fragmented Lives*. Harmondsworth: Penguin.
Enos, W.F., Conrath, T.B. & Byer, J.C. (1986). Forensic examination of the sexually abused child. *Paediatrics* 78, 385-98.
Everstine, D.S. & Everstine, L. (1983). *People in Crisis: Strategic Therapeutic Interventions*. New York: Brunner.
Eysenck, H.J. (1964). *Crime and Personality*. London: Routledge & Kegan Paul.
Fairtlough, A. (1983). *Responsibility for Incest: A Feminist View*. Norwich: University of East Anglia.
Faller, K.C. (1984). Is the child victim of sexual abuse telling the truth? *Child Abuse and Neglect* 8, 473-81.
Farrell, B.A. (1981). *The Standing of Psychoanalysis*. Oxford: OUP.
Farrell, C. (1978). *My Mother Said ... The Way Young People Learned about Sex and Birth Control*. London: Routledge & Kegan Paul.
Feldman, M.P. (1977). *Criminal Behaviour: A Psychological Analysis*. Chichester: Wiley.
Feldman, M.P. & MacCulloch, M.J. (1971). *Homosexual Behaviour: Therapy and Assessment*. Oxford: Pergamon.
Feldman, M.P. & MacCulloch, M.J. (1980). *Human Sexual Behaviour*. London: Wiley.

Field, L.H. & Williams, M. (1971). A note on the scientific assessment and treatment of the sexual offender. *Medicine, Science and the Law* 11, 180-1.

Finkelhor, D. (1978). *Psychological, Cultural and Family Factors in Incest and Family Sexual abuse.* Manuscript, University of New Hampshire.

Finkelhor, D. (1979a). *Sexually Victimized Children.* New York: Free Press.

Finkelhor, D. (1979b). What's wrong with sex between adults and children? Ethics and the problem of sexual abuse. *American Journal of Orthopsychiatry* 49, 692-97.

Finkelhor, D. (1980a). Sex among siblings: a survey on prevalence, variety, and effects. *Archives of Sexual Behavior* 9, 171-94.

Finkelhor, D. (1980b). Risk factors in sexual victimization of children. *Child Abuse and Neglect* 4, 265-73.

Finkelhor, D. (1981a). Sex between siblings: sex play, incest and aggression. In Constantine & Martinson (eds), *Children and Sex.*

Finkelhor, D. (1981b). The sexual abuse of boys. *Victimology* 6, 76-84.

Finkelhor, D. (1982). Sexual abuse: a sociological perspective. *Child Abuse and Neglect* 6, 95-102.

Finkelhor, D. (1983). Removing the child – prosecuting the offender in cases of sexual abuse: evidence from the National Reporting System of Child Abuse and Neglect. *Child Abuse and Neglect* 7, 195-205.

Finkelhor, D. (1984). *Child Sexual Abuse: New Theory and Research.* New York: Free Press.

Finkelhor, D. (1986). *A Sourcebook on Child Sexual Abuse.* Beverley Hills, Ca.: Sage.

Finkelhor, D. & Araji, S. (1983). *Explanations of Pedophilia: A Four Factor Model.* Manuscript, University of New Hampshire.

Finkelhor, D. & Browne, A. (1985). The traumatic impact of child sexual abuse: a conceptualization. *American Journal of Orthopsychiatry* 55, 530-41.

Finkelhor, D. & Hotaling, G.T. (1984). Sexual abuse in the National Incidence Study of Child Abuse and Neglect: an appraisal. *Child Abuse and Neglect* 8, 23-33.

Finkelhor, D. & Russell, D. (1984). Women as perpetrators. In Finkelhor, *Child Sexual Abuse: New Theory and Research.*

Fitch, J.H. (1962). Men convicted of sexual offences against children: a descriptive follow-up study. *British Journal of Criminology* 3, 18-37.

Ford, C.S. & Beach, F.A. (1952). *Patterns of Sexual Behavior.* London: Eyre & Spottiswoode.

Forseth, L.B. & Brown, A. (1981). A survey of intrafamilial sexual abuse treatment centers: implications for intervention. *Child Abuse and Neglect* 5, 177-86.

Forward, S. & Buck, C. (1978). *Betrayal of Innocence: Incest and its Devastation.* Harmondsworth: Penguin.

Foucault, M. (1977). *Discipline and Punish.* London: Allen Lane.

Foucault, M. (1979). *The History of Sexuality*, Vol. 1: *An Introduction.* London: Allen Lane.

Foucault, M. (1986). *The History of Sexuality*, Vol. 2: *The Use of Pleasure.* Harmondsworth: Viking.

Fox, C. & Weaver, C. (1978). Group work with sexual offenders (an alternative approach). *Probation Journal* 25, 84-6.

Fox, R. (1980). *The Red Lamp of Incest.* London: Hutchinson.

Fraser, M. (1976). *The Death of Narcissus.* London: Secker & Warburg.

Freeman, M.D.A. (1983). *The Rights and the Wrongs of Children.* London: Frances Pinter.

French, L.A. & Wailes, S.N. (1982). Perception of sexual deviance: a bi-racial analysis. *International Journal of Offender Therapy and Comparative Criminology* 26, 242-9.

Freud, A. (1981). A psychoanalyst's view of sexual abuse by parents. In Mrazek & Kempe (eds), *Sexually Abused Children and their Families.*

Freund, K. (1967). Erotic preference in pedophilia. *Behaviour Research and Therapy* 5, 339-48.

Freund, K. (1971). A note on the use of the phallometric method of measuring mild sexual arousal in the male. *Behavior Therapy*, 2, 223-8.

Freund, K. (1976). Diagnosis and treatment of forensically significant anomalous erotic preferences. *Canadian Journal of Criminology and Corrections* 18, 181-9.

Freund, K. (1981). Assessment of pedophilia. In M. Cook & K. Howells (eds), *Adult Sexual Interest in Children.* London: Academic Press.

Freund, K. & Costell, R. (1970). The structure of erotic preference in the nondeviant male. *Behaviour Research and Therapy* 8, 15-20.

Freund, K., Langevin, R. & Zajac, Y. (1974). Heterosexual aversion in homosexual males: a second experiment. *British Journal of Psychiatry* 125, 177-80.

Freund, K. *et al.* (1972). The female child as a surrogate object. *Archives of Sexual Behavior* 2, 119-33.

Freund, K. *et al.* (1973) Heterosexual aversions in homosexual males. *British Journal of Psychiatry* 122, 163-9.

Freund, K. *et al.* (1974). The phobic theory of male homosexuality. *Archives of General Psychiatry* 31, 495-9.

Freund, K. *et al.* (1975). Heterosexual interest in homosexual males. *Archives of Sexual Behavior* 4, 509-18.

Frisbie, L.V. (1959). Treated sex offenders and what they did. *Mental Hygiene* 43, 263-7.

Fritz, G.S., Stoll, K. & Wagner, N.N. (1981). A comparison of males and females who were sexually molested as children. *Journal of Sex and Marital Therapy* 7, 54-9.

Fromuth, M.E. (1986). The relationship of childhood sexual abuse with later psychological and sexual adjustment in a sample of college women. *Child Abuse and Neglect* 10, 5-15.

Frude, N. (1982). The sexual nature of sexual abuse: a review of the literature. *Child Abuse and Neglect* 6, 211-23.

Furniss, T. (1983). Mutual influence and interlocking professional-family process in the treatment of child sexual abuse and incest. *Child Abuse and Neglect* 7, 207-23.

Gaddini, R. (1983). Incest as a developmental failure. *Child Abuse and Neglect* 7, 357-8.

Gaffney, G.R. & Berlin, F.S. (1984). Is there hypothalamic-pituitary-gonadal dysfunction in paedophilia? *British Journal of Psychiatry* 145, 657-60.

Gagne, P. (1981). Treatment of sex offenders with medroxyprogesterone acetate. *American Journal of Psychiatry* 138, 644-6.

Gagnon, J.H. (1965a). Female child victims of sex offenders. *Social Psychology* 13, 176-92.

Gagnon, J.H. (1965b). Sexuality and sexual learning in the child. *Psychiatry* 28, 212-26.

Gagnon, J.H., & Simon, W. (eds) (1967). *Sexual Deviance*. New York: Harper & Row.

Gagnon, J.H., & Simon, W. (eds) (1974). *Sexual Conduct*. London: Hutchinson.

Garfinkel, H. (1967). *Studies in Ethnomethodology*. Englewood Cliffs, New Jersey: Prentice-Hall.

Gauld, A. & Shotter, J. (1977). *Human Action and Its Psychological Investigation*. London: Routledge & Kegan Paul.

Gebhard, P.H. & Gagnon, J.H. (1964). Male sex offenders against very young children. *American Journal of Psychiatry* 121, 576-9.

Gebhard, P.H. *et al.* (1965). *Sex Offenders: An Analysis of Types*. New York: Harper & Row.

Geiser, R.L. (1979). *Hidden Victims: The Sexual Abuse of Children*. Boston: Beacon Press.

Gelder, M. (1979). Behaviour therapy for sexual deviations. In I. Rosen (ed), *Sexual Deviation*. Oxford: OUP.

Gellner, E. (1985). *The Psychoanalytic Movement*. London: Granada.

General Synod (1979). *Homosexual Relationships: A Contribution to Discussion*. London: CIO.

Giarretto, H. (1976). The treatment of father-daughter incest: a psycho-social approach. *Children Today* 5(4), 2-5, 34-5.

Giarretto, H. (1977). Humanistic treatment of father-daughter incest. *Child Abuse and Neglect* 1, 411-26.

Giarretto, H. (1978). *Integral Psychology in the Treatment of Father-Daughter Incest*. Ph.D. Dissertation. California Institute of Asian Studies, San Francisco.

Giarretto, H. (1981). A comprehensive child sexual abuse treatment program. In Mrazek & Kempe (eds), *Sexually Abused Children and Their Families*.

Giarretto, H., Giarretto, A. & Sgroi, S.M. (1978). Co-ordinated community treatment of incest. In Burgess *et al.* (eds), *Sexual Assault of Children and Adolescents*.

Gibbens, T.C.N. & Prince, J. (1963). *Child Victims of Sex Offences*. London: Institute for the Study and Treatment of Delinquency.

Giddens, A. (1976). *New Rules of Sociological Method*. London: Hutchinson.

Giddens, A. (1979). *Central Problems in Social Theory*. London: Macmillan.

Giddens, A. (1982a). *Sociology: A Brief but Critical Introduction*. London: Macmillan.
Giddens, A. (1982b). Trends in the philosophy of the social sciences. In B. Dufour (ed), *New Movements in the Social Sciences and Humanities*. London: Temple Smith.
Giddens, A. (1984). *The Constitution of Society*. Cambridge: Polity Press.
Gladue, B.A., Green, R. & Hellman, R.E. (1984). Neuroendocrine responses to estrogen and sexual orientation. *Science* 225, 1496-99.
Goffman, E. (1963). *Stigma: Notes on the Management of Spoiled Identity*. Englewood Cliffs: Prentice-Hall.
Goodman, R.E. (1983). Biology of sexuality: inborn determinants of human sexual responses. *British Journal of Psychiatry* 143, 216-20.
Goodwin, J. (1981). Suicidal attempts in sexual abuse victims and their mothers. *Child Abuse and Neglect* 5, 217-21.
Goodwin, J. (1982a). *Sexual Abuse: Incest Victims and Their Families*. Boston: John Wright.
Goodwin, J. (1982b). Use of drawings in evaluating children who may be incest victims. *Children and Youth Services Review* 4, 269-78.
Goodwin, J. & DiVasto, P. (1979). Mother-daughter incest. *Child Abuse and Neglect* 3, 953-7.
Goodwin, J., Cormier, L. & Owen, J. (1983). Grandfather-granddaughter incest: a trigenerational view. *Child Abuse and Neglect* 7, 163-70.
Goodwin, J., McCarthy, T. & DiVasto, P. (1981). Prior incest in mothers of abused children. *Child Abuse and Neglect* 5, 87-95.
Goodwin, J., Sahd, D. & Rada, R.T. (1982). False accusations and false denials of incest: clinical myths and clinical realities. In J. Goodwin (ed), *Sexual Abuse: Incest Victims and Their Families*. Boston: John Wright.
Goodwin, J., Simms, M. & Bergman, R. (1979). Hysterical seizures: a sequel to incest. *American Journal of Orthopsychiatry* 49, 698-703.
Gooren, L. (1986a). The neuroendocrine response of luteinizing hormone to estrogen administration in heterosexual, homosexual and transsexual subjects. *Journal of Clinical Endocrinology and Metabolism* 63, 583-8.
Gooren, L. (1986b). The neuroendocrine response of luteinizing hormone to estrogen administration in the human is not sex-specific but dependent on the hormonal environment. *Journal of Clinical Endocrinology and Metabolism* 63, 589-93.
Gosselin, C. & Wilson, G. (1980). *Sexual Variation*. London: Faber & Faber.
Gross, M. (1979). Incestuous rape: a cause for hysterical seizures in four adolescent girls. *American Journal of Orthopsychiatry* 49, 704-8.
Groth, A.N. (1978). Pattern of sexual assault against children and adolescents. In Burgess *et al.* (eds), *Sexual Assault of Children and Adolescents*.
Groth, A.N. (1979). Sexual trauma in the life histories of rapists and child molesters. *Victimology* 4, 10-16.
Groth, A.N. (1982). Review of *Perspectives on Paedophilia*. *Child Abuse and Neglect* 6, 240.
Groth, A.N. & Birnbaum, H.J. (1978). Adult sexual orientation and attraction to underage persons. *Archives of Sexual Behavior* 7, 175-81.
Groth, A.N. & Birnbaum, H.J. (1979). *Men Who Rape: The Psychology of the Offender*. New York: Plenum Press.
Groth, A.N. & Burgess, A.W. (1977). Motivational intent in the sexual assault of children. *Criminal Justice and Behavior* 4, 253-64.
Gruber, K.J. (1981). The child victim's role in sexual assault by adults. *Child Welfare* 60, 305-11.
Gruber, K.J. (1984). The social-situational context of sexual assault of female youth. *Victimology* 9, 407-14.
Gruber, K.J. & Jones, R.J. (1981). Does sexual abuse lead to delinquent behavior? A critical look at the evidence. *Victimology* 6, 85-91.
Gruber, K.J. & Jones, R.J. (1983). Identifying determinants of risk of sexual victimization of youth: a multivariate approach. *Child Abuse and Neglect* 7, 17-24.
Hall, E.R. & Flannery, P.J. (1984). Prevalence and correlates of sexual assault experiences in adolescents. *Victimology* 9, 398-406.
Hall, R. (1985). *Ask Any Woman: A London Inquiry into Rape and Sexual Assault*. Bristol: Falling Walk Press.

Hamblin, A. & Bowen, R. (1981). Sexual abuse of children. *Spare Rib*, 106, 6-8.

Harré, R. (1974a). Some remarks on 'rule' as a scientific concept. In T. Mischel (ed), *Understanding Other Persons*. Oxford: Blackwell.

Harré, R. (1974b). Blueprint for a new science. In N. Armistead (ed), *Reconstructing Social Psychology*. Harmondsworth: Penguin.

Harré, R. (1974c). The condition for a social psychology of childhood. In M.P.M. Richards (ed), *The Integration of a Child into a Social World*. Cambridge: CUP.

Harré, R. (1977a). Rules in the explanation of social behaviour. In Collett (ed), *Social Rules and Social Behaviour*.

Harré, R. (1977b) The ethogenic approach: theory and practice. In L. Berkowitz (ed), *Advances in Experimental Social Psychology*, Vol. 10. New York: Academic Press.

Harré, R, (1978a). Accounts, actions and meanings – the practice of participatory psychology. In M. Brenner, P. Marsh & M. Brenner (eds), *The Social Contexts of Method..* London: Croom Helm.

Harré, R. (1978b). Architectonic man: on the structuring of lived experience. In R.H. Brown & S.M. Lyman (eds), *Structure, Consciousness and History*. Cambridge: CUP.

Harré, R. (1979). *Social Being: A Theory for Social Psychology*. Oxford: Blackwell.

Harré, R. (1983). *Personal Being*. Oxford: Blackwell.

Harré, R. (1984). Social rules and social rituals. In H. Tajfel (ed), *The Social Dimension*, Vol. 1. Cambridge: CUP.

Harré, R. & Secord, P.F. (1972). *The Explanation of Social Behaviour*. Oxford: Blackwell.

Harré, R., Clarke, D. & De Carlo, N. (1985). *Motives and Mechanisms: An Introduction to the Psychology of Action*. London: Methuen.

Hartman, V. (1965). Group psychotherapy with sexually deviant offenders (pedophiles) – the peer group as an instrument of mutual control. *Journal of Sex Research* 1, 45-57.

Hawton, K. (1983). Behavioural approach to the management of sexual deviations. *British Journal of Psychiatry* 143, 248-55.

Heath, S. (1982). *The Sexual Fix*. London: Macmillan.

Heim, N. (1981). Sexual behavior of castrated sex offenders. *Archives of Sexual Behavior* 10, 11-19.

Heim, N. & Hursch, C.J. (1979). Castration for sex offenders: treatment or punishment? A review and critique of revent European literature. *Archives of Sexual Behavior* 8, 281-305.

Henn, F.A., Herjanic, M. & Vanderpearl, P.H. (1976). Forensic psychiatry: profiles of 2 types of sex offenders. *American Journal of Psychiatry* 133, 694-5.

Henriques, J. *et al.* (1984). *Changing the Subject*. London: Methuen.

Herdt, G.H. (ed.) (1982). *Rituals of Manhood. Male Initiation in Papua New Guinea*. Berkley, Ca.; University of California Press.

Herman, J. (1981). *Father-Daughter Incest*. Boston: Harvard University Press.

Herman, J. & Hirschman, L. (1977). Father-daughter incest. *Signs* 2, 735-56.

Herman, J. & Hirschman, L. (1981). Families at risk for father-daughter incest. *American Journal of Psychiatry* 138, 967-70.

Hippchen, L.J. (ed) (1978). *Ecologic-Biochemical Approaches to Treatment of Delinquents and Criminals*. New York: Van Nostrand Reinhold.

Hobbs, C.J. & Wynne, J.M. (1986). Buggery in childhood – a common syndrome of child abuse. *The Lancet*, 4 October, 792-5.

Hollway, W. (1984). Gender differences and the production of subjectivity. In Henriques *et al.*, *Changing the Subject*.

Howard League (1985) *Unlawful Sex: Offences, Victims and Offenders in the Criminal Justice System of England and Wales*. London: Waterlow.

Howells, K. (1979). Some meanings of children for pedophiles. In M. Cook & G. Wilson (eds), *Love and Attraction*. Oxford: Pergamon.

Howells, K. (1981). Adult sexual interest in children: considerations relevant to theories of aetiology. In M. Cook & K. Howells (eds), *Adult Sexual Interest in Children*. London: Academic Press.

Howells, K. & Wright, E. (1978). The sexual attitudes of aggressive sexual offenders. *British Journal of Criminology* 18, 170-4.

Hsu, F.L.K. (1971). Psychosocial homeostasis and Jen: conceptual tools for advancing psychological anthropology. *American Anthropologist* 73, 23-44.

Hunter, R.S., Kilstrom, N. & Loda, F. (1985). Sexually abused children: identifying masked presentations in a medical setting. *Child Abuse and Neglect* 9, 17-25.

Hyde, M. & Kaufman, P.A. (1984). Women molested as children: therapeutic and legal issues in civil actions. *American Journal of Forensic Psychiatry* 5, 147-57.

Illich, I. (1975). *Medical Nemesis: The Expropriation of Health*. London: Calder & Boyars.

Ingleby, D. (ed) (1980). *Critical Psychiatry: The Politics of Mental Health*. New York: Pantheon Books.

Ingram, M. (1981). Participating victims: a study of sexual offences with boys. In Constantine & Martinson (eds), *Children and Sex*.

Isherwood, P. (1981). Conspiracy and corruption. *Spare Rib*, 104, 31.

Jackson, S. (1982). *Childhood and Sexuality*. Oxford: Blackwell.

James, J. & Meyerding, J. (1978). Early sexual experience as a factor in prostitution. *Archives of Sexual Behavior* 7, 31-42.

James, J., Womack, W.M. & Stauss, F. (1978). Physician reporting of sexual abuse of children. *Journal of the American Medical Association* 240, 1145-6.

Jersild, J. (1956). *Boy Prostitution*. Copenhagen: G.E.C. Gad.

Jersild, J. (1967). *The Normal Homosexual Male versus the Boy Molester*. Copenhagen: NYT Nordisk Forlay Arnold Busck.

Johnson, C.L. (1981). Child sexual abuse: case handling through public agencies in the southeast of the USA. *Child Abuse and Neglect* 5, 123-8.

Johnston, M.S.K. (1979). The sexually mistreated child: diagnostic evaluation. *Child Abuse and Neglect* 3, 943-51.

Jones, D.P.H. & Krugman, R.D. (1986). Can a three-year-old child bear witness to her sexual assault and attempted murder? *Child Abuse and Neglect* 10, 253-8.

Jones, D.P.H. & Melbourne-McGraw, J. (1987). Reliable and fictitious accounts of sexual abuse to children. *Journal of Interpersonal Violence* 2, 27-45.

Jones, G.P. (1982). The social study of pederasty: in search of a literature base: an annotated bibliography of sources in English. *Journal of Homosexuality* 8, 61-93.

Jones, J.G. (1982). Sexual abuse of children: current concepts. *American Journal of Diseases of Children* 136, 142-6.

Jones, R.J., Gruber, K.J. & Timbers, G.D. (1981). Incidence and situational factors surrounding sexual assault against delinquent youths. *Child Abuse and Neglect* 5, 431-40.

Jorné, P.S. (1979). Treating sexually abused children. *Child Abuse and Neglect* 3, 285-90.

Julian, V. & Mohr, C. (1979). Father-daughter incest: profile of the offender. *Victimology* 4, 348-60.

Justice, B. & Justice, R. (1980). *The Broken Taboo: Sex in the Family*. London: Peter Owen.

Karlen, A. (1971). *Sexuality and Homosexuality: The Complete Account of Male and Female Sexual Behaviour and Deviation, With Case Histories*. London: MacDonald.

Karlen, A. (1980). Homosexuality in History. In J. Marmor (ed), *Homosexual Behavior*. New York: Basic Books.

Karpman, B. (1950). A case of paedophilia (legally rape) cured by psychoanalysis. *Psychoanalytic Review* 37, 235-76.

Karpman, B. (1954). *The Sexual Offender and His Offenses: Etiology, Pathology, Psychodynamics and Treatment*. New York: Julian Press.

Kelly, G.A. (1955). *The Psychology of Personal Constructs*, Vol. 1 & 2. New York: Norton.

Kelly, G.A. (1969). *Clinical Psychology and Personality: The Selected Papers of George Kelly*. New York: John Wiley & Sons.

Kelly, G.A. (1978). Confusion and the clock. In F. Fransella (ed), *Personal Construct Psychology 1977*. London: Academic Press.

Kempe, R.S. & Kempe, C.H. (1978). *Child Abuse*. London: Fontana/Open Books.

Kempe, R.S. & Kempe, C.H. (1984). *The Common Secret: Sexual Abuse of Children and Adolescents*. New York: W.H. Freeman.

Kercher, G.A. & McShane, M. (1984a). The prevalence of child sexual abuse victimization in an adult sample of Texas residents. *Child Abuse and Neglect* 8, 495-501.

Kercher, G.A. & McShane, M. (1984b). Characterizing child sexual abuse on the basis of a multi-agency sample. *Victimology* 9, 364-82.

Kinsey, A.C., Pomeroy, W.B. & Martin, C.E. (1948). *Sexual Behavior in the Human Male.* Philadelphia: W.B. Saunders.

Kinsey, A.C. *et al. Sexual Behavior in the Human Female.* Philadelphia: W.B. Saunders.

Kirschner, R.H. & Stein, R.J. (1985). The mistaken diagnosis of child abuse. *American Journal of Diseases of Children* 139, 873-5.

Knopp, F.H. (1984). *Retraining Adult Sex Offenders: Methods and Models.* Syracuse: Safer Society Press.

Kohlenberg, R.J. (1974). Treatment of a homosexual pedophiliac using in vivo desensitization: a case study: *Journal of Abnormal Psychology* 83, 192-5.

Kraemer, W. (ed) (1976). *The Forbidden Love: The Normal and Abnormal Love of Children.* London: Sheldon Press.

Kroth, J.A. (1979). Family therapy impact on intrafamilial child sexual abuse. *Child Abuse and Neglect* 3, 297-302.

Kurland, M.L. (1960). Pedophilia erotica. *Journal of Nervous and Mental Disease* 131, 394-403.

LaBarbera, J.D., Martin, J.E. & Dozier, J.E. (1980). Child psychiatrists' view of father-daughter incest. *Child Abuse and Neglect* 4, 147-51.

Laing, R.D., Phillipson, H. & Lee, A.R. (1966). *Interpersonal Perception.* London: Tavistock.

Landis, J.T. (1956). Experiences of 500 children with adult sexual deviation. *Psychiatric Quarterly Supplement* 30, 91-109.

Langevin, R. (1983). *Sexual Strands: Understanding and Treating Sexual Anomalies in Men.* Hillsdale, New Jersey: Lawrence Erlbaum Associates.

Langevin, R. (ed) (1985). *Erotic Preference, Gender Identity, and Aggression in Men: New Research Studies.* Hillsdale, New Jersey: Lawrence Erlbaum Associates.

Latham, T. (1981). Facing sexual issues with the family. *Journal of Family Therapy* 3, 153-65.

Law, S.K. (1979). Child molestation: a comparison of Hong Kong and western findings. *Medicine, Science and the Law* 19, 55-60.

Lawson, H. (1985). *Reflexivity: The Post-Modern Predicament.* London: Hutchinson.

Lempp, R. (1978). Psychological damage to children as a result of sexual offences. *Child Abuse and Neglect* 2, 243-5.

Lester, D. (1972). Incest. *Journal of Sex Research* 8, 268-85.

Lévi-Strauss, C. (1969). *The Elementary Structures of Kinship.* Boston: Beacon Press.

Lewis, C.S. (1961). *A Grief Observed.* London: Faber & Faber.

Lewis, D.O. & Balla, D.A. (1976). *Delinquency and Psychopathology.* New York: Grune & Stratton.

Lindberg, F.H. & Distad, L.J. (1985a). Post-traumatic stress disorders in women who experienced childhood incest. *Child Abuse and Neglect* 9, 329-34.

Lindberg, F.H. & Distad, L.J. (1985b). Survival responses to incest: adolescents in crisis. *Child Abuse and Neglect* 9, 521-6.

Litin, E.M., Griffin, M.E. & Johnson, A.M. (1956). Parental influence in unusual sexual behavior in children. *Psychoanalytic Quarterly* 25, 37-55.

Lloyd, J. (1982). The matrix of incest: an overview of three inter-related systems – the family, the legal and the therapeutic. *Journal of Social Welfare Law*, January, 16-28.

Lloyd, R. (1979). *Playland.* London: Quartet Books.

London Rape Crisis Centre (1984). *Sexual Violence: The Reality for Women.* London: Women's Press.

Longo, R.E. (1982). Sexual learning and experience among adolescent sexual offenders. *International Journal of Offender Therapy and Comparative Criminology* 26, 235-41.

Lukianowicz, N. (1972). Incest I: Paternal incest II: other types of incest. *British Journal of Psychiatry* 120, 301-13.

McCaghy, C.H. (1967). Child molesters: a study of their careers as deviants. In M.B. Clinard & R. Quinney (eds). *Criminal Behavior Systems: A Typology.* New York: Rinehart & Winston.

McCormack, A., Janus, M.D. & Burgess, A.W. (1986). Runaway youths and sexual victimisation: Gender differences in an adolescent runaway population. *Child Abuse and Neglect* 10, 387-95.

MacCulloch, M.J. & Waddington, J.L. (1981). Neuroendocrine mechanisms and the aetiology of male and female homosexuality. *British Journal of Psychiatry* 134, 341-5.

McFadyean, M. (1985). Sex and the under-age girl. *New Society*, June 14.

MacFarlane, K. (1978). Sexual abuse of children. In J.R. Chapman & M. Gates (eds), *The Victimization of Women*. Beverley Hills, California: Sage Publications.

MacFarlane, K. & Korbin, J. (1983). Confronting the incest secret long after the fact: a family study of multiple victimization with strategies for intervention. *Child Abuse and Neglect* 7, 225-40.

McGeorge, J. (1964). Sexual assaults on children. *Medicine, Science and the Law* 4, 245-53.

McGuire, R.J., Carlisle, J.M. & Young, B.G. (1965). Sexual deviations as conditioned behaviour: a hypothesis. *Behaviour Research and Therapy* 2, 185-90.

McMullen, R.J. (1987). Youth prostitution: a balance of power. *Journal of Adolescence* 10, 57-69.

MacNamara, D.E.J. (1965). Male prostitution in American cities. *American Journal of Orthopsychiatry* 35, 204.

Maisch, H. (1973). *Incest*. London: Deutsch.

Malinowski, B. (1927). *Sex and Repression in Savage Society*. London: Routledge & Kegan Paul.

Mann, E.M. (1985). The assessment of credibility of sexually abused children in criminal court cases. *American Journal of Forensic Psychiatry* 6, 9-15.

Mannarino, A.P. & Cohen, J.A. (1986). A clinical-demographic study of sexually abused children. *Child Abuse and Neglect* 10, 17-23.

Marmor, J. (1980). Overview: the multiple roots of homosexual behavior. In J. Marmor (ed), *Homosexual Behavior*. New York: Basic Books.

Marshall, W.L. (1973). The modification of sexual fantasies: a combined treatment approach to the reduction of deviant sexual behavior. *Behavior Research and Therapy* 11, 557-64.

Marshall, W.L. & Barbaree, H.E. (1978). The reduction of deviant arousal satiation treatment for sexual aggressors. *Criminal Justice and Behavior* 5, 294-303.

Martin, M.J. & Walters, J. (1982). Family correlates of selected types of child abuse and neglect. *Journal of Marriage and the Family* 44, 267-76.

Martinson, F.M. (1977a). Eroticism in childhood: a sociological perspective. In E.K. Oremland & J.D. Oremland (eds), *The Sexual and Gender Development of Young Children: The Role of the Educator*. Cambridge, Massachusetts: Ballinger.

Martinson, F.M. (1977b). Sex education in Sweden. In E.K. & J.D. Oremland (eds), *The Sexual and Gender Development of Young Children: The Role of the Educator*. Cambridge, Mass: Ballinger.

Masson, J.M. (1984). *Freud – The Assault on Truth: Freud's Suppression of the Seduction Theory*. London: Faber & Faber.

Masters, R.E.L. (1966). *Forbidden Sexual Behavior and Morality*. New York: Matrix House.

Mayhall, P.D. & Norgard, K.E. (1983). *Child Abuse and Neglect: Sharing Responsibility*. New York: John Wiley & Sons.

Mead, M. (1935). *Sex and Temperament in Three Primitive Societies*. London: Routledge & Kegan Paul.

Mead, M. (1949). *Male and Female: A Study of the Sexes in a Changing World*. London: Victor Gollancz.

Mednick, S.A. & Christiansen, K.O. (eds) (1977). *Biosocial Bases of Criminal Behavior*. New York: Gardner Press.

Mednick, S.A. & Finello, K.M. (1983). Biological factors and crime: implications for forensic psychiatry. *International Journal of Law and Psychiatry*, 6, 1-15.

Mednick, S.A., Gabrielli, W.F. Jr. & Hutchings, B. (1984). Genetic influences in criminal convictions: evidence from an adoption cohort. *Science* 224, 891-4.

Meeks, L.B. & Heit, P. (1982). *Human Sexuality*. Philadelphia: Saunders.

Meiselman, K.C. (1978). *Incest: A Psychological Study of Causes and Effects with Treatment Recommendations*. San Francisco: Jossey-Bass.

Meiselman, K.C. (1980). Personality characteristics of incest history psychotherapy patients: a research note. *Archives of Sexual Behavior* 9, 195.

Meldrum, J. & West, D.J. (1983). Homosexual offences as reported in the press. *Medicine, Science and the Law* 23, 41-53.

Mey, B.J.V. & Neff, R.L. (1982). Adults-child incest: a review of research and treatment. *Adolescence* 17, 717-35.

Mian, M. *et al.* (1986). Review of 125 children 6 years of age and under who were sexually abused. *Child Abuse and Neglect* 10, 223-9.

Miller, A. (1985). *Thou Shalt Not Be Aware*. London & Sydney: Pluto Press.

Mills, C.W. (1959). *The Sociological Imagination*. New York: OUP.

Mills, J. (1985). Breaking the last taboo. *The Listener*, October 31, 11-12.

Mohr, J.W. (1962). The pedophilias: their clinical, social and legal implications. Originally published in *Canadian Psychiatric Association Journal* 7, 255-60. Reprinted in B. Schlesinger (ed) (1977), *Sexual Behaviour in Canada: Patterns and Problems*. Toronto: University of Toronto Press.

Mohr, J.W. (1981). Age structures in pedophilia. In M. Cook & K. Howells (eds), *Adult Sexual Interest in Children*. London: Academic Press.

Mohr, J.W., Turner, R.E. & Jerry, M.B. (1964). *Pedophilia and Exhibitionism*. Toronto: University of Toronto Press.

Money, J. (1980a). *Love and Love Sickness: The Science of Sex, Gender Difference, and Pair-Bonding*. Baltimore: Johns Hopkins University Press.

Money, J. (1980b). Genetic and chromosomal aspects of homosexual etiology. In J. Marmor (ed), *Homosexual Behavior*. New York: Basic Books.

Money, J. (1983). Paraphilias: phyletic origins of erotosexual dysfunction. In S.G. Shoham (ed), *The Many Faces of Crime and Deviance, Israel Studies in Criminology*, Vol. 6, New York: Sheridan House.

Moody, R. (1980). *Indecent Assault*. London: Word is Out/Peace News.

MORI (1984). *Childhood: Research Study Conducted for Gambles Milne Ltd*. London: Market & Opinion Research International.

Mrazek, P.B. & Kempe, C.H. (eds) (1981). *Sexually Abused Children and Their Families*. Oxford: Pergamon.

Mrazek, P.B. & Mrazek, D.A. (1981). The effects of child sexual abuse: methodological considerations. In Mrazek & Kempe (eds), *Sexually Abused Children and Their Families*.

Mrazek, P.B., Lynch, M. & Bentovim, A. (1981). Recognition of child sexual abuse in the United Kingdom. In Mrazek & Kempe (eds), *Sexually Abused Children and Their Families*.

Mrazek, P.B., Lynch, M.A. & Bentovim, A. (1983). Sexual abuse of children in the United Kingdom. *Child Abuse and Neglect* 7, 147-53.

Mulcock, D. (1954). A study of 100 non-selected cases of sexual assaults on children. *International Journal of Sexology* 7, 125-8.

Nash, C.L. & West, D.J. (1985). Sexual molestation of young girls: a retrospective survey. In D.J. West (ed), *Sexual Victimization*. Aldershot: Gower.

Nava, M. (1984). Drawing the line: a feminist response to adult-child sexual relations. In A. McRobbie & M. Nava (eds), *Gender and Generation*. Basingstoke: Macmillan.

Nedoma, K., Mellan, J. & Pondelickova, J. (1971). Sexual behaviour and its development in pedophilic men. *Archives of Sexual Behavior* 1, 267-71.

Nelson, J.A. (1981). The impact of incest: factors in self-evaluation. In Constantine & Martinson (eds). *Children and Sex*.

Nelson, S. (1982). *Incest: Fact and Myth*. Edinburgh: Stramullion.

Newman, L. (1982). Behind closed doors – the terrors of sexual abuse. *19*, September, 34-6.

Newman, L. (1983). Sexual abuse within the family. *19*, May, 35-40.

Newsweek (1984). A hidden epidemic: special report on sexual abuse. *Newsweek*, May, 34-40.

Newton, D.E. (1978). Homosexual behavior and child molestation: a review of the evidence. *Adolescence* 13, 29-43.

Nolan, J.D. & Sandman, C. (1978). Biosyntonic therapy: modification of an operant conditioning approach to paedophilia. *Journal of Consulting & Clinical Psychology* 46, 1133-40.

North, M. (1972). *The Secular Priests*. London: Allen & Unwin.

NSPCC (1984a). *Developing a Child-Centred Response to Sexual Abuse: A Discussion Paper.* London: NSPCC.

NSPCC (1984b). *The Characteristics of the Sexually Abused Child and its Family.* London: NSPCC.

NSPCC (1986). *Incidence of Child Sexual Abuse.* London: NSPCC.

O'Carroll, T. (1980). *Paedophilia: The Radical Case.* London: Peter Owen.

Ortiz y Pino, J. & Goodwin, J. (1982). What families say: the dialogue of incest. In Goodwin (ed), *Sexual Abuse: Incest Victims and Their Families.*

Ortmann, J. (1980). The treatment of sexual offenders: castration and anti-hormone therapy. *International Journal of Law and Psychiatry* 3, 443-51.

Pacht, A.R. & Cowden, J.E. (1974). An exploratory study of five hundred sex offenders. *Criminal Justice and Behavior* 1, 13-20.

Panton, J.H. (1978). Personality differences appearing between rapists of adults, rapists of children and non-violent sexual molesters of female children. *Research Communications in Psychology, Psychiatry and Behavior* 3, 385-93.

Papatheophilou, R., James, S. & Orwin, A. (1975). Electroencephalographic findings in treatment-seeking homosexuals compared with heterosexuals: a controlled study. *British Journal of Psychiatry* 127, 63-6.

Parker, T. (1969). *The Twisting Lane: Some Sex Offenders.* London: Hutchinson.

Parker, W. (1985). *Homosexuality Bibliography: Second Supplement 1976-1982.* Metuchen, N.J.: Scarecrow Press.

Parton, N. (1985). *The Politics of Child Abuse.* Basingstoke: Macmillan.

Paul, D.M. (1977). The medical examination in sexual offences against children. *Medicine, Science & the Law* 17, 251-58.

Paul, D.M. (1986). What really did happen to Baby Jane? – The medical aspects of alleged sexual abuse of children. *Medicine, Science and the Law* 26, 85-102.

Paulson, M.K. (1978). Incest and sexual molestation: clinical and legal issues. *Journal of Clinical Child Psychology* Fall, 177-80.

Peters, J.J. (1976). Children who are victims of sexual assault and the psychology of offenders. *American Journal of Psychotherapy* 30, 398-421.

Petrovich, M. & Templer, D.I. (1984). Heterosexual molestation of children who later became rapists. *Psychological Reports* 54, 810.

Pettit, P. (1976). Making actions intelligible. In R. Harré (ed), *Life Sentences.* London: John Wiley & Sons.

PIE (1976). *Paedophile Information Exchange Survey of Members.* London: PIE.

PIE (1978). *Paedophilia: Some Questions and Answers.* London: PIE.

Pierce, R.L. (1984). Child pornography: a hidden dimension of child abuse. *Child Abuse and Neglect* 8, 483-93.

Pierce, R.L. & Pierce, L.H. (1985a). Analysis of sexual abuse hotline reports. *Child Abuse and Neglect* 9, 37-45.

Pierce, R.L. & Pierce, L.H. (1985b). The sexually abused child: a comparison of male and female victims. *Child Abuse and Neglect* 9, 191-9.

Pinkava, V. (1971). Logical models of sexual deviations. *International Journal of Man-Machine Studies* 3, 351-74.

Pinta, E.R. (1978). Treatment of obsessive homosexual pedophilic fantasies with medroxyprogesterone acetate. *Biological Psychiatry* 13, 369-73.

Plummer, K. (1975). *Sexual Stigma: An Interactionist Account:* London: Routledge & Kegan Paul.

Plummer, K. (1979). Images of pedophilia. In M. Cook & G. Wilson (eds), *Love and Attraction.* Oxford: Pergamon.

Plummer, K. (1980). Self-help groups for sexual minorities: the case of the paedophile. In D.J. West (ed), *Sex Offenders in the Criminal Justice System.* Cambridge: Institute of Criminology, University of Cambridge.

Plummer, K. (1981a). Pedophilia: constructing a sociological baseline. In M. Cook & K. Howells (eds), *Adult Sexual Interest in Children.* London: Academic Press.

Plummer, K. (1981b). The paedophile's progress: a view from below. In Taylor (ed), *Perspectives on Paedophilia.*

Plummer, K. (1981c). Homosexual categories: some research problems in the labelling perspective of homosexuality. In K. Plummer (ed), *The Making of the Modern Homosexual*. London: Hutchinson.

Plummer, K. (1984). The social uses of sexuality: symbolic interaction, power and rape. In J. Hopkins (ed), *Perspectives on Rape and Sexual Assault*. London: Harper & Row.

Polanyi, M. (1958). *Personal Knowledge: Towards a Post-Critical Philosophy*. London: Routledge & Kegan Paul.

Polanyi, M. (1966). *The Tacit Dimension*. London: Routledge & Kegan Paul.

Polanyi, M. (1969). *Knowing and Being: Essays by Michael Polanyi*. London: Routledge & Kegan Paul.

Pomeroy, J.C. Behar, D. & Stewart, M.A. (1981). Abnormal sexual behaviour in the pre-pubescent child. *British Journal of Psychiatry* 138, 119-25.

Powell, G.E. & Chalkley, A.J. (1981). The effects of paedophile attention on the child. In Taylor (ed), *Perspectives on Paedophilia*.

Power, D.J. (1976). Sexual deviation and crime. *Medicine, Science and the Law* 16, 111-28.

Power, D.J. (1977). Paedophilia. *The Practitioner* 218, 805-11.

Prentky, R. (1985). The neurochemistry and neuroendocrinology of sexual aggression. In D.P. Farrington & J. Gunn (eds), *Aggression and Dangerousness*. Chichester: John Wiley & Sons.

Quinsey, V.L. (1973). Methodological issues in evaluating the effectiveness of aversion therapies for institutionalized child molesters. *The Canadian Psychologist* 14, 350-61.

Quinsey, V.L. (1977). The assessment and treatment of child molesters: a review. *Canadian Psychological Review* 18, 204-20.

Quinsey, V.L. (1979). Assessment of the dangerousness of mental patients held in maximum security. *International Journal of Law and Psychiatry* 2, 389-406.

Rabinow, P. (ed) (1984). *The Foucault Reader*. Harmondsworth: Penguin.

Rada, R.T. *et al.* (1983). Plasma androgens in violent and nonviolent sex offenders. *Bulletin of the American Academy of Psychology and Law* 11, 149-58.

Rader, C.M. (1977). MMPI profile types of exposers, rapists and assaulters in a court services population. *Journal of Consulting and Clinical Psychology* 45, 61-9.

Rance, L. & Lloyd, C. (1986). Why child molesters cannot be left alone. *Sunday Observer*, July 6, 46.

Read, D.A. (1979). *Healthy Sexuality*. New York & London: Macmillan.

Reinhart, M.A. (1987). Sexually abused boys. *Child Abuse and Neglect* 11, 229-35.

Reiss, A.J. (1961). The social integration of queers and peers. *Social Problems* 9, 102-20.

Renshaw, D. (1983). Understanding and treating incest. In W.E. Fann, I. Karacan, A.D. Pokorny & R.L. Williams (eds), *Phenomenology and Treatment of Psychosexual Disorders*. Lancaster: MTP Press.

Renvoize, J. (1982). *Incest: A Family Pattern*. London: Routledge & Kegan Paul.

Rice, M.E. & Quinsey, V.L. (1980). Assessment and training of social competence in dangerous psychiatric patients. *International Journal of Law and Psychiatry* 3, 371-90.

Ricoeur, P. (1981). *Hermeneutics and the Human Sciences*. Cambridge: CUP.

Righton, P. (1981). The adult participant. In B. Taylor (ed) *Perspectives on Paedophilia*. London: Batsford.

Rist, K. (1979). Incest: theoretical and clinical views. *American Journal of Orthopsychiatry* 49, 680-91.

Roche, P.Q. (1950). Sexual deviations. *Federal Probation*, 14, 3-11.

Rogers, C.M. & Terry, T. (1984). Clinical intervention with boy victims of sexual abuse. In I. Stewart and J. Greer (eds), *Victims of Sexual Aggression*. New York: Van Nostrand Reinhold.

Romanyshyn, R.D. (1982). *Psychological Life: From Science to Metaphor*. Milton Keynes: Open University Press.

Rooth, G. (1973). Exhibitionism, sexual violence and paedophilia. *British Journal of Psychiatry* 122, 705-10.

Rosen, I. (1979a). The general psychoanalytical theory of perversion: a critical and clinical study. In I. Rosen (ed), *Sexual Deviation*. 2nd ed. Oxford: OUP.

Rosen, I. (1979b). Perversion as a regulator of self-esteem. In I. Rosen (ed), *Sexual Deviation*.

2nd ed. Oxford: OUP.

Rosenfeld, A.A. (1977). Sexual misuse and the family. *Victimology* 2, 226.

Rosenfeld, A.A. (1978). Sexual abuse of children. *Journal of American Medical Association* 240, 43.

Rosenfeld, A.A. (1979). Endogamic incest and the victim-perpetrator model. *American Journal of Diseases of Children* 133, 406-10.

Rosenfeld, A.A., Nadelson, C.C. & Krieger, M. (1979). Fantasy and reality in patients' reports of incest. *Journal of Clinical Psychiatry* 40, 159-64.

Rosenfeld, A.A. *et al.* (1977). Incest and sexual abuse of children. *Journal of Child Psychiatry* 16, 327-39.

Rossman, G.P. (1973). Literature on pederasty. *Journal of Sex Research* 9, 307-12.

Rossman, G.P. (1979). *Sexual Experience Between Men and Boys*. London: Temple Smith.

Roybal, L. & Goodwin, J. (1982). The incest pregnancy. In Goodwin (ed), *Sexual Abuse: Incest Victims and Their Families*.

Rubin, R. & Byerly, G. (1983). *Incest: The Last Taboo: An Annotated Bibliography*. New York: Garland.

Rush, F. (1980). Child Pornography. In L. Lederer (ed), *Take Back the Night: Women on Pornography*. New York: William Morrow.

Russell, D.E.H. (1983). The incidence and prevalence of intrafamilial and extrafamilial sexual abuse of female children. *Child Abuse and Neglect* 7, 133-46.

Russell, D.E.H. (1984a). *Sexual Exploitation: Rape, Child Sexual Abuse, and Workplace Harassment*. Beverly Hills: Sage.

Russell, D.E.H. (1984b). The prevalence and seriousness of incestuous abuses: stepfathers versus biological fathers. *Child Abuse and Neglect* 8, 15-22.

Ryan, G. (1986). Annotated bibliography: adolescent perpetrators of sexual molestation of children. *Child Abuse and Neglect* 10, 125-31.

Sagarin, E. (1977). Incest: problems of definition and frequency. *Journal of Sex Research* 13, 126-35.

Sandfort, T.G.M. (1982). *The Sexual Aspect of Paedophile Relations*. Amsterdam: Pan/Spartacus.

Sandfort, T.G.M. (1984). Sex in pedophiliac relationships: an empirical investigation among a nonrepresentative group of boys. *Journal of Sex Research* 20, 123-42.

Sandfort, T.G.M. (1987). *Boys on their Contacts with Men*. Elmshurst, N.Y.: Global Academic.

Sartre, J-P. (1974). *Between Existentialism and Marxism*. London: NLB.

Sayers, S. (1985). Mental illness as a moral concept: the relevance of Freud. In R. Edgley & R. Osborne (eds), *Radical Philosophy Reader*. London: Verso.

Schachter S. & Singer, J.E. (1962). Cognitive, social and physiological determinants of emotional states. *Psychological Review* 69, 379-99.

Schlesinger, B. (ed) (1977). *Sexual Behaviour in Canada: Patterns and Problems*. Toronto: University of Toronto Press.

Schlesinger, B. (1982). *Sexual Abuse of Children: A Resource Guide and Annotated Bibliography*. Toronto: University of Toronto Press.

Schofield, M. (1965a). *The Sexual Behaviour of Young People*. London: Longman.

Schofield, M. (1965b). *Sociological Aspects of Homosexuality: A Comparative Study of Three Types of Homosexuals*. London: Longman.

Schultz, L.G. (1979). The sexual abuse of children and minors: a bibliography. *Child Welfare* 58, 147-63.

Schultz, L.G. (1981). Child sexual abuse in historical perspective. *Journal of Social Welfare and Human Sexuality* 1, 21-35.

Schultz, L.G. & Jones, P., Jr. (1983). Sexual abuse of children: issues for social service and health professionals. *Child Welfare* 62, 99-108.

Schuman, D.C. (1986). False accusations of physical and sexual abuse. *Bulletin of the American Academy of Psychiatry and the Law* 14 (1), 5-21.

Scott, E.M. (1977). The sexual offender. *International Journal of Offender Therapy and Comparative Criminology* 21, 255-63.

Selby, J.W. *et al.* (1980). Families of incest: a collection of clinical impressions. *International*

Journal of Social Psychiatry 26, 7-16.

Sereny, G. (1984). *The Invisible Children: Child Prostitution in America, Germany and Britain*. London: Deutsch.

Sgroi, S.M. (1977). 'Kids with clap': gonorrhea as an indicator of child sexual assault. *Victimology* 2, 251-67.

Sgroi, S.M. (1982). *Handbook of Clinical Intervention in Child Sexual Abuse*. Lexington: D.C. Heath.

Shaw, R. (1978a). The persistent sexual offender: control and rehabilitation. *Probation Journal* 25, 9-13.

Shaw, R. (1978b). The persistent sexual offender – control and rehabilitation (a follow-up). *Probation Journal* 25, 61-3.

Shepher, J. (1983). *Incest: A Biosocial View*. New York: Academic Press.

Sheridan, A. (1980). *Michel Foucault: The Will to Truth*. London: Tavistock.

Shotter, J. (1970). Men, the man-makers: George Kelly and the psychology of personal constructs. In D. Bannister (ed), *Perspectives in Personal Construct Theory*. London: Academic Press.

Shotter, J. (1973a). Prolegomena to an understanding of play. *Journal for the Theory of Social Behaviour* 3, 47-89.

Shotter, J. (1973b). Acquired powers: the transformation of natural into personal powers. *Journal for the Theory of Social Behaviour* 3, 141-56.

Shotter, J. (1974). The development of personal powers. In M.P.M. Richards (ed), *The Integration of a Child into a Social World*. Cambridge: CUP.

Shotter, J. (1975). *Images of Man in Psychological Research*. London: Methuen.

Shotter, J. (1978). Towards a social psychology of everyday life: a standpoint 'in action'. In M. Brenner, P. Marsh & M. Brenner (eds), *The Social Contexts of Method*. London: Croom Helm.

Shotter, J. (1981). Telling and reporting: prospective and retrospective uses of self-ascriptions. In C. Antaki (ed), *The Psychology of Ordinary Explanations of Social Behaviour*. London: Academic Press.

Shotter, J. (1982a). Consciousness, self-consciousness, inner games and alternative realities. In G. Underwood (ed), *Aspects of Consciousness*, Vol. 3. *Awareness and Self-Awareness*. London: Academic Press.

Shotter, J. (1982b). Contemporary psychological theory – human being: becoming human. In B. Dufour (ed). *New Movements in the Social Sciences and Humanities*. London: Temple Smith.

Shotter, J. (1983). 'Duality of structure' and 'intentionality' in an ecological psychology. *Journal for the Theory of Social Behaviour* 13, 19-43.

Shotter, J. (1984). *Social Accountability and Selfhood*. Oxford: Blackwell.

Siegel, J. (1981). Intrafamilial child sexual victimization: a role training model. *Journal of Group Psychotherapy, Psychodrama and Sociometry*, 1981 (author's reprint).

Silbert, M.H. & Pines, A.A. (1981). Sexual child abuse as an antecedent to prostitution. *Child Abuse and Neglect* 5, 407-11.

Silbert, M.H. & Pines, A.M. (1982). Victimisation of street prostitutes. *Victimology* 7, 122-33.

Singer, M. (1979). Perspective on incest as child abuse. *The Australian and New Zealand Journal of Criminology* 12, 3-14.

Smith, P. (1987). A place of safety? *New Society*, 21 August, 18-19.

Spodak, M.K., Falck, Z.A. & Rappeport, J.R. (1978). The hormonal treatment of paraphiliacs with depo-provera. *Criminal Justice and Behaviour* 5, 304-14.

Sroufe, L.A. & Ward, M.J. (1980). Seductive behaviour of mothers of toddlers: occurrence, correlates, and family origins. *Child Development* 51, 1222-9.

Stanko, E.A. (1985). *Intimate Intrusions: Women's Experience of Male Violence*. London: Routledge & Kegan Paul.

Steele, B.F. & Alexander, H. (1981). Long-term effects of sexual abuse in children. In Mrazek & Kempe (eds), *Sexually Abused Children and Their Families*.

Stoller, R.J. (1974). Hostility and mystery in perversion. *International Journal of Psychoanalysis* 55, 425-34.

Stoller, R.J. (1976). *Perversion: The Erotic Form of Hatred*. Hassocks, Sussex: Harvester Press.

Stone, L.E., Tyler, R.P. & Mead, J.J. (1984). Law enforcement officers as investigators and therapists in child sexual abuse: a training model. *Child Abuse and Neglect* 8, 75-82.

Storr, A. (1964). *Sexual Deviation*. Harmondsworth: Penguin.

Summit, R. (1983). The child sexual abuse accommodation syndrome. *Child Abuse and Neglect* 7, 177-93.

Summit, R. & Kryso, J. (1978). Sexual abuse of children: a clinical spectrum. *American Journal of Orthopsychiatry* 48, 237-51.

Sword, R.O. (1978). Sexual deviancy. In M.U. Barnard, B.J. Clancy & K.E. Krantz (eds), *Human Sexuality For Health Professionals*. Philadelphia: W.B. Sanders.

Szasz, T.S. (1970). *Ideology and Insanity*. London: Marian Boyars.

Szasz, T.S. (1971). *The Manufacture of Madness*. London: Routledge & Kegan Paul.

Szasz, T.S. (1977). *The Theology of Medicine*. Baton Rouge: Louisiana State University Press.

Szasz, T.S. (1978). *The Myth of Psychotherapy*. Oxford: OUP.

Tasto, D.L. (1980). Pedophilia. In W.J. Curran *et al.* (eds), *Modern Legal Medicine, Psychiatry and Forensic Medicine*. Philadelphia: F.A. Davis.

Taylor, B. (1976). Motives for guilt-free pederasty: some literary considerations. *Sociological Review* 24, 97-114.

Taylor, B. (ed), (1981). *Perspectives on Paedophilia*. London: Batsford.

Taylor, C. (1977). What is human agency? In T. Mischel (ed), *The Self: Psychological and Philosophical Issues*. Oxford: Blackwell.

Taylor, L. (1972). The significance and interpretation of replies to motivational question: the case of sex offenders. *Sociology* 6, 23-39.

Tedesco, J.F. & Schnell, S.V. (1987). Children's reactions to sex abuse investigation and litigation. *Child Abuse and Neglect* 11, 267-72.

Tesser, A. & Reardon, R. (1981). Perceptual and cognitive mechanisms in human sexual attraction. In M. Cook (ed), *The Bases of Human Sexual Attraction*. London: Academic Press.

Thomas, G. & Johnson, C.L. (1979). Developing a program for sexually abused adolescents: the research-service partnership. *Child Abuse and Neglect* 3, 683-91.

Thompson, N.L., West, D.J. & Woodhouse, T.P. (1985). Sociolegal problems of male homosexuals in Britain. In D.J. West (ed), *Sexual Victimisation*. Aldershot: Gower.

Tierney, K.J. & Corwin, D.L. (1983). Exploring intrafamilial child sexual abuse: a systems approach. In D. Finkelhor, R.J. Gelles, G.T. Hotaling & M.A. Strauss (eds), *The Dark Side of Families*. Beverley Hills: Sage.

Time (1980). Attacking the last taboo. *Time*, April 14, 53. European edition.

Time (1981). Cradle-to-grave intimacy. *Time*, September 7, 31. European edition.

Tindall, R.H. (1978). The male adolescent involved with a pederast becomes an adult. *Journal of Homosexuality* 3, 373-82.

Tolsma, F.J. (1957). *De betekenis van de verleiding in homofiele ontwikkelingen*. Amsterdam: Psychiatric Juridical Society.

Toobert, S. Bartelme, K.F. & Jones, E.S. (1959). Some factors related to pedophilia. *International Journal of Social Psychiatry* 4, 272-9.

Trankell, A. (1972). *Reliability of Evidence*. Stockholm: Beckmans.

Trigg, R. (1985). *Understanding Social Sciences*. Oxford: Blackwell.

Tsai, M., Feldman-Summers, S. & Edgar, M. (1979). Childhood molestation: variables related to differential impacts on psychosexual functioning in adult women. *American Journal of Abnormal Psychology* 88, 407-17.

Tsang, D. (ed) (1981). *The Age Taboo*. Boston: Alyson; London: Gay Men's Press.

Tucker, N. (1985). A panic over child abuse. *New Society*, October 18, 96-8.

Tyler, R.P. & Stone, L.E. (1985). Child pornography: perpetuating the sexual victimization of children. *Child Abuse and Neglect* 9, 313-18.

Ullerstam, L. (1967). *The Erotic Minorities: A Swedish View*. London: Calder & Boyars.

Van den Berg, J.H. (1972). *A Different Existence: Principles of Phenomenological Psychopathology*. Pittsburgh: Duquesne University Press.

Van den Berg, J.H. (1978). *Medical Power and Medical Ethics*. New York: Norton.

Van Wyk, P.H. & Geist, C.S. (1984). Psychosocial development of heterosexual, bisexual and

homosexual behavior. *Archives of Sexual Behavior* 13, 505-44.
Virkkunen, M. (1974). Incest offences and alcoholism. *Medicine, Science and the Law* 14, 124-8.
Virkkunen, M. (1975). Victim-precipitated pedophilia offences. *British Journal of Criminology* 15, 175-80.
Virkkunen, M. (1976). The pedophilic offender with antisocial character. *Acta Psychiatrica Scandinavica* 53, 401-5.
Virkkunen, M. (1981). The child as participating victim. In M. Cook & K. Howells (eds), *Adult Sexual Interest in Children*. London: Academic Press.
Walker, N. (1977). *Behaviour and Misbehaviour: Explanation and Non-Explanation*. Oxford: Blackwell.
Walmsley, R. & White, K. (1979). *Sexual Offences, Consent and Sentencing*. London: HMSO.
Walmsley, R. & White, K. (1980). *Supplementary Information on Sexual Offences and Sentencing*. London: HMSO.
Walters, D.R. (1975). *Physical and Sexual Abuse of Children: Causes and Treatment*. Bloomington: Indiana University Press.
Ward, E. (1984). *Father-Daughter Rape*. London: Women's Press.
Waterman, C.K. & Foss-Goodman, D. (1984). Child molesting – variables relating to attribution of fault to victims, offenders, and nonparticipating parents. *Journal of Sex Research* 20, 329-49.
Weaver, C. and Fox, C. (1984). The Berkeley sex offenders group: a seven-year evaluation. *Probation Journal* 31, 143-6.
Weber, M. (1947). *The Theory of Social and Economic Organization*. New York: Free Press.
Weber, M. (1971). *The Interpretation of Social Reality*. London: Michael Joseph.
Weeks, J. (1985). *Sexuality and its Discontents*. London: Routledge & Kegan Paul.
Weinberg, M.S. & Bell, A.P. (eds) (1972). *Homosexuality: An Annotated Bibliography*. New York: Harper & Row.
Weinberg, S.K. (1955). *Incest Behavior*. New York: Citadel Press.
Weiss, J. *et al.* (1955). A study of girl sex victims. *Psychiatric Quarterly* 29, 1-27.
Wells, L.A. (1981). Family pathology and father-daughter incest: restricted psychopathy. *Journal of Clinical Psychiatry* 42, 197-202.
West, D.J. (1977). *Homosexuality Re-Examined*. London: Duckworth.
West. D.J. (1980). Treatment in theory and practice. In D.J. West (ed), *Sex Offenders in the Criminal Justice System*. Cambridge: Institute of Criminology, University of Cambridge.
West, D.J. (1981). Adult sexual interest in children: implications for social control. In M. Cook & K. Howells (eds), *Adult Sexual Interest in Children*. London: Academic Press.
West, D.J. (1982). Victims of sexual crime. *British Journal of Sexual Medicine*, January, 30-5.
West, D.J. (1983a). Sex offences and offending. In M. Tonry & N. Morris (eds), *Crime and Justice: An Annual Review of Research*, Vol 5. Chicago: University of Chicago Press.
West, D.J. (1983b). Homosexuality and lesbianism. *British Journal of Psychiatry* 143, 221-6.
West, D.J. (1984a). The victim's contribution to sexual offences. In J. Hopkins (ed), *Perspectives on Rape and Sexual Assault*. London: Harper & Row.
West, D.J. (1984b). Homosexuality and social control. In *Sexual Behaviour and Attitudes and their implications for Criminal Law*. Proceedings of the 15th Criminological Research Conference, Council of Europe. Strasbourg: Secretariat memorandum prepared by the Directorate of Legal Affairs.
Westermarck, E. (1891). *The History of Human Marriage*. London: Macmillan.
Whitehouse, M. (1978). *Whatever Happened to Sex?* London: Hodder & Stoughton.
Whitehouse, M. (1982). *A Most Dangerous Woman?* Tring: Lion Publishing.
Whitehouse, M. (1985). *Mightier Than The Sword*. Eastbourne: Kingsway.
Will, D. (1983). Approaching the incestuous and sexually abusive family. *Journal of Adolescence* 6, 229-46.
Wilson, G.D. (1978). *The Secrets of Sexual Fantasy*. London: Dent.
Wilson, G.D. & Cox, D.N. (1983). *The Child-Lovers*. London: Peter Owen.
Wilson, P. (1981). *The Man They Called a Monster: Sexual Experiences Between Men and*

Boys. North Ryde, New South Wales: Cassell Australia.

Winch, P. (1958). *The Idea of a Social Science*. London: Routledge & Kegan Paul.

Wittgenstein, L. (1953). *Philosophical Investigations*. Oxford: Blackwell.

Wolfe, D.A. *et al.* (1986). Evaluation of a brief intervention for educating school children in awareness of physical and sexual abuse. *Child Abuse and Neglect* 10, 85-92.

Wolfenden Report (1957). *Report of the Committee on Homosexual Offences and Prostitution*. London: HMSO.

Wolters, W.H.G. *et al.* (1985). A review of cases of sexually exploited children reported to the Netherlands State Police. *Child Abuse and Neglect* 9, 571-4.

Woodling, B.A. & Heger, A. (1986). The use of the colposcope in the treatment of sexual abuse in the pediatric age group. *Child Abuse and Neglect* 10, 111-14.

World Health Organization (1977). *International Classification of Diseases*. Geneva: WHO, London: HMSO.

Wright, R. & West, D.J. (1981). Rape: a comparison of group offences and lone assaults. *Medicine, Science and the Law* 21, 25-30.

Wyatt, G.E. (1985). The sexual abuse of Afro-American and White-American women in childhood. *Child Abuse and Neglect* 9, 507-19.

Wyatt, G.E. & Peters, S.D. (1986a). Issues in the definition of child sexual abuse in prevalence research. *Child Abuse and Neglect* 10, 231-40.

Wyatt, G.E. & Peters, S.D. (1986b). Methodological considerations in research on the prevalence of child sexual abuse. *Child Abuse and Neglect* 10, 241-51.

Yates, A. (1978). *Sex Without Shame*. London: Temple Smith.

Yates, A. (1982). Children eroticized by incest. *American Journal of Psychiatry* 139, 482-5.

Yates, A., Beutler, L.E. & Crago, M. (1985). Drawings by child victims of incest. *Child Abuse and Neglect* 9, 183-9.

Yeudall, L.T. (1977). Neuropsychological assessment of forensic disorders. *Canada's Mental Health* 25, 7-15.

Yeudall, L.T. (1980). A neuropsychosocial perspective of persistent juvenile delinquency and criminal behavior: discussion. *Annals of the New York Academy of Sciences* 347, 349-55.

Zilbergeld, B. (1979). *Men and Sex: A Guide to Sexual Fulfilment*. London: Souvenir Press.

Index of Names

Subject Index